THE
TUDORS
AND
EUROPE

THE
TUDORS
AND
EUROPE

JOHN MATUSIAK

First published 2020

The History Press
97 St George's Place, Cheltenham,
Gloucestershire, GL50 3QB
www.thehistorypress.co.uk
© John Matusiak, 2020

The right of John Matusiak to be identified as the Author
of this work has been asserted in accordance with the
Copyright, Designs and Patents Act 1988.

British Library Cataloguing in Publication Data.
A catalogue record for this book is available from the British Library.

ISBN 978 0 7509 9187 2

Typesetting and origination by The History Press
Printed and bound in Great Britain by TJ International Ltd.

CONTENTS

I

CONTOURS AND CONNECTIONS

1

PEOPLES, PERCEPTIONS, PREJUDICE: TUDOR ENGLAND AND THE DISCOVERY OF 'EUROPE'

Why should Europe be so called, or who was the first author of this name, no man has yet found out.

From the introduction by Abraham Ortelius to his atlas of 1570, *Theatrum Orbis Terrarum*

In an impassioned oration of 1599, the French scholar and political philosopher Louis Le Roy bewailed the condition of 'our common mother Europe', which, 'as though in answer to Mohammedan prayers', now found herself 'soaked in her own blood'. Some three decades or so earlier, the religious reformer John Calvin had also spoken of '*Europae concussio*' – 'the shattering of Europe' – as he reflected upon the divisions that he, in no small measure, had actually helped to propagate. Yet when England's first Tudor ruler readied for battle on Bosworth Field in the high summer of 1485 with the intention of ending once and for all the meandering thirty-year contest that we now call the Wars of the Roses, the vast majority of his 8,000-strong force, including those very continental mercenaries whom he had enlisted to his cause, neither recognised nor remotely comprehended any such term as 'Europe'. Nor, indeed, would matters alter appreciably for the majority of Englishmen over many decades to come. For when Falstaff staked his claim in Act IV of *Henry IV, Part 2*, to being 'simply the most active fellow in Europe' – 'an I had but a belly of indifferency' – Shakespeare's intentions remained purely comedic, as he sought to lay bare the underlying ignorance of the braggart knight who, like most of his contemporaries, equated 'Europe' with little more than what later generations might have considered 'Timbuktu'.

As early as 1471, in fact, the astronomer Johannes Müller had seen fit
to declare Nuremberg 'the middle point of Europe', while in 1505 Jakob
Wimpheling became another to employ the expression in his eulogy for
Strasbourg's splendid cathedral:

> I would say that there is nothing more magnificent on the face of the earth
> than this edifice. Who can admire this tower sufficiently? Who can ade-
> quately praise it? With its stone tracery, its sculptured columns, its carved
> statues which describe so many things, it exceeds all buildings in Europe
> in beauty.

But if a negligible minority of mainly French and German writers were
slowly sleepwalking their way towards a broader sense of identity beyond
their national boundaries, the process proved markedly more tentative on
the English side of the Channel – and for good reason. For although the
fighting was sporadic, the armies small and the material losses inconsiderable, the tortuous struggle between the two rival branches of the Plantagenet
line during the second half of the fifteenth century had nevertheless been
more than sufficiently disruptive to ensure that Henry VII's new kingdom
remained an inward-looking and comparatively insignificant backwater on
the Continent's damp and misty fringe. The Crown, after all, had become little
more than a political football when Henry VI lost his throne to Edward IV at
Towton in 1461, only to retrieve it in 1470 with the help of Edward's former
henchman, Warwick the Kingmaker. Nor had things improved eight years
later when the restored king once more made way for his resurgent rival. And
in the meantime England's entire strategic relation to 'Europe' had altered
accordingly in the wake of the events of 1453 when she was forced to forsake
the last of her French lands, excepting Calais.

For it was only at this point, at the end of the Hundred Years War, that
England, without realising it, became once again an island of the sort that
it had been before 1066 – that is, an autonomous political unit, territorially
and psychologically distinct from Europe. Until this turning point, despite
the Channel, the North Sea and the Straits of Dover, the kingdom had
been intimately linked with France in particular, to the extent indeed that
the long conflict between the two realms had actually taken place at what
amounted to a more or less provincial level. In other words, England – or
more specifically its elites – perceived the Anglo–French domain as a single
entire unit that became, in consequence, both battlefield and prize until the
two sides gradually disentangled themselves from the huge field of operations that had sapped their resources for so long. Even then, however, the
notion of England's physical linkage to Europe through France was not dead,

as Henry VIII subsequently revived the dreams of his Lancastrian forebears, and sallied forth once more with bold ambitions to recapture the French Crown – notwithstanding the warning delivered to the House of Commons by Thomas Cromwell in 1523 that a war of conquest 'would cost just as much as the whole of the circulating money in the country'. Such a policy, he suggested, was likely to force England to adopt a leather currency, which would become especially problematic if the king were taken prisoner and ransom became necessary, since 'the French … would probably refuse to return the English king on payment of leather, as they refused even to sell their wine except on payment of silver'. In the event, no such expedient proved necessary, as the second Tudor's ambitions foundered on reality's reef even more decisively than Henry V's had ultimately done before him, and Calais finally fell to the French Crown eleven years after his death. Its return was insincerely promised at the Treaty of Cateau-Cambrésis in 1559, and the last Tudor ruler of England would briefly gain possession of Le Havre before its recapture in 1562. But more than a century earlier, the die had already been effectively cast. Thereafter, the Channel, the Straits of Dover and the North Sea were not so much a gateway to the perceived natural inheritance of England's ruling class as a heaving watery bulwark protecting the island from alien influences and hostile foes.

In 1477, the Burgundian ruler of the Netherlands, England's ancient ally, finally yielded possession of the Somme towns, Picardy, and the ancestral Duchy of Burgundy to France; and fifteen years later another old ally, the Duchy of Brittany, was, likewise, annexed to the French Crown. Together these events stripped away the wide belt of possessions and friendly or satellite territories that had formerly served as a land buffer against invasion, and left the entire southern coast of the Channel from Brest to Boulogne directly in French hands – all of which was certain to bring far-reaching changes not only in England's domestic economy and internal politics, but, no less importantly, in her broader perception of the world beyond her waters. For with Edward IV's eventual death in 1483, and the subsequent succession of his brother, Richard III, the dynastic merry-go-round had begun yet another giddy circuit, which ended only when Henry Tudor, great-grandson of a fugitive Welsh brewer wanted for murder, at last made his way from French protection to Market Bosworth in England's midland heart to stake his own flimsy claim to primacy. Outnumbered by two to one, he would ultimately triumph in a particularly foul and inglorious fray fought on blood-soaked fen and moorland, only to inherit a kingdom that had arguably grown more insular than at any previous point in its history.

And how, of course, was it ever likely to have been otherwise when self-interest and endemic lawlessness had robbed his subjects of any broader

vision or direction? 'The French vice is lechery and the English vice treachery', ran the saying at the time, and no impartial observer could surely
have doubted at least the second half of this maxim when the first Tudor
cautiously mounted his throne. For it was no coincidence that one contemporary parliamentary petition justly complained how '... in divers parts
of this realm, great abominable murders, robberies, extortions, oppressions
and other manifold maintenances, misgovernances, forcible entries, affrays
and assaults be committed, and as yet remain unpunished'. On the contrary,
estate jumping, abduction of heiresses and casual brigandage had become, in
effect, a modish pastime for the high-born Englishmen depicted to this day
on their tombs and brasses in plate armour. Indeed, no less a figure than Sir
Thomas Malory who had written in *Morte D'Arthur* 'that we fall not through
vice and sin, but exercise and follow virtue', found himself in prison in 1485
for sheep stealing, sacrilege, extortion, rape and attempted murder. And in
such circumstances it seemed only natural that England's first Tudor ruler
should continue to limit his horizons and abandon temporarily his predecessors' medieval ambitions to win and hold dominions abroad, settling instead
for a safer status as ruler of a kingdom 'off' rather than 'of' Europe, while
securing alliances, where possible through marriage, as a guarantee of firm
government and sound finance at home.

While that process unfolded, moreover, his subjects, just like the residing majority of their contemporaries overseas, would continue to consider
themselves members of 'Christendom' rather than 'Europe'. In 1565, just
under half a century after Martin Luther had put paid once and for all to
the universalist pretensions of the Roman Catholic Church, a devout citizen of Milan nevertheless saw fit, on the advice of his confessor, to include
in his family devotions, a prayer that 'us and all of Christendom' be kept
'in perfect union and love'. And so it was with the young Cornishman
Peter Mundy, who as late as 1620, having laboured his way back across
the Turkish-dominated Balkans after a trip to Constantinople, passed the
boundary of the Venetian enclave of Spalato (Split), to declare with no little
relief how 'wee were no sooner past it, but we entered into Christendome,
then seeming to be in a new world'. Long before both men wrote, of course,
the realistic prospect of a *Corpus Christianorum* united by its beliefs and aspirations, first adumbrated by Charlemagne more than eight centuries earlier,
was already effectively defunct, to be finally laid to rest amid the ashes of
the Thirty Years War of the following century. But the notion persisted stubbornly throughout a long process of transition, which was reflected, aptly
enough, in 1590 by the alternating references of the much-travelled English
squire Sir John Smythe to the countries of western 'Europe' and the 'nations
of the occidental parts of Christendom' – not to mention the Italian Jesuit

Michele Lauretano's coining of the phrase 'the Christendom of Europe' in 1572.

Certainly, the old medieval term carried with it comforting connotations of what amounted to a sacred sheep-fold, within which the Continent's peoples shared at least the residing ideal of a common faith, while 'Europe', by contrast, appeared to embody no intrinsic unity beyond the geographical landmass that it represented and, as the sixteenth century progressed, an emerging sense of the moral and civilising superiority of the states and peoples that comprised it. Nor, in particular, did it seem to foster any special understanding or mutual appreciation, let alone collective consciousness, among the residents of its competing kingdoms, as was clear from the observations of one Venetian visitor to England in 1497:

> The English [wrote the author of the so-called Italian Relation] are great lovers of themselves, and of everything belonging to them; they think that there are no other men than themselves, and no other world but England; and whenever they see a handsome foreigner, they say that 'he looks like an Englishman', and that it is a great pity that he should not be an Englishman.

Just over a century later, moreover, in 1598, a German commentator would make almost the identical point, highlighting how his English hosts, upon seeing a foreigner 'very well made or particularly handsome', were inclined to reflect how 'it is a pity he is not an Englishman'. Doubtless, an Elizabethan audience of *The Merchant of Venice* two years earlier would have been fully conversant with the stereotypes underlying the spirit of Portia's list of suitors, in which the Italian from Naples – that unrivalled nursery of riding schools – 'doth nothing but talk of his horse', and the Frenchman 'is every man in no man'. 'If I should marry him,' she continues, 'I should marry twenty husbands', while the weakness of Germans was drink, leading her to conclude disdainfully: 'I will do anything, Nerissa, ere I will be married to a sponge.'

In Portia's view, predictably, the Englishman 'is a proper man's picture'. 'But alas,' she declares with an injection of impartiality not often evident among many of her contemporaries, 'who can converse with a dumbshow'. And if the traveller Fynes Moryson was at least prepared to reflect favourably upon the fact that 'the Germans do not make water in the streets' after his extensive travels on the Continent from May 1591 to May 1595, and to acknowledge the skill of his Teutonic hosts as artificers, even he could not resist adding how:

> I think that to be attributed not to their sharpness of witt, but to their industry, for they use to plod with great diligence upon their professions.

They were, he concluded, 'somewhat inclining to the vice of Dullness' – a regrettable but altogether less rancid national characterisation than those afforded by Thomas Nash to other 'Europeans' in his novel of 1594, *The Unfortunate Traveller*, in which the hero, an exiled English earl in Rome, holds forth energetically about the shortcomings of a range of his foreign counterparts. What is to be learned in France, he rails, save 'to esteeme of the pox as a pimple', in Spain save to copy a 'ruffe with short strings like the droppings of a man's nose', in Italy 'save the art of atheism, the art of epicurising, the art of whoring, the art of poisoning, the art of sodomitry', in Holland save how 'to be drunk and snort in the midst of dinner'. 'No,' concludes the Earl, 'beleeve me, no bread, no fire, no water doth a man anie good out of his owne country.'

At the same time, the corrupting influence of the foreigner was an equally familiar Tudor theme. Hans, the first Netherlander to be portrayed on the English stage, in the morality play *Wealth and Health* of *c.* 1557, was duly depicted – once again entirely in accordance with the audience's preconceptions – as a lurching drunkard. And notwithstanding nearly two subsequent generations of English admiration for Dutch art and music – not to mention ongoing co-operation with the northern Netherlands as a military ally from 1585 onwards – this same stereotype could still be trotted out by Sir John Smythe with no apparent inkling of the irony involved in a fellow-Protestant pot calling a continental kettle black. Writing only five years after the outbreak of war with Spain, which England's Dutch allies had already been waging since 1568, Smythe would nevertheless note how 'this detestable vice' of drunkenness had 'taken a wonderful root' within his own country 'that in times past was wont to be of all other nations of Christendom the most sober'. By contrast, a French scholar such as Joseph Scaliger was at least prepared to acknowledge from his quiet seat in Leiden how the Netherlands was not without 'some good people' and that the country people, men and women, and almost all the servant girls can read and write'. But English commentators, in the main, remained stubbornly ungenerous.

And if a weakness for alcohol was widely held to have infected England's shores from across the North Sea, so the contagion of decadence and moral collapse from Italy was frequently highlighted with no less vigour. Three years before the death of Elizabeth I, an English translator of Livy reflected mournfully upon the current condition of the classical poet's homeland, 'so farre degenerate are the inhabitants now from that ancient people, so devoute, so virtuous and uncorrupt in old time'. But it was Roger Ascham, author of the widely influential educational handbook *The Scholemaster*, who had first gone so far in 1570 as to claim that the Italianate Englishman was nothing less than 'a devil made flesh' – a view echoed by the German Barolomew Sastrow, who later quoted it as a familiar proverb. 'Italy now,' Ascham maintained, 'is not that Italy that it was wont to be, and therefore not so fit a place, as some do count it, for young men to fetch either wisdom or honesty from thence' – a sentiment that would help explain, perhaps, why Giordano Bruno was jostled and insulted during his stay in England between 1583 and 1585, and one that also pointed the way ultimately to John Webster's two great tragedies of 1612 and 1623 in which Italians poisoned their victims in four different ways: by the leaves of a book, the lips of a portrait, the pommel of a saddle and an anointed helmet.

Yet it was a companion of Frederick, Duke of Württemberg, writing in 1592, who recorded how the English 'care little for foreigners, but scoff and laugh at them', making it small wonder, of course, that those on the receiving end should sometimes have responded in kind. In deprecating the tendency of English women to disdain the advances of his fellow-countrymen, for example, a Spaniard of 1554 duly saw fit to observe how, given 'the sort of women they were', this was 'an excellent thing for the Spaniards'. Four years later, meanwhile, a Frenchman who, along with his peers, had been treated to taunts of knave and dog, and branded a son of a whore, readily concluded that the English were more false and lacking in conscience than snakes, crocodiles and scorpions, while another gibe to have a long history was the aristocratic Italian Pietro della Valle's dismissal of the English ambassador in Constantinople as 'a better shopkeeper than a soldier'. Some Englishmen such as George Pettie, the translator of Guazzo, were, it is true, mildly apologetic for the arrogance of their own countrymen, blaming it on the changed behaviour of the English when they crossed the Channel. England, wrote Pettie, 'is the civilest countrey in the worlde: and if it be thought otherwise by strangers, the disorders of those traveylers abrode are the chiefe cause of it'. But a Mantuan diplomat would nevertheless write home from London to confirm that the land of his current domicile, though a would-be paradise, was actually inhabited by devils, while, in spite of Henry VIII's best efforts to patronise Italian artists, craftsmen and military engineers, Benvenuto Cellini – who was happy to work in France – flinched at the very prospect of living amongst 'such beasts as the English'.

The medieval notion – half superstition, half belief among the French – that English invaders sported tails rolled up inside their breeches, had, it is true, faded in the second half of the fifteenth century, only to resurface in a propaganda poem of 1513 when Henry VIII set forth across the Channel in hope of emulating his conquering forebears. The same poem, too, had spared no venom in describing the marauding foe as hideous, loathsome, stinking toads. But when English troops subsequently sacked towns like Ardres and turned their dwellings to charcoal, it was hardly surprising, of course, that French children, long reared on stories about the Hundred Years War when the 'Goddams with tails' had pillaged and plundered their land, should once again have regurgitated the myths of their elders. For most English troops remained belchingly contemptuous of French peasants, whom they believed to be so backward and exploited that they drank only water and tended their masters' fields unshod, while even in times of fleeting peace, French merchants in London were both cheated and intimidated, and deprived of even their most basic dignities. Forbidden to attend English cloth fairs, stripped and searched at every opportunity and imprisoned as spies if found loose upon the streets at night without a candle, they were left in no doubt either that the English king's incursion upon their homeland in 1513 would not be his last. For no more than one year later, not only in a newly built armoury at Greenwich, but also in rented houses and cellars throughout the capital, German craftsmen were soon busy fashioning weapons of all descriptions for the next invasion, from the finest iron brought specially from Innsbruck.

As late as 1603, the Duc de Sully, when on an embassy to London, would warn Henri IV how 'the English hate us, and with a hatred so strong and so widespread that one is tempted to number it among the natural dispositions of this people'. And it was small consolation that his hosts were, of long tradition, far from limited in their antipathies, since not only Frenchmen but all foreigners in England's capital were susceptible to intimidation and indeed violence, as the German mercantile community of the so-called 'Steelyard' on the north bank of the Thames, by the outflow of the Walbrook where Cannon Street station now stands, would discover to their cost in the autumn of 1497. By that time, according to the account provided by Edward Hall's chronicle, the King of England had already 'not only banished all Flemish wares and merchandise out of his realm and dominions', but gone on to light the blue touch paper for what followed by restraining 'all English merchants from their repair and traffic into any lands and territories of the king of the Romans [i.e. Germany] or the Archduke his son'. And the results were indeed explosive, since 'the restraint made by the king', we are told, 'sore grieved and hindered the [English] merchants being adventurers':

For they [Hall continues], by force of this commandment, had no occupying to bear their charges and support their countenance and credit. And yet one thing sore nipped their hearts, for the Easterlings [i.e. Germans] which were at liberty brought into the realm such wares as they were wont and accustomed to do and so served their customers throughout the whole realm. By reason whereof the [English] masters being destitute of sale and commutation neither retained so many covenant-servants and apprentices as they before were accustomed and in especial Mercers, Haberdashers and Clothe workers, nor yet gave their servants so great stipend and salary as before that restraint they used to do. For which cause the said servants intending to work their malice on the Easterlings, the Tuesday before St Edward's day came to the Steelyard in London and began to rifle and spoil such chambers and warehouses as they could get into. So that the Easterlings had much ado to withstand and repulse them out of their gates.

Ultimately, indeed, only the actions of the Lord Mayor — as well as the intervention of English carpenters and blacksmiths 'which came to their aid by water out of the borough of Southwark' – saved the embattled foreigners. But 'above eighty servants and apprentices (and not one householder)', Hall tells, were nevertheless found guilty, and their leaders 'sent to the Tower and there long continued'.

Nor was this the last episode of its kind. For in 1517 the xenophobic riot of 'Evil May Day' would involve further assaults and looting of foreign shop owners by apprentices of the capital's craft guilds who had long envied the prosperity of foreign communities, and been stirred once more by agitators stoking widespread fears of unemployment through foreign competition. Already in April 1516, bills had been posted upon the door of St Paul's cathedral, as well as at the church of All Hallows in Barking, suggesting that the king himself had been lending money to Florentine merchants, who were then using it to trade at advantage over their English competitors. And such was Henry VIII's concern at the resulting stir that he subsequently ordered an enquiry to be made in every ward of the City, so that the handwriting of all apprentices could be checked. Yet the sullen antipathy of the London mob could not be quelled for long, and no gathering for the particular purpose of unleashing an anti-foreign crusade could have been more fitting than the motley crowd of merchants and shopkeepers, apprentices and bargees, who, during the Easter and Whitsuntide holidays, crowded round the pulpit of St Mary Spitall, to take in the customary sermons, which were also preached before the mayor and aldermen of the city.

So it was that on the Tuesday of Holy Week, a canon of St Mary's by the name of Dr Beale saw fit to lay the blame for the increase in the capital's poverty squarely upon the shoulders of grasping aliens. God had given England to Englishmen, he fumed in the old familiar manner, and 'as birds would defend their nest, so ought Englishmen to cherish and defend themselves and to hurt and grieve aliens for the common weal' – with the result that only a few days later, on 28 April, Beale was taken at his word when some foreigners were buffeted in the streets and thrown into a canal. And this was not the end. For although arrests were made by order of the mayor, a rumour soon spread that on May Day the whole of the capital would rise and all foreigners be slain, prompting Thomas Wolsey in the meantime to send for the

mayor and give orders that on the eve of the fatal day every Londoner should
stay indoors between the hours of nine o'clock in the evening and seven the
following morning.

Nevertheless, as a certain Alderman Munday was attempting to enforce
the order in Cheapside, an angry crowd of watermen and apprentices, cart-
ers and priests, drawn from every quarter of the city began to run amok. The
jails were forced open and even Newgate was made to yield up those men
who had already been imprisoned for the patriotic cause. Thus reinforced, the
crowd proceeded to surge through St Nicholas' shambles towards the liberty
of St Martin's-le-Grand – one of the principal resorts of London's foreign
colony – where none other than Thomas More, then serving as under-sheriff
of London, tried in vain to reason with them. For, as the uneasy parley was
unfolding, the foreign inhabitants of the threatened buildings chose to seize
the initiative with a volley of stones and other missiles, at which point the
fury of the rioters finally span out of control. Sacking and plundering as they
went, they first wrought vengeance upon St Martin's and then steamed off to
loot the foreigners of Cornhill and Whitechapel.

In the process, the king's French secretary, Meautis, barely escaped with
his life, though the Italian merchants who came under heaviest attack were,
by contrast, too well armed to be pillaged with impunity, and it was largely
due to their resistance and Wolsey's personal influence that the forces of
order finally rallied. Doubtless in recognition of his own unpopularity, the
cardinal had initially strengthened his residence at York Place with men
and ordnance, before arranging for the lieutenant of the Tower to shoot
some rounds of artillery into the crowded streets. At the same time, he
also alerted the Earl of Shrewsbury to be ready with reinforcements, while
the Howards, leading some 1,300 troops, set about the task of restoring
order, since the apprentices, who were ready enough to loot a foreigner's
house or bludgeon a peaceful Flemish merchant or two, were altogether
less inclined to come to close quarters with trained soldiers. Instead, those
who were able to do so wisely made good their escape, though thirteen
were eventually tried upon a far-fetched charge of high treason, and for
some time afterwards the city gates would be gruesomely decorated with
their quartered remains.

Mob violence on such a scale was, it must be said, rare. But ill feeling, in
the capital especially, continued to surface against a variety of real or imagined
offences associated with outsiders. Low-standard price-cutting, the forging
of trademarks, and the seduction of honest citizens' wives were, for example,
perennial complaints, as even the more law-abiding found themselves accused
in a no-win situation of keeping themselves aloof from the native community
among whom they dwelt and reaped their profits. 'Though they be demised

or borne here among us,' ran one late sixteenth-century accusation, 'yett they keep themselves severed from us in church, in government, in trade, in language and marriage', while Andrew Boorde's depiction of a north Italian merchant in 1542 was merely one more pebble in the mountain of unfavourable portrayals of Italians in general: 'I am a Lombard and subtyll craft I have/ To decyve a gentleman, a yeman or a knave.' No more trustworthy than Jews and no less harmful than Scots and Irishmen, it seems, the Italians, like all other foreigners in England's capital, were to be kept at bay within their huddled communities, and derided accordingly on those rare occasions that they might choose to venture forth.

Not, of course, that chauvinist prejudices were the unique preserve of English men and women. On the contrary, sixteenth-century 'Europe' was awash with such preconceptions, stereotypes and antagonisms. Whether, for instance, Henry VIII really was ever stricken by what the English called the French disease, the French termed the Italian pox, the Italians dubbed the Spanish complaint and the Spanish, in their turn, duly designated the English disease, remains doubtful. But the moral of the varying terminology was plain enough to discern, and no less impervious to cure, for that matter, than the dreaded ailment of syphilis itself – one victim of which, Ulrich von Hutten, seemed keen to salve with a diet of diatribes more than worthy of the most scathing Englishman:

> I send you more salutations [he wrote from his sickbed in 1517] than there are thieves in Poland, heretics in Bohemia, boors in Switzerland ... pimps in Spain, drunkards in Saxony, harlots in Bamberg, children of Sodom in Florence.

And similar, if sometimes less earthily expressed, sentiments were common across the Continent's kingdoms, usually incorporating an unfavourable contrast between the virtues of the author's homeland and the vices of neighbours. 'On the whole,' wrote Louis le Roy in 1576, 'the Spanish are haughty ... the English and Scots proud, the Greeks cautious and subtle, the Italians wary, the French bold.' Likewise, the late medieval Spanish *Poem of Alexander* had highlighted the superiority of the Iberian temperament, though in doing so acknowledged the martial prowess of the French emphasised by Le Roy more than a century later:

> The people of Spain are vital and active,
> The French we see as bold warriors,
> The English are braggarts with false hearts,
> The Italians [Lombardos] are cowards, the Germans thieves.

And as the tide of vitriol swirled, so even the standard bearers of what might be optimistically construed as a budding European consciousness found it difficult to forgo their own generalising sideswipes at the national character-istics of their less worthy counterparts. For even Erasmus, that arch-advocate of peace and brotherhood, would nevertheless pigeon-hole the Germans as feckless and crude, the French as violent beneath a veneer of refinement, the Italians as vain and devious. While Kharon the ferryman, he declared, might willingly carry Spaniards across the Styx because they were abstemious, the English, by contrast, were resolutely banned from passage, so crammed were they with food that the boat was likely to sink under their load.

In 1536, foreshadowing Shakespeare's Portia, the protagonist of Pietro Aretino's *Dialogue in which Nanna teaches her daughter Pippa to be a whore* alerts her eager protégé to the differences in behaviour to be expected from her French, German, Spanish and Swedish clients, while precisely a decade later the Venetian ambassador to Charles V was meticulous in reporting the pitfalls to be anticipated from the employment of troops from different lands. 'Now that the country has become commercial, and is filled with beautiful and luxurious cities,' he wrote of the Dutch, 'the ancient valour has degenerated.' But it was for the Germans that his profoundest misgivings were reserved:

> The insolence of this nation is almost incredible. They are impious towards God, and cruel to their neighbour ... They are fearless of death, but can neither foresee, nor take advantage of any passing occurrence. In the assault of a city, where much skill and dexterity is required, they are the worst people that can be: and in the case of a skirmish their interminable baggage is always in the way. They are most impatient of hunger and thirst, and will insist upon being paid at the appointed moment.

Nor did stereotyping of this kind cease as one travelled to the eastern reaches of the Continent, which, as the comments of the Polish diplomat Christopher Warszewicki made clear when his Latin treatise, *On Ambassadors and Embassies*, appeared in 1595, were already closely integrated into the affairs of the West. Altogether more sober in its assessments, the book never-theless adumbrated the national variations that all sixteenth-century writers considered, in effect, 'natural':

> The position in Moscow is suited to wary men, for there 'the Greek faith' is practised and nothing can be done without lengthy disputes ... To Spain, individuals of calm temperament should be sent ... In Italy it is right that the state be represented by civilised and courteous men ... France is a place for versatile men of speedy intellect ... In England, handsome,

high-born envoys are best suited, for the English have a great respect for that sort of person, telling them apparently that it is a pity they are not Englishmen themselves. In Germany, diplomats need to keep their promises, the Germans being famed from time immemorial for their constancy and perseverance.

Altogether more curious, however, was the claim of Carlos García who, in reflecting upon the Treaty of Vervins between France and Spain in 1598, would confess how he had often wished that he had interviewed midwives in both countries to determine whether the glaring differences in temperament and attitudes might at least be partially explained by variations in the delivery methods for babies. The French, he suggested, grasp an intellectual point quickly, and then let it drop, which makes them more practical, while the Spanish absorb inferences slowly, enjoying the process of pondering. This is why, he contended, 'there are few native Spaniards who practise mechanical skills, as weavers, cobblers, tailors', and why, to the distress of travellers, there were so few innkeepers. 'But for the French to understand something,' García continues, 'is to turn it to practical advantage', with the result that 'they hate inactivity' and thus not only 'immerse themselves in all sorts of manufactures', but apply themselves also to study of the law rather than to the less practical study of scholastic theology. This much, he concludes, is clear:

> … the French are choleric, the Spanish patient; the French are sprightly, the Spaniards slow to act; the former are volatile, cheerful and impetuous, the latter are ponderous, sombre and introspective; the French eat a lot, the Spanish little; the French are givers, the Spaniards savers – one could go on comparing the one with the other and find nothing but contraries.

Yet if García's *The Antipathy between the Spanish and French Peoples* is altogether more successful in highlighting contrasts than offering explanations and solutions, it at least represented not only a commendably balanced but earnest early attempt at analysis on the basis of external as opposed to innate influences. Nor was it entirely alone in its efforts, since climate, too – not to mention cosmic influence – was perceived increasingly widely as part of the general reason why the inhabitants of one country were so different from others:

> There is no help for it [claimed Stephano Guazzo in 1574] but you must … thinke that every nation, land and countrie, by the nature of the place, the climate of the heaven, and the influence of the starres hath certaine vertues and certaine vices which are proper, naturall and perpetuall.

It was on this basis therefore, as Giovannia Botero elaborated in 1589, that 'a Spaniard doubles his energy when he goes to France, while a Frenchman in France becomes languid and dainty':

> Those who live in northern countries but not in the extreme north [he confidently asserted], are bold but lack cunning; southerners on the other hand are cunning but not bold ... The former are simple and straightforward, the latter shy and artful in their ways. They are as the lion and the fox; whereas the northerner is slow and consistent in his actions, cheerful and subject to Bacchus, the southerner is impetuous and volatile, melancholy and subject to Venus ... Mountain-dwellers are wild and proud, valley people soft and effeminate. Industry and diligence flourish in barren lands, idleness and refinement in fertile ones.

But if such attempts at geographical determinism lent an objective veneer of sorts to the debate, they nevertheless continued in the main to reinforce the ongoing tendency of contemporaries to rank the conduct of nationalities demeaningly, particularly when it came to standards of civilised behaviour. Early in the fifteenth century, the Florentine Leonardo Bruni had congratulated his fellow countryman Poggio Bracciolini on bringing back to Italy a manuscript of Quintilian from a Swiss monastery to 'deliver him from his long imprisonment in the dungeons of barbarians'. And a similar superiority and self-satisfaction extended especially to specific groups, such as the native Irish and Russians, who represented, it was said, parts of Europe impervious not only to orderly government but decorous manners of any kind – a sphere in which even supposedly enlightened commentators might not be entirely impartial. For when Erasmus noted in *De Civilitate morum puerilium libellous* (1530) – the first treatise in western Europe on the moral and practical education of children – that it was a custom of Spaniards to brush their teeth with urine, the Dutchman's apparent fastidiousness was by no means unconnected to the growing opposition to his works in the Iberian peninsula and, in particular, the liberal Catholicism he condoned.

As Europeans rankled under the load of their political and economic rivalries, moreover, they bristled with no less passion than Tudor Englishmen at the peaceable introduction of foreigners into positions of privilege and power within their own lands. When the future Holy Roman Emperor Charles V inherited the Crown of Spain in 1516, for example, he caused virulent and lasting offence by bringing with him a corps of officials and advisers from his native Burgundy, while Catherine de' Medici's lavish patronage of Italians, her former compatriots, caused widespread resentment in France between 1559 and 1589. At its peak, in the 1570s, Henri Estienne produced a diatribe against 'the new Italianised French language' and reprimanded courtiers for aping Italian mannerisms, since 'the French are not by nature given to gestures and do not like them'. And in the meantime, further afield in Poland, the arrival of Bona Sforza in 1518 after her marriage to Sigismund I had lit the slow fuse of what can only be described as a floodtide of italophobia later in the century. Royal attempts to exert some measure of centralised control over the self-patrolled anarchy of the Polish nobility were directly interpreted as the imposition of Italian, 'Machiavellian', political theory, while resentment at the economic success of Italian immigrants, exacerbated by tax exemptions on their import–export dealings, led to mockery of them as effeminates with big brains topping feeble bodies. As their unwelcome visitors thrived in mining, publishing and the growing commerce in luxury goods, Poles continued to denounce them as unmanly 'lute players' and sent their sons to German rather than Italian universities.

Not long after the death of Elizabeth I, the Englishman Fynes Moryson was at least able to denote the existence of certain distinctions between 'Italians':

The Milanese [he wrote in 1617] are said to be little jealous and to hate fat women; the Mantuans to love women that can dance; the Florentines to love a modest woman, and one that loves home; the Neapolitans to love a stately high-minded woman. Those of Lucca are said to love constantly, the Venetians contrarily, and to desire fat women with great dugs.

But generalisations – and almost invariably unfavourable ones at that – remained the order of the day for all national types, notwithstanding the fact that, occasionally at least, there were fleeting glimpses of empathy, even sympathy, between Europeans, as with the brutal sacking of Rome on 6 May 1527 when the rampant German and Spanish troops of Charles V provoked widespread horror and disgust. 'Never,' wrote one outraged commentator, 'was Rome so pilled neither by Goths nor Vandals' after relics and sacred shrines had been destroyed, virgins spoiled and wives ravished, and perhaps a quarter of the entire population killed by frenzied soldiers who, besides their other misdeeds, were said to have 'punished citizens by the privy members to cause them to confess their treasure'. Even more extraordinarily, however, Italians soon came to settle down with remarkable indifference under Spanish rule in the 1530s in the formerly independent Duchy of Milan, just as they had done in the kingdom of Naples since the beginning of the century. Though in literature, resentment found a timid outlet in portrayals of vainglorious Spaniards and their bragging troops, well-to-do Italians nevertheless freely adopted Spanish costume and manners with more than passing enthusiasm, and beyond the Alps too, there were some early inklings of growing intercourse and acceptance. For on the broader level, the increasing traffic across the Continent of diplomats, merchants, artists and scholars all played their part in encouraging a modicum of mutual understanding. All countries also employed foreign mercenaries and, ironically enough, at least among the officers within rival forces, friendships and mutual admiration were not unheard of, as is clear from Pierre de Brantôme's *Lives of the Captains* and, indeed, a whole range of military memoirs.

Even so, it was not until around 1600, it seems, that voices were raised more generally against the free-for-all consolations of snap judgements and routine prejudice, since by then the pressing need for international peace and the sense of responsibility of more widely educated men was at last encouraging a less blinkered vision. The German cosmographer Johann Rauw noted in 1597, for instance, how 'the old saying is true: no country is worth three pennies more than any other'. And the very early stirrings of a significant sea change were evident elsewhere, too. 'There is hardly a nation under the sun that has no special faults and merits,' wrote the Dutchman Karel von Mander in 1604 when recommending the virtue of travel for artists, while four years later Joseph Hall – though once more acknowledging that 'the French are commonly called rash, the Spaniard proud, the Dutch drunken, the English busy-hands, the Italian effeminate, the Swethens timorous, the Bohemians inhuman, the Irish barbarous and superstitious' – nevertheless went on to ask, 'is any man so sottish as to think that France hath no staid man at all in it, Spain no meacock [weakling], or Germany none that lives so soberly?'

Nor, it must be said, were the actions of Hall's Tudor compatriots towards foreigners invariably as harsh as their words or occasional outbursts of violence might suggest. Certainly, the eventual association of Protestantism with patriotism and economic expansion afforded Flemish refugees in the second half of the sixteenth century an altogether different reception from that dealt out to aliens during the Steelyard riots of October 1497 or the Evil May Day disorders twenty years later. 'You would never believe,' wrote Clais van Wervekin to his wife, 'how friendly the people are together and the English are the same and quite loving to our nation ... Send my money and the three children. Come at once and do not be anxious.' This was from Norwich in 1567, and Protestant patriotism was likewise the force that created the English intervention in the Dutch wars against Spain when, in May 1572, the first three hundred men, paid for by public subscription, left London to help the privateering Sea Beggars newly established in Flushing.

Sheer self-interest, too, might sometimes act as a restraint upon any more typical inclination towards xenophobia. Earlier, in January 1528 for example, textile workers had rioted in Somerset, Wiltshire and East Anglia when English sales in the Netherlands and Spain were disrupted by Thomas Wolsey's declaration of war against Charles V, while opposition to Henry VIII's divorce from the emperor's aunt, Catherine of Aragon, was just as firmly underpinned by the fall in short-cloth exports from London to Antwerp, which had stood at 75,000 in 1529 before tumbling to 66,000 at the height of the marriage crisis. In 1525, likewise, the tax known as the 'Amicable Grant' stirred overwhelming opposition – to the extent that royal councillors were jostled in the streets by irate crowds who denounced the war with France as a waste of money, likely to conquer 'not one foot' of the ancient enemy's territory. Sir Thomas Boleyn was roughly handled in Maidstone, while the new Duke of Norfolk, who had succeeded his father the previous year, was met with stiff opposition at Lavenham and Sudbury in particular. And as Cambridge students rioted at the prospect of foreign conflict, so Huntingdonshire and Essex also rumbled, along with the men of Chelmsford and Stansted who refused to pay, causing certain commissioners to report how 'some fear to be hewn in pieces if they make any grant'.

In this case, of course, it was 'Captain Poverty' rather than compassion or any sense of commonality that explained Englishmen's reluctance to wreak havoc upon helpless French peasants. But at a spiritual level, undeniably, some large groups of anonymous Tudor folk felt at one time or another that their experience of life only made sense in association with the beliefs of a broader, united Christendom, as in 1536 when the Pilgrimage of Grace shook Thomas Cromwell's protestantising government to its foundations and, to a lesser extent, in 1569 when the rebellion of the Northern Earls had a not altogether dissimilar impact. Even so, of course, the forces of religion and commerce cut both ways, and were always more likely to fuel further vilification of foreigners among Shakespeare's 'mutable rank-scented many', especially when commercial exclusion went hand-in-hand with what Tudor Englishmen, high and low alike, interpreted as manifest collusion between Rome and Spain. Ironically, in 1549 the so-called 'Prayer Book' rebellion had originated in Cornwall partly as a result of vexation at the introduction of Protestant innovations derived from the Continent, but as the second half of the century wore on, it was invariably Catholicism's relationship with Spain, and in particular the papacy's association with Spain's commercial monopoly in the New World, dating back to the Treaty of Tordesillas in 1494, that confirmed the darkest suspicions of English men and women – suspicions amplified exponentially as a result of sentences such as those pronounced against Sir John Hawkins' sailors by the Inquisition's *auto da fe* in February 1574:

William Collins, of Oxford, age 40, seaman, ten years in the galleys; John Farenton, of Windsor, 49, gunner, six years in the galleys; John Burton, of

Bar Abbey, 22, seaman, 200 lashes and six years in the galleys; Paul de Leon
of Rotterdam, 22, seaman, 200 lashes and six years in the galleys; William
Griffin, of Bristol, 24, seaman, 200 lashes and eight years in the galleys;
George Ribley, of Gravesend, 30, seaman, burnt at the stake, but first strangled; John Moon, of Looe, 26, seaman, 200 lashes and six years in the galleys;
John Lee, of 'Sebria' [*sic*], 20, seaman or gunner, 200 lashes and eight years
in the galleys; William Brown, of London, 25, steward, 200 lashes and six
years in the galleys; Thomas Goodal, of London, 30, soldier, 300 lashes and
ten years in the galleys; John Gilbert, of London, 29, seaman, 300 lashes
and ten years in the galleys; Roger Armar, of Gueldres (Netherlands), 24,
armourer, 200 lashes and six years in the galleys; Michael Morgan (alias
Morgan Tillert), of Cardiff, 40, seaman, 200 lashes and eight years in the
galleys; John Brown, of Ireland, 28, seaman, 200 lashes and eight years in
the galleys; John Williams of Cornwall, 28, 200 lashes and eight years in the
galleys; Robert Plinton, of Plymouth, 30, 200 lashes and eight years in the
galleys; John Grey, Englishman, 22, gunner, 200 lashes and eight years in the
galleys; George Dee, Englishman, 30, seaman, 300 lashes and eight years in
the galleys.

In the wake of Hawkins' account of his fight at San Juan de Ulúa in
September 1568, moreover, the smouldering antagonisms, hitherto checked
by politics, were allowed ever freer play, as Spanish Catholicism was alternately
dismissed as mere hypocrisy or damned as an outright encouragement to vice.
'For matter of religion,' wrote Sir Walter Raleigh in his account of Sir Richard
Grenville's death at the Battle of Flores in 1591, 'it would require a particular volume, if I should set down how irreligiously they cover their greedy
and ambitious pretences with that veil of piety,' while James Wadsworth, the
English double agent, informed his readers how:

> the Spaniards were and are little better than Atheists, only making use of the
> Pope for their own particular ambitions and ends, as to confirm and estab-
> lish him in unlawful monarchies, and under colour of Religion to make
> Subjects become slaves.

More serious still from the moralist's perspective was the assertion of Sir
Francis Drake's chaplain, who claimed that 'the poisonous infection of Popery'
is introduced wherever the Spanish go, and that there is therefore no city, village or house in the Indies 'wherein (amongst the other like Spanish virtues)
not only whoredom, but the filthiness of Sodom, not to be named among
Christians, is not common without reproof'. According to Raleigh's lieutenant, Lawrence Keymis, this was to be explained by the fact that Spaniards

considered themselves 'well and surely blessed, however they live, if their towns and houses be religiously crossed'.

Yet in 1555, while Mary Tudor still shared the Crown of England with Philip II, some Englishmen like Richard Eden, translator of Peter Martyr's *The Decades of the Newe Worlde*, were nevertheless ready to declare how the kings of Spain 'are more deserving of the name of hero than those men of antiquity who are generally accounted such', since in 'enlarging the Christian world' they had set an example for all nations. For Eden, furthermore, the repression associated with Spanish rule was actually nothing less than commendable, particularly in relation to the Indians of their subject American lands whose:

> bondage is such as is much rather to be desired than their former liberty which was to the cruel cannibals rather a horrible licentiousness than a liberty, and to the innocent so terrible a bondage, that in the midst of their fearful idleness, they were ever in danger to be a prey to those manhunting wolves. But the Spaniards as ministers of grace and liberty, brought unto these new gentiles the victory of Christ's death whereby they being subdued by the worldly sword, are now made free from the bondage of Satan's tyranny.

Plainly, what was resolutely construed as wickedness by the time of the Spanish Armada could still be construed as piety just over three decades earlier amid the swirling eddies of political circumstance. But as fever mounted steadily against the 'dark Popish Domdaniel' of Spain during the reign of Elizabeth I, so two books, perhaps more than any others, achieved particular popularity and, in doing so, stirred English audiences to new heights of outrage. One was a curious volume entitled *A Discovery & Plaine Declaration of sundry Subtill practices of the Holy Inquisition of Spain* by 'Reginaldus Gonsalvius Montanus' – an unknown figure probably connected in some way with the Lutheran community of Seville, which was destroyed in that city during 1557–58 – and the other was John Foxe's *Actes and Monuments*, which in 1570 incorporated an appended section in recognition of the growing interest in Spanish wrongdoing. Both works took pains to emphasise what Foxe termed 'the extreme dealing and cruel ravening of these Catholic Inquisitors of Spain, who, under the pretended visor of religion, do nothing but seek their private gain and commodity, with crafty defrauding and spoiling of other men's goods'. But Foxe, in particular, was keen to highlight the 'brutish and beastly madness' entailed by the Inquisition's activities in cases like that of the English merchant Nicholas Burton who, on 5 November 1560, was seized while discussing commercial matters and placed in Cadiz jail. After questioning, not as to his faith but only with regard to the location of his goods, he was held without charge for fourteen days before being taken to Seville and burnt on 20 December. Likewise, both Foxe and Montanus, as well as Richard Hakluyt the Younger, recorded the case of another merchant, John Fronton, who lost his goods for omitting the final *Sancta Maria mater Dei ora pro nobis peccatoribus* in saying his Ave Maria, though the most memorable tale of its kind came perhaps from Sir Walter Raleigh, who reputedly discovered some Spaniards about to walk off with an innocent Fleming's worldly treasures. When the poor fellow protested that he was a good Catholic, the rascally Iberians nevertheless declared that while he himself was undoubtedly of the True Faith, his goods were heretic and therefore subject to confiscation.

As William Warner paraphrased it in *Albion's England* (1602), 'This Spanish Inquisition is a Trap so slyly set/As into it Wise, Godly, Rich, by Blanchers base are met.' Elsewhere, Fox tells us how Spain's Inquisitors were equally capable of extorting their own countrymen and exacting similar punishments to those meted out upon English victims. In one story, we hear how a maker of holy images was offered a fraction of the going price for one of his wares, and, unaware of the purchaser's identity, swore to smash his work rather than sell it so cheaply. Whereupon, goaded beyond endurance, the poor fellow made good his word, only to be arrested immediately as a desecrator of sacred images. Later burned, his fate was suitably exploited by Foxe to reinforce the recurring theme:

> The abuse of this inquisition is most execrable. If any word shall pass out of the mouth of any, which may be taken in evil part, yea, though no word be spoken, yet if they bear any grudge or evil will against the party, incontinent they command him to be taken, and put into a horrible prison, and then find out crimes against him at their leisure, and in the meantime, no man living is so hardy as once to open his mouth for him.

All things, Foxe tells us, were done 'hugger mugger and in close corners, by ambiages, by covert ways and secret counsels', and while Montanus describes prisoners treated worse than dogs, imprisoned together in holes, several at a time, and subject to the use of hot coals – notwithstanding the fact that such a torture was expressly forbidden by the Instructions of Valencia of 1561 – Foxe himself embroiders his own account with a description of cells in which the wretched prisoner 'cannot see so much as the ground where he is, and is not suffered either to read or to write, but there endureth in darkness palpable, in horrors infinite, in fear miserable, wrestling with the assaults of death':

Add moreover to the distresses and horrors of the prison [Foxe concludes], the injuries, threats, whippings and scourgings, irons, tortures and racks which they there endure, sometimes also they are brought out, and showed forth to the people as a symbol of rebuke and infamy. And thus they are detained there, some many years, and murdered by long torments, and whole days together are treated more cruelly out of all comparison, than if they were in the hangman's hands to be slain all at once.

For Montanus's translator, Thomas Skinner:

… the monstrous racking of men without order of law, the villainous tormenting of naked women beyond all humanity, their miserable death without pity or mercy, the most reproachful triumphing of the Popish Synagoge over Christians as over Paynims and Ethnics … ought surely … to move us to compassion.

And his appeal, along with others like it, not only struck home potently, but ensured the steady emergence of figures like Francis Drake as national folk heroes – notwithstanding the fact that the very term 'nation' was still of limited currency at that time.

For in England as elsewhere, the word was hardly ever used before the seventeenth century to refer to all the inhabitants of a particular country. Instead, either it pertained to men of a particular category, regardless of their origin, as in the educationalist Roger Ascham's denunciation in 1570 of 'the barbarous nation of scholemen', or it was applied to a discrete body of foreigners living abroad. In universities where there were large numbers of foreign students, such as Bologna, Padua, Paris and Montpellier, the partly self-governing sections into which they were divided were known as 'nations'. And the same was true when the banished Italian merchants of Lyons – mainly Florentine in origin – petitioned Henri IV in 1494 for a restoration of their privileges there, appealing in the name of 'the Florentine nation'. Where other forms of expression were used to specify what might be considered some inchoate sense of nationhood, they were invariably employed in exhortation rather than routinely: in other words, to arouse a feeling of common identity rather than to reflect a pre-existing one. Thus, Rudolf Agricola might speak of 'our Germany' and Martin Luther of 'we Germans', while Niccolò Machiavelli appealed emotively to 'Italy' and 'the Italians', and Guillaume Budé paid homage to the 'Genius of France'. But for most 'Germans', as the saying went, 'Hesse was fatherland and Bavaria abroad', and the same was no less true of Florentines, Neapolitans, Milanese and Venetians, not to mention Parisians, Gascons, denizens of Provence, citizens of Languedoc or any other region of the patchwork of local communities constituting early modern France. Far more acutely aware of 'foreigners' than of their own 'national' identity, the sentiment of nationhood therefore only rang true within a country at exceptional moments of danger from outside threats, and even then such rallying calls from the centre faded to whispers and eventually to silence wherever men slowly passed along unmade roads into regions with their own forms of speech and patterns of local loyalties. As such, ironically enough, it was only gut reactions to 'them' that gradually served to forge a more refined notion of 'us' whether as Englishmen, Frenchmen, Germans, Italians or, ultimately indeed, as 'Europeans'.

Nor, of course, was this surprising when it is remembered that in all languages 'foreigner' had, in any case, a double meaning – applying not only to aliens but also to 'outsiders' from as little as 10 or 20 miles away who arrived to compete for jobs or burden local charitable services. 'Countries' were, indeed, still little more than congeries of regional and local identities themselves, and the approach of a popular German geography textbook – Johannes Honter's *Rudimenta Cosmographica* of 1542 – was typical of its day, illustrating rivers, mountains and major cities but no borders, and reflecting in its place names, all in Latin, the provinces of the Roman and medieval worlds rather than contemporary political realities. On the map of France, significantly, 'Burgundia Gallia' (Burgundy) and Brittania Celtica (Brittany) are printed in larger capitals than 'Francia', which is itself inscribed above 'Lutecia' (Paris). Neither was it coincidental that, upon nearing the French capital in 1517, one Italian traveller commented gratefully how he had at last entered 'the real France', or that ten years later Thomas Bedyll would remark in a letter to Thomas Cromwell how 'London is the common country of all England'.

Certainly, the importance of a uniform mode of speech in characterising the inner coherence of a country was recognised as early as 1492, when the first grammar of the Spanish language was presented to a surprised Queen Isabella by its author, the humanist Antonio de Nebrija, who is said to have justified its adoption because, 'Madam, language is the instrument of empire.' On similar grounds, an edict issued by Francis I in 1539 proposed that the form of French spoken in the Paris region should be adopted as the official language across the entire kingdom. And as early as 1490, though mainly for entrepreneurial reasons, William Caxton had also sounded the call for a common language in England. For how else as a printer specialising in translations, he complained, was he to choose 'between plain, rude and curious forms' of the native tongue? In making his case, moreover, he instanced a London merchant who could not make himself understood in East Anglia. But he might easily have cited any one of a number of outlying regions, the most obvious of which was Cornwall, where, at the outset of Henry VII's reign, the county was still divided into three distinct linguistic blocs: West Cornwall, inhabited by a population of Celtic descent, which was mostly Cornish speaking; the western part of East Cornwall, inhabited by a population of Celtic descent, which had largely abandoned the Cornish dialect in favour of 'English'; and the eastern part of East Cornwall populated by people of Anglo–Saxon descent, which was entirely English speaking. And though philological studies suggest that the Cornish language had been in retreat since the Middle Ages, the western rebels of 1549 would nevertheless declare in Article 8 of their demands how they disapproved of the introduction of the new Prayer Book on the grounds that 'we the Cornyshe men (whereof certen of us understande no Englysh) utterly refuse thys newe English'.

Under the circumstances, a nation that had difficulty in communicating with itself was always less likely to acquire the languages of its foreign neighbours – and particularly the spoken variant. In 1554 men of Littlebourne in Kent were still using the term 'countrymen' only for fellow villagers. And while gentlemen were less parochial in outlook, differences in speech resulting from such insularity were hardly less pronounced among the well-born than the humble. Among Elizabeth I's courtiers, Sir Christopher Hatton habitually wrote – and very likely said – 'axe' for 'ask', while the Earl of Leicester wrote 'hit' for 'it', and Raleigh, Aubrey was told, 'spake broad Devonshire to his dying day', notwithstanding 'his conversation with the learnedest and politest persons'. True, such local differences were receding, with the result that even in Cornwall most people had become at least bilingual by the end of the century – 'unless', in the words of John Norden, 'it be some obscure people, that seldome confer with the better sorte'. But in Wales the problem was more entrenched still, as reflected in the complaint of one Welsh Catholic priest who protested in the mid-century against the missionary efforts of his Protestant counterparts in the hills and valleys of his birthplace. 'What should English men do there,' he declared, 'which have not the languadge?' And nor would Henry VIII's attempts to solve the issue by compulsion prove any more successful than attempts to regularise the language elsewhere. Indeed, in 1549 William Thomas still saw fit to note in his *Historie of Italie* the 'great diversitie of speech, as with us between a Londoner and a Yorkshyreman', and to contrast this with Italian gentlemen who all spoke the 'courtisane' tongue and had no regional accents.

In Italy too, meanwhile, Machiavelli had seen fit in 1516 to lament that Tuscan, the classic tongue of Dante, Petrarch and Boccaccio, was under challenge from those who ignored the example of Florence and who 'confound her language with those of Milan, Venice and the Romagna and with all the filthy usages of Lombardy'. His concern, it is true, was largely literary, but its vigour owed something to his distress that the peninsula's regions, sharply distinct from one another, could not unite against the 'barbarian' foreigners', France, Spain and Germany, and their invading armies. And his misgivings were demonstrated aptly enough in 1538, when a military engineer from Bergamo, Venice's subject city in Lombardy, was dismissed from Venetian service because, in spite of his undoubted skills, his dialect was so distinctive that 'he had the defect of not being able to communicate his ideas'.

So far as the printed word was concerned, there was, in fact, a marked advance in the uniformity of languages. But while such gaping divergences continued to prevail in spoken discourse, the development of national consciousness would always be dilatory. It was a Frenchman, Charles de Rouelle, who complained that in travelling across his homeland in the mid-sixteenth century, he encountered no fewer than eight different ways of saying 'yes' and 'no'. And dialects were not simply a matter of aberrant pronunciation, but of divergent syntax and vocabulary. It was all very well for Johann Rauw to observe in 1597, for example, that in a journey of 'ninety-three days … you would walk the circumference of Germany as far as the German language is spoken', but he ignored both the differences between southern and northern Germany, as well as those within each. Indeed, when the first north German translation of the Bible was published in 1479, it was presented in double columns to take account of the Frankish and Saxon forms of the language. Furthermore, even the surge of books and pamphlets accompanying the Reformation, and directly aimed at a mass readership, had produced little change a century later.

But while national consciousness continued in the main to languish, the same was becoming less true paradoxically for the notion of 'Europe' itself – all of which was reflected in a growing preoccupation among artists, poets and scholars like the Florentine Angelo Poliziano with the Greek myth of Europa, a Phoenician princess impregnated by Zeus, 'transformed for love into a handsome white bull', whose divinely sired progeny were said to have become the inheritors of the Continent. The source of this fable, Ovid's *Metamorphoses*, was already well known to medieval writers, and it was no mere coincidence that in 1471, around the very time that Poliziano was rekindling the tale, a woodcut in a treatise on the virginity of the Holy Mother should have shown Europa leaning forward to touch a bull in an image that paralleled earlier depictions of the Madonna and a unicorn. Later, in 1512, a pen-and-ink drawing by the Nuremberg artist Peter Fischer the Younger adopted a similar theme, though by then Albrecht Dürer had already immortalised it with another woodcut, *The Rape of Lucretia*, produced in 1495. From that time forth, in every medium from painting to pottery, relief sculpture to enamel, the story gradually gathered pace, captured on the one hand in objects such as a majolica dish of the 1550s held by the British Museum, in which the bull firmly parts the maiden's legs while Cupid looks on approvingly, and most supremely of all by Titian's supremely confident portrayal of 1559–62, painted for Philip II of Spain whose family by that time dominated almost half of the Continent's western and central portions.

That Europeans perhaps shared something more than their Christianity had been hinted at, too, by an editor of the first printing press to be established in Italy in 1465, who saw them as successors of the Roman Empire and thereby 'men of the Latin world'. But it was more significant still, perhaps, that, in reviewing the Protestant isolation following Elizabeth I's succession to her Catholic sister, Mary, in 1558, the Spanish ambassador in London should actually refer to England as 'the sick man of Europe' – and no less indicative of the evolving trend that twenty years later an entry in the *Geographical Encyclopaedia* of the great Brabantian cartographer Abraham Ortelius simply reads 'For Christians, see Europeans'. While the Frenchman, Guillaume Postel, might in 1561 frown upon the indecency of paying homage to a liaison involving a bull and a woman, his suggestion that 'Europe' should be renamed 'Japetie' – after Japeth, the son of Noah, who had populated the area after the Flood – had clearly proved futile. Instead, in an age of revived Latinity, the newly discovered continent of 'Europe' would have to be feminine in precisely the way encapsulated on the title page of Ortelius's famous atlas of 1572. Sternly ensconced on a throne beneath an arbour, she holds in one hand the sceptre of world domination, while the other extends over an orb, of globe-like dimensions, marked with the Christian cross. Below, and obviously subservient to her are three other female characters, a richly clad Asia, a semi-naked Africa, and a nude America holding up a human head as a witness to her cannibalism.

And here again, of course, the evolving perception of Europe's distinctness from 'others' was key. Visiting the governor of the new English colonies along the James River in 1640, David de Vries, born in La Rochelle in 1593 to Dutch parents, would be welcomed with a glass of Venetian wine and sit down with an English colonist who, like him, had also been in the East Indies in the 1620s. 'I looked at him well,' de Vries recounted, 'and he at me', before hearing the colonist remark 'that mountains could not meet one another, but men who see the world can'. By their clothes, their food, their demeanour, these individuals were self-consciously European – men who, 'having steered the four corners of the earth', were now more aware of their common cultural heritage than they could ever have been a century earlier. Landing at St John's, Newfoundland, in 1620, after marvelling at the monumental icebergs he encountered en route, de Vries had been struck by the Dutch, Basque, Portuguese and English vessels that were now fishing and trading in those waters. And if he was left in any doubt at that point about the features they shared, notwithstanding peculiarities of language, custom and habit, such doubts were progressively overcome by his curious encounters with the local Indians among whom he went on to live at some length.

By then, too, the early seventeenth-century English collector of travel narratives, Samuel Purchas, had made himself spokesman for the idea of what amounted to a common European identity. 'Asia,' he wrote, 'yeerely sends us her spices, silks and gemmes; Africa her gold and ivory; America … [is] almost everywhere admitting European colonies.' In every department of life, predictably, whether it be the liberal arts or the mechanical ones (like 'the many artificiall mazes and labyrinths in our watches'), superiority, as far as he was concerned, belonged to 'wee in the West'. It was 'ours' and belonged to 'us' by right, notwithstanding the awkward fact that the Turks remained masters of Greece and the Balkans, as well as much of Albania and the whole of Bosnia. By the 1530s, indeed, Sultan Suleiman had already added the epithet 'Lord of Europe' to his numerous other titles, as his all-conquering janissaries moved up from Bucharest, Belgrade and Budapest to within a few days' march of Vienna. There, it is true, they were held for the moment. But in a medal struck at about the same time, the figure of the Emperor Charles V was shown supported by an angel and haunted by Suleiman's turbaned profile. Nor would the status quo alter during Samuel Purchas's lifetime.

Yet their encounters with Turks, no less than their dealings with the native peoples of the Americas and the Indies, further convinced Europeans of their common distinctiveness. To those who viewed the Ottoman Empire from outside, of course, its rulers were above all responsible for the kind of monstrous inhumanity that even their European contemporaries found alien. What Christian monarch, for example, might have strangled all nineteen of his brothers – as Mahommed III had done – to prevent any challenge to his succession? European rulers, it is true, burned, tortured and maimed, but only Turks impaled, ramming a pointed stake up through the anus and out between the collarbones, regardless of age or sex, to leave the skewered victim suspended above ground as a warning to others. Indeed, images by German artists like Erhard Schoen of the siege of Vienna in 1529 and later Imperial–Turkish wars peppered the landscape with such writhing figures. And whenever a Turk featured in an English or French play in the later sixteenth century, he invariably appeared laden with dreadful associations, however facetiously employed, so that while Elizabeth I might see fit to endorse trading relations with Constantinople in 1581 through the Turkey Company, she was nevertheless quick to condemn her official ambassador Edward Barton for accompanying Mahommed III on his war of 1593 against Austria, on the grounds that 'he had borne the English armes upon his tent … in the Turkes campe against Christians'.

Not all self-comparisons with Turks were, in fact, so favourable to the Europeans who made them. For in addition to their comparative tolerance of other religious views, the sultan's subjects continued to take their own faith seriously enough for the Protestant radical Thomas Müntzer to remark in the 1520s that if a devout Turk came to worship in Catholic Europe in search of added grace 'he would gain about as much as a midge could carry on his tail'. And there was like acknowledgement, for that matter, of the spotlessness of Turkish homes and the emphasis upon hygiene, including the cleanliness of turbans in particular, which provided so many highlights in the narrative paintings of Vittore Carpaccio. The discipline and patient endurance of Turkish soldiers was manifest to those who encountered them on the field of battle, while a passing observation made by Pietro della Valle, a visitor to Constantinople, contrasted the fidgety, self-preening behaviour of Europeans at a grand reception with the decorous stillness that prevailed in Turkey. While the guests from Europe spent their time 'hurrying about, as if on important business, walking from one end of the rooms to another, and then returning, and then going back yet again, either alone or accompanied, with nothing else to do', their Turkish counterparts looked on impassively, finding their visitors' behaviour 'very strange'.

Once again, significantly, the emphasis was upon the Turks' 'otherness', and the growing awareness of a common European 'us' was only reinforced by further encounters with unfamiliar cultures. The Hindu devotion to their idols 'puts us Christians to shame for the laziness with which we exert ourselves in the cult and service of the true God', wrote della Valle as his travels proceeded, while Francis Xavier's Jesuits continually contrasted Japanese customs with European after the saint's first mission in 1549. When defecating, one priest noticed, 'we sit, they crouch', while Xavier himself was particularly preoccupied with Japanese writing. 'I am sending you,' he informed his superiors at home, 'a copy of the Japanese alphabet; their way of writing is very different from ours because they write their lines from the top of the page down to the bottom.' The reason for this, Xavier continued, had been explained to him by a convert named Paul who 'explained that as the head of a man is at the top and his feet are at the bottom, so too a man should write from top to bottom'. And while Xavier makes no specific mention of 'Europe' or 'Europeans', by 1584 Alessandro Valignano's *Historia del Principo y Progresso de la Compania de Jesus en las Indias Orientales (1542–64)* was replete with such references. For, after noting the superiority of Japanese politeness 'not only to other eastern peoples but also to Europeans as well' and observing how Japanese children learn more quickly and do not fight or hit one another 'like European boys', Valignano went on to declare how:

> it may truly be said that Japan is a world the reverse of Europe; everything is so different and opposite that they are like us in practically nothing. So great is the difference in their food, clothing, honours, ceremonies, language, management of the household, in their way of negotiating, sitting, building, curing the wounded and sick, teaching and bringing up children, and in everything else, that it can be neither described nor understood ... To see how everything is the reverse of Europe, despite the fact that their ceremonies and customs are so cultivated and founded on reason, causes no little surprise to anyone who understands such things.

Contact with Africa, too, had done no less to stir an appreciation of Europeanness, as African slaves rowed gondolas for their Venetian owners, and negro servants were treated as pets in wealthy households throughout the northern Mediterranean, leaving the hero of the early picaresque Spanish novel *Lazarillo de Tormes* (1554) undismayed when his mother took a negro as a lover. In 1596, Elizabeth I complained that there were too many 'blackamoores' competing with needy Englishmen for places as domestic servants, while Shakespeare's *Othello* represented a comparatively sympathetic, if nevertheless alarming, middle way between the frequent depictions of Africans in literature as evil. More representative of Tudor opinion in general, perhaps, was Ben Jonson's *Masque of Blackness*, in which a courtier representing the River Niger comes to London with his black daughters to see how far the English sun might 'blanch an Ethiop'. Assured that this will undoubtedly happen in the altered climate, the River retires happy in the conviction that his daughters will become white and therefore in European eyes more beautiful.

Plainly, the impact of travel, exploration and discovery was beginning by the end of the sixteenth century to leave its mark upon Englishmen just as it had done rather earlier upon newly self-conscious Europeans. And just as the English sense of a common 'us' had been prompted by a heightened awareness of a European 'them', so a growing awareness of a common European culture, over and beyond the national differences that moulded the prejudices of the majority, was also emerging. When Francis Bacon produced *The History of the Reign of Henry VII* in 1622, he would refer to the monarch's tomb in Westminster Abbey – designed by the Italian Pietro Torrigiano – as 'one of the stateliest and daintiest monuments *in Europe*', on the safe assumption that his readers would know precisely what he meant. And he had been on equally sure ground with his observations in *The Advancement of Learning* (1605) regarding England's involvement in the 'affairs of Europe'. In the extended Latin version of that book, indeed, he would freely refer to 'Nos Europäi' – 'we Europeans' – and in doing so reflect an evolving mindset distinct in a range of ways from the perceptions and attitudes of his compatriots who had witnessed the dawn of the Tudor age more than a century earlier. Yet if Bacon embraced the apparent sea change with precisely the kind of enthusiasm that might be expected from such a high-minded proponent of 'progress', there still persisted among most of his countrymen a residing sense of England's distinctiveness. For rulers and ruled alike, indeed, England remained an island realm 'off' rather than 'of' Europe, sundered, as the poet John Gylford put it in 1611, from the 'transmarine nations' and, more importantly still, secure from the regular convulsions that continued to trouble what he nevertheless termed 'the CONTINENT'.

2

MAPS, CITIES, DYNASTIES, STATES

From my tender youth I had a great desire to see foreign countries, not to get liberty (which I had in Cambridge in such measure, as I could not well desire more), but to enable my understanding, which I thought could not be done so well by contemplation as by my experience; nor by the ear or any sense so well, as by the eyes. And having once again begun this course, I could not see any man without emulation, and a kind of virtuous envy, who had seen more cities, kingdoms and provinces, or more courts of princes, kings and emperors than myself.

From Fynes Moryson, *An Itinerary* (1591–97)

If awareness of Europe's common cultural identity would emerge only falter-ingly during the sixteenth century, the Continent's existence as a geographical abstraction nevertheless long pre-dated the arrival of the first Tudor upon his throne in 1485. Strabo's *Geography* of *c.* AD 10 was familiar to scholars of the Middle Ages well before it encouraged Columbus to believe that Asia could be reached directly by sailing westwards across the Atlantic. And with the book's emphasis upon the wide range of Europe's micro-climates and their products, as well as its concentration of towns and cities, and above all the orderly, law-abiding lives of its inhabitants, the foundations were duly laid for that abiding sense of superiority that, by 1570, was being voiced anew by those like the cartographer Abraham Ortelius. From Strabo's perspective, Europe was, 'both varied in form and ideally adapted by nature for the devel-opment of excellence in men and governments', while Ortelius considered its 'stately cities, townes and villages' so 'pleasant and so beautiful', and the peoples of its 'severall nations' so blessed with 'courage and valour' that their native continent was, without doubt, 'superior unto other parts of the world'. Criss-crossed by trade routes from east to west, supposedly self-sufficient in all the food, metals and human resources necessary for its defence, Europe was already well on its way, it might seem, to becoming what the philosopher Hegel later termed 'the centre and end' of History itself.

Yet by 'Europe' Strabo had meant only the Mediterranean, and the geographical information contained in the maps of his medieval successors had in any case remained almost wholly subsidiary to their two symbolic functions: to remind the viewer that God had created a world comprising a circle of lands whose centre was Jerusalem; and to reinforce the belief that what mattered principally was not where but who Europeans were – which meant Christians first and last. The earliest surviving geographical representations, dating from the eleventh century, are in this respect all depictions of religious heritage rather than physical space, and it was only natural, therefore, that the accuracy of these so-called 'TO' maps (named from the stylised T-form of the waters separating the continents and the ocean surrounding the entire world) should have suffered accordingly. Subsequently, the maker of the late thirteenth-century Hereford map of the world would still inscribe 'Europa' across Africa and vice versa, and pay little regard to their relative size. And even two hundred years further on – by which time study of the second-century-geographer Ptolemy was leading to a new generation of maps centred upon the Indian Ocean – Europe continued to be presented most frequently as little more than a waif-like extension of Asia.

But from the early sixteenth century, thanks to a new mathematical interest in cartographical projections that could take account of the curvature of the earth, backed up by more accurate assessments of degrees of latitude, and the unprecedented expansion of knowledge of the world's surface, Europeans became able to intuit, with increasing degrees of accuracy, the geographical expanse in which they lived. In the process, the production of maps became nothing less than an outright craze as the new century progressed, with statesmen employing them for strategic purposes, and rulers commissioning them as symbols of power – framing, hanging and painting them on walls, rolling and folding whole collections of them in chests or on shelves, admiring them in woven tapestries, and making them part of their everyday mental furniture. Duke Cosimo de' Medici of Florence, for example, had a large room dedicated to cartography as part of his refurbishment of the Palazzo Vecchio, with the result that the walls of the Sala delle Carte Graphiche are lined to this day with fifty-four maps: twenty-three drawn by Stefano Bonsignori, and a further thirty-one completed by Ignazio Danti between 1563 and 1575. By which time, the fruits of such enthusiasm had already proven revolutionary, after Martin Waldseemüller produced in 1511 the first map of Europe to be independent of both the Jerusalem and the Ptolemaic traditions.

Soon after its reissue nine years later, moreover, Waldseemüller's map was to be followed by a string of others, which in 1554 culminated in the 5ft engraved *Europe* of the Flemish mathematician and cartographer Gerardus Mercator. The largest representation to that time of any continent, Mercator depicted, in fact, a conventionally triumphalist image, with Europe's plains, forests and mountain chains clearly marked, and so crammed with towns and cities that southern Italy appeared as populous as its northern counterpart, and Hungary no less densely peopled than France. Portugal's towns, likewise, seemed equally numerous to those of the Netherlands. Yet if such inaccuracies were regrettable, the overall message remained undeniable – that Europe was not only awash with natural resources and man-made centres of activity, but a discrete entity steadily subordinating the rest of the globe to its energies. Henceforth, the idea of the atlas became firmly entrenched in the budding European consciousness, as sales mushroomed and they became must-have items for any gentleman of sophisticated pretensions. For although Ortelius's *Theatrum*, with its total of fifty-three maps in all, was probably the most costly of all books published in the sixteenth century, it had nevertheless run to a total of forty editions by the century's end, and stimulated the market for cheaper versions like Matthias Quadt's *Atlas of Europe*, published in a smaller format in 1594, which contained not only a representation of Europe as a whole but fifty others from which only Russia, Norway and Ireland were missing.

At the same time, a steady stream of regional maps also poured forth from gifted amateurs, as triangulation by means of compass, plane table and the alidade (sight rule) became commonplace, and illustrated handbooks offered suitable instruction on how enthusiasts might employ not only symbols for towns, cities, castles and river crossings, but distance scales as well. Yet in England, significantly, interest in cartography remained comparatively dilatory and narrow in scope – particularly where representations of Europe as a whole were concerned. In 1579, Christopher Saxton completed the first national compilation of maps of the kingdom's regions, and by 1602 George Owen would write in his *Description of Pembrokeshire* how such maps 'are usual with all noblemen and gentlemen, and daily perused by them for their better instruction of the estate of this realm'. More famous still among Tudor cartographers was John Speed, whose *Theatre of Great Britain* eventually appeared in 1612. But when Mercator's great *Atlas Sive Cosmographicae Meditationes de Fabrica Mundi et Fabricati Figura* was published in England in 1595 and dedicated to Elizabeth I, it had no English rival remotely worthy of the name. Aside from its sixteen maps of Britain, another twelve dealt with the poles and the northern European and Baltic States, which English cartographers had hitherto ignored. And it was a further sign of England's intellectual insularity, perhaps, that while Elizabeth's chief minister, Sir William Cecil, duly commissioned maps of the east coast of Ireland and parts of the mainland of the British Isles by his countryman Lawrence Nowell, he was nevertheless compelled to rely for a broader European perspective upon a copy of Ortelius' *Theatrum*, which by 1573 also contained as a supplement the first map of Wales, created by Humphrey Llwyd.

In the meantime, the crowning glory of all Tudor cartography had undoubtedly been the collection of 1555 commissioned by Queen Mary for her husband, Philip II of Spain, which consisted of a dozen double-sided maps, all of exceptional quality, but produced once again by a foreigner: in this case the Portuguese Diogo Homem, who had fled to England from his homeland after implication in murder. Intended as a fabulous gift for her spouse, Mary had spared no expense in employing the services of arguably the most widely renowned cartographer of the century, and the result was a pictorial masterpiece ranking among the most beautifully illustrated works of its kind, with mythic, historic and country-specific figures, flags and coats of arms, as well as large and famous cities presented in small vignettes, employing gorgeous colours and elaborate decorative frames. Yet monstrous creatures were still depicted swimming in uncharted, non-existent waters, alongside legendary African kings ruling from the foothills of mythical mountains, reflecting the ongoing limitations of Homem's actual knowledge. And the world of *The Queen Mary Atlas* – dominated by the great maritime powers of Spain and Portugal, and embellished with ornate compass roses gesturing enigmatically to the East – plainly betrayed its creator's origins and intentions throughout, as Islamic banners in North Africa and the Balkans cast a threatening shadow over the borders of Christian Europe.

These borders, however, remained fuzzy for rulers and cartographers alike, since Europe was not only a physical space lacking clear-cut frontiers as a land mass, but a cultural one, too, still of imprecise definition. And to compound matters, even as late as the 1520s, no European universities – excepting a handful in Germany, where Ptolemy was introduced – offered geography as a prescribed field of study. 'I have been asked,' wrote a humanist physician in Zurich in the early 1490s, 'to describe the regions of our Confederation and their environs so that you may realise ... how useful such a description is to all those princes who are about to take the field with their armies.' But while Leonardo da Vinci and artists like him had recently begun to depict landscapes and project their spatial thinking to the wider prospect of a bird's-eye view or, wider and higher still, to a detailed map of a whole province, English armies still got lost – as the Duke of Suffolk found to his cost during his French campaign of 1523. And if Columbus had been bold enough to declare twenty years earlier that 'the world is small' – albeit with the qualification that 'I mean it is not as large as people say it is' – it was still more than large enough to perplex and, on occasion, bamboozle its rulers, especially at a time when international borders themselves were so often hotly disputed, and outposts of one ruler's jurisdiction could often be located well within the territory of a neighbour. In 1543, the ultimately unfulfilled Treaty of Greenwich, proposing a marriage between Edward VI and Mary, Queen of Scots, promised to unite England and Scotland sixty years before King James VI and I actually did so. But for centuries the border between the two kingdoms was ill-defined – an effective no man's land of ceaseless raids and deadly feuds – and similar imprecision pertained elsewhere. Indeed, throughout all Europe political boundaries were in such flux, continually reshaped by the strategies of marriage and war, and by the accidents of royal fertility and untimely death, that no map attempting to show them was printed until 1602.

If frontiers were fissile, however, states themselves were not only real but evolving both in England and elsewhere at a striking rate, and steadily consolidating their control over the 50 million souls that constituted early modern Europe's total population. Of these, possibly 85 per cent in western Europe – nearer 95 per cent in the east – lived in villages or isolated farmsteads and were primarily engaged in agriculture, since industry was so limited in range and small scale. In areas such as south-east Germany, where mining and metallurgy were major operations, as well as Holland, which specialised in shipbuilding and fish processing, and Flanders and northern Italy where cloth manufacture was organised on highly intensive capitalist lines, there had, it is true, been significant developments. And some of the earliest applications of surplus capital had also been made in the cities stretching from central Italy to Lombardy and then down the Rhine to the North Sea. But in early sixteenth-century Europe as a whole, towns nevertheless remained the exception rather than the rule, while 'big' ones were those often boasting no more than 10,000 inhabitants. Since there were few other towns of even moderate size in the whole of southern Europe, Naples, with a population of well over 100,000, was a particularly striking anomaly, as was Paris – the greatest metropolis of the west – which boasted at least 150,000 inhabitants, and was beginning to expand its walls into the future Faubourg St Germain. Lyons, however, was only half its size and well below that came French towns of the next rank, such as Reims or Bourges with 10,000. Germany, meanwhile, contained no cities above the size of Cologne at 40,000 and Nuremberg, Augsburg or Magdeburg at 30,000, and Spain no urban centre larger than Salamanca at possibly 100,000. Castile, Burgos, Toledo and Seville had populations of over 50,000, and Madrid – not yet a capital city – 12,000. But beyond these, numbers tumbled precipitously in those areas that made the Spanish kingdom a byword among contemporary travellers as the most deserted and uncouth backwater in all western Europe.

Elsewhere, no Portuguese town could rival the kingdom's capital, Lisbon, at 40,000, while the contrast between Stockholm at 6,500, Bergen at 6,000, and other Swedish and Norwegian towns was greater still. And the same applied to Moscow, with perhaps 150,000, and other Russian towns, of which Novgorod alone was of significant size. In Holland, only Leiden, Amsterdam, Delft and Haarlem passed 10,000; in Switzerland, only Geneva with 12,000– 15,000. And after Naples, the largest cities in Italy as a whole were Venice with some 100,000 inhabitants, Milan with approximately the same, and Florence with 70,000. Certainly, there was no reason for the European pilgrim or trader to feel superior upon arrival in Constantinople, which required eight heavily laden grain ships each day to feed its 100,000 or so inhabitants, or Aleppo and Damascus with 65,000 and 57,000 respectively, let alone Cairo, for which there are no reliable figures, but which seemed to Italian visitors to be capable of housing the entire combined populations of Rome, Venice, Milan and Florence. And if Italians might be suitably dumbstruck by such places, there was better reason still for Tudor travellers to marvel at the comparative insignificance of their own towns, since London had no more than 60,000 inhabitants, after which came Norwich with 12,000 and Bristol with 10,000. Coventry and perhaps a dozen other English towns had around 7,000, along with a few, like Northampton and Leicester, which had 3,000. But the great majority contained as few as 200 inhabitants or less, while even the 810 market towns of Henry VII's realm had populations ranging from no more than 300 to 1,200.

Plainly, early Tudor England, with a total population amounting to perhaps 2.3 million in the 1520s and 2.8 million by 1545, was effectively a demographic minnow by comparison with many other European states like France, which grew from some 7 or 8 million in 1450 to about 16 million a century later, not to mention Spain at just over half that figure, Russia – though figures are very uncertain – at possibly 9 million, and even Poland at 3.5 million. Measured against a peak of perhaps some 5 million before the Great Pestilence of the late fourteenth century, the implications for England's international status were obvious, and prompted numerous mid-Tudor observers in particular to be acutely aware of their country's 'depopulation'. Around 1535 Thomas Starkey, for example, asserted how 'in tyme past … the cuntrey hath byn more populous, then hyt ys now'. But in 1548 John Hales expressed the problem more urgently, observing that 'the people of this realm … is greatly decayed', while one year later John Coke declared that much of England was 'waste, desert and salvaige grounde, not inhabyted'. At that very time, it is true, Sir Thomas Smith was of the opinion that the overall number of people was nevertheless 'still encreasinge' and had been for some time – a fact that some contemporaries ascribed to 'younger marriages than of old', as well as 'the banishment of single-living votaries', i.e. clerical marriage. Nor was Smith ultimately proved wrong, since by 1584 Richard Hakluyt was in no doubt whatsoever 'that throughe our longe peace and seldome sickness … we are growen more populous than ever heretofore', and by the end of Elizabeth I's reign, the population had indeed just exceeded 4 million.

But the uncomfortable fact remained that when the Tudor age dawned, Burgundy boasted the same population as Henry VII's realm, and even the kingdom of Naples, as well as the Papal States, numbered perhaps no more than one third less. Indeed, only Portugal, at 1 million, and Switzerland and Sweden, both with around 750,000, had fewer people among the European powers of major significance. And if France towered above its old enemy in this respect, allies too, like Spain and above all the Holy Roman Empire, could never perceive their English counterparts as genuinely co-equal when demographic realities contrasted so starkly with the aspirations and bombast of figures like Henry VIII. For the Empire alone, which encompassed among its multiple territories those of modern-day Germany, incorporated some 12 million subjects rising to 14 million by the middle of the century. And the trend across Europe was similarly ever upward, negating any apparent catch-up that might have been anticipated from declining death rates in Elizabethan England. After the severe mortality of the last two years of Mary Tudor's reign, resulting from a nationwide influenza epidemic on the heels of three bad harvests, the stagnation of the 1570s was followed by sustained growth, so that Sir Humphrey Gilbert complained ultimately how his country was now 'pestered with people'. But more than fifty years earlier, in his *German Chronicle* of 1538, Sebastian Franck was already observing of his own homeland how 'there are so many people everywhere, no one can move'. 'If God does not inflict a war in which many die,' he went on, 'we shall be forced – chosen by lot or some such way – to travel like the gypsies in search of a new land.' And the Empire's population, like that of France and Spain, would indeed continue to grow at a time when the general principle that size mattered remained as undeniable as ever.

Even so, no account of the balance of forces between Tudor England's main European rivals can fail to highlight that this principle also involved a potential paradox – and nowhere more so, indeed, than in the case of the Holy Roman Empire itself. For if, in terms of scale and historic pedigree, the Empire appeared arguably the greatest of all western European states and therefore the obvious starting place for any survey of the Continent's political status quo, in practice it hardly existed at all. 'Of the power of Germany,' wrote Niccolò Machiavelli in *Ritratto delle cose della Magna*, 'none can doubt,

for it abounds in men, riches and arms … But it is such as cannot be used.'
And the inadequacies of the Holy Roman Empire did indeed reflect a primary principle of contemporary geopolitics. For while the evolving states
of Europe had to be large enough to intimidate competitors, the most successful players in the Continent's power games also needed to be sufficiently
compact to be united. Certainly, both France and Spain, which were already
emerging as coherent and comparatively stable nation states, were cases in
point. But the Holy Roman Empire, as a multi-ethnic and multilingual state,
not only sprawled, but lacked any natural centre around which national feeling could readily coalesce. Governed since 1438 by an elected Habsburg
emperor in conjunction with a motley assortment of dukes, counts, mar-
graves, lords, archbishops, 'prince-bishops', 'Imperial Knights' and urban
oligarchs representing some eighty or so 'Imperial Free Cities', the 'Holy
Roman Empire of the German Nation', as it was formally known, was in
fact as variable in complexion as it was vast in extent, stretching from the
Alps in the south to the Baltic in the north, and from France in the west to
Hungary and Poland in the east. And in consequence, its Habsburg rulers
would remain little more than territorial princes of their own traditional
Austrian heartlands, enjoying great theoretical prestige while facing stubborn resistance within their broader Imperial territories to any attempts to
impose centralised control.

In 1521, two years after his succession, the most powerful emperor of all,
Charles V, would boldly assert how 'the Empire from of old had not many
masters, but one, and it is our intention to be that one'. Yet he, like his predecessors, would prove unequal to the task of consolidation and reform, since
the task of administering the vast mosaic over which he nominally ruled was
rendered insurmountably difficult by the existence of some 1,000 separate
autonomous units within its jurisdiction – all varying considerably in size and
stature and all jealously protective of their 'liberties'. Territories like Saxony,
Brandenburg and Bavaria, each with populations of over a million by the
century's end, were, on the one hand, worthy of consideration as unified and
discrete 'states' in their own right, but there were also micro-princedoms
such as Anhalt, only a little larger than Essex, and divided between no fewer
than four rulers. Hesse, Trier and Württemberg, too – each with populations of 400,000 in 1600 – had undergone similar fragmentation as a result
of ingrained antipathy to the principle of primogeniture, and even the
Palatinate – another of the major Imperial princedoms with a population of
perhaps 600,000 – was itself divided into two major components: the 'Lower'
Palatinate, a rich wine-growing district between the rivers Mosel, Saar and
the Rhine, and its so-called 'Upper' counterpart, a relatively poor agricultural area between the Danube and the kingdom of Bohemia, which had

itself fallen under Habsburg control in 1526 while remaining an autonomous entity within the Empire as a whole.

By and large all these units paid faithful allegiance to their emperor. But all were equally anxious to protect their traditions and prerogatives in the face of the ongoing Habsburg quest for more effective central control or, as many feared, absolute hegemony. And in the meantime there was no more striking illustration of the Holy Roman Emperor's dependence upon his leading subjects than his relationship to the seven most powerful of all – the so-called 'Electors' who, since the Golden Bull of 1356, had been responsible for his appointment in the first place. Together, the Duke of Saxony, the Margrave of Brandenburg, the King of Bohemia, the Count-Palatine of the Rhine, and the archbishops of Mainz, Cologne and Trier determined the successor to the Imperial throne. Furthermore, the consolidation and centralisation that became characteristic of western Europe in the sixteenth century was to be found in Germany at the princely rather than the Imperial level. For the electors, as well as their more important counterparts like the dukes of Bavaria and indeed some of the lesser ones, had fashioned their own privy councils and financial chambers, and come to employ administrators who had been trained in Roman Law, which emphasised the rights of the ruler over those they ruled. By contrast, at a time when any effective national ruler needed an organised administration, an army and a regular system of taxation, the Holy Roman Emperor possessed none of these things – or even, for that matter, a common currency to run throughout his dominions. Instead, what limited power the Habsburgs possessed was theirs purely as rulers of Austria and its associated territories.

As such, it required no imagination to appreciate that the Holy Roman Empire, as it existed at the dawn of the Tudor period, was effectively a mere shadow of the original '*Imperium Christianum*' envisioned under Charlemagne after his coronation by Pope Leo III on Christmas Day 800, at which time the Vatican had intended to extend its own authority by legitimising the new state through a nominal connection to the original Roman Empire, and thereafter making the emperor its secular arm. Yet for all its diversity and divisions, its anomalies, complexities, quirks and contrasts, this self-same sprawling entity, governed traditionally from its Habsburg nerve centre in Vienna, was still widely perceived as the linchpin of Europe. So much so, indeed, that both the King of France and indeed Henry VIII himself saw fit to contest the election of Emperor Maximilian's grandson Charles in 1519. In the event, the crushing impracticality of the English ruler's enterprise became rapidly apparent to his representative, Richard Pace, soon after the hapless envoy's arrival at Frankfurt. For when Pace asked the banker, Hermann Rinck, to make the customary arrangements for bribing the electors, Rinck discovered at once that they would insist on being paid in cash unless any bond was issued under the Great Seal of England. More dauntingly still, the Englishman was also told of the enormous sums that would be required to advance his royal master's cause, since in addition to the money already expended by the King of France, Charles himself had made available another 1.5 million gold florins. To cap all, the Archbishop of Mainz had demanded 52,000 florins for his vote before increasing his price to 120,000. And while Rinck was of little use in mustering cash upon this scale, especially when Charles had the full elemental force of the Fugger banking family at his disposal, Pace also found himself in risk of his life from armed bands intent upon preventing the succession of a foreigner.

Ultimately, therefore, common sense would prevail, though not before the King of England had agonised at length over his decision to abandon the chase for such a valuable prize. 'As touching his enterprise of the Empire,' wrote John Clerk to Wolsey at one o'clock in the morning on the eve of Henry's withdrawal, 'I have reasoned as deeply as my poor wit would serve me, not varying from your instructions; but His Grace, as methinketh, considereth no jeopardies.' Nevertheless, by next morning the dead weight of the facts had impressed themselves even upon the monarch who fondly dreamed of becoming 'arbiter of Europe'. Instead, he would have to settle for the more modest path laid down by his father, though at the very time when Henry VII became king some two-and-a-half decades earlier, his Imperial counterpart was indeed approaching the kind of influence that made his throne so alluring an acquisition – not least because Maximilian I, son and heir to Emperor Frederick III, had in 1477 married Mary of Burgundy, daughter of Charles the Bold, after the ill-judged aggression of Louis IX of France had driven her to seek protection wherever it might be found. As a result, Maximilian acquired the greater part of the Burgundian inheritance, which included the Rhineland possessions of Franche Comté, Luxemburg and the Netherlands, and thereby added immeasurably to the traditional Austrian Habsburg lands on the Danube, encompassing Carinthia, Styria and the Tyrol.

That the marriage should have been sealed primarily in the name of the Habsburg dynasty rather than in that of the Empire they ruled, reflected, however, the dual priorities of the Habsburgs as territorial rulers in their own right as well as emperors. Indeed, as head of the House of Habsburg, the emperor held numerous key interests that extended beyond the Empire and might well on occasion run counter to its needs, so that upon Maximilian's own election after his father's death in 1493, his priorities lay largely with family interests and his hereditary estates rather than Imperial authority per se. Nor would the same be any less true of his own successor and grandson,

Charles V – all of which had significant ramifications. For if the Empire was hampered by its many masters – i.e. the rulers of its many components – it would be stricken, too, by the divided loyalties of the emperors themselves, whose Habsburg origins necessarily entailed further burdensome obligations for the Empire as a whole, as Maximilian's marriage to Mary of Burgundy amply demonstrated. For although the match opened up new possibilities for Austria in the west, it also ensured the enduring enmity of France to the wider Empire, which was now added to the ongoing Habsburg preoccupation with the Danube and the Turks – a concern that had been especially evident since the fall of Byzantium in 1453, and was further compounded by the events of the 1470s when the Sultan's borderers had raided into Styria, Carinthia and the Friuli, lighting Muslim fires that could be seen from the tops of the towers of Venice.

Sultan Selim the Grim (1512–20) would, it is true, focus Ottoman energies away from Europe, by marching unsuccessfully on Persia in 1514 after its ruler, Shah Ismail Safawi, broke the old tradition of toleration between the Sunni majority and Shi'ite minority in the Muslim world by imposing Shi'ism on his subjects by force. Over the next three years, Selim would also go on to conquer Syria, Arabia and the inoffensive Mamluk sultans of Egypt. But his son Suleiman the Magnificent (1520–66) nevertheless swiftly returned with a vengeance to renew the traditional holy war against Christendom, and in his first dozen years not only seized Belgrade and Rhodes, but smashed Hungary, killing its king in battle, before besieging Vienna twice. Drawing on the Islamic principle of 'holy war' (*ghâzâ*) – especially after acquiring Mecca and other Islamic holy shrines, and absorbing the Mamluks – the Ottoman sultans had already inherited the title of 'servant of the two sanctuaries' and the old caliphate protection for the House of Islam (*dâr-al'Islâm*), with aspirations to convert the entire world. Likewise, from the time of Sultan Mehmed II onwards in the previous century, the Ottoman Porte had also continued to nurture the *imperium* acquired with the capture of Constantinople, which was stridently affirmed by the Italian portrait painter Gentile Bellini's depiction of Mehmed as the descendant of Alexander the Great, complete with the inscription 'emperor of the world' (*Imperator Orbis*) at the bottom of the painting. And by 1529, when Suleiman installed John Zápolya on the throne of that part of Hungary he had conquered – using the very Crown seized by the Ottomans just before it was about to be smuggled to Vienna – such claims to universal primacy seemed every bit as convincing as those advanced by any Holy Roman Emperor.

In 1560, indeed, the Imperial ambassador at Constantinople, the Flemish humanist Ghislin, wrote pessimistically of the comparative imbalance in power:

On their side are the resources of a mighty empire ... experience and practice in fighting ... habituation to victory, endurance of toil, unity, order, discipline, frugality and watchfulness. On our side is public poverty, private luxury ... broken spirit, lack of endurance and training ... Can we doubt what the result will be?

Styling himself 'Distributor of the Crowns of the Great Monarchs of the World', Suleiman had by then long ceased to sit cross-legged upon a divan to receive ambassadors, and opted instead to occupy a jewel-encrusted throne. By 1532, furthermore, Venetian goldsmiths had completed work on a ceremonial warrior's helmet for the sultan, consisting of four concentric crowns – one more than that of the papal tiara – which was deliberately designed to outshine the claims to *imperium* of both the pope and the Holy Roman Emperor. The sight of it in 1532, it was said, turned Habsburg envoys into 'speechless corpses' at a time when Christian listening posts on the Ottoman world in Vienna and Venice were awash with troubling reports of Turkish intentions to conquer Rome. And as rumours swirled, Ottoman geomancers and image-makers drew on the millenarian expectations that were common currency in Mediterranean lands among Jews and Christian converts to Islam, presenting Suleiman as a Muslim messiah (*mahdi*) whose reign would usher in the last days before the coming of the Islamic millennium projected for 1591–92. In anticipation of an imminent Ottoman onslaught, Ferrante Gonzaga supervised the building of 137 towers around the coast of Sicily, while Charles V's envoy in Naples, Pedro de Toledo, began a similar programme of watchtowers and defensive emplacements. Throughout the Italian peninsula, indeed, as well as eastern Europe, the growing anxiety was transmitted by printed broadsheets, ordinances for military levies, debates in councils of state, preaching, images and popular songs.

Already cast by Pope Leo X as the enemies of Christ in his bull *Constituti iuxta* of April 1517, the Turks were similarly depicted by Charles V almost twenty years later as the 'perpetual enemy of our Holy Catholic faith'. But the remedy to their threat was by no means obvious – particularly to the Venetian senators whose maritime empire had shrunk before their advance. 'Every time we have made war upon the Turks,' said one of them in 1538, 'we have lost.' And although the end of the Jagiellon line of kings in Hungary had added Bohemia and a slice of Hungary to the Habsburgs' hereditary lands in Austria, leaving this complex of territories the bulwark of Europe, it was of small consolation – not least because it required heavy and expensive fortification, which assumed an especially pressing significance for Emperor Charles V, irrespective of the fact that his Ottoman enemies were intermittently stricken with problems of their own. Distracted, on the one hand, by

Shi'ite aggressors of the Persian Safavid dynasty to the east, the Turks were in fact weakened further by Suleiman's ineffectual successor, Selim the Sot (1566–74), as well as social upheaval in Asia Minor. Yet they remained dauntingly strong, since Turkish advances in central Europe had been accompanied by equivalent strides in the Mediterranean, where full-scale campaigns – involving the capture of Rhodes in 1522, the failed siege of Malta in 1565, the conquest of Cyprus in 1571 and regular sweeps by the Ottoman fleet – were combined with raiding on the Christian coast by the corsairs of Algiers and the gradual extension of the sultan's patronage over the independent kingdoms of North Africa.

By then, as the successors of both Henry VII and his son confined themselves to worthy words of Christian solidarity from their distant island haven, the main burden of defence would be borne by Venice and Spain, who eventually gained their most notable triumph at the naval battle of Lepanto in 1571. But more than half a century earlier, Henry VIII, too, had found himself fixated by notions of crusade at a time when it was still not finally appreciated that Christendom would never again raise its banners of war in the Holy Land. Indeed, Thomas Wolsey's so-called 'Peace of London' or 'universal peace' between England, France, the Holy Roman Empire, Spain and the Papacy in 1518 had been premised upon nothing less than a general settlement of all disputes involving the states of western Europe, as the prelude to a united military campaign against the Turks in response to the subjection of the Holy Land by Selim the Grim two years earlier. As a mark of the treaty's solemnity, Wolsey had not only celebrated sung mass at the high altar of St Paul's on Sunday, 3 October, with a splendour that defied exaggeration, but followed it with a state banquet at the Bishop of London's palace that was said to have been more sumptuous than any feast 'given by Cleopatra or Caligula'. Moreover, when Cardinal Campeggio had first arrived in England the year before, to preach the necessity of a crusade, Wolsey's royal master had displayed no hesitation in proclaiming that he would place everything in his possession at the pope's disposal. His personal wealth and treasure, his royal authority and even his kingdom itself, Henry declared, might all be gladly rendered up in the sacred cause of defending Christendom against the infidel, though upon hearing of Emperor Maximilian's offer to assume the role of commander-in-chief, he laughed out loud at the suggestion and proceeded to observe that the Venetians should be more fearful of the King of France than any Turkish sultan.

In the meantime, however, the object of the King of England's amusement had nevertheless found time to demonstrate his superior wisdom in politics closer to home by continuing his Habsburg forebears' policy of waging the Holy Roman Empire's battles, wherever possible, by means of the marriage bed. 'Let others wage war', ran the time-honoured Habsburg maxim, 'but thou, O happy Austria, marry; for those kingdoms which Mars gave to others, Venus gives to thee.' And so it was that in the very same year that Maximilian I became the last emperor to attempt to be crowned in Rome, the way opened for arguably the most momentous match of all, after Charles VIII of France, in recognition that he would be unable to extend his rule to the north-west without excessive cost, had ceded Flanders to him in return for a guarantee that the old Burgundian lands around Dijon were to remain an integral part of the French kingdom. Thereafter, in 1496, the emperor duly arranged the marriage of his son Philip to Joanna, the daughter of Ferdinand and Isabella of Spain, with the most fateful of all consequences, since the resulting son, Charles, was to unite in his own person the existing Austrian and Burgundian lands with Spain, which encompassed not only Castile and Aragon but Navarre, the Balearic Islands, Sardinia, Sicily and Naples.

In due course too, as both Charles I of Spain and Emperor Charles V, the same boy would go on to guarantee that not only Spain, Austria and Burgundy but also the Holy Roman Empire would be ruled by members of the same Habsburg dynasty, creating a power bloc larger than any in Europe since the days of Charlemagne. Well-planned marriages and an equally well-executed Imperial election brought Charles the Burgundian Netherlands in 1506, followed by Spain in 1516, and then the Austrian lands and Imperial Crown three years later, while his brother Ferdinand – to whom he delegated control of Austria in 1520–21 – went on to gain Bohemia and the rump of non-Ottoman Hungary in 1526. Later again, Charles's son Philip not only married Mary Tudor, but ruled as King of England from 1554 to 1558, leaving Ferdinand's own son Charles to come as near as any suitor ever did to gaining the hand of England's Queen Elizabeth. And in the meantime, as the patchwork garment of the Habsburg domains was spreading its countless threads across Europe, so Spanish conquistadores were steadily consolidating their Habsburg monarch's grip upon the New World, sending back growing quantities of gold and silver to fund his enterprises in Europe, which received a further boost in 1580 when Spanish troops marched into Portugal, claiming the Crown for Philip II by descent through his mother. With it came the Portuguese trading empire from Brazil and West Africa to Goa and the Moluccas.

By any standards, it was an extraordinary ascent for a dynastic House that had only assumed its imperial status in the first place because the subsidiary rulers of the Holy Roman Empire considered it insufficiently powerful to dominate them. Indeed, there had seemed a distinct element of absurdity in the decision of Charles V's lacklustre great-great grandfather, Emperor Frederick III, to adopt as his emblem the Latin acrostic device AEIOU

(*Austriae est imperare orbi universe*, Austria will rule the world). But as the six-teenth century progressed, there seemed scant reason to many why Habsburg power, bolstered by the immense agglomeration of territories that had come its way, including the New World on the other side of the Atlantic, should not continue to expand until it embraced the whole of Christendom within its orbit. Both Charles V and his son Philip II – who ruled Spain from 1558 after his father, shortly before his death, had left the Imperial Crown to his other son, Ferdinand – were convinced, after all, that the remarkable resources bestowed upon them were entirely God-given, so that they might fulfil the crusading ambitions of their forebears, whether against the Turks or the per-nicious influence of Protestant heresy, which would take root in Germany and elsewhere from the second decade of the sixteenth century onwards. Nor was this the limit of their agenda. For from the perspective of the Habsburgs, and in particular the men who advised them, their universalist pretensions seemed nothing less than the basis for an impending golden age, one redolent of the *Pax Romana* to which the Renaissance of classical learning and clas-sicising art had been turning such attention for so long.

Among those facing the prospect of imminent subjugation, however, such pretensions naturally represented not only an apocalyptic threat but a clarion call to desperate resistance. Above all, the rulers of France were only too conscious of Habsburg territories to the north, east and south, which represented a noose being drawn tighter and tighter around them. And with this in mind, Charles V's contemporary, Francis I, would exert every effort to break out of the stranglehold – fighting his Habsburg enemies in Italy, intriguing against them in Germany as the Empire dissolved into religious disunity, and even joining hands ultimately with their Turkish foes. For this, from the perspective of the Valois kings of France, was not only a life or death struggle, waged to preserve their freedom, but a tug of war, too, between the past and the future, in which Charles personified the medieval concept of supranational authority while Francis embodied the notion of the modern nation state acknowledging no superior. At one level, the interminable con-flict that followed encapsulated the incompatibility of Christian idealism with Machiavellian realism – not least because the 'most Christian' kings of France also laid claim in their own right to the moral leadership of Christendom as the true heirs of Charlemagne 'the Frank'. But it also involved, in much less abstract terms, a straightforward struggle for power's sake between two great dynasties, in which the odds – notwithstanding the apparent imbalance in comparative resources and, in particular, the eventual familial link between the Holy Roman Empire and Spain – were surprisingly evenly stacked.

Across the Pyrenees in the later fifteenth century, as the new Tudor dynasty was setting out to consolidate its own authority in England, Spain too had stood at the parting of the ways. Local rulers, local liberties and local privileges were threatened, on the one hand, with centralised control or outright destruction by a unified national state, as was happening to the north in France; or local differences might ultimately prevail, causing fragmentation to increase and finally confirm the land's status as little more than a 'geographical expression', like Italy to the east. At that time, 'Hispania' was still the mapmaker's label of convenience for the jagged corner of Europe that jutted out into an unexplored ocean, and the historian's name for a famous province whose unity had not long survived the downfall of the Roman empire – a shadow of what once had been. Throughout the Middle Ages, indeed, the Hispania of the cartographers had served merely to lend a fictitious unity to a complex of crowns and kingdoms encompassing Castile and León, Navarre, Aragon, Portugal and the Moorish kingdom of Granada. Each had its own history, its own institutions and its own ways, and in so far as the Christian kingdoms preserved any semblance of the unity of Roman times, it lay only in one residing common notion: namely, that all were brothers in the crusade against the Islamic onslaught that had finally brought about the collapse of the old Visigothic kingdom of Spain in the eighth century.

Thereafter, in the wake of repeated assaults by Arabic forces, it seemed likely for an extended period that the so-called 'Moors' might occupy the entire peninsula. But Christian resistance continued in the north, and provided the nucleus from which, first, the kingdom of León emerged and later Castile, which eventually split off to become a separate kingdom in its own right. Other regions, too, had managed to maintain their independence – among them Portugal, which became an independent entity in the twelfth century, as well as the Basque kingdom of Navarre, and Catalonia, which later became part of Aragon. Yet in the early years of the eleventh century it was still not certain that any of these Christian states would survive, until the impetus of the Arab invasions eventually slowed and allowed the process of reconquest – *Reconquista* – to begin with the capture of Toledo in 1085. Even so, the Moorish kingdom of Granada, with a population of around 1 million, continued to survive after its Islamic inhabitants were first confined to it in 1242. And nor did successive attempts to unify the various Christian kingdoms – by either brute force or marriage – enjoy enduring success, mainly because the absence of an established system of primogeniture ensured that any precarious unity was invariably lost upon the death of a ruler. Indeed, even after León was finally incorporated into Castile in the early thirteenth century, and the *Reconquista* revived with the capture of Valencia, the enlarged kingdom of Castile – constituting around 62 per cent of Spanish territory and boasting a population of perhaps 5 million, which dwarfed its other Christian neighbours – became convulsed by internal struggles between magnates and the

Crown, which, during the fourteenth century, drew the other peninsula states as well as foreign ones into what became a quagmire of permanent civil war.

In the meantime, the kingdom of Aragon, with a population of around 0.8 million, had nevertheless expanded into the western Mediterranean, with the powerful support of its Catalonian mercantile oligarchy, absorbing Sardinia, Sicily and southern Italy, and incorporating them into an Aragonese trading zone. Yet Aragon's comparative economic success, founded upon Catalonia's cloth-making industry, was not matched by her counterparts and, in particular, Castile where the prolonged struggle against the Moors had elevated the glorification of martial and spiritual values above those of commerce and enterprise. Remote from the rest of Europe, Castile would live for centuries, in fact, in a world of its own, its gaze turned in upon itself, its energies directed towards the Infidel, and its pastoral, nomadic society organised predominantly for war. It was a realm, in essence, where the pattern of life was largely determined by those who fought and those who prayed – as epitomised by the three military–religious orders of Calatrava, Alcantara and Santiago, and the concept of the *Hidalgo*, the knight who lived for war and glory and despised all other forms of activity. The result was the comparative neglect of arable land – most of which was owned by the nobility, the military orders, the Church and the monastic orders – and an over-dependence upon the wool trade and the nomadic shepherds who every year brought some 2½ million sheep from their summer pastures in the north to their winter grazing grounds in the south to the flourishing town of Medina del Campo, the centre of the wool trade.

By the middle of the fifteenth century, in fact, there were certain signs of change, as Castile's woollen exports to northern Europe expanded and a vigorous urban society took root in Cantabria, living on newfound wealth and acquainting itself with ideas, which were flowing into the country from the north. Yet this, by and large, remained the limit of Castilian commercial enterprise, and this was the situation when Ferdinand of Aragon (1452–1516) and Isabella of Castile (1451–1504) were brought together in 1469 in a marriage that would succeed at last in creating a unified kingdom of Spain where all earlier attempts had failed. Hailed in history as Spain's 'Catholic Monarchs' – *los reyes Católicos* – they faced a daunting task, and it was not until 1479, the same year in which Ferdinand became King of Aragon, that Isabella was finally able to consolidate her own position, after which the couple ruled in effect as joint sovereigns. Even so, their problems continued. For on the west coast of the Iberian Peninsula, Portugal was not only already a nation, but slightly bigger than Aragon and a traditionally hostile power that had helped promote a punishing civil war against Isabella in Castile. Indeed, Portugal was to remain a serious stumbling block for any would-be unifier of its nearest neighbour, particularly when Portuguese expansion around Africa to the Indies was achieved in 1497 – and even more so at a time when the kingdom of Granada remained stubbornly unconquered. Nor was this all. For to the north, the small kingdom of Navarre lay partly in France, which was further antagonised by Aragon's rule of Sicily and claims to the kingdom of Naples in southern Italy – claims that had, in any case, only served to stretch Aragonese resources to the limit.

In some respects, the issues facing Ferdinand and Isabella were not dissimilar to those preoccupying Henry VII of England. In each case, there was the pressing problem of lawlessness and a disputed succession to manage. But for Spain's 'Catholic Monarchs' there was also the imminent prospect of a Portuguese invasion to deal with at the very time that, according to the chronicler Andrés Bernáldez, 'no justice was left in the land':

> The common people [Bernáldez complained] were exterminated, the crown property alienated, the royal revenues reduced to such slight value that it causes me shame to speak of it; whence it resulted that men were robbed not only in the open fields but in the cities and towns, that the regular clergy could not live in safety, and that the seculars were treated with no respect, that sanctuaries were violated, women raped, and all men had full liberty to sin as they pleased.

Unlike Spain, furthermore, England enjoyed not only the good fortune of a temporary respite from military entanglements but also the blessing of a royal marriage between its new Tudor monarch and Elizabeth of York, which would do much to underpin the drive for political stability. By contrast, the circumstances of Isabella's marriage to Ferdinand had actually seemed to betoken their weakness, since the events leading up to the wedding, which took place in the morning of 19 October 1469 at a private residence in Valladolid, were, to say the least, unusual. Certainly, there was little hint of a love match, though the 19-year-old bride, plain and not strikingly feminine, eventually grew fond enough of her husband to be jealous of his numerous infidelities. Equally, it was not a dynastic arrangement imposed on the couple from above. On the contrary, ignoring the opposition of her brother Henry IV, and resisting suitors from Portugal, France and England, Isabella chose for herself to marry Ferdinand, notwithstanding the fact that they were related by consanguinity and would soon be excommunicated. With a forged dispensation and under threat of arrest from her brother, the princess had ultimately been rescued from her home at Madrigal by the Archbishop of Toledo, while her bridegroom had reached Valladolid only a few days before the ceremony after an even more eventful journey from Zaragoza, travelling by night through hostile territory with a handful of attendants disguised as merchants, and narrowly escaping death from a stone hurled by a sentinel from the battlements of Burgo de Osma.

At the time that bride and groom met for the first time on 15 October, their poverty was such that they found themselves compelled to borrow to meet the wedding expenses. And even this was by no means the limit of their difficulties, since Louis XII of France, perceiving the grave threat to his own country posed by a union of the reigning Houses of Castile and Aragon, was anxious to prevent the ceremony occurring, as were enemies nearer home, including Castilian grandees bitterly opposed to a matrimonial alliance that promised to strengthen the Crown's authority. Hoping to dispossess Isabella, they were rallying to the cause of her brother Henry's alleged daughter, Juana *la Beltraneja*, and though their efforts were eventually frustrated, there remained the equally formidable obstacle that the political differences between Castile and Aragon should be so pronounced. For while Castile had a single representative assembly, or *Cortes*, whose membership and frequency of meeting were both dependent on the Crown, four such bodies existed in Aragon, which was itself comprised of three constituent kingdoms. In each case, consent was required for all new taxes and laws, and to compound matters, Aragon also boasted a hereditary justiciary whose task was to uphold the law and the legitimate interests of the subject against the encroachments of royal government.

'We who are as good as you,' ran the customary oath of the Aragonese nobility to its ruler, 'swear to you who are no better than us to accept you as our king and sovereign lord provided you observe all our liberties and laws. But if not, not.' And if the political status quo in Castile and Aragon was markedly different, so too, of course, were the economic and indeed social conditions pertaining in both kingdoms. For although the nobles of Aragon were as proud as those of Castile, they were also poorer and therefore in reality less powerful. Geographically, Castile not only had the advantage of its central position but was three times as large as that of Aragon and its component states. At the same time, merchants and townspeople played a far more important role in Aragon, though their prosperity, still based upon the commercial empire that Catalonia had built up in the western Mediterranean, was by this time eroded by the activities of the Genoese. Even the expansion of Castile's language, not to mention the renaissance of her culture, reflected her superiority, since Castilian had already become the written language of the Basques, while Catalan, the most robust of the non-Castilian languages, was steadily retreating as a literary medium.

In key respects, therefore, Aragon was very much the junior partner in its federation with Castile, so that when Ferdinand married Isabella, he readily agreed to live in his wife's kingdom, ruling Aragon through a council that was itself resident in Castile. Nor was there doubt that Isabella would play the leading role in encouraging the gradual reconquest of the peninsula from the Moors, as well as the accompanying task of ensuring the purification of her peoples from all taint of unorthodoxy and heresy. For Ferdinand, whose reputation for cunning and duplicity led Machiavelli to dub him 'the foremost king in Christendom', was content to consolidate his power at home and to add to his territories by timely intervention in European affairs, leaving Isabella to indulge her intense sense of religious mission. Indeed, the King of Aragon made no secret of his cynical exercise of statecraft and the store he set upon it above honour and the finer sentiments of his spouse. On the contrary, as England's Henry VIII would find on more than one occasion, he took pride in subterfuge, and to such a degree that when Louis XII of France complained how he had been twice deceived by him, his response was unabashed. 'He lies,' came the retort, 'it is the tenth time.'

Yet it was this very combination of contrasting personalities, aided in no small measure by a chain of almost miraculous events, which not only overcame each of the inauspicious auguries at the time of Ferdinand and Isabella's marriage, but literally carried the name and reputation of Spain to the ends of earth while Tudor England confined its horizons largely to survival. Inheriting distinct and seemingly incompatible kingdoms, shattered by social and political strife, Spain's Catholic monarchs nevertheless tapped into the hidden potential of their separate realms and left to their Habsburg successors the makings of a potent nation state: united, peaceful and powerful beyond any in Europe. For while the vigour and endurance of the Castilians made possible the discovery and conquest of a vast overseas empire, it was the techniques of government and administration inherited from the Aragonese that ensured its organisation and survival. Likewise, it was the European wars undertaken by Ferdinand in defence of Aragonese interests that would serve to canalise the energies of a proud and triumphant nation, in precisely the way that Isabella's religious zeal established a further springboard for all else that followed, since the triumphant conclusion of the age-old crusade against the Moors of Granada in 1492 would both free Spain at last from the internal wars that had dogged it, and release the energies of those crusading warriors subsequently seeking new worlds to conquer.

Over the course of time, the threat from Portugal would fail to materialise, and allow its newly united neighbour to be drawn progressively into a process broadly mirroring developments across the Continent – not least in Tudor England where Henry VII keenly emulated his counterparts in the quest for law, order and financial solvency by reining in 'over-mighty' subjects in the interests of centralised control and uniformity. Key to all in Spain's consolidation, however, was firstly the adoption of Roman Law encompassing the principle, enshrined in the *Leyes de Toro* of 1505, that 'what pleases the prince has force'; and even more importantly the creation of an overseas empire that would soon altogether dwarf the narrower horizons of Henry VII's realm. For only six months after the fall of Granada, Christopher Columbus at last received the backing he had been requesting for years to make the first recorded European contact with the West Indies. And only one year later, the Spanish pope, Alexander VI, gave his homeland authority over all lands more than 100 leagues west of the Cape Verde Islands, before finally drawing the boundary 370 miles to the west by the Treaty of Tordesillas of 1494. By the end of the same year, the Canary Islands had been conquered, and between 1508 and 1510 Oran and other points on the North African Mediterranean coast were captured from the Muslims. By which time the *Casa de Contratación* (House of Trade) had been established at Seville to control all American trade, and Columbus himself was already a man of the past, broken upon the wheel of his own endeavours after failing to colonise Hispaniola (Haiti) and establish a commercial monopoly.

Yet by the time of his death in 1506, the purported discoverer of America had nevertheless sown the seed for Spain's forthcoming 'Golden Century', which required with hindsight only one further ingredient. For upon the demise of Isabella two years later, as if to emphasise the essentially personal nature of the union between Castile and Aragon, she was succeeded not by her husband Ferdinand but by their daughter Joanna, wife of Emperor Maximilian's son Philip. Over some years, in fact, Spain's rulers had been arranging the marriage of their offspring in what appeared to be a deeply laid plot to encircle France, and this last match seemed, in effect, to complete the task. Already the eldest son John had been married to Maximilian's daughter Margaret, and in 1502 negotiations were also opened for what would prove to be the fateful union between Catherine of Aragon and Arthur of England, son and heir of Henry VII. But where Joanna was concerned, a considerable threat also existed that Spain's dominions might one day pass to the vain and foolish youth that her husband Philip had undoubtedly proved himself upon his first visit to her homeland in 1502. With a train of Flemish advisers whose arrogance sorely offended the native Spaniards, the emperor's son had strutted, postured and gaffed indiscriminately. And nor, it seemed, could Spain's long-term security be any more guaranteed by Joanna herself, whose husband's chronic unfaithfulness eventually aroused her to an hysteria not far short of madness. In the event, only the greatest guile and skill – as well as luck – could nullify the threat to the unity and independence that Ferdinand and his deceased wife had sought so strenuously to bring about. But in all three respects, the King of Aragon proved equal to the challenge. For in playing his cards astutely, he was duly declared regent for his daughter, before his hapless son-in-law – thoroughly outwitted and outplayed – conveniently expired at Burgos in September 1506.

True, the problem of the Castilian succession had still not altogether evaporated, since Joanna's heir, the future Charles V of the Holy Roman Empire, was being educated as a Fleming in the distant Netherlands, which he had inherited from his father as part of the Burgundian inheritance. Indeed, if Ferdinand could have overridden the well-established rules of succession, he would undoubtedly have settled the throne upon Charles's younger brother, Ferdinand, who was being raised as a Spaniard. But there proved no scope for such bold action, and the king confined his remaining energies instead to the acquisition of the frontier kingdom of Navarre, which he duly achieved in 1515 after his marriage to Germaine de Foix of Navarre's royal house. The following year, on 23 January, he died at Madrigalejo, to be replaced by his grandson, who duly became Charles I of Spain and later, in 1519, the Holy Roman Emperor after the death of his Habsburg grandfather Maximilian. Hampered by his inability to speak Spanish and the need to spend so much of his reign abroad, Charles's succession would prove, in fact, a significant source of resentment among his new subjects until he learned to govern them as a Spaniard. Yet this he managed. And with his consolidation of power eventually complete in both Spain and Empire, his potential seemed limitless, stoking afresh those residing fears of Habsburg domination that were nowhere more apparent than in France, where the impact of prolonged conflict with England during the previous century had already exacted a heavy toll.

Before the Hundred Years War, by any general measure, the prosperity of France – and especially its northern regions – had been outstanding. Indeed, by the early fourteenth century the country's good fortune appeared to have outstripped all other lands in Europe, making it, in Froissart words, the 'fairest kingdom of the world after the kingdom of heaven'. By 1360, however, this same plentiful realm had become, in the words of Petrarch, 'a heap of ruins', and eighty years later Thomas Basin, Bishop of Lisieux, was still observing that 'all was a desert' between the Loire and the Somme. 'A few patches of cultivated land or a vineyard might here and there be seen,' he commented, 'but only rarely, and never save in the immediate neighbourhood of a castle or a walled town'. In its agonies, the place had become a prey to wolves and to displaced wandering mercenaries known, appropriately enough, as *routiers*, and in the meantime, the population had fallen to one half – in some places even one third – of its former level. As elsewhere, the marshes of Poitou reverted to their natural condition, and woods steadily overtook the untilled fields, so that in Saintonge and other places the people were said to have reflected for long afterwards how 'the forests came back to France through the English'.

Doubtless, some of the accounts were prone to exaggeration, but the widespread desolation is borne out vividly enough by the legal evidence of the time, which abounds in contracts dealing only in wasted lands.

Yet France's impressive recovery before the end of the century – and even in the latter stages of the war itself – remained all the more remarkable for this very fact. For, according to some estimates, as much as one-third of the kingdom was reclaimed for cultivation between 1480 and 1510, and the same outburst of renewed agricultural activity was to be sustained throughout the sixteenth century – to such a degree, indeed, that by 1565 Jean Bodin was testifying to the flourishing state of the countryside. Nor, too, was agriculture the only area of France's economic resurgence, as the cloth industry underwent considerable expansion – notably at Rouen, at Montvilliers, in the Caux country, and at Bourges and Paris – while the exploitation of coal, iron, silver and lead resources made significant headway after Charles VIII's decision in 1445 to employ Saxon and Bohemian miners to work the silver-bearing ores of Beaujolais and Lyonnais. In 1471, Louis XI created a bureau of mines with powers to grant concessions and prospect for ore, and the result was an influx of German miners who likewise assisted in the creation of numerous small iron centres in many localities, such as the Bocage and Perche districts of Brittany and Normandy, as well as the Champagne country and in Nivernais and elsewhere. And as industrial production revived, so trade, too, appeared to advance on all fronts, thanks to ordinances concerning the coinage between 1435 and 1451, and, not least, the security of French roads.

In 1462, under royal patronage, Lyons created its famous fairs, which took a part of international traffic away from Geneva by tapping the trade flowing along the great route from Flanders to Italy, while another fair was established at Rouen for the specific purpose of competing with Antwerp. At Lyons, too, as well as Tours, Italians were encouraged to develop silk manufacture – which, in the words of one ordinance, 'all idle people ought to be made to work at' – and in 1470, as confirmation of the strength of French commerce, an exhibition of the kingdom's goods was actually organised in London during the brief restoration of Henry VI. Aigues-Morte on the Mediterranean and La Rochelle on the Atlantic acquired a monopoly of the import of spices, while Charles VIII sent trade missions as far afield as Morocco, and concluded similar arrangements with Denmark and several German principalities, as well as Castile and Aragon. Along the fertile valleys of long-established agriculture in the great upland of the Central Massif, where the fertility of the volcanic soil enabled cultivation well above the usual limits, there had been further revival. And in those areas where a different language, Provençal or *Langue d'Oc*, predominated, as opposed to the *Langue d'Oil* of the north, the familiar theme was repeated, reflected likewise in the west, where the ruined vineyards of Médoc and Bordelais around the marshes of the Gironde estuary, linked so closely to England through its wine trade, had also experienced rapid renewal after years of dislocation.

More notable still, arguably, was the building of ships and harbours – first at Bordeaux and later in the reign of Louis XII at Marseilles in the newly acquired district of Provence, where the king had plans to gain control of the Mediterranean trade. And in the meantime, most significantly of all perhaps, there emerged an awakening of national consciousness, spurred on in no small measure by those who benefited most obviously from the altered conditions: the bourgeois mercantile class who now bought castles, acquired official posts in the law courts and in finance, and became ennobled to form the first cohort of the so-called *noblesse de la robe*. Jacques Cœur, son of a merchant–furrier of Bourges, had been only one of many to emerge during the final stages of the Hundred Years War with lined pockets and high ambitions. His firm, situated first at Montpellier, then at Marseilles, had gone on to trade with the Mediterranean ports, as well as the Levant and Egypt, both exporting and importing, and harvesting rich profits from armaments and commissions on every kind of product, including cloths, carpets, silks, spices and perfumes. His fleet carried precious merchandise – as well as slaves – and, in due course, Jacques Cœur became, too, an industrialist, possessing a factory at Florence, a dye works at Montpellier, mines in Lyonnais, and a collection of paper mills. Such was his fortune, indeed, that he was able to buy thirty manors, and become not only the king's financial agent and counsellor, but also banker to the Treasury.

So it was not for nothing, perhaps, that Cœur had chosen as his motto *A vaillans cuers riens impossible*, 'To a valiant heart, nothing is impossible', since, for those with an eagle eye for profit, France at the dawn of the Tudor period, unlike its English counterpart, was truly a land of opportunity – and one well set to assert itself more broadly over the years ahead. For if France's economic recovery both during and after the Hundred Years War was notable, its political revival had proved hardly less impressive. And the driver of both, in no small measure, was its ruler from 1461 to 1483 – a nervous, impulsive, suspicious, tricky, cynical, superstitious figure, incapable of pronouncing the letter *r*, who nevertheless set his kingdom on the road to becoming a nation state of the kind never emulated by any Habsburg emperor. Covering himself with sacred medals, murmuring paternosters at every opportunity, while claiming he could seduce or buy all the saints in Paradise, Louis XI would take crucial steps to unify his realm by a combination of ruthless repression, economic expansion and a genius for diplomatic intrigue. He had two of his greatest nobles – the Count of St-Pol and the Duke of Nemours – cynically executed; he

incarcerated a cardinal, his old favourite, Jean La Balue; and when the town of
Arras hesitated to take his side, he put its aristocratic leaders to the sword and
expelled its inhabitants. Yet it was he who installed silk weaving, first at Lyons,
then at Tours, and he who not only conferred important privileges on the
fairs at Lyons, but attracted traders and foreign craftsmen in any way he could
and concluded commercial treaties with Portugal, England and Germany's
Hanseatic League. And when Charles the Bold of Burgundy sought to realise
his dream of a Lotharingian 'Middle Kingdom' by taking Alsace and Lorraine,
in order to ensure the link between his Burgundian domains and Flanders, it
was Louis who exhorted the Duke of Lorraine to defend his independence
and roused the Swiss cantons to protect Alsace, with the result that Charles
was defeated by the Swiss at Granson and Morat in 1476, before being killed
at Nancy the following year.

Ultimately, in fact, the man dubbed 'the universal spider' by his vanquished enemy would lose much of the Burgundian inheritance to the
Habsburgs by pressing Burgundy's new ruler too hard and driving her into
his enemy's hands. For as a result of the Treaty of Arras of 1492, by which
he retained that part of the Duchy of Burgundy lying within the French
border, along with Picardy and the so-called Somme towns, he nevertheless surrendered Gelderland, Utrecht, Liége and Lorraine, which regained
their independence, while the rest – Flanders, Artois and Franche Comté,
the free county of Burgundy outside the French frontiers – passed, as we
have seen, to the Habsburgs. Two hundred years later, therefore, Louis XIV's
main efforts would still be devoted to obtaining these areas. And if, in the
meantime, Edward IV of England had been bought off by the so-called
'merchant's peace' of Picquigny in 1475, by which the King of England
obtained a lump sum of 75,000 crowns, as well as 50,000 crowns a year
and the betrothal of the dauphin to his daughter, nor should it be forgotten
that the underlying hostility between the two realms remained unhealed.
Indeed, when both kings met on a bridge as a token of their reconciliation
by the treaty, they did so through a wooden grille halfway across, for mutual
fear of assassination.

But if Louis XI was certainly capable of failure – and it is hard to overlook,
above all, his fatal lack of foresight in allowing the House of Habsburg to seat
itself in the west – it remains impossible to deny his overriding achievement
in laying the foundations for what Machiavelli considered 'among the best
ordered and governed kingdoms of our time'. Before long, it would be imi-
tated by the Tudor rulers of England and Catholic monarchs of Spain, and in
the longer term it would ultimately break the House of Habsburg decisively.
Yet even by the end of Louis' reign, as Machiavelli acknowledged in admiration, the French king's authority was supreme:

It towered over the great vassals, and even the provincial and popular elements, commanding peace, compelling obedience, concentrating in itself all the interests of the nation, terrible from the suddenness with which it punished, everywhere present, taking counsel from no one, firmly established in itself.

And if the sight of drowned burgesses floating down French rivers in sacks labelled 'Make way for the King's justice' was less than gratifying, nor could it be denied that, at the height of his powers, not only was the Lord Chancellor of England in Louis' pay, but the monarch of France was also reputed to have more influence in the Empire than the Emperor Maximilian himself – not least because he also boasted a diplomatic service modelled on the most effective elements of those developed by the states of Italy. By the time of his death, he had been consumed once and for all by his neuroses, deluded by the belief that he was becoming a leper, and immuring himself in his palace at Tours, where the grounds were studded with sentries and mantraps. But as he lay surrounded by ineffective remedies, including the ring of St Zenobius and the blood of turtles from the Cape Verde Islands – not to mention the services of a hermit brought all the way from Calabria in southern Italy – he could seek solace, too, from the firm knowledge that his successors could rely upon a powerful army, numbering 16,000, including 6,000 Swiss mercenaries, which were the best – and most expensive - troops in Europe.

Thereafter, under a succession of forcefully ambitious kings, which included not only Charles VIII (1483–98) and Louis XII (1498–1515), but their two successors, Francis I (1515–47) and Henri II (1547–59), French assertiveness on the continental stage would be undiminished. For together, these rulers continued to assert their rights as overlords to parts of the Burgundian inheritance within the ancient borders of France, and proved equally keen, when opportunity offered, to extend their possessions eastwards into territory under Imperial control – in Lorraine and the Franche-Comté. At the same time, in wielding their inherited rights of succession, they would challenge the status of Milan as a fief of the Holy Roman Empire, and dispute with no less vigour Spanish control of Naples. Bolstered by the Pragmatic Sanction of Bourges, which had declared in 1438 that the payment of annates to Rome was to cease and that French clergy, subject to royal permission, should elect their own nominees as abbots and bishops, Louis XI's Valois successors were to stand out no less stridently against papal domination than against their secular rivals. And if France's fears of subjugation by her Habsburg enemy were matched, at least in part, by a bold assertion of her own more expansive ambitions, so these ambitions were also reinforced by the further expansion of military resources at her disposal over the years ahead: her standing army of noble cavalry, her expanding companies of Swiss and German mercenary infantry, the state-of-the-art artillery train that she would perfect, and the heavy regular taxation that the French king's subjects continually bemoaned.

Under the circumstances, it was small wonder that successive Habsburg rulers of both Spain and the Holy Roman Empire deemed France their most powerful and consistent enemy, or that grounds for conflict between Habsburgs and Valois should have proven so plentiful. Charles V's councillor Granvelle confided to an English ambassador 'that he hadde his sleve full of querelles against the French whenne ever th'empereur list [liked] to break them'. And war did indeed break out between Francis I and Charles V in 1521, though this was but one more episode in a conflict dating back to 1494, which would ultimately run through four separate phases spanning four separate decades. Invariably the storm centre was Italy, and when Italy's riches and divisions first tempted the French southward towards the end of the fifteenth century, it could hardly have been otherwise. For while Germany, Spain and France were different in their languages, customs and political institutions, they were nevertheless still essentially agrarian societies in which wealth and power derived from ownership of land and in which trade, however widespread and increasingly important, remained a secondary activity. But in northern Italy, by contrast, towns dominated the countryside and an urban civilisation had developed in which commerce, manufacture and the untold prosperity that resulted were mainstays. Standing midway on the major European trade route from the Levant, where the riches of the Orient became available to the markets of all Europe, Italy had become, in fact, not only the Continent's commercial hub, but home to an entrepreneurial élite comprising the first finance capitalists of the day. And nor were northern Italy's giants – Venice, Milan, Florence – simply cities in any conventional sense, since the need for food and security had driven them to extend their control far into the surrounding countryside (the *contado*), to render them, in effect, 'city-states', all independent one from the other and ruled either by merchant oligarchs, as in Venice and Florence, or by the will of a despot, as in Milan. Only in the south, in the kingdom of Naples, did a recognisably feudal society exist, complying with conditions elsewhere in Europe.

Most renowned and enticing of all Italy's city-states was Venice, sitting astride the commercial axis of Europe, which extended from the Levant, up the Adriatic, across the Alps and down the Rhine into the Continent's heart. Venetian merchants traded cotton and spices from the Levant in return for metals – especially copper, from central Europe – while the state-owned Venetian galley fleet made regular journeys through the Straits of Gibraltar to England and the Netherlands. Yet as a result of her inability to feed her large population, Venice remained vulnerable to the Ottoman Turks who controlled the regions that sustained her, and her diplomacy reflected the delicate balance she was forced to maintain between her western Christian commitments, on the one hand, and the pressing need to keep open her life-lines. As such, the merchant families who not only dominated the Senate and so-called Council of Ten but appointed the doge as nominal ruler were faced with an ongoing paradox: the need to sustain and expand their commercial dominance while scrambling by all and any means to withstand the looming threats from without, since not only the Turks but other foreign powers and even Venice's jealous Italian neighbours were an ongoing source of potential danger. Ostensibly at the height of her prosperity when Philip de Commynes visited the city in 1494 and marvelled at its splendid buildings and lavish entertainments, Venice was nonetheless increasingly vulnerable – ominously overstretched in reality by the very success during the first half of the fifteenth century that had extended her frontiers from the Alps to the Po, and from the Adda to the Isonzo.

Pope, Emperor, Milan, Mantua and Ferrara were in fact all the poorer for Venice's advance, and all were both envious and fearful of her unabated desire for further territory. At the same time, Venice's overseas interests and unwill-ingness to surrender primacy made her mostly reluctant to combine with her neighbours in Italy's broader defence and earned her a reputation for selfish absorption in her own affairs. In 1455, she had entered a formal league with Milan, Florence, the Papacy and Naples, the object of which was to preserve the balance of power within the peninsula and maintain Italian inde-pendence. But, like other combinations of its kind, this one had not lasted, leaving Italy fragmented and Venice herself exposed to increasing danger. For under the influence of popes like the Borgia Alexander VI, the papacy, which remained the focal point of all Italian politics, had become merely one Italian state among many, intent upon becoming a strong temporal power and desir-ous above all of territorial expansion, while to the north of the papal states none of the numerous duchies and republics, including the more powerful, were stable. Florence, home of banking and the woollen industry, had long been riddled by strife, which would peak under the influence of the viru-lent preaching of the Dominican Girolamo Savonarola against the reigning duke, Piero. And though, by 1434, the banker Cosimo de' Medici had become Florence's effective ruler, he held no formal title beyond *Pater Patriae* – 'Father of the Country' – and maintained only a façade of republican government, while Pisa, which had fallen under Florentine rule, sought every opportunity to free itself from control of its inland overlord on the Arno. The internal tensions involving the merchant oligarchy that had brought the Medici to power in the first place remained unresolved, and Milan, likewise, had once more succumbed to despotism after the dictatorship of its Visconti dukes was successfully overthrown in 1477. Hired by the city's republican leaders to rescue it from the threat of Venice, the mercenary captain, Francesco Sforza, subsequently proceeded to subjugate the government on his own behalf. And although both he and his successors would thereafter build on a princely scale and stage lavish entertainments to make their government acceptable to Milan's citizens, their glittering alternative to the republican government of Venice and what amounted to the political halfway house of Florence seemed no more capable of stability in the long term than its predecessors.

Under such circumstances, Italy clearly invited invasion, particularly when both of the Habsburg and Valois giants had dynastic claims of their own to justify intervention on various grounds and when other Italian states were in no better condition to resist. Of the remaining states of the north, for example, Genoa was a republic rich in trade but similarly dogged by internal dissent, while Savoy remained an Alpine duchy generally remote from the affairs of its counterparts and more or less under the influence of France. Yet the paradox of Italy's outstanding economic success and abject political weakness, which lay at the root of her tragedy, could hardly have been more fortunate for the newly established Tudor dynasty far to the west. For while the emergence of the two great monarchies of Habsburg and Valois finally ruled out any hope of England recovering her lost possessions or even resuscitating her lost satellites, their protracted struggle for Italy nevertheless brought valuable breathing space, and the additional prospect of a subsidiary role as a significant player in the finely poised balance of power that resulted. The continual fighting, in particular the introduction of firearms, ensured from this point forth that armies were not only to become steadily more permanent and more professional but larger and vastly more expensive, so that even the major participants broke their credit in maintaining them. And it was this above all that ensured early Tudor England's security against all statistical odds. For while the emperor could expect an income of perhaps £1,100,000 per annum and the King of France some £800,000, the ordinary revenue of their English counterpart, before the breach with Rome and exclusive of grants from Parliament, was seldom much more than £150,000. Couple to this England's slender demographic resources, and it was apparent that her rulers could neither afford nor man the kinds of force necessary to compete on any kind of even basis – especially when her southern coast, all along the 350 miles from Land's End to Dover and beyond, now lay open to direct attack and necessitated the absorption of most of the levies of the southern and eastern counties into home defence, just as the levies of the northern shires had been long committed to watching the Scottish border.

But while the Continent's two great leviathans fought themselves to a standstill to the far-off south, England was nevertheless able to rest comparatively easily – at least under its first Tudor ruler who, unlike the second, was prepared to settle for the role of good steward at home rather than that of constitutional innovator or dashing knight-errant abroad. In 1497 the Milanese ambassador Soncino had analysed the sources of Henry VII's growing strength:

> Everything favours the king, especially an immense treasure, and because all the nobles of the realm know the royal wisdom and either fear him or bear him an extraordinary affection.

One year later the Spaniard Ayala told King Ferdinand how his English counterpart's government was 'strong in all respects', while in 1500 Soncino was able to observe further that 'England has never been so tranquil and obedient as at present'. 'If only the minds of men would remain constant,' added the papal tax collector Silvestro Gigli all too innocently; prestige, prosperity and safety seemed assured at last.

3

TRAVEL, TRAVELLERS, COMMUNICATION

I do not know how your lordship fares for letters from Spain; for myself, I have heard nothing from the king concerning the affairs of the Netherlands since 20 November last … His Majesty's service has suffered greatly by it.
Message from Don Luis de Requesens to Don Diego de Zuñiga, Philip II's ambassador at Paris, sent from Antwerp, 24 February 1575

In the spring of 1508, with little more than a year of Henry VII's life remaining, Thomas Wolsey found himself dispatched on a delicate diplomatic mission to England's closest European neighbour, Scotland, whose international status had risen sharply in recent years. Indeed, its king, James IV, had not only determined from the outset of his reign to make his realm one of Christendom's leading nations, but succeeded admirably to that end. He had built a navy, opened gunpowder factories in Fife, intervened boldly in international politics and, for good measure, even gone on in 1503 to marry the King of England's elder daughter, Margaret. His court was appropriately splendid too, and included, amongst other notables, the poets William Dunbar and David Lindsay, not to mention a bevy of beautiful ladies, several of whom he successfully seduced. Somewhat paradoxically, perhaps, James was nevertheless very religious and, despite the time he expended upon women, hunting and diplomacy, he still managed, we are told, to attend Mass several times a day, receiving for his trouble the title of Defender of the Faith from the papal legate at Holyrood Abbey in 1507. In the meantime, he not only founded two new dockyards for the thirty-eight ships of his navy – including the carrack *Great Michael*, which, at 1,000 tons, was then the largest ship in the world – but built lavishly, encouraged medical and scientific study, welcomed the establishment of Scotland's first printing press in 1507, and upon the advice of his chancellor, William Elphinstone, passed what has been described as Scotland's first education act, which directed that all barons and freeholders of substance should send their eldest sons and heirs to school for a specified time. Plainly, if ever a ruler merited the title 'Renaissance prince', it was he. But though his realm boasted three universities as compared to England's two, and its scholars taught in universities throughout the Continent, it remained for the people of its southern neighbour an almost mythical land inhabited by 'wild Scots' and bounded in the north, or so it was supposed, by a great and impenetrable barrier of snow and ice.

For Tudor Englishmen, indeed, there could hardly have been a stranger or more exotic land, or, for that matter, a more menacing one. A decade earlier, King James had supported Perkin Warbeck, pretender to the English throne, and carried out a brief invasion of England on his behalf in September 1496, before laying siege to Norham Castle the following year, with his grandfather's famous bombard Mons Meg. And even after the subsequent Treaty of Perpetual Peace with England in 1502, which sealed his marriage to the English king's daughter, James had kept his options open, refusing to repudiate Scotland's 'auld alliance' with France that had already lasted over three hundred years. More than this, he had sent his cousin, the Earl of Arran, and Arran's brother, Patrick Hamilton, to France to negotiate a renewal of that alliance, though for Scots, even more so than Englishmen, communication with the French was far from straightforward. For if James's envoys travelled by sea, they risked finding themselves forced by rough weather to shelter in an English port, while travel by land involved either permission from the English government or, alternatively, the hazard of making the journey without guarantees of safe conduct. In the event, Arran and Hamilton took the last option and paid the price accordingly. For although they reached France uneventfully, they were apprehended at Kent on their return journey and taken to Henry's court to be detained as 'honoured guests'. The result was a vigorous complaint from the King of Scotland about the treatment of his two representatives and a further swipe at the English authorities in Northumberland for their failure to surrender Scottish fugitives.

Always tense, Anglo–Scottish relations had therefore taken a serious turn for the worse, and it was this that prompted Wolsey's dispatch to Edinburgh on a mission made even more difficult by the sheer logistical difficulties involved in reaching Scotland in the first place, since the journey was a forbidding one requiring at least a fortnight's hard going, even in the most favourable conditions. On the rough and muddy roads north, in fact, 40 miles a day was the furthest distance that any traveller could normally hope to cover, and the situation was little more satisfactory elsewhere. Nor would it improve significantly over the years to come. A statute of 1530 eventually empowered Justices of the Peace to inquire into the state of bridges – their upkeep being regarded as an act of charity – and to see that nearby parishes contributed to the maintenance of 300ft of highway at either end of their boundaries. But the danger of being way-laid by robbers, particularly on the approaches to major towns, remained considerable, with the result that roads in early Tudor England and indeed Europe as a whole would continue to be used more frequently for the movement of goods and beasts than the carriage of people. Significantly, England's first printed road table of 1541 listed only nine long-distance routes: the so-called 'highways' linking London with the chief provincial cities and thence with the remoter regions. But no cross-country roads were mentioned at all, since those that did exist were merely tracks linking village with village, often obliterated by encroaching farmers or flooding – as indeed were many highways.

To compound matters, sleeping arrangements for longer-distance travellers were also far from straightforward, since inn-keeping, except in larger towns, was not a common occupation in the early sixteenth century and strangers were rarely guaranteed a warm welcome, which explains the often exagger-ated estimates of monastic hospitality in remoter parts of the country. In some cases, too, even less formal provision of shelter for wayfarers was positively discouraged, as was the case at Elmley Castle in Worcestershire where a vil-lage by-law of 1537 stipulated 'that no tenant … shall harbour any stranger or vagabond under pain of 3s. 8d'. And while Wolsey, on his long journey north, did at least enjoy the company of Lord Darcy of Templehurst – an older cour-tier and privy councillor then serving as Warden of the Eastern Marches who became perhaps the only true friend the future cardinal ever made during his many years at court – the luxury of his own bed was by no means guaran-teed, even for a royal emissary. Indeed, Wolsey had first been thrown into the closest kind of acquaintance with Darcy as a result of the inadequate arrange-ments resulting from the itinerancy of the royal court. For the two men had long been sleeping companions on arduous royal progresses to remote and inhospitable locations, and the trip to the wild and lawless Border between England and Scotland was without doubt the most remote and inhospitable location of all. Darcy, touchingly, would later write to his friend referring to him as his 'bedfellow' and reflecting upon the discomforts they experienced together on their courtly travels. He would also recall the long hours they had spent beneath the covers revealing their minds and ambitions to each other and talking over their frustrations, each promising to help the other as far as he could.

But if there were cosy bedtime compensations to be had en route, the fact remained that sixteenth-century travel, especially abroad, was invariably an arduous business, offering few home comforts even to the most privileged. When the Earl of Northumberland travelled to France on military campaign in 1513, he brought with him not only an imposing noble pedigree, but all the creature comforts and necessities befitting a man of his substance. These included a feather bed and mattress for his pavilion, with cushions of silk and worsted hangings, a close carriage drawn by seven horses, and two chariots requiring eight horses each. Four carts, drawn by seven horses apiece, were also part of his train, along with a teeming throng of servants led by a steward, a chamberlain, a gentleman usher of the chamber, a master of horse, carvers and cupbearers, a herald and a pursuivant. On the same campaign, too, Wolsey would be another enjoying the advantages of rank, as the army endeavoured early in its progress to rest for the night in driving rain somewhere between the townships of Fréthun and Old Coquelles on its muddy way to the fortress of Thérouanne. For while common soldiers huddled in their thousands under the open skies beneath dripping bushes and windswept trees, Wolsey's tent, which was known as the Inflamed House, occupied more than 1,700sq ft – about half as much again as the records show for Charles Brandon, second-in-command of the entire army. And there were other hallmarks of privilege as well, not the least of which was that most prized of status symbols, a personal indoor toilet or 'stool place', something provided for only four other members of the king's retinue: the captain of the yeoman of the guard, the treasurer at war, the lord chamberlain and the master of the horse.

Yet in spite of such sophistications, the sixteenth-century tent was altogether more vulnerable to the elements than its present-day counterpart, and in spite of the fact that virtually all of those on the 1513 expedition were custom-made for the task, the accounts of Richard Gibson – Master of the King's Hales, Tents and Pavilions – include several references to the doubling of walls and addition of partitions to combat the damp and cold. No less vexatious either was the inordinate length of time involved in any excursion, even to the closest of neighbours like Scotland, as Wolsey was certainly to find in 1508 while both he and Darcy continued to edge their way northwards, punctuating their journey as was customary with business stops along the way to obviate the need for return visits later. After making their way up the Great North Road by Ware, Huntingdon and Grantham, they were forced, for example, to tarry first at York with the Abbot of St Mary's, who acted as the government's banker in that region, to arrange for the payment of wages and for the supply of provisions to the border garrisons. After which, they stopped at Newcastle to discuss with the Earl of Northumberland his somewhat ineffectual attempts to suppress the lawlessness of the border country, before moving on to inspect the fortresses at Norham and Berwick. By which time, the party had still not entered Scotland and embarked upon the last leg of its journey: a two-day haul via Dunbar and Haddington to Edinburgh along a road that was more commonly trudged by English armies than diplomats. At the end of it all, after waiting five days in Berwick for his guarantee of safe conduct, Wolsey finally reached Edinburgh on 28 March, only to find the king inspecting a gunpowder factory, as a result of which, it was another five days before an audience was finally arranged. 'There was never,' complained the future cardinal, 'a man worse welcome into Scotland than I.'

Not only in England and Scotland, however, was the lot of the sixteenth-century traveller a daunting one. For in Europe at large, hospitable towns were few and far between, and only on the chief trade routes were inns to be found – at intervals averaging 10 to 15 miles – as travellers wound their way at speeds that hardly varied until the coming of the railways. From Paris to Calais took just over four days, to Brussels just over five, to Metz six, to Bordeaux seven, to Toulouse eight to ten, to Marseilles ten to fourteen and to Turin ten to fifteen. From Venice, on the other hand, it still took Philippe de Commines six days to reach Asti, notwithstanding the fact that 'the road was the best in the world', while other travel times from Venice averaged four days to Rome (though there is a record of a courier completing the journey non-stop in a day and a half), to London twenty-six, to Madrid forty-two, and to Constantinople forty-one. Even these, moreover, were times taken by merchants or diplomats in a hurry, though along routes where an organised postal service operated, some further speed might be achieved, with the result that in 1516 letters sent from Brussels via the postal system operated by the Taxis family usually reached Paris in summer in thirty-six hours, and Lyons in just over three days. To Rome required just over ten, though all depended ultimately upon the weather, which explains why the norm of the overland postal service between Amsterdam and Antwerp at the end of the sixteenth century varied between three and nine days, and to Danzig between twenty-four and thirty-five days. On the roads from Danzig to Lisbon, the variation ranged from thirty-two to as many as fifty-three days.

In consequence, the arrival or imminent arrival of the mails frequently amounted to an obsession, not least because the post, insofar as any recognisable system existed at all, had neither a fixed hour nor even a fixed day. 'I am waiting for the regular Flanders mail to go past at any hour,' Thomas

Perrenot de Chantonnay, Spain's ambassador to France, noted anxiously in December 1561, while the French diplomat Cardinal de Rambouillet recorded in January 1570 how it was a waste of time for Charles IX to send him letters, 'because of the knavery and negligence of the postmasters in carrying Your Majesty's dispatches ... which is such and so great ... that the said dispatches often spend a month or six weeks on the road between the Court and Lyons'. 'When I receive them,' he continued, 'the time when I could have availed myself of them and had occasion to execute the orders contained in them is often, to my very great sorrow, past ...'

The theme, indeed, was unremitting in the diplomatic correspondence of the day. Henri III's agent in Spain related in February 1584 how he had been without news of his government for two weeks and that many letters 'have remained at Burgos coming from the direction of Valladolid'. Two mails might fail to make a connection, or couriers, forewarned of brigands, might refuse to travel at night. But the effect was the same, leaving the viceroy of Naples without direction, or the Venetian ambassador at Madrid without news from Italy for sixty days. A letter from Spain to Italy was as likely to go by Bordeaux and Lyons as by Montpellier and Nice, while a letter sent to Henri IV by Monsieur de Villiers, his ambassador in Venice in April 1601, arrived at Fontainebleau by way of Brussels. Even news of the epoch-making victory over the Turks at Lepanto on 7 October 1571 only reached Venice on 18 October, Naples on the 24th, Lyons on the 25th, Paris and Madrid on the 31st.

Under such circumstances, it was hardly surprising that across the Channel, Tudor England should have been all the more tightly sealed from its neighbours when travel times within its own borders were no better. Not until 1637, in fact, did an English regulation specify that post-letters were to travel in summer at 7 miles an hour and in winter at 6. But little progress ensued and as late as 1666 the average speed of letters from Plymouth, Chester and York to London was still no more than 4 miles an hour. In Peru, by comparison, it had taken an Inca mail-runner three days to complete the journey from Lima to Cuzco, though a seventeenth-century post-horse would take twelve to cover the same distance. Indeed, so efficient was the Inca delivery system that fresh fish could be run up from the coast, over a distance of some 350 miles, in two days, though in England's case, of course, there was the added obstacle of a treacherous sea crossing to contend with, as Catherine of Aragon found to her cost upon her journey to England in 1501. Delayed first by an attack of fever and then by a sudden, though local, Moorish uprising in her native land, which had prevented her father from accompanying her to the coast, Catherine's journey had finally begun in May across interminable stretches of her flat, arid homeland, as well as its sometimes hilly and mountainous regions, often in blistering heat. But after her embarkation at Corunna, there had been such fierce hurricanes from the turbulent Bay of Biscay that her sea captains found themselves compelled to put back to Spain – their topmasts and rigging destroyed and one ship unaccounted for – before setting sail again in September, this time from Laredo at the eastern end of the Basque coast, on the month-long journey to England. Thereafter, upon sighting Ushant in bright weather, the diminutive princess encountered further shattering storms off Brittany, breaking never more than three or four hours apart and accompanied by terrific thunder and lightning, which paralysed both her and her entourage with fear. Spars and masts alike were carried away by seas so high that, as the Licentiate Alcares reported to the bride-to-be's mother, 'it was impossible not to be afraid'.

Years later, Catherine's associates would recall how she had spoken of the delays and terrors of the voyage as an ill omen, and the risks and rigours of the English Channel would remain notorious long after her ordeal. But sea travel in general posed problems that continue to stretch the credulity of most modern observers. When Henry VII mounted his throne, ships plying the south coast of England still kept very close to land for fear of pirates, though it was always the weather, ultimately, that remained the most forbidding threat of all. Over a century later, in January 1610, a Venetian ambassador on his way to England waited fourteen days at Calais facing waves so high that no ship dared venture out, while the year before, according to Alberti Tommaso, a Venetian ship bound for Constantinople had been forced to stand for eighteen days off the open beach of Santa Anastasia in the shelter of Chios, waiting for the weather to abate. Almost as perplexing was the consequent unpredictability of sea travel, so that a voyage from the Sea of Marmora to Venice, which Pierre Belon was able to achieve in just thirteen days, might in another instance require no less than half a year. One Venetian roundship, sailing in October–November 1570, made the journey from Crete to Otranto in twelve days, though a similar vessel left Alexandria on 7 January 1564, only to reach Messina on 5 April – a journey totalling eighty-eight days. Similarly, in May–June 1561, another roundship sailed almost the entire length of the Mediterranean from Crete to Cadiz in a month, only for two galleys to set sail from Algiers in July 1569 and take seventy-two days to reach Constantinople. One particular boat that sailed from Malta to Tripoli in nine days in January 1564 took seventeen days for the return journey, and similar variations held true for sea voyages in general, whether they took place in the icy chill of the North Sea or Baltic or on the crossing from Marseilles to Spain, which was often undertaken in secret by hapless – and perennially complaining – French ambassadors.

Apart from infrequent and widely scattered communities of fishermen and isolated bands of salt evaporators, the sea coast of Europe was in fact largely deserted, its rocks and marshes acting, to all intents and purposes, as a *cordon sanitaire* that travellers or traders only penetrated to embark or disembark. And as a consequence, even maritime countries such as Portugal and Venice suffered from a shortage of sailors, at a time when the sea itself was widely perceived as a wreckers' world: one written about only in terms of trepidation, and largely unpainted, too, save as the background to a miracle or a foreground to the welcoming quays of a port. Inland, similarly, Europe's mountains were treated as zones of fear, just like the forests still covering so much of the Continent, which were rarely explored unless by huntsmen or fugitives from justice. Such, indeed, were the real or imagined hazards and inconveniences of long-distance journeys that the Venetian government, which had the most elaborate diplomatic network of any, had no choice but to impose heavy penalties as a means of keeping its hard-pressed agents on the move. In 1506, Francesco Morosini wrote from Turin to say that in crossing the Alps from France several of his suite had died in snowstorms. Next year the papal legate returning from a meeting between Louis XII and Ferdinand of Aragon at Savona had been seasick – 'even to the point of blood' – before arriving in Rome so weakened that he contracted a fever and died. And when Cardinal Lorenzo Campeggio bade farewell to his two children on 25 June 1528, bound for London to preside over Henry VIII's divorce proceedings, he faced an excruciating, gout-ridden odyssey, which would not culminate until 28 October when he was finally greeted by booing London crowds. Rotten food and surly muleteers only added to the inconvenience for contemporary wayfarers, along with constant exposure to wind and rain at a time when waterproof clothing was non-existent and the roads were too rutted for the kind of heavy closed carriages that John Stow suggests did not become common in England until 1555.

Yet notwithstanding the tribulations involved, long-distance travel did indeed continue to occur. In fact, some English merchants not only made Spain a frequent visiting place, but resided there, especially in the early part of Henry VIII's reign, when they lived, mainly in Seville, on the friendliest terms with their hosts. The ledger of Thomas Howell, for instance, illustrates how he traded in dyestuffs, mordants and Seville oil, all of which were so essential for English clothiers, while Robert Thorne and Robert Barlow were two other figures resident in Seville, who sent their shipments to the Indies in the same manner as Spaniards. Other English merchants were also to be found in a range of northern ports, including Bilbao, Fuenterrabia, Pasajes, Portugalete, Laredo, Santander, El Ferrol and El Corunna. Bilbao, chief centre for the Spanish wool *flotas*, seems in fact to have been especially attractive for many Englishmen, including individuals such as Thomas Traves and John Shaa, as well as Nicholas Wilford, who helped negotiate the sums due to Thomas Wolsey from Spain in 1527. At least two other English merchants, Thomas Holland and Roger Jefferson, are known to have been married in the town, and John Joyce was buried there, while in Renteria, a small port between San Sebastian and the French frontier, lived Thomas Batcock, perhaps the best established Englishman in those parts, who was many times employed on diplomatic and commercial matters by his government. Batcock, too – who had a relative in the service of a member of Charles V's council – may have been one to marry in Spain, since he is known to have declared on one occasion that none of his children could write English, while else-where, as in San Sebastian, several resident English merchants would later receive sentences from the Inquisition for upholding Henry VIII's claims to ecclesiastical supremacy.

Even before the Tudor period, moreover, the dukes of Medina Sidonia had actively encouraged English traders to conduct business from the little port of San Lucar de Barrameda at the mouth of the Guadalcavir. The Andalusia Company, established in 1531 specifically for commerce with Spain, had its headquarters there and an English church was built on lands provided by the dukes. Cadiz, the chief Andalusian port of call for Levant traders of all nations, was another focal point for English merchants, and even as late as 1539, by which time Anglo–Spanish relations had soured to the brink of war, Englishmen such as Thomas Pery were still attempting to maintain their links on the Spanish mainland. A citizen and clothworker of London, where he lived in Fenchurch street in the parish of St Denis, Pery, who was born around the turn of the century, had been trading to Spain for some years, making Ayamonte his headquarters during visits, while leaving his wife, Alice, to manage his affairs at home. And he was still in Spain on 9 October 1539 when a local priest and several other Spaniards confronted him in his ware-house at the dwelling of his host, Gômez Malmazeda. 'What a goode crysten is yowre kinge of Ynglande to pwte down the monasterys and to take awaye the belles?' said the priest. And the upshot, following a denial by Pery that he himself was a heretic, was his arrest in Lepe on 11 October, where he remained chained by the left leg for eleven days 'as thowgh I had byne the strongest thyfe in the world'. Ultimately, Pery's ordeal would last another four months before he was finally released after the loss of his goods and threats of burning. He might indeed have died, he wrote later, had it not been for the good offices of a certain Mr Harrison and John Field, two other leading English merchants still resident in Seville who had helped him 'of cheryte', since the Spaniards had not left him a single blanket or garment to his back, 'Gode amend them'.

Among the trickle of early Tudor travellers to Europe, however, there was also a smattering of adventurers, including the man indirectly responsible, it might be said, for Pery's ordeal in the first place. For in December 1503, at around the age of 18, Thomas Cromwell was serving with the French army in Italy as either a soldier or page. Having fought that month at the Battle of Garigliano, moreover, Cromwell was to remain in Italy in the service of the Florentine banking family of Frescobaldi and travel widely there, operating mainly in Florence, but also in Pisa and Venice. Significantly, it was during his Italian sojourn that he came into contact with a range of new ideas and approaches, and readily absorbed the emerging rationalistic ethos of the day. This was reinforced by his subsequent visits to leading mercantile centres in the Low Countries, where he not only developed a network of contacts but learnt several languages. Thereafter, at some point, he returned to Italy, since records of the English Hospital in Rome indicate that he stayed there in June 1514, while documents in the Vatican Archives also suggest that he was an agent for the Archbishop of York, Cardinal Christopher Bainbridge, and handled English ecclesiastical issues presented before the Roman Rota. Certainly, it was a remarkable odyssey for a brewer's son from Putney, which rendered him, in effect, a prime example of how travel could indeed broaden the outlook of at least a minority of Englishmen. For by the time of his return he had not only been introduced to Marsiglio of Padua's seminal work, *Defensor Pacis*, which emphasised the primacy of the secular ruler in ecclesiastical affairs, but encountered the writings of various religious reformers. Equally importantly, his considerable commercial experience had firmly reinforced his natural tendency to think in terms of efficiency and outcomes rather than hidebound traditions, equipping him admirably for his later role as architect and enforcer-in-chief of Henry VIII's breach with the Catholic Church.

But while Cromwell was equipping himself on his travels with the necessary tools to put paid once and for all to England's links with Rome, there were others, equally, who set forth from their island home for the express purpose of serving the Holy See at a time when papal appeals for assistance against the advance of Islam in the eastern Mediterranean and along the Danube valley were growing in volume. According to a contemporary Durham register, for instance, three men – from Brancepeth, Chester-le-Street and Morpeth – made vows of commitment in 1499 in response to a crusading indulgence issued by the pope the previous year. And nor should it be forgotten that the Holy City remained a popular destination in its own right for English pilgrims throughout the reign of Henry VII and into the reign of his son, before the breach with the papacy finally staunched the flow. Records of the English College in Rome, for example, reveal a constant stream of visitors who were received in the so-called English Hospital there: eighty-two in the six months from November 1504 to May 1505; 202 in the year between May 1505 and May 1506; and 205 in the year before that. Not all, it is true, were necessarily pilgrims, since some described as merchants and sailors may well have been in Rome in the normal course of their work. But a letter to Thomas Wolsey written in 1518 made clear that increasing numbers of pilgrims were indeed creating extra costs for the hospital. And there is evidence, too, that Wolsey's countrymen were continuing to make their way to other sacred sites – albeit in lower numbers than formerly.

For unlike Rome itself, some of the old pilgrim routes, like that to St James of Compostella, which had once attracted the more intrepid brand of English visitor, had long been declining in popularity – not least as the habit grew of paying others, usually by bequest, to go as proxies. During a single day in 1493, the gatekeepers at Aix-la-Chapelle recorded 142,000 visitors to the Shrine of the Sacred Blood, but there are likely to have been few Englishmen among them, and though English pilgrims continued to wind their way to Rome, the death there of 30,000 people in 1500, a year of plague as well as of Jubilee, seems likely to have checked the flow thereafter. Instead, resorts like Walsingham, Canterbury, Glastonbury, Hailes Abbey, the tomb of Henry VI and a host of others increasingly filled the vacuum. The first, indeed, had generated a nationwide cult and enlisted substantial royal patronage from the time of Henry III through to the reign of Henry VIII himself, so that by 1513 even Erasmus was overwhelmed by what he witnessed at the so-called Slipper Chapel, where visitors left their shoes before tramping barefoot the final mile to the shrine itself. 'When you look in,' he wrote, 'you would say it is the abode of saints, so brilliantly does it shine with gems, gold and silver.' On an altogether smaller scale, Suffolk alone boasted at least sixteen sites attracting considerable numbers of pilgrims: at Beccles, Cherington, Eye, Ipswich, Ixworth, Melford, Mildenhall, Mutford, Norton, Stoke-by-Clare, Stowmarket, Sudbury, Thetford, Weston, Woodbridge and Woolpit. And with a similar proliferation of holy places throughout the length and breadth of the kingdom, what further incentive was there to risk the considerable dangers and inconveniences of continental travel – even with divine favour or salvation itself in mind?

For most Englishmen, therefore, long-distance movement of any kind remained largely internal, and consisted predominantly of unskilled farm labourers, forced by adverse economic circumstances to journey in search of work, though in Europe, by contrast, an early modern form of what might, at some stretch, be considered the 'free movement of labour' was already under way. Crucial to this process was Europe's rapid population growth, which frequently outpaced the demand for agricultural and urban labour, particularly in areas such as Castile, the mountains of central Europe and the less fertile islands and coasts of the Mediterranean. Inflation, rising rents, heavy taxation and the depredations of war also forced rural labourers from their villages. And the result was a steady passage of men seeking jobs – not least as soldiers in the mercenary companies necessitated by the endemic wars of the period. Albanian mercenaries, for example, were found as far afield as Spain, though most sought service in Italy where they were relied upon particularly by Venice. Called 'stradiots' – from the Italian *strada* – because they were always on the road, they were joined from various impoverished regions by others of all nationalities wandering in search of wars which those more prosperous were unwilling to fight themselves. Luck and a captain short of men could, in fact, turn a tramp into a soldier overnight, though Croatians, Scandinavians and, most notably, the so-called '*landsknechts*' of Germany earned merited reputations as high-calibre troops able to command accordingly high sums for their services from a range of European governments. And in the meantime, thousands of French rural labourers also crossed the Pyrenees each summer to help with the harvest. As such men and countless others like them travelled, they too not only interacted with their hosts but frequently married and settled, assimilating their culture while familiarising the resident population with their own.

Equally apparent was the unchecked flow of skilled labour across mainland Europe's flimsy borders. Many towns, for example, and even wealthier villages, came to enjoy the services of itinerant clockmakers, while churches, too, often grew up at the hands of non-native masons. In 1515, there were no clockmakers in Geneva, but from 1550 they came as refugees from France, and by 1600 the city had twenty-five to thirty master clockmakers. In Zürich, a third of all apprentices came from distant foreign parts, mainly Germany, while in Frankfurt, even before the new century had begun, some 56 per cent of locksmiths who came to work and train had arrived from over 150km away. The great mosques of Constantinople were built by European craftsmen, just like the guns that had shattered the city's walls in 1453, and a whole host of other trades were also in the hands of artisans who travelled in and between Europe's states unimpeded by border controls. Printing was one example, as was proof-reading. We hear much, too, of itinerant actors, jugglers and musicians, and catch glimpses even of itinerant professional football players, particularly in Italy, where the first recognisable traces of the organised sport began. And then again, of course, there were the most iconic wanderers of all, the gypsies. Treated most tolerantly in Scotland and Scandinavia, they were expelled from Spain – by law if not in

fact – in 1499, and from Burgundy in 1515. Henry VIII would also banish
them and sanction the execution of those who remained. But in spite of such
harassment, they continued to flourish on mainland Europe and added their
own exotic brand of culture to the early cosmopolitan ethos evolving there.
A gypsy band played at the wedding of Matthias Corvinus and Beatrice of
Aragon in Buda in 1476, while on Corfu, under Venetian protection, a hundred gypsies formed a community exempt from both galley service and the
usual obligations of peasant status.

Rather more welcome and hardly less common on Europe's roads were the
students and scholars flowing to prestigious universities in Italy especially, but
also to places as far afield as Paris, Louvain, Heidelberg, Kraków and elsewhere,
since degrees could be built up piecemeal by residence at one university after
another. For each student there was, in effect, an ideal curriculum available,
devised according to personal taste on the basis of the reputations of famous
teachers, who were to be followed by moving not from one lecture hall to
another but from one country to another. Renewed interest in Latin, Greek
and Hebrew had, after all, produced a new and revolutionary mood in scholarship, both secular and Christian, and to take advantage of it, scholars found
themselves hurrying from one seat of learning to another: to confer with colleagues; to exploit an eager publisher; or to settle for a while under the wing
of a sympathetic patron as the 'New Learning' bubbled through the rocks of
traditional scholasticism. One of the more common uses of the term 'nation' at
this time was, as we have seen, to designate the various groupings of university
students to their common places of origin, and it was no mere coincidence
that Thomas More should have seen fit to write in defence of the restless itinerancy of Europe's most famous scholar of all, Desiderius Erasmus, who 'defies
stormy seas and savage skies and the scourges of land travel' and goes 'through
dense forest and woodland, over rugged hilltops and steep mountains, along
roads beset with bandits … tattered by the winds, spattered with mud, travel
weary'. As a result, More wrote, his Dutch friend 'both learns and gives', for 'as
the sun spreads its rays, so wherever Erasmus is he spends his wonderful riches',
though More himself was another Englishman who forewent the opportunity
for European travel, settling instead for two years at Oxford between the ages
of 14 and 16, before being deprived of his allowance for wasting time on such
extraneous studies as Greek, and finishing his studies at Lincoln's Inn.

Not altogether surprisingly, the vast majority of English students
also continued, like their forefathers, to wend their way to Oxford and
Cambridge for the kind of traditional education that demonstrably
failed in the main to attract the kind of foreign clientele so notable in
the best universities abroad. Nor was it insignificant, perhaps, that in 1556
Ottavio Maggi still believed that a good ambassador should speak what

had become the three main languages of diplomacy – Latin, French and Italian – together with German and even Turkish, but not English, though by then the most privileged English men and women were already in the early stumbling stages of adapting to the challenge of mastering foreign tongues. In the early years of Henry VIII's reign, indeed, knowledge of French became a sign of good breeding, and the publication of manuals of instruction in that language by John Palsgrave and Alexander Barclay encouraged the trend, prompting Thomas More in his *Epigrammata* to lampoon the resulting shortcomings of those involved, with a specific section entitled 'In Anglum Gallicae linguae affectatorum':

> With accent French he speaks the Latin tongue
> With accent French the tongue of Lombardy,
> To Spanish words he gives an accent French,
> German he speaks with his same accent French,
> In truth he seems to speak with accent French,
> All but the French itself. The French he speaks
> With accent British.

Even so, by 1550 French was spoken by all courtiers, as Gallic sensibilities became the benchmark in every matter of good taste, governing dress, cooking, wines, deportment, dancing and even the Italian art of fencing, for, although Italians had perfected it, the technique reached England through the offices of French masters, as, it seems, did equestrian skills, if Shakespeare's reference in *Hamlet* to the Norman Lamord's talents in both areas is any guide. As early as 1518, Edward Hall had described in his *Chronicle* how a group of young English noblemen returned from the French court in 1518 completely derisive of all things English – a theme echoed by More in his observations on the behaviour of such gallants:

> He struts about
> In cloaks of fashion French. His girdle, purse,
> And sword are French. His hat is French.
> His nether limbs are cased in French costume.
> His shoes are French. In short, from top to toe
> He stands the Frenchman.

And more than half a century later, Thomas Nash would declare in *The Unfortunate Traveller* (1597) how he could tell a long sojourner in France by his strange manner of speaking English, though by then the French language itself had become altogether more than a matter of mere affectation.

Certainly, both Queen Elizabeth and her closest adviser, William Cecil, were fluent in both French and Italian, as was the Earl of Leicester. It was said of Cecil, in fact, that he 'never read any books or praiers, but in Lattin, French and Italian: very seldome in Englishe'. And the numbers of diplomats and writers who had spent time in Venice or Padua absorbing Italian culture and literature also increased as the century progressed. Sir Thomas Hoby, who translated Castiglione's *Courtier*, and Sir Philip Sidney are cases in point, though Edmund Spenser, who was inspired to write *The Faerie Queen* in imitation of the Italian romances of Ariosto and Tasso, never visited the homeland of his heroes. Knowledge of Italian was spread, too, by William Thomas's *Principal Rules of the Italian Grammar* (1550), which Sir Walter Mildmay arranged to have published as 'a necessary book for the public', while the demand for instruction in foreign languages was also met professionally by growing numbers of immigrant refugees. The most notable, Claude de Sainliens, settled in London as a schoolmaster about 1565 and anglicised his name to Claudius Holybrand, publishing a number of very successful manuals in the form of dialogues: *The Frenche Schoolemaister* (1573), *The Italian Schoolemaister* (1573), and *Campo di Fior: the Flourie Fielde of Foure Languages*.

No English ruler, it is true, could match the linguistic gifts of Scotland's James IV or, for that matter, his general inquisitiveness regarding the nature of language per se. For as well as being the last king of his country to speak Gaelic, James was a renowned polyglot, and prepared, it seems, to send two of his children to be raised by a mute woman alone on the island of Inchkeith, with the aim of determining if language was learned or innate. In July 1498, the Spanish envoy, Pedro de Ayala, reported to Ferdinand and Isabella that James:

> speaks the following foreign languages: Latin, very well; French, German, Flemish, Italian, and Spanish … He likes, very much, to receive Spanish letters … The King speaks, besides, the language of the savages who live in some parts of Scotland and on the islands … His knowledge of languages is wonderful.

The ambassador noted, too, how James 'has read many Latin and French histories, and profited by them, as he has a very good memory'. By comparison, neither Henry VII nor even his much-vaunted successor were a remote match, notwithstanding the latter's undoubted accomplishments under his French tutor, the humanist Bernard André. But at least the internationalisation of cultural and artistic styles, which had long been gathering pace in Europe, did not leave either monarch entirely untouched. And nor could it have been otherwise when 'high culture' was set at such store for the image of contemporary rulers, and when native English talent remained in comparatively short supply. For both men, especially in light of the flimsy origins of the Tudor dynasty, the quest for courtly splendour remained a high priority. And if the latest and most accomplished talent lay abroad, so English rulers, too, would have little choice but to go in search of it.

With this in mind, Henry VII employed Flemish stained-glass workers, and another Fleming to design some of his coinage, while the bronze screen around his funeral monument by the Italian Pietro Torrigiano was the work of a Dutchman. Keener still in his efforts to enhance his court by cultural imports was Henry VIII who, among other things, captured the services of the renowned Venetian organist, Dionisio Memmo, calling him over from S. Marco to London in 1516. Yet when Thomas Wolsey became the first man in England to employ distinguished artists and sculptors from Italy on a large scale, he did so at a time that lagged significantly behind their employment elsewhere. At his urging, agents scoured the markets of Flanders, France, Italy and Venice for all kinds of rich art, and the Florentine Giovanni da Maiano came to work at Hampton Court in 1521 to make a series of terracotta roundels depicting the heads of Roman emperors, which cost, we are told, £2 6s 8d each. Finer still was the panel over the gateway of the Clock Tower, showing Wolsey's cardinal's hat, archiepiscopal crosses and legatine pillars. Completed by Italian craftsmen as a fitting accompaniment to the clock itself – which had been designed by the German Nicholas Cratzer, and built by the French clockmaker Nicholas Oursian who became naturalised in 1541 – the sum total was an exterior façade making Hampton Court broadly comparable in grandeur to various structures abroad.

But it was notable that at the other end of the Continent, Ivan III had already introduced Italian craftsmen to work on the final stages of the Kremlin almost half a century earlier. The Uspensky Sobor, indeed, was completed by Aristotile Fioraventi in 1479, while the diamond-faceted Granovitaia Palace, designed by Solari with the decoration of Ferrarese palaces in mind, was finished in 1491. In Poland, likewise, not only were Italian scholars introducing Roman Law and the study of Greek and classical Latin to Kraków university, but Italian architects were working on both the city's cathedral and the royal palace of Wawel. By comparison, Hampton Court remained a decidedly parochial project, with original plans drawn up by the Englishman Ellis Smith, which were finally completed by Henry Redmayn, ably assisted by William Reynolds – the same master mason who had finally completed the tower at Wolsey's Magdalen College. Most of the timberwork was prepared under the direction of the master carpenter, Humphrey Cook, while the building materials themselves were as solidly native as the men who used them: stone from Reigate and Barnet, timber from Reading and Weybridge, lime from Ruislip and red bricks baked in nearby kilns by Richard Reculver, costing 3*s* per thousand. Even the majority of Hampton Court's fine gold and silver objects were purchased from London's finest goldsmiths, who were predominantly of Lombard origin.

Away in Spain, meanwhile, Italians were also setting their mark upon court culture through the patronage of Ferdinand and Isabella – an imprint broadened by the organisation of their household, which had resulted in the employment of Italian tutors not only for the royal princesses but at the school for young aristocrats that the king and queen took under their protection. Foreign troops, musicians, cooks, saddlers, dressmakers and surgeons were all a notable feature of the Spanish royal establishment, which was also, by nature of the kingdom itself, highly itinerant. And the result was the steady exposure of at least the noble class to unfamiliar influences of precisely the kind that were equally prominent in France, where Leonardo da Vinci had died in 1519. To complete his château at Amboise, Charles VIII employed Italian architects, painters, sculptors, wood carvers, marquetry workers, upholsterers, armourers and an organ maker, while in 1500 Louis XII added faience workers from Forli, complete with their kilns. Afterwards came the architects Francesco Laurana, Fra Giocondo, Giuliano da San Gallo and Domenico da Cortona, as well as foreign musicians, particularly cornettists and trombone players, to the court of Francis I. Josquin des Prez, doyen of the period's composers, was another migrant – from his home in Hainault – who spent most of his time in France, dying there in 1521, after working in Milan, the papal chapel in Rome, and at the court of Ercole d'Este in Ferrara. By contrast, as the Tudor dynasty found its feet, the only English musician of significant continental repute was John Hothby who taught for twenty years in Lucca, and died in 1487.

At the same time, the urge to seek out foreign lands for curiosity's sake was always less evident among Englishmen until, perhaps, the last third or so of the century, and never, even then, to the degree typified by the likes of Antonio Pigafetta who joined Magellan's expedition in August 1519 'to go and see with my own eyes', or Lodovico Varthema who set off for Mecca in 1502 disguised as a Moslem pilgrim, 'longing for novelty'. Instead, excursions to distant lands were not so much a passion as an arduous necessity incumbent upon men like Richard Pace, whose wanderings as a scholar and diplomat confirmed not only the full rigours of European travel, but the equally undeniable fact that, in spite of its geographical location, England could never neglect her connection to the European state system and its vagaries. For battles in far-off Italy, the deaths of emperors and popes, and the twists and turns of the balance of power would continue to affect English fortunes both suddenly and unexpectedly. And whenever they did, envoys such as Richard Pace would continue to venture forth, braving storm-tossed seas, precipitous mountain ranges, dangerous roads and often-times frosty hospitality in their kingdom's interests – conveying messages, gleaning information, bartering for advantage and, where necessary, deploying considerable sums of money in the acquisition of allies. A frequently thankless occupation of the highest intensity and considerable personal risk, the sixteenth-century emissary's lot was never an easy one, and in Pace's particular case, it would entail strains that by the time of his death in 1536 had helped reduce him, it seems, to mental collapse. But it was also a role, as Pace's career confirms, that could bring with it the kind of wide-ranging repute, inconceivable under other circumstances for Englishmen of comparatively humble origins.

In Thomas Cromwell's correspondence, his name was written 'Pacey', in John Foxe's 'Pacy', while in one of Wolsey's instructions, he is referred to as 'Passe' – a spelling also employed by a Spanish ambassador. Elsewhere, in the French translation of a sermon by Wolsey, printed in Paris soon after he delivered it, the spelling was rendered 'Pacee', and the variations continued internationally in tandem with his ubiquity. To Margaret of Austria, he was 'Paseo', while the Venetians usually dubbed him 'Il Pazeo' or 'Ricardo Paceo', or occasionally 'Panzeo'. Erasmus latinised his name into 'Pacœus', though his own translation was 'Paceus', and Sebastiano Giustiniani, the Venetian ambassador, who knew him well, opted for 'Rizardo Pazoto'. Only Shakespeare, in fact, in a brief reference in *King Henry VIII* to 'Doctor Pace', spells his surname according to the modern convention. But if spellings are inconsistent, the undeniable conclusion is not: namely, that Richard Pace, who features only marginally in most popular treatments of Tudor history these days, was nevertheless a widely known figure among his European contemporaries, and a prime example of that comparatively rare phenomenon among early Tudor Englishmen – someone intimately acquainted with other countries' habits and affairs.

Imbued with high principle, good nature and exceptional intelligence, Pace was, as might be expected, a remarkable linguist and a man of tremendous tenacity, though his health was always poor, and he was prone, it seems, to anxiety and excitability – qualities exacerbated, no doubt, by his enforced decision to opt for the priesthood, and by his subsequent choice to turn to the service of prelates and the Crown, to fill his empty pockets. For Erasmus, who knew him well, he was fitter to serve the Muses than the State, and though a pious man, he seems to have had little of the cleric in him. Yet if he was not without deficiencies, he became well enough known in diplomatic circles for one contemporary to note how a Venetian ambassador came before the pope wearing a black gown trimmed with black satin 'made in the style adopted by Paceo, the English ambassador'. Elsewhere, too, we hear of how he met the doge of Venice in what appears to have been his trademark long black satin gown trimmed with sables, but that when news reached him there of the final humiliation of his enemy the King of France at Pavia in 1525, he was sporting a doublet of cloth of gold, and a gold chain, like the other ambassadors present. Nor should this change surprise us, since this, after all, was still the individual widely acknowledged in Imperial circles as a likely successor to Thomas Wolsey, and a man who had the self-confidence beneath his dour black robes to tell Charles V on one occasion how he considered himself sent into the world to be the cause of France's ruin. Francis I himself, moreover, was so interested in Pace that he asked for a description of his person and stature – which, alas, was never forthcoming – while one Venetian diarist considered him sufficiently significant to record whenever he looked pleased at some fresh news.

What, then, were the origins, drives and experiences of this rarity among early Tudor Englishmen: a cultured cosmopolitan traveller, equally at home among Europe's leading intellectuals or amid the murky machinations of international power-politics? A useful starting place is Hampshire, since it is there that he is first mentioned and it was to the New Forest that he retired in chronic ill health towards the end of his life. Long before then, however, according to the account contained in his book *De Fructu qui ex Doctrina Percipitur*, Pace had distinguished himself as a scholar, first under the pupilage of Thomas Langton, Bishop of Winchester, and subsequently at Queen's College, Oxford, and then Padua. As a result, he may even have begun his first journey to war-torn Italy as early as 1496, at the age of around 13, or possibly in 1498, at a time when a flickering prospect of peace in the north of the country appeared temporarily. The usual route was to cross the Channel to Calais, or a Flemish port, and proceed through Flanders and Liège, up the Rhine, over the Alps by the Brenner Pass, through Trent to Verona. Indeed, scores of Flemish painters went that way during the sixteenth century, and on to Rome, walking all the way in some instances, unless a lift was offered on road or river. But while Pace may have been afforded the advantage of a horse, carriage or wagon for at least some of the way, he was certainly not rich enough to travel to Padua in anything other than the kind of extreme discomfort that would become so familiar to him as his life unfolded.

Nor, on his journey, could the young scholar have failed to witness another of the potential scourges awaiting any early modern traveller, one in fact that not infrequently proved the most prolific slayer of all: pestilence.

For even in times of fleeting peace, the effects of conflict upon war-torn Italy were still ever-present in the form of famine and plague. And by the time of Pace's arrival, his new home was not only in the full throes of political dismemberment, but stricken by contagion. 'Italy,' wrote Giucciardini, looking back on the period, 'had at no Time enjoy'd a State of such compleat Prosperity and Repose, as in the year 1490, and some time before and after.' But around the very moment that young Richard Pace set out, the peace was rudely shattered. And with the Spaniards in possession of Naples, the French in control of Milan, and the pope caught increasingly desperately between the two, the land had become riven by dissent, disloyalty and widespread despair. Florence, on the one hand, had largely lost its political importance, while Venice, though still great, was for that very reason soon to be broken at any cost by invading rivals. And as the Venetians eventually retreated from their mainland possessions and withdrew to the lagoons at the advance of Louis XII and Emperor Maximilian, even this was not the limit of their homeland's agonies, since the resentment of their Italian rivals, as well as the Ottoman threat, remained ongoing.

As such, it was small wonder, perhaps, that Pace would develop such a lifelong love for his own homeland, speaking of England as 'his natural country' and relishing its distinctness from other realms through which he travelled. Yet if he found himself alone among his Italian hosts, as is suggested by the lists of the university at Padua, which actually include no other English names throughout the period from 1480 to 1500, he was not to be daunted by the new culture in which he found himself. On the contrary, the young scholar appears to have thrived upon it, transferring first to Bologna before the autumn of 1500 after a bequest from his patron Thomas Langton yielded an annual sum of £10 a year for seven years, and then subsequently residing in Venice, where we hear of him delivering an oration on the study of Greek, which – unusually for so young a scholar – was then published in Basel. At Ferrara, thereafter, Pace also met Erasmus who described him as 'a young man so well equipped with knowledge of the two literatures [i.e. Latin and Greek], as to be able by his genius alone to bring honour to England', though by then an important decision was pending. For in 1508 Langton's legacy ended, and even Pace, now an accomplished man in his mid-twenties, was faced with concluding his prolonged Italian sojourn and making an imminent return to England.

Nor was it an inopportune moment to do so, for in April 1509 the French, in league with the pope, rushed to overwhelm Venice, routing her army at Agnadello the following month, and marauding through the vineyards on the bank of the Adda. But the self-same battle, ironically enough, would also guarantee Richard Pace's future and ensure his continued travels on the

Continent in years to come, since England, under Henry VIII, would now no longer remain in the kind of splendid isolation from events abroad that Henry VII had been so keen to maintain. More indisputably than ever, France had utterly outgrown England, and now her threat was palpable. Extending her influence from the Atlantic to the Mincio, she held Milan and Genoa, while Ferrara, Mantua and Florence followed her counsel slavishly. Worse still, she already had ships that could threaten Naples, and was also able to hire a mighty fleet from Genoa. And though the ducal families of Burgundy and Austria had in the meantime been united in the infant Archduke Charles, who would later become ruler of both Spain and the Holy Roman Empire, none of this was yet guaranteed. In consequence, every English priority now shifted towards Europe, and increased, accordingly, the urgent need to enlist those rare Englishmen with intimate knowledge of European ways. Whether Henry VIII allied himself with the pope, the emperor or Venice, he would require skilled emissaries. Should he attempt, likewise, to advance Wolsey's candidature for the papacy, enlist the services of Swiss or German mercenaries, or ultimately seek the Imperial throne for himself, he would need reliable messengers and negotiators. And in this regard few were better qualified, irrespective of his comparative youth, than Richard Pace, who had already spent more than a decade abroad.

Accordingly, when Cardinal Christopher Bainbridge was entrusted to represent the King of England in Rome, with a view to forming an alliance that would protect the Church and drive the French from Italy, it was only natural that he should be supported by a suitable staff – duly enlisted from the brightest and best. And so it was that Richard Pace now became Bainbridge's secretary, soon securing his place as England's best-known roving ambassador for the better part of two decades. During that time, Pace's travels were as extensive and informative as those conducted by any Englishman – on land at least – during the entire first half of the sixteenth century. While he was at Rome with Bainbridge, for instance, the poet Ariosto came as the Duke of Ferrara's ambassador to the pope, along with Baldassare Castiglione from the Marquis of Mantua, and Alberto Pio from the emperor, rubbing shoulders with all members of the English delegation. Along the Borgo, Pace came to see, too, what was left of old St Peter's and the first portion of the new basilica, at the very time that Martin Luther was also at large in the Holy City, declaiming later that 'if there is a hell, then Rome is built upon it'. When hostilities began over the affairs of Ferrara, Pace witnessed the panic and horror of war at first hand, while in 1522, during the heat of the summer that was always a much-lamented ordeal for Englishmen, he was also present when a particularly destructive form of plague appeared, as a result of which there were heathenish rites for him to muse upon. For when a Greek led through the city a bull that he claimed to have cast under a spell, Pace was on hand to record its sacrifice in the Colosseum in an effort to appease the hostile demons who had sent the pestilence in the first place. And as Pace continued in the meantime to busy himself with diplomatic business, so he also managed to maintain his scholarly commitments, causing the doge to thank Wolsey for dispatching to Italy a man so famous for learning and virtue.

By the end of 1518, moreover, the object of the doge's praise was clearly a man of increasing material substance, for on Christmas Eve thirty-two silver tankards were apparently stolen from his house at Santa Maria Formosa. Four years earlier he had exerted himself to the utmost in seeking out the assassin of Cardinal Bainbridge, who had been poisoned at the papal court by a priest named Rinaldo di Modena. And the rewards for his diligence followed rapidly. For he was collated Archdeacon of Dorset soon after, and by 1516 appointed not only as Wolsey's personal secretary but as a secretary of state, having already engaged at Wolsey's behest in lengthy negotiations at Zurich in support of Emperor Maximilian's activities against the French in northern Italy. On this latter occasion, the emperor and his ministers had proven so avaricious and duplicitous that even Pace was stretched to breaking point. In dealing with 'such people', he finally declared, 'Christ himself should with difficulty obtain anything without money'. And in return for his efforts, Pace had also been made to suffer the full brunt of Maximilian's 'hospitality' – so much so that he barely lived to tell the whole frustrating tale. Verbal abuse, capricious threats of banishment and frequent house arrest all came Pace's way, before he eventually became the target of an unsuccessful attempt at murder by poisoning. As if for good measure, he had also found himself temporarily imprisoned by the French after their victory at the Battle of Marignano.

In the meantime, Pace had left a series of letters, which graphically describe the incidents of his mission: the insatiable greed of the Swiss; the caprices and embarrassments of Maximilian himself; as well as the indiscretion of Sir Robert Wingfield, brother of the English ambassador at the Imperial court, who had recommended him to Wolsey upon his brief return to England that spring. More importantly still, in the midst of his cares and misadventures, Pace had also found time to start work on his treatise, *De Fructu*, which was begun, as he tells us in the preface, in a public bath (*hypocausto*) at Constance, far from books or learned society. In the event, it was a work that ruffled some feathers. The people of Constance, for example, were to find fault with some of Pace's observations on the drunkenness prevailing among them, and for a time too, it seems, even Erasmus, his friend of long-standing, was offended by a passage that the Dutchman misinterpreted as a sideswipe at his personal poverty. But while Constance bristled and Erasmus smarted, Pace himself could well afford his growing sense of superiority, since he was already describing himself on the title page of *De Fructu* as the king's 'first secretary', and enjoying the kind of visibility and patronage that his Dutch counterpart was always seeking in vain.

On Sunday, 3 October 1518, when the so-called 'universal peace' between England and France was about to be ratified by a marriage contract between the French infant heir and the almost equally infantine Princess Mary of England, it was Pace who made 'a good and sufficiently long oration' on the blessings of peace before a gorgeous throng in St Paul's Cathedral. Only one year later, furthermore, upon the death of Maximilian on 12 January 1519, Pace was dispatched on his most important mission to date, to sound out the electors of the Holy Roman Empire in support of Henry VIII's potential candidacy for the Imperial throne. Tireless as ever, the scholar–diplomat would obtain audiences with the Imperial electors in June and July but gained no support for his royal master, and attributed his ultimate failure to his late arrival on the field. 'Here', said Pace of the Imperial Crown, 'is the most dearest merchandise that ever was sold; and after mine opinion, it shall be the worst that ever was bought, to him that shall obtain it.' But if he was outspoken in his reservations, he had nevertheless remained unstinting in his efforts – to the extent, indeed, that he had taxed his already fragile health to the limit, suffering a severe attack of fever in Germany, which recurred in November, a few months after his return. And on this occasion, his collapse was not to be temporary. For, during the summer of 1520, he wrote to Wolsey explaining that he was seriously ill in both mind and body.

Even so, when Leo X died on 2 December 1521, Pace was promptly dispatched to Venice, in an unsuccessful attempt to bolster Wolsey's bid for the papacy. Nor was it any coincidence thereafter that the ailing diplomatist once again sought much-needed rest at Constance, taking the opportunity in spite of his exhaustion to translate some short treatises of Petrarch into Latin. In the preface to the resulting book, he spoke not only of the pestilence in Rome at that time, but once more of his own infirmity. And it was not long afterwards that his final mission abroad was to break him once and for all. For, while dispatched to the Franco–Italian border to seal arrangements for an assault on Provence by the Duke of Bourbon, Pace found himself ascending the Alps from Borgo through the highest and most terrifying mountains he had ever seen – not only thirsty and hungry, but on either horseback or foot from midnight to midnight. Antonio de Leyva, the Spanish general who was also present, was carried all the way on the shoulders of his men. But for Pace, there was no such relief. At one point, indeed, he had not 'dared to turn his horse for all worldly riches, nor even look down for the proclivity and deepness of the valley'. And having traversed the Alpine pass over the Col di Tenda, 'so upright to ascend and stand that it made us creep on all four', Pace later complained from Lucca in July of the 'molestious passage' of his baggage. Yet the reward for his efforts was not only the ultimate failure of Bourbon's campaign, but the growing resentment of Wolsey, it seems, who resented the favour shown him by the king, and accused him of overestimating Bourbon's chances of success. Certainly, Pace was both wounded and concerned by Wolsey's ill will, which clearly played a further part in exacerbating his condition, so that by October 1525, the Doge of Venice himself was urging Pace's recall on health grounds, though no permanent improvement was forthcoming thereafter. On the contrary, coadjutors were appointed for him in his deaneries on 21 August 1526, in spite of which his mental malady increased, so that by 1527 he had been removed from the deanery of St Paul's to Sion, near Twickenham, where he seems to have been kept under some form of restraint, as a result of what was described in February 1536, shortly before his death, as 'mental imbecility'.

Precisely how far the exertions of his travels serve to explain Pace's wretched end is, of course, unknown. Yet for all the strain involved, within half a century of his death, travel in Europe had come to be seen increasingly as the defining hallmark of a small handful of wealthier, more accomplished English noblemen. Indeed, even in the difficult days of 1581, amid mounting Anglo–Spanish hostility, William Cecil did not hesitate to speed the Earl of Northumberland's son abroad, with a stock of advice and directions. And by the century's close, much published advice was also available about the courtly arts to be acquired on the Continent, not to mention the inordinate cost of travel, which continued to be well outside the reach of all but the most affluent:

> If he travel without a servant [wrote Robert Dallington in 1598 in his *Method for Travel*], £80 is a competent proportion except he learn to ride. If he maintain both these charges, he can be allowed no less than £150: and to allow above £200 were superfluous and to his hurt. The ordinary rate of his expense is 10 gold crowns a month for his fencing, as much his dancing, no less his reading, and 10 crowns monthly his riding except in the year. I allow for apparel, books, travelling charges, tennis play and other extraordinary expenses.

But if Dallington and others like him perceived the kind of 'education' afforded by such journeys as little more than an extension of the casual social round already disquieting some critics, it was equally apparent in

Elizabethan England that such journeys could serve an altogether more worthy function as an important preparation for young men seeking advancement within the State. In fact, for individuals like Henry Cheke, who sent back regular 'observations' when on his travels in the 1570s, the ability to accumulate and convey useful information to their country's government was seen as nothing less than the final stage in their apprenticeship for high office.

Returned as MP for Peterborough in 1571, at the age of 23, Cheke received a clerkship of the Privy Council five years later, and soon afterwards set out on an eighteen-month tour of France and Italy, for which he was eventually rewarded with the post of secretary to the Council of the North. And Cheke, it seems, was only one of a number of such political climbers, laden with directives from their superiors to provide accounts of cities and fortifications, methods of government and the attitude of peoples towards their rulers, as well as details of ecclesiastical organisation and law courts, schools and universities and how they were run. In some instances, financial assistance might be forthcoming, though more often than not such journeys were perceived as a hopeful investment for the individuals concerned. And there was also, in most cases, a generally patriotic element involved, as Philip Sidney made clear to his younger brother who was about to set off on his own adventures. 'Your purpose,' he wrote, 'being a gentleman born, is to furnish yourself with the knowledge of such things as may be serviceable to your country.'

The elder Sidney, moreover, was well placed to proffer such advice, since he himself had set off in 1572, at the age of 19, on an extensive tour of Europe lasting nearly three years. Son of the Lord President of the Council in Wales, educated for some years at Shrewsbury School and for a year or so more at Christchurch, he had been dispatched in the company of a sound Protestant tutor and three servants to travel to Paris in the train of the Lord High Admiral. At which point, he came under the supervision of the English ambassador, Francis Walsingham, and narrowly missed involvement in the Massacre of St Bartholomew, which occurred while he was staying at Walsingham's house in the thick of the violence. Thereafter, it was Walsingham, moreover, who seems to have assumed responsibility for the remainder of Sidney's itinerary, arranging for him to visit one leading Protestant scholar after another. The learned publisher Andrew Wechel at Frankfurt, Henri Estienne at Heidelburg, and Johann Sturm at Strasburg all became personal acquaintants, as well as Hubert Languet in Vienna, who supervised Sidney's later studies and long remained in touch. A tour in Hungary and then Italy was followed by a short spell at Padua University, though the dangers of Rome were studiously avoided before a return through Germany and Poland with visits to Prague and Antwerp. Finally returning to England in 1575, Sidney would also set out two years later for a secret assignation in Prague with the exiled Jesuit, Edmund Campion, by which time he was already admirably equipped for prominence at the Elizabethan court not only as poet, courtier and scholar, but soldier too. For, fittingly enough, he would die a hero's death on mainland Europe at the Battle of Zutphen in the Netherlands in 1586, dying from a gangrenous wound in the thigh incurred twenty-six days earlier.

At the time of his death, Sidney was still only 31 – a particularly striking example of the growing geographical liberation of young Elizabethans, intent upon honing their intellects and personalities abroad by travels quite distinct in nature from the so-called 'grand tour' of a later generation. For Sidney's wanderings, too, were conducted with a specific outcome in mind, which had little to do with expanding the mind for fashion, gentility or self-fulfilment's sake. Writing in 1583 to his kinsman John Dutton esquire, Sir Christopher Hatton informed him of the return from abroad of 'my cousin and servant your son' and that 'her majesty doth very graciously accept of the gentleman's travel … with assurance, that he will prove a man meet to be hereafter employed in service, to the benefit of his country'.

Similarly, it was no mere whim that led Francis Bacon, future Lord Chancellor of England, to interrupt his legal studies at Gray's Inn for the opportunity of visiting France in 1576 in the company of Sir Amyas Paulet, the English ambassador. Still only 15 years old, Bacon spent the next three years visiting Blois, Poitiers, Tours, Italy and Spain, and gaining an invaluable grounding in language, statecraft and civil law while performing routine diplomatic tasks. On at least one occasion, too, he delivered diplomatic letters to England for Walsingham, Cecil and Leicester, as well as for the queen, while all the time absorbing valuable political instruction as a result of his evolving acquaintance with the state of government and society in France under Henri III.

A little later, the English author, diplomat and politician Henry Wotton would follow a parallel path, though at a slightly older age. For, after taking an MA at Oxford and coming into his inheritance at the age of 22, he too, as Izaak Walton put it in 1672:

> laid aside his books and betook himself to the useful library of Travel, and a more general conversation with mankind, employing the remaining part of his youth, his industry and fortune to adorn his mind.

Leaving England around 1589 Wotton set out with the specific intention of preparing for the kind of diplomatic career that ran in his family, and his travels appear to have lasted for as many as nine years, taking him to France and Geneva for one year, to Germany for three and Italy for five. At Altdorf, furthermore, he met Edward, Lord Zouch, to whom he later addressed a series of letters over the years 1590 to 1593 that contained not only much political and other news, but an invaluable record of his journey, which speaks volumes not only for his energy but for the expanding horizons of late Tudor Englishmen. Progressing by way of Vienna and Venice to Rome, he managed, it seems, to contract a considerable debt to Isaac Casaubon, with whom he stayed in Geneva, though the burden was more than justified by what followed. For he had also undertaken to supply information to Robert Devereux, 2nd Earl of Essex – whose service he entered upon his return – for the specific purpose of supplying intelligence of affairs as far afield as Transylvania, Poland, Italy and Germany. In 1602, in fact, Wotton was living in Florence when a plot to murder James VI of Scotland came to the ear of the Grand Duke of Tuscany, with the result that he was entrusted not only with letters warning the king of the danger, but with supposedly tried and trusted Italian antidotes against poison. Travelling to Scotland via Norway under the pseudonym Ottavio Baldi, he was well received by James, and remained three months at the Scottish court, retaining his Italian incognito.

Yet unlike Wotton and others of similar outlook, there was also a further type of Elizabethan traveller, smaller in number and driven less by patriotism and ambition than by a simple wish to learn of the world around them out of sheer fascination: travellers, as it were, for travel's sake, who, merely half a century earlier, were not only unheard of but almost inconceivable among their English counterparts. Chief among this new breed was, perhaps, Fynes Moryson who 'from his tender youth' exhibited 'a great desire to see foreign countries'. Born in 1566 at Cadeby in Lincolnshire, he had matriculated at Peterhouse, Cambridge, in 1580 and obtained a fellowship four years later, specialising in civil law. But by 1589 he had obtained the necessary licence to travel and after extensive preparation in London, he took ship at Leigh, near Southend, on 1 May 1589, on an expedition around Europe that would take up the greater part of the next six years. By the end of 1591 he reached Prague, where he dreamt of his father's death on the day of the event, only to find news confirmed at Nuremberg during a year's leisurely tour through Germany. After which he retraced his steps to the Low Countries in preparation for a far more extensive excursion still, which would see him briefly enrol as a student at Leyden University on 7 January 1593, and subsequently pass through Denmark and Poland to Vienna, before entering Italy by way of Pontena and Chiusa in October of the same year. After visiting Naples, he also thoroughly explored Rome, where he paid visits to cardinals Allen and Bellarmine, and was given, notwithstanding his Protestant sympathies, every facility for viewing the Vatican's antiquities. The cities of north Italy occupied him from April 1594 to the beginning of 1595, and in the early spring of 1595 he also obtained an interview with Theodore Beza at Geneva, before journeying hurriedly through France, to catch a glimpse of Henri IV at Fontainebleau.

Along the way, unsurprisingly, Moryson experienced all the usual inconveniences and hazards associated with European travel in Richard Pace's day. At the village of Derwaldhan in Germany he recorded how 'at eight o'clock in the night, the horses being spent, my self wearied', his coach and its party of female travellers came upon 'a kind of barn', which proved to be the local inn. Upon entry – 'not without sighs' – Moryson tells us:

> no man returned salutation to us: the women my companions, drew out victuals they had brought to eat, I being fasting to that hour, with great fear and trembling of the heart, expected that at least they would give me some raw bacon or dried puddings. But they thought nothing less. At last I desired an egg or two for my supper. The servant answered that the old woman was in bed, and that he knew not the mystery, whether any eggs were in the house or no …

Nor were the sleeping arrangements any preferable to the fare on offer, since Moryson subsequently spent the night lying 'on a dog's bed in straw' in a single room in the company of 'the women, virgins, men, maids and servants', and situated at the furthest distance from the stove, which, in the event, he proved to be glad of, 'delighting more in sweet air, than the smoke of a dunghill'. Next day, he arose 'no less sleepy than I was', though the meagre hospitality on offer at Derwaldhan seemed enviable by comparison to his reception en route to Paris. For he had already been warned at Metz that 'the journey would be very dangerous to me, in respect that the army being broken up, all France would be full through all parts of scattering troops of soldiers, returning to their own homes'. And surely enough, near Châlons where Moryson found himself travelling on foot in the company of a 'poor man' whom he had hired to carry his cloak and 'little baggage', the inevitable happened.

According to Moryson's account of the episode, after he had 'scarce entered France', he did indeed encounter demobilised troops, whereupon 'suddenly the mischiefs fell upon me, which my friends at Metz foretold me':

> When I had passed half this day's journey, I met with a dozen horsemen, whose captain demanded of me my name and country. I answered that I

was a Dutch man, and the servant of a Dutch merchant, who stayed for me
at Châlons, whither I was then going. He (as it seemed to me) thinking it
dishonourable to him, if he should assault a poor fellow, and a stranger, did
let me pass, but before I came to the bottom of the hill, I saw him send
two horsemen after me, who wheeling about the mountains, that I might
not know they were of his company, suddenly rushed upon me, and with
fierce countenance threatening death, presented their carbines to my breast.
I having no ability to defend me, thought good not to make any the least
show of resistance, so they took my sword from my guide, and were content
only to rob me of my money …

In fact, after selling his horse at Metz for sixteen French crowns, Fynes had
retained some coins 'in the bottom of a wooden box' and covered them with
'stinking ointment for scabs', which deterred his assailants from searching further. And it was this, it seems, that left him with at least sufficient funds 'to
keep me from begging in a foreign country', though before his eventual landing at Dover on 13 May 1595, he would be stricken by another ever-present
torment for the Tudor traveller, foul water, which left him with 'three days'
sickness of vomiting and looseness'.

Nevertheless, before the year was out, Moryson expressed an 'itching
desire' to see Jerusalem, 'the fountain of religion', as well as Constantinople,
'of old the seat of Christian emperors'. In the company of his brother Henry,
he would also reach Tripoli, Aleppo and Antioch. But it was his journeys in
twelve European countries that were the subject of the book that eventually secured his fame as, quite literally, a trailblazer among English travellers.
Published eventually in 1617, *An Itinerary [by Fynes Moryson, Gent.], containing his ten years Travels through the twelve Dominions of Germany, Bohmerland,
Sweitzerland, Netherland, Denmark, Poland, England, Scotland, and Ireland*, dealt
with a panorama of topics encompassing plans of the chief cities he visited,
as well as 'the rates of hiring coaches and horses from place to place with
each day's expences for diet, horse-meat, and the like'. Observations on
geography, national costume, character, religion, and constitutional practice
were also included. And though the work delights too much, perhaps, in
statistics respecting the mileage of the author's daily journeys, or the varie-
ties in the values of the coins he encountered, it remains invaluable not
only as a historical source, but much more importantly still as a symbol of a
changed outlook.

A century earlier, as Tudor England set about the task of regaining its
feet after half a century of civil war, such a work was unthinkable. By the
time of Elizabeth I's death, however, windows that hardly existed in the
days of her grandfather had been flung wide open. For Europe, both as

a concept and geographical entity, was as real to the queen, her ministers and increasing numbers of her subjects, as it was to those more intrepid souls who actually visited or above all traded with it in ever greater numbers. Equally strikingly, Europe had become bigger as well as better known, encompassing not only those long-familiar kingdoms that set the limits of Henry VII's horizons, but realms far more mysterious still – the chief of which was Russia.

4

TRADE

But yf they come for wolles, for our clothes, carseys [kerseys], corne, tinne, lead ... and such substanciaull and necessarie things, let them bring in againe flax, tar, oyle, fish and such other ... Geve them an aple for the best juell they have about them.

Sir Thomas Smith,
Discourse of the Common Weal (1549)

On 28 February 1557 Londoners were treated for the first time to the spectacle of a Russian ambassador entering their city. For it was upon that occasion that Ossip Nepea, representative of Tsar Ivan IV, made his way amid high ceremony from 'Smithfield barres' to 'his lodging situate in Fant church streete', accompanied by Lord Montague and the Lord Mayor and the capital's Aldermen 'in their skarlet'. As he passed, Richard Hakluyt tells us, Nepea was greeted, 'with great plausibilities of the people running plentifully on all sides and replenishing all streets in such sorte as no man without difficultie might pass'. And the eagerness of the London crowds was hardly to be marvelled at, since Russians represented one more curious novelty brought to light by Tudor England's newly expanding horizons. Only four years earlier a little group of Englishmen led by Richard Chancellor had reached the White Sea coast, where they were well received by the tsar – an achievement that rightly ranks as one of the great geographical discoveries of the period. And to nearly all the people greeting Nepea with such enthusiasm, Russia still meant little more than a vast and shadowy realm cursed by a hideous climate and populated by uncouth men and fantastic beasts – notwithstanding the fact that elsewhere in Europe, Russia's links were long-standing. As early as the eleventh century, indeed, several Russian princesses had married European rulers, including Henri I of France, and, in the meantime, the country had also attracted considerable attention from no less a figure than Pope Gregory VII, who hoped for its conversion to Catholicism. Trade with the Danube valley and south Germany had developed steadily, while Kiev and Novgorod acquired international importance as commercial centres. And although the Tatar conquest of the early thirteenth century had brutally severed many of Russia's external bonds, Novgorod, in particular, had continued throughout to maintain her commercial relationships with the Baltic.

By the fifteenth century, moreover, as the Grand Duchy of Moscow began to assert its independence of the 'Tatar yoke' during the half-century before Challoner's expedition, Europeans had once again penetrated Russia's fringes in significant numbers. Step by step, craftsmen, technicians and soldiers from the West had gradually begun to implant in the country some of the ideas and practices of their own lands. And with them came embassies: from Venice and the Holy Roman Emperor, interested in the possibilities of a joint offensive against the Turks or Poles; from Sweden and Denmark, driven by the Baltic trade; from popes still fondly clinging to the hope of a reunion between Orthodox and Catholic Christendom. In 1493, Grand Duke Ivan III made with Denmark what amounted to Russia's first west European alliance, and by the early decades of the sixteenth century, Muscovy, as it was generally known in the West for the next two hundred years, had begun to play a modest but sometimes appreciable role in the calculations of most European statesmen and diplomats. In 1519, Grand Duke Vasili III had subsidised the Teutonic Knights in a war against Poland, and in 1532 there were reports of the adhesion of the 'Kings of Russia' to a general league against the Emperor Charles V. There had, too, been cultural bridge building: the provision for the first time in Russia of a complete version of the Bible, based on the Vulgate; the translation into Slavonic of a small number of classical works; the infiltration of certain western religious ideas; even the adoption in Moscow of some of the court ceremonial practices of the Dukes of Burgundy.

Yet in this slow and uneven process, England had played no appreciable part. Instead, the architects, doctors, metal-workers, and canon-founders who began the infusion of western techniques into Russia in the later fifteenth and early sixteenth centuries were usually Italians or Germans, sometimes Jews or Greek. Nor did any English embassy appear at Moscow or any English diplomat set foot in Russia until after the middle of the century, though a mysterious Scot, dubbed 'Master David', had visited the country several times between 1496 and 1514 as 'herald' of the King of Denmark. At a fancy dress ball in Parliament Hall at Westminster in 1510, the Earl of Wiltshire and Baron Fitzwalter, had, it is true, appeared in what was purported to be Russian dress. But the description of their costume – 'two long gounes of yellowe satin, traversed with white satin … after the fashion of Rusland, with furred hates of grey on their hedes, either of them having an hatchet in their hands and bootes with pykes turned up' – makes it clear that they had no real knowledge of the country or its people. And the few references to be found in geographies of the early sixteenth century merely confirm the level of English ignorance. Andrew Boorde, for instance, in his well-known *Fyrst Boke of the Introduction of Knowledge* made no reference at all to Russia, and his very limited awareness of any area beyond the eastern boundaries of the Holy Roman Empire can be seen in his claim that 'the speech of Hungary is corrupt Italien, corrupt Greke, and Turkysh'. Similarly, Roger Barlow's *Brief Summe of Geographie*, written in about 1540, places Russia with splendidly exotic vagueness, 'hard by the mountains sarmaticos and riscos', and 'by the mountains of ercynia'.

By the 1580s, however, the situation had been altered by what was to become over time a new and ultimately transformative force: the growth and diversification of English trade. For Richard Chancellor's journey to Moscow and Ivan the Terrible's subsequent opening of Russia to English commerce were followed by the creation in 1555 of the Muscovy Company, which soon assumed a prominent place among the chartered companies of the age. While no more than four ships were sent by the company to Russia in any year up to 1567, by 1570 thirteen were sent to the port of Narva alone. In 1582, eleven, and in the following year ten, ships were sent to St Nicholas; in 1599 and 1602 eleven and ten ships respectively were sent to the new port of Archangel, which had by then replaced it. And the increase in traffic was more than reflected in the profits that, from the 1560s, English merchants had gleaned from the goods (mainly cloth) that they exported to their new partner. Equally, Russian wax, hemp and other products commanded a good market in England, and it was not out of friendship, but as a private speculation, that Nepea and his suite brought with them large quantities of oil and furs. By 1587, when imports of all commodities from Russia were at the record level of £13,530 13s 4d, more than a quarter of the total expenses of the navy were for rope purchased from the Muscovy Company, while the war waged by Ivan the Terrible over two decades, from 1558–83, not only generated valuable sales of war materials for English merchants but brought their dwellings under the personal protection of the tsar within the so-called *Oprichnina* – that part of Russia under his direct control.

As such, the revolution in English attitudes, which was by no means confined to Anglo–Russian commerce, could hardly have been more marked – particularly when the limitations of English trade at the start of the Tudor period are fully appreciated. 'England,' wrote one foreign observer in 1557, 'is frequented by all the nations of Europe, from Poland onward, and lately even by Muscovy and Russia ... so it is considered commodious, delightful and wealthy above all other islands of the world.' Yet seventy years earlier, foreign carriers had long been in control of a considerable portion of England's overseas trade, and in the fifteenth century there had been an actual shrinkage in the areas to which English merchants were able to trade directly in English ships. The great commercial league of north German cities, known as the Hansa or Hanseatic League, had driven English traders out of the Baltic and Scandinavia and almost out of Iceland. At the same time, they had shut down English trading establishments at Danzig and Bergen and secured a practical monopoly of English commerce with those regions. The reason, quite simply, was the civil war that had resulted in Edward IV's expulsion by the Lancastrians in 1470 and subsequent restoration with the assistance of shipping and mercenaries supplied by the Hanseatic League. In repayment, Edward had agreed by the Treaty of Utrecht of 1474 to give the League's members a privileged position over his own subjects. And though they had promised to give the English a reciprocal freedom in their territories in return for the privileges accorded to their own London headquarters – the so-called 'Steelyard' – no such goodwill was actually forthcoming. On the contrary, realising the strength of its sea power in comparison to England's and fully aware that its policy of promoting invasion and revolution could be tried again if need arose, the League had proceeded to leave England virtually excluded from direct trade with Scandinavia and the Baltic.

In the meantime, moreover, Italian traders had proceeded to consolidate a not dissimilar stranglehold upon England's Mediterranean trade. Although a few English adventurers had taken ships through the Straits of Gibraltar, their sailings were disorganised, and Venetian, Genoese and Florentine vessels had filled the vacuum decisively. Venetian galleys, exceptional among contemporary merchantmen for being state-owned and keeping regular timetables, made Southampton their usual port of call, mistrusting the as yet ill-buoyed and ill-charted passage past the Goodwin Sands and into the Thames estuary. They were the largest oared vessels of their time, stronger than the more nimble fighting galleys, and equipped with a sail plan for use with fair winds, as well as long sweeps for progress at other times. And they were joined for trade with England by Genoese carracks, which were then the largest trading ships of any kind in Europe and were afterwards to give Henry VIII's shipwrights the model for the finest craft of his new navy. Heavily armed and manned, both types of ship were expensive to run, and the prices of the wares they carried were enormous. But it was they, rather than English vessels manned by English masters and seamen, that nevertheless brought into the kingdom the textiles of the Middle East, the malmsey and sweet wines of Greece and Candia (Crete), the currants of the Levant, and the spices and luxuries of the Orient, purchased from Arab traders at Alexandria. Superfine cloth, glass, armour, and other luxury items from the cities of Italy, together with alum for English cloth manufacture from deposits owned by the pope, which then constituted the chief supply in Europe, were also among their cargoes. And when their holds were emptied to the satisfaction of the numerous business houses maintained in London by Italian merchants, it was them that carried out, along with tin and other goods, the wool and woollen cloth of England to be dyed and finished in the workshops of Venice and northern Italy – just as the Hansards in their turn took away much of the cloth from London to the workshops of Antwerp and Flanders, notwithstanding the fact that the English Merchant Adventurers and wool Staplers dominated the trade itself. Even in the wine trade to Bordeaux and Gascony, as with London and West Country cloth exports to Spain, foreign carriers played a crucial part.

To compound matters, the Iceland fishery, which produced an appreciable proportion of England's food supply, had been disrupted by a long quarrel with the King of Denmark. Cod from Norway and stockfish (dried fish) from Iceland had in fact been reaching English markets – above all London – from the fifteenth century onwards. And while the first English boats to reach Icelandic waters came from Norfolk ports such as Cromer and Blakeney as early as 1412, Hull in particular had also accumulated an immense trade in stockfish as well as other types. Indeed, in Richard II's time, the de la Pole family had largely founded its great wealth upon the Hull fishing industry, which had left its indelible mark upon the town in a whole range of other ways, too – not the least of which was its very appearance. For, since a catch of stockfish was comparatively light, the ships of Hull would ballast themselves in stormy weather with 'great coble stone' out of Iceland, which, as John Leland recorded, came eventually to pave the whole town's streets. Yet by the dawn of the Tudor period, fisheries had become another area where English interests had been seriously undermined by unfavourable terms of trade, reducing English fishermen, in effect, to the position of interlopers on Icelandic shores. In the process, not only was an important source of the kingdom's food supply seriously compromised, but so too was the rate of exchange between English cloth and Scandinavian sea produce in general.

On almost all commercial fronts, therefore, the choice facing Henry VII was as simple as it was stark, and so were the consequences of failure, for unless a remedy was found for his kingdom's mercantile weakness, his very political survival was at stake. As such, he had no choice but to expand the markets for England's all-important cloth exports, in order to create employment and profit. At the same time, however, he had also to transfer control of his kingdom's exports to native interests, while creating seamen, shipwrights and shipyards fit for the task of developing a truly competitive mercantile marine. Only thus could adequate wealth accumulate and be enjoyed in safety, and only thereby could the Tudor dynasty be steadily consolidated. The problems had long been recognised and discussed, but the necessary measures had never been more than fitfully attempted. Henceforth, however, mercantilism would have to be embraced wholeheartedly, so that the interests of English wool – as represented by landowners, staplers, cloth-makers, or cloth exporters – might prevail accordingly. For the Merchant Adventurers of London and the south-east and east coasts, as well as the clothiers of the West Country, the Midlands and East Anglia, and farmers who provided the wool – not to mention the families in countryside and towns who spun and wove it – a solution was simply essential. And the foundation for this solution, as England's first Tudor ruler shrewdly comprehended, was to be laid in Parliament, the gathering place not only for his kingdom's wisest and finest subjects but for the controllers of its predominant trade.

It is probable, in fact, that England's coastal and inland commerce was worth at least ten times as much as all her overseas trades put together, and very likely considerably more in the first half of the sixteenth century. Indeed, even in the late seventeenth century, Gregory King's analysis of the English economy concluded that, out of a total national product amounting to £50.8 million at that time, exports stood at merely £4.3 million, or around 8.5 per cent of total production. The largest sector by far, both then and in Henry VII's day, was agriculture, and the vast majority of the output of foodstuffs and raw material was consumed domestically. Only wool (and later cloth) was of appreciable significance for sale abroad, along with some coal and a little lead and tin, which were still mainly produced for the home market. Yet the richest men in England other than the greatest landowners were merchants who engaged in foreign trade, and these men, such as the Springs of Lavenham, the Marlers of Coventry, the Canynges of Bristol, and the great merchants of London, too numerous to mention, all carried substantial political weight. None would have been a tenth as rich from inland trade alone, and their wealth, unlike that of the landed magnates, was more liquid, enabling them to become important sources of loans to their importunate Tudor rulers. A depression in the export trade, or equally obviously its manipulation by alien merchants for foreign profit, could hit them all. And it was no coincidence, therefore, that during the Wars of the Roses, the Yorkist inclinations of great cities like London, as well as small clothing centres in Berkshire – soon to be home of one of the most famous sixteenth-century clothiers, John Winchcombe – had been heavily influenced by hopes for stronger government and better trade. Now, however, these same men looked for no less from the first Tudor, and to his credit, Henry VII was not backward in satisfying their expectations.

In the shipping world, the expansion of tonnage was promoted by the relatively simple policy of reviving and applying a system of bounties to the owners of large ships. Henceforth, a merchant who built or acquired a vessel exceeding a specified burden became entitled to a considerable remission of duties on the goods shipped in her. But Henry appreciated too, of course, that unless new ships could earn their keep by finding markets, few would be built, and with this in mind he therefore promoted in the Parliament of 1485–86 a Navigation Act requiring that Englishmen should not transport their goods in foreign vessels when English ones were available. Additionally, it was laid down that one entire and important trade – that with Bordeaux – should be reserved to domestic shipping, as a result of which Gascon wine and woad from Toulouse were henceforth imported only in English, Irish or Welsh ships with crews manned predominantly by subjects of the king. Introduced as a temporary measure, the Navigation Act was made permanent in 1489, impacting significantly upon Spanish shipping in particular, but causing similar outcries from the Hansards, whose complaints give clear proof of the efficiency of the act's introduction.

Yet in spite of general indignation, the problem of the Hanseatic League was not in fact directly addressed by Henry until the Navigation Act had been implemented, and only then after he had confirmed the existing Hanse privileges by letters patent in April 1486. Doubtless, he desired to repudiate the one-sided terms of Edward IV's previous agreement, but his fear that Hanseatic sea power might be employed in favour of an opponent made caution essential. And it was for this reason that he opted to yield nominal acquiescence to Edward's concessions while utilising every legal device at his disposal to whittle them away. Already, the Navigation Act had curtailed the Hanse's carrying trade from Bordeaux. But in the meantime a fruitful quibble was raised by Henry's customs officers on the interpretation of '*suae merces*', the phrase in the original treaty describing the goods on which the League was to pay lower duties. Naturally enough, the Hanse merchants saw fit to claim that it covered all the merchandise that they brought into England, while their opponents now contended that *suae merces* applied only to wares produced in Hanseatic cities, to the exclusion of those acquired elsewhere. Though insufficient cause for the League to risk fomenting war and using its ships to carry élite mercenary troops from Germany in support of Henry's enemies, it was a clear signal of a new, more assertive approach to commercial relations, which would characterise the rest of the reign. And though the *suae merces* controversy was to continue for decades, this in itself was testament to the subtlety of the first Tudor's overriding objective of exploiting his comparatively meagre hand to maximum advantage – probing, challenging, pressing at every opportunity, while avoiding an all-out conflict he could ill afford to wage.

Certainly, Henry VII's Hanseatic rivals would not be bowed easily, though English pirates went unpunished upon capturing their ships, and public hatred of Germans escalated to the point where they could not walk safely in the streets of England's capital. When Hull refused to admit the Hansards in 1488, Henry turned a blind eye, just as he would do five years later, providing scant compensation for mob attacks on the London Steelyard, and accompanying this with a demand for £20,000 as security that the League would not undermine English trade in the Netherlands. But when Henry brought them to a meeting at Antwerp in 1491 in the hope of amending Edward IV's treaty of 1474, he found them unbending in their refusal to allow reciprocal freedom of access to his ships in the Baltic and north German markets. Indeed, he obtained nothing more than a limited concession for English trade at Danzig – which the city itself went on to reject – at the price of renewing the entire 1474 treaty. Later, when the Tudor navy had become the linchpin of the nation's forces, a 'King's merchant' would be stationed at Danzig permanently to buy the cables and cordage, tar and timber so indispensable to the fitting out of ships in western Europe. But this was still in the future, and when Henry reached agreement with Riga in 1499 upon its rift with the Hansa, this too became a dead letter after the breach proved temporary. Worse still, when the White Rose pretender, the Earl of Suffolk, became a fugitive in Germany, the English king was forced in 1504 to confirm Hansard privileges just as he had at the outset of his reign.

But if the ongoing harassment of the League, which ensued upon the disappearance of Suffolk's threat, also achieved little, the King of England's quarrel had at least yielded the resolution of a pressing problem elsewhere. For Henry could not, as Francis Bacon later put it, 'afford to have trade sick', and it was not only in England that the Hansa was unpopular. On the contrary, the King of Denmark, who also ruled Norway along with Iceland, was equally at odds with his overbearing German neighbours, and responded gladly to English overtures for the conclusion of the long-standing maritime war in northern waters that had hitherto marred relations between the two kingdoms. The resulting treaty of 1490, following on from the efforts of an English delegation dispatched by Henry, not only gave his subjects full facilities in the Iceland fishery, but also the right to hold premises of their own at the staple town of Bergen in Norway and in other ports. Thereafter, English fishermen

would be able to ply their trade in the Icelandic fishery under the King of
Denmark's protection. And in the process, the treaty of 1490 also ensured that
English access to the Baltic would escape restriction in the bottleneck of the
Danish Sound.

Elsewhere, there had been progress, too, against England's Italian rivals in
the Mediterranean where, from the middle of the fifteenth century, a small
number of English ships had been making incursions. Now they were starting to go direct to Crete and the Levant for the wines that the Venetians
normally carried to London and Southampton, prompting a tax from
Venice in 1488 of four ducats per butt upon all wines carried in foreign
vessels. In effect, the whole issue of English access to the Mediterranean
was undisguisedly at stake, and the opportunity was not to be wasted, as
Henry first imposed an extra duty on Venetian-borne malmsey to England,
and followed it with a proposal to Florence in 1490 that the wool supply
to all Italy should be sent almost entirely to the Florentine port of Pisa,
and carried only in English ships – a masterstroke that Florence, as a great
cloth-weaving but not a great ship-owning city, could hardly refuse. At the
same time, the export of wool to Venice was to be restricted to 600 sacks
a year, carried likewise only in English ships. And when consuls were duly
appointed to represent the English mercantile community in Pisa, the
threat finally became sufficient for the Venetians to waive their opposition
to Henry's vessels in the Levant, paving the way for an English trade that
would prove particularly lucrative until it was disrupted for a time in the
mid-sixteenth century by the growth of Turkish and Algerian sea power and
piracy, which led, among other things, to the much-vaunted flight of the
Aucher on its way to Chios in 1552.

By benefiting from such measures, the loyalty of London merchants in particular was guaranteed, and became one among many factors ensuring the
commitment of Henry VII's subjects to his government. But these were not
the only instances of the king's success in commercial affairs, as he set about
the task of ensuring reasonable conditions for English ships once they had
reached their overseas markets. His first care, in fact, was always to confirm
and if possible extend the right of English merchants to trade freely in the
Netherlands, since the Netherlands had long been England's principal overseas market, or at least distributing centre. And in this respect, his success was
crucial, for during the reigns of both himself and his son, the remarkable
growth of Antwerp drew more and more of England's growing cloth production there. The improvement of access by water up the River Scheldt,
and the comparative ease and cheapness of overland and river communications with the Rhineland and south Germany, made Antwerp in fact a natural
meeting place for English exporters and their German customers from the

mid-fifteenth century onwards. But it became even more so when the political turbulence involving the cities of Bruges and Ghent and the new Habsburg overlords of the Netherlands reduced the appeal of Flemish cities as trading centres. Many Italian merchants, moreover, followed the English and in 1488 Antwerp's new primacy was effectively sealed by Emperor Maximilian's requirement that all 'nations' of foreign traders transfer their business there from Bruges.

In 1499, the King of Portugal's agent, who had already moved with the rest of his counterparts eleven years earlier, finally relocated his headquarters to Antwerp permanently, and in August 1501 the first consignment of spices arrived from Lisbon, ensuring for the next fifty years Antwerp's status as the entrepôt for Portuguese spices for all north-western and central Europe. And with this the city finally sealed its exalted status as the meeting point and exchange centre for all four of the great international and intercontinental trades of the day. From the Baltic area the Hansards brought the corn, timber, hemp and tar that the Iberian and Mediterranean countries as well as the Netherlands increasingly needed. From Augsburg, Frankfurt, and other cities of southern and western Germany came metals, especially copper and silver. From Spain and Portugal respectively came fine wool and spices. And from England – carried by native Merchant Adventurers and Staplers, as well as Hansards – arrived cloth to be sold, finished and distributed over northern, central and even eastern Europe. Italian silks, French and Spanish wines, and Netherlands linens were all among the commodities making Antwerp the greatest mart of Europe, while alum, the essential mordant in the cloth dyeing industry, was officially stapled there. And to assist the smooth running of business, there was a parallel expansion of banking, credit and insurance facilities, as south German financiers such as the Fuggers, Welsers and Hochstetters of Augsburg, as well as Italian ones including the Affaitadi of Cremona, installed permanent agents, most of them well established by 1510.

Even so, the item most central to Antwerp's greatness, remarkably perhaps, would prove to be English cloth. One contemporary estimated that it accounted for nearly a third of all imports to the city – a statistic that convinced English merchants its prosperity or otherwise lay in their hands. And in consequence – before Vasco da Gama reached India or the Portuguese royal agent finally deserted Bruges – they had not hesitated to play off Middelburg, Bergen-op-Zoom, and other towns against it. Indeed, by maintaining their right to trade to any of those towns, the English were able to extort privileges from all without committing themselves exclusively to any, though as the predominance of Antwerp grew inexorably and the power of Burgundy's Habsburg dukes – always supporters of loyal Antwerp against rebellious

Ghent and Bruges – came to be asserted more and more effectively, so the opportunities for English merchants to bargain for themselves receded. Worse still, as Henry VII saw fit from time to time to manipulate trade in the interest of politics, they found themselves reduced increasingly to instruments, if not victims, of his foreign policy. And never more so, perhaps, than in the late summer of 1493, when Emperor Maximilian and the Netherlands refused to curb the activities of Perkin Warbeck, pretender to the Crown of England. In response, Henry forbade the Merchant Adventurers to trade to Antwerp or other Low Countries ports, and ordered them to join the Staplers in using Calais as their base.

The result, unsurprisingly, was damage to the comparatively backward economy of England that at least matched any loss or distress to the Netherlanders, particularly as the Hansards were quick to step into the breach after the Netherlands government took the logical step of imposing a counter-embargo of its own in May 1494. Yet it remained Henry VII's rivals nevertheless who gave way just under two years later after Warbeck's failure, and amid mounting pressure on Maximilian and Philip of Burgundy to enlist the King of England's support in their negotiations with France. Indeed, the economic provisions of the agreement known as *Intercursus Magnus*, drawn up in February 1496, amounted in effect to little less than a charter of liberty for English merchants, who were subsequently allowed to sell their goods wholesale and without restriction in any part of Philip's dominions except Flanders. No longer subjected to new tolls and duties in excess of those prevailing during the previous fifty years, they were also promised speedy and fair justice in Philip's courts. And they were to benefit likewise from the clarification of rules affecting inspection of cargoes, punishments for fraudulent dealing, recovery of debts, carriage of arms and contraband, and almost every conceivable matter over which disputes might subsequently arise.

Plainly, if Henry had sacrificed trade to his dynastic necessities in 1493, he amply repaid the debt three years later. But the benefits of the new arrangements were no less marked for Antwerp either, which was soon on its way to achieving a greatness that would extend to the middle of the next century. Symbolic of this primacy was the establishment in 1531 of a new bourse that eventually became the model for London's Royal Exchange. Thereafter, as Antwerp grew during the next half century into a thriving metropolis with more than 100,000 inhabitants, including 10,000 foreign merchants of mostly Spanish and Portuguese origin, the city would serve, too, as the more general model for all other urban centres with similar ambitions. Daily, the merchants and exchange dealers of the Antwerp bourse would meet to transact their commercial and financial business in the building's rectangular open space, enclosed by a colonnade covered with star and net vaults, and surmounted by high-rise 'pagoda towers' that served, appropriately enough, as lookouts for the harbour. Before long, as the city's primacy continued to evolve, every nation came to occupy a more or less permanent place in Antwerp's stock market, with representatives forming permanent communities, often with their own officials and residences. And best-organised and closest-knit of all among these were the English and Portuguese, who, along with the Spanish and Italians, enjoyed special status and privileges. By contrast, groups such as the south Germans were neither so fully organised nor so numerous, notwithstanding the importance of firms like the Fuggers, while the Hansards did not take up corporate residence till 1569, by which time both their own and indeed Antwerp's days of greatness had gone forever.

In the event, the foundations of the city's heyday had proved less secure than appearances suggested, since so much depended upon the continued flow of goods brought by foreigners, and in particular their ongoing presence within its walls. It was for this reason that all visitors had been accorded an absence of restrictions that was, to say the least, unusual by sixteenth-century standards. And while Antwerp's 'modernity' should not be exaggerated, its freedom from the kind of xenophobia that swept London during the Evil May Day riots of 1517 remained one of its most distinctive features. Yet for all its virtues and power, the decline of Europe's commercial hub would prove almost as precipitous as its rise, since neither its own cloth-finishing industry nor its printing works nor the enterprise of its own native merchants, who traded extensively with Spain and ventured on occasion to both the New World and India, were sufficient to guarantee its security. For when depression struck the English cloth trade and the Portuguese spice trade in the 1550s, and the great German merchant bankers were shattered by the Habsburg bankruptcy of 1556, the great flow of goods that had constituted Antwerp's life blood duly began to dry up. The religious persecution sweeping France in 1555 assisted the process, and the so-called 'Spanish Fury' of 1576, when Requesens' mutinous troops destroyed so much of the city, effectively finished it. Thereafter, the closure of the Scheldt by northern Dutch rebels in 1585 was merely a final nail in the coffin that had been fashioned more than three decades earlier when the English cloth exports, underpinning Antwerp's greatness more than any other commodity, suddenly faltered.

Key to England's cloth trade throughout Antwerp's dominance had been the 'company' of the Merchant Adventurers of London – an amorphous and ill-defined organisation that had grown up among English merchants trading to the Netherlands during the thirteenth and fourteenth centuries. Including outport merchants as well as Londoners, the grants made to the company by both countries came, in fact, to include all Englishmen trading to the Netherlands, although by 1500 a distinct group had emerged, dominated by men from the capital, and led by a single Governor. Possessed of its own coat of arms, the organisation had also come by then to pre-empt the title 'Adventurers' that had formerly applied to any merchant (other than the so-called 'Staplers' of Calais) trading overseas. And a complementary process had also been at work among London's great livery companies – Mercers, Drapers, Grocers, Haberdashers and others – all of whom shared a like interest in the export of unfinished and undyed cloth. For the purpose of negotiating with governments, it made sense for these too to merge over time within the same single body, which coalesced ultimately around the Mercers. The latter not only formed the largest group, but were able to supply an appropriate meeting place for the evolving organisation, along with a clerk, a minute book and a treasure chest. The result was formal recognition in 1486 when an Act of the Common Council of London recognised the 'Adventurers' in their newly comprehensive and more organised structure.

The official seat of their government lay always, in fact, in the Netherlands, where elections were held, important regulations were ratified, and meetings of the General Court – the full assembly of members – were conducted. But since some two-thirds of merchants active in the Netherlands, along with the company's Governor and at least eight of its twelve-man executive, were Londoners, there can be no reasonable doubt where the effective centre of authority lay. Indeed, even when in time the greater merchants ceased to visit the Netherlands in person, and were represented by their agents, provincial merchants in the separate companies of places such as Newcastle, York and Bristol could do no more than vainly protest at the measures imposed by the dominant majority. And in the meantime the Mercers continued to maintain their ascendancy inside the London group throughout the first half of the century, notwithstanding the fact that after 1526 the minutes of the Adventurers were separated from those of the Mercers, and the Governor of the Company was no longer invariably drawn from among them. It was they, after all, who continued to account for around 40 per cent of Londoners' cloth exports right up to 1547, and they, too, who consequently continued to control the organisation's official machinery.

Curiously, perhaps, the early years of the Adventurers had seen them attempting to break into the European cloth market via Zeeland and Brabant. They had also tried Utrecht for a time and considered Middelburg before finally fixing upon Antwerp, where the merchants of Cologne, the main distributors of English cloth in Germany, could be found. After which, the wealth of some Adventurers, such as the Greshams, the Holleses and the Osbornes, who came to constitute almost patrician families within the capital, grew apace, irrespective of the fact that, even at the height of their greatness, their business strategy was not without shortcomings. For, far from adventuring, at least in the modern sense of the word, they pursued primarily a safety-first policy of easy profits in an assured market, avoiding not only voyages of discovery but, equally, the development of more familiar markets closer to home. The sea passage from London to Antwerp was, after all, effectively the shortest trade route of its kind, and nor did the Merchant Adventurers encourage any diversity in England's export trade, preferring instead simply to expand sales of woollen cloth. They did not innovate in the sphere of company organisation, merely copying their general structure and many of their regulations from the Staplers of Calais, and they were slow too, as we shall see, to adopt new devices of commercial technique like maritime insurance that was already firmly established on the Continent.

In their defence, of course, the Merchant Adventurers had little incentive to forsake a tried and trusted market for the uncertainties of new ones when sales of cloth appeared to be thriving so appreciably. In the years 1510–15, for example, exports ranged from 76,000 to 93,000 cloths per year, while the combined value of both cloth and wool exports was about £104,000 per annum, notwithstanding the fact that by the end of Henry VIII's reign wool exports would fall rapidly in the wake of heavy taxation and the demands of home industry. In the Netherlands, moreover, the Adventurers had expended much money and energy in obtaining privileges and concessions not only from the municipal government of Antwerp but from Bergen and Middelburg, where they enjoyed tax reliefs and judicial immunities. As a result, they held in the Netherlands a position corresponding to that of the Hansards in England – making them not only better off than native competitors but susceptible to similar jealousies and resentments. Their shipments were so continuous and secure, indeed, that neither war nor piracy, embargo nor sequestration, would prevent a London merchant like Thomas Kitson from sending at least one shipment of cloth from the Netherlands every year from 1512 to 1539. And in consequence, notwithstanding some severe short-term fluctuations, the cloth trade expanded continuously up to 1551, from just over 50,000 cloths annually in the first few years of Henry VII's reign to over 120,000 in Henry VIII's last years. Profit margins, likewise, continued to run high, so that Kitson, for example, made a gross profit of between 20 and 25 per cent in 1521–23, while the accounts of Thomas Gresham for the years 1546–51 suggest net profits on his whole business of nearly 15 per cent, meaning that he could expect to double his capital every five years.

In the meantime, relations with England's other great trading company, the Merchants of the Staple of Calais – which held not only a monopoly of the export of tin and lead, hides, butter and cheese, but also of raw wool and fleeces – were frequently less than cordial, since the pickings for both sides were potentially rich and the risks considerable. The term 'staple' was derived, in fact, from the Latin term *stabile emporium*, meaning 'a fixed mart', the existence of which at Calais allowed the government to monitor trade and levy taxation more easily. But in the first half of the fourteenth century, before the town's conquest by England in 1347, Bruges and Antwerp had performed a similar role until a group of twenty-six traders were incorporated as the Company of the Staple at Calais in 1363, and the company's role and influence expanded accordingly in both London and the provinces. As a result, the Merchants of the Staple became some of the wealthiest men in the kingdom – and some of the greatest commercial gamblers, too, if the level of so-called 'desperate debts' recorded in merchant inventories, such as that of William Wigston, are any guide. A merchant of the Staple based in Leicester, Wigston died in 1536 with more than £3,500 owed to him by foreign merchants in Antwerp, Malines, Bruges and Delft, and therefore written off as 'desperate'. Nor, it seems, was he by any means a rarity within his organisation, since other inventories of the period frequently display similar debts ranging in some cases from less than a tenth of the whole money due to as much as two-thirds, the higher figures being almost invariably the result of war or rumours of war overseas or some other interruption of trade.

The same, meanwhile, was equally true for the Staplers' chief rivals. Gregory Isham, for example, a comparatively 'rich' Merchant Adventurer, had a working capital of perhaps £3,000, but gross debts of £8,000–£9,000 at Antwerp and at London when he died in 1588, leaving only £88 in plate and £145 in ready cash for his heirs. And notwithstanding the absence of international credit facilities, which were not formally recognised in England until 1571, merchants of all kinds also found themselves subject to other complications, demonstrated by the example of William Harborne who, in 1580, arranged for wine to be bought in Crete and shipped to the Baltic by way of London. Clearly expecting the venture to be safe and profitable – a hefty assumption in its own right – he found himself involved in complex conversions involving Venetian and Polish currency dealers. Yet what he and others like him rarely counted upon was the scale of subterfuge involving their own compatriots – all of which was amply encapsulated in the ongoing tension between Merchant Adventurers and Staplers, especially after 1516 when the latter found themselves compelled to join the Adventurers if they wished to take part in the Netherlands cloth trade. From some perspectives, the dispute between the two companies at this time amounted to little more than shadow-boxing, since many Staplers were already Adventurers and the gradual decline of their company meant in any case that they could not compete in the long term with their more powerful rivals. Yet the testy relationship between the two groups represented one more example of the cut-throat morality of Anglo–European trade, and a further demonstration of the Adventurers' unhealthy tendency to concentrate commercial activity in their own hands when those hands were tightly tied to a precarious single market.

Should that market falter, of course, it was not only the comfortable expectations of a grandee such as Thomas Gresham that might suffer, but the fortunes of all those involved in the cloth chain that supplied his kind. And the warning signs of precisely the type of crisis that finally broke in 1551 were already visible during the final years of Henry VIII, notwithstanding the earlier boom from which Gresham in particular had benefited so lucratively. Between 1542 and 1544 cloth exports for London alone averaged 99,000 cloths, rising to 119,000 in 1545–47, and peaking as high as 133,000 in 1550. Yet the boom was partly artificial in character, prompted by debasement of the coinage in England, beginning in 1543, which produced a rapid price inflation that at first stimulated trade. For a time, English cloth was relatively cheap for the foreign purchaser, since prices still moved more slowly than the rate of exchange on the Antwerp Bourse. But this could not go on indefinitely and by the spring of 1550 the Antwerp market had reached saturation point, leaving the Adventurers unable to sell their cloth amid an orgy of mutual recrimination in which the older and richer merchants blamed their younger and less experienced counterparts and both groups blamed the clothiers for providing shoddy goods that would not sell.

Worse still, the crisis of over-production was exacerbated by additional debasements of the coinage, which ensured that the exchange rate between London and Antwerp now moved rapidly to the disadvantage of sterling, reaching a nadir in July 1551. The hoarding of coins in England made it difficult for English merchants to meet debts at both Antwerp and Calais, and when the government launched ill-timed efforts to bring about deflation in the summer of 1551, they served merely to produce further financial confusion. Indeed, even when the currency correction did take effect finally, the main effect was simply to raise the price of cloth in the Netherlands at the worst possible time, and thereby kill off once and for all any lingering hopes for a prompt recovery in the market. Equally, when Bordeaux was identified as an alternative outlet, the result, as early as September, was a similar glut of cloth there also, as English traders flocked in desperation to offload their wares. The city, remarked one of them, was thronged with 'such sort of merchants as I think came not out of England many a day'. And as if this were not enough, two other blows had already been dealt to lessen any other chance of an upturn. For in 1550 Charles V had launched a new campaign against Protestantism in the Netherlands, which resulted in threats to English 'heretics' to abandon Antwerp, while in March of the following year an outbreak of sweating sickness struck particularly heavily at the heart of the London merchant community.

In one fell swoop, the dangers of putting all the kingdom's commercial eggs in one basket had become apparent as a seemingly indestructible market collapsed, in effect, under the weight of its own success. But the slump in the cloth trade, disastrous as it proved, was by no means the only structural problem relating to England's trade with Europe, particularly during the reign of Henry VIII. For if cloth sales had continued to boom well into his reign, and would partially recover from the collapse of 1551 as a consequence of diversification into other markets, there was nevertheless no overall growth of English commerce with Europe. Customs duties on exports from 1485 to 1509 amounted to £37,440, and between 1509 and 1547 to £37,804. In fact, the only significant alteration concerned the expansion of some of those English ports involved in European trade at the expense of others. Above all, London's share grew from 49.5 per cent to 66.1 per cent, while customs receipts at locations including Boston, Bristol, Exeter and Hull all slipped back marginally and those at Ipswich were slashed. Most strikingly of all, duties at Southampton were more than halved during the reign of Henry VIII, falling from £7,000 a year in the time of Henry VII, to £2,033 by 1535–40 and by 1540–45 to as low as £633 a year.

To some extent, the change in Southampton's fortunes was due to improvements in shipbuilding, rigging and piloting, which precluded the need for a long and hazardous journey up the Channel and round the Kent coast, while making navigation of the Thames estuary safer. But there had been changes too in the town's wide hinterland as the collection of wool for export dwindled in favour of local cloth industries in the Cotswolds, Wiltshire and Berkshire, which marketed largely through London. And it was London's increasing dominance over its provincial neighbours that not only underlay Southampton's troubles but represented one of the most outstanding features of England's evolving commercial relationship with Europe at this time. In the case of a handful of ports like Newcastle where coal, grindstones, canvas, rough and tanned leather, and lead continued to flow out relatively unchecked, the fall in customs receipts was comparatively negligible. Coal from Newcastle, in fact, continued to make its way not only to France but even as far as the Mediterranean, causing one English merchant to reflect with satisfaction upon France's dependence in particular, since 'they can neither make stele-work or metal work, nor wyer-work, nor goldsmith-work, nor guns, nor no manner of thing that passeth the fier'. But so long as cloth dominated England's commercial relations with Europe, as it did until the late seventeenth century, so London would grow ever more dominant over its provincial competitors, such as they were. And in the year ending Michaelmas 1565, for which figures survive, cloth still accounted for 78 per cent of English exports, and wool, sheep fells (hides) and textiles of all kinds for over 90 per cent. By which point, London accounted for 88 per cent of all cloth exports, while the only other significant items exported in the year were lead (2.4 per cent), tin (2.3), grain (1.4) and skins (1.0).

For one Venetian, writing in 1513, English cloth was 'one of the most important foundations of trade in the world'. And not for the first time among his countrymen, he exaggerated. Yet it was hardly insignificant that in 1582, Richard Hakluyt was still maintaining how there was 'no commoditie of this realme that may set so many poore subjects on worke' as cloth, or that William Camden, looking back on Elizabethan trade with the Netherlanders of both north and south, should have observed that 'the English wooll hath been to them the true Golden Fleece'. Clearly, the lesson of 1551 had not altered the country's dependence upon its primary export any more than later shocks of 1563–64, 1568–73 or 1586–87 would do. On the contrary, though the bell had by then already tolled for Antwerp, and the Baltic in particular was opening up increasingly as England's commercial window on Europe, the status of the all-important Anglo–Netherlands trade remained paramount not only economically, but as the guiding principle of Tudor foreign policy from the 1490s to the 1570s. Throughout, the objective was to seek and retain the friendship of the Habsburgs, who 'as the House of Burgundy' were lords of the seventeen provinces of the Low Countries. And in consequence every English sovereign and chief minister sought alliance first and foremost with the Habsburgs rather than with the Valois kings of France or their German Protestant counterparts. For William Cecil no less than Thomas Wolsey, indeed, English foreign policy would actually remain more subject to the dictates of English cloth exports than to considerations of religion or even, arguably, the balance of power itself.

It was no small irony, therefore, that so much of Henry VII's constructive work for English commerce in Europe should have been so decisively undermined by his heir. Put quite simply, Henry VIII inherited a healthy trading position from his father, not to mention a substantial – if sometimes exaggerated – personal fortune, only to squander both in extravagant and almost wholly fruitless wars. The jump of more than 20 per cent in cloth exports achieved during the first Tudor's reign continued, it is true, for the first decade of the next. But it was followed by some twenty years of falling revenue, reflecting the inevitable shrinkage as a result of conflict. Not only open warfare, but incessant rumours of wars and fears of impending closure of overseas markets also brought trade to a standstill at times, notably in the 1520s. And the results were palpable. From 1521 to 1529 the average annual yield of the customs fell from £42,643 to £35,305; then from 1530 to 1538 down to a little over £32,000. As exports dwindled, furthermore, the wool subsidy decreased by an average of nearly £10,000 a year, though buoyant cloth exports in good times continued to mask the full scale of the problem. For the annual average of customs revenue in the last nine years of the reign was still under £39,000, rather less than it had been in the latter half of the previous reign some fifty years earlier. And the dip in exports was occurring, of course, at the very time that the king was launching the series of coinage debasements that would finally pre-empt the crisis of 1551 under his young successor.

The Suffolk cloth industry, more dependent than any other on foreign markets, was particularly resistant to the heavy war taxation of 1523–25, while the Amicable Grant of 1525 for the prolongation of war with France roused even fiercer opposition all over the kingdom. In East Anglia, some 20,000 men of Suffolk and Essex, supported by the scholars of Cambridge, assembled in May before the rising was finally quelled and the proposal for the grant dropped. Then, in 1528, there was further trouble over the mere rumour of war. Corn prices had reached their highest level in living memory after the disastrous harvest of the previous year, and the prices of dairy produce were the highest for thirty years. So when rumours spread that an ongoing commercial tussle with the Netherlands was about to flare into open hostilities, the clothiers of Suffolk and merchants of London could not hold off for long. It was mooted that English merchants were being detained in Flanders, and as Suffolk clothiers laid off men, the Duke of Norfolk duly summoned before him at Stoke-by-Nayland forty of the region's most substantial clothiers, exhorting them to keep their employees in work. At the same time, Wolsey summoned a great number of the London mercantile community, to inform them of the king's 'high displeasure', and to warn that he was actually prepared to take the cloth trade into his own hands. In the process, though open war never ensued, exports dropped in 1528–29 by some 25 per cent.

Nor were these the only side effects of Henry VIII's all too frequent bellicose posturings. His third French War of 1542–44, for instance, saw the growth of uncontrolled privateering, as a result of which honest merchants on both sides of the Channel found themselves ruined by the capture and pillage of their ships at sea. The most sensational case was the seizure, in 1545, of the treasure ship *San Salvador* by Robert Reneger – a particularly displeasing feature of which from the Spanish viewpoint was Reneger's subsequent reception at the English court, which, like Drake's in 1580, involved the culprit's undisguised adulation. In the following year, to add salt to the wound, Spanish shipping underwent further attack within the north-east port of Munguia, so that even before the end of Henry VIII's reign the prevailing atmosphere was already beginning to resemble that more normally associated with his younger daughter's rule some four decades later. And in this case there was an added complication, since both Bristol and Southampton were rapidly losing ground to London, and London was tending, with ominous consequences for the future, to concentrate its trade increasingly on Antwerp, making any marked decline in Anglo–Spanish relations potentially more damaging than ever.

Occasionally, it is true, there were glimpses of sound sense amid the turmoil. In October 1542, for example, English and French fishermen arranged an independent truce 'during herring time', and letters to the effect went forth from Dieppe and Calais to the king in London. Nor on this occasion were they countermanded, since the food supply, it seems, was much too valuable to both sides to be jeopardised even by rulers who never went hungry themselves. And fishmongers and fishermen, of course, carried no little sway in both overseas commerce and domestic politics. Six mayors of London out of twenty-four in the period 1350–74, after all, had been, as John Stow reminds us, 'jolly fellows' of the fish trade, and well back into the fifteenth century, Cornish exports of fish were second in importance only to those of tin. Indeed, by the early years of Elizabeth's reign, the export of pilchards to the Catholic countries of southern Europe had developed on such a large scale that when Nicholas Ball, merchant of Totnes in Devon, died comparatively young in 1586, he had made his fortune not in cloth, but by exporting the 'silly small fish', caught in millions during the season, to Portugal and the Mediterranean. Within four months of Ball's demise, moreover, his wife had been snatched into marriage from under the nose of a rival by the canny Exeter merchant Thomas Bodley, whose Bodleian Library at Oxford was eventually established in 1598, largely on funds gained from his bride's rich maritime legacy.

Yet if Bodley's opportunism was not without broader benefit for posterity, the initiative of other Englishmen sometimes wrought havoc in the shorter term upon the livelihoods not only of foreigners but even their own compatriots. John Johnson and his partners, for example, had a vigorous interest in the herring trade from Dunkirk and Calais down to Dieppe and other Normandy ports, but they were only one group among many who suffered from the attacks of their privateering countrymen in the 1540s, as wars launched by Henry VIII continued to demonstrate that the commercial shockwaves from conflict were effectively uncontainable. Ultimately, in 1549 Johnson's ships were among forty or fifty hoys and other vessels 'bound with herrings into France' that were intercepted by raiders, who by then had infested the whole eastern and southern coast. More significantly still, the privateers' lawless actions brought damaging reprisals from other victims of their activities when, after continual complaints from the French and Imperial ambassadors in London, an eventual ban on herring boats was accompanied by what one contemporary described as 'the general arrest in Antwerp of all our English merchants' bodies and goods'.

Palpably, peace alone could ensure the underlying health of England's trade with Europe, and after the decline of Antwerp only innovation in seeking new outlets and expanded development of exports beyond cloth could fully guarantee the kingdom's economic security in the long term. Even at the period of greatest dependence upon Anglo–Netherlands trade, between about 1520 and 1550, Englishmen had not abandoned all their other markets. Trade with France, for example – especially of cloth in exchange for woad, salt and canvas – by no means entirely ceased between the interruptions for Henry VIII's wars, and in 1559–60 wine, mostly French, accounted for nearly 10 per cent of all English imports. Spain, too, had been increasing in importance as a source of iron, and there was a modest but significant trade with Scotland, as Scottish merchants made their way down the east coast to ports like Lynn and Boston, exchanging their fish for grain. But after the collapse of 1551, cloth exports recovered to a new peak in 1554 before falling again to settle by the end of the decade at a steady level of 100,000 to 110,000 cloths a year, which they maintained for most of Elizabeth I's reign. And as a result, the Merchant Adventurers were continuing to emphasise in 1561 how it was 'more commodiouse to the merchant' to sell at Antwerp – where they enjoyed an 'English House' as their headquarters, and an 'English quay' permanently at their disposal – than to trade directly with other places. For in the same year, too, they gave evidence that much of the cloth they were still exporting to Antwerp continued to find its way to more distant markets, including not only Italy and Spain, but Hungary and Morocco.

Nor should it be forgotten that the 100,000 or so cloths sent yearly to Antwerp around 1560 were worth at least £575,000, and that these figures were for traditional broadcloths sent to traditional markets, taking no account of the lighter, so-called 'new draperies' exported in increasing quantities over the final third of the century. The paradox, however, was that English trade still found itself hamstrung by an over-dependence on cloth at a time when imports of what many contemporaries considered unnecessary items were increasing. In the 1530s, Thomas Starkey had complained how English cloth was being exported merely to pay for wine, combs, girdles, knives, 'and a thousand such trifling things' that could either be ignored altogether or made at home to increase employment, while in 1549, there were similar complaints from Sir Thomas Smith against the number of imports 'that we might ether clene spare, or else make them within oure owne realme'. High on Smith's lists were items such as glass, paper, pottery, gloves, ink-horns and playing cards, all of which were leading to the kind of unfavourable balance of trade that should, he believed, be avoided at all costs. Foreign 'trifles', includ-ing fruit, should be exchanged, he argued, only for English 'trifles' and English fruit. And his arguments made a lasting impression on his colleague William Cecil, who by about 1564 was already increasingly concerned about the kingdom's overwhelming dependence upon cloth exports to Antwerp.

Knowing full well, of course, that concentration on one outlet gave Philip II of Spain – who had ruled the Netherlands since 1555 – undue power to 'annoye this realme', Cecil argued, too, that 'the people that depend upon makyng of cloth ar of worss condition to be quietly governed than the husband men'. Fortunately, there had been no widespread disorder in the clothing counties in 1551–52 comparable to the agrarian risings of 1548–49. Yet the organised power of cloth merchants was of a different order to the 'Toms, Dicks and Harries' who had joined Robert Ket's rebels, and a similar crisis in future might have untold political consequences. As such, a diver-sification of cloth export markets to include Germany, Scandinavia, Russia, Narva in Estonia, Portugal, Italy and Turkey made the soundest possible sense, just as it seemed no less obvious to Cecil of the need to prevent his coun-try from being 'overburdened with unnecessary forrayn wares'. Around 1580, moreover, he was still arguing for a reduction in imports of items like silk, wine and spices, by which time Philip's trade embargoes of 1563–64 and 1568–73 had indeed dealt severe blows to English exports. Talk of replac-ing the Adventurers' 'staple' at Antwerp by a home staple at London, Ipswich, Hull, York or Southampton, to which foreign buyers could freely resort from any country to buy English cloth, had likewise fallen on deaf ears. And high-flown hopes of autarky, though mildly fanned by a statute of 1563 restricting the import of foreign luxuries such as books, hats and handkerchiefs, could in any case hardly answer England's pressing need for flax, linen and canvas for shipbuilding, which accounted for 17 per cent of English imports in 1559–60, let alone the iron goods and Italian textiles, which represented about 6 per cent each.

Ultimately, in fact, it was only hard necessity that eventually persuaded Elizabethan merchants to abandon Antwerp step by step. The bankruptcies of the French and Spanish crowns in 1557 and the outbreak of the Dutch revolt against Spain, which shook the city's prosperity, were followed by its sack in 1576 and the closure of its sea outlet by the Protestant rebels themselves in 1585. And although the bulk of English cloth exports continued to be sent by the Merchant Adventurers to their Netherlands and German markets, there proved no alternative other than to supplement and finally replace the convenient Antwerp staple. The first move was forced, in fact, by the Spanish regent of the Netherlands, who suspended the cloth trade in November 1563 in the hope of putting pressure on the English government by causing

unemployment and economic dislocation. But by March 1564, when the
Netherlanders sued to heal the breach, realising that Antwerp needed the cloth
trade even more than the English did, Queen Elizabeth had already arranged
to send the English cloth fleet to Emden in East Friesland, a German port
just beyond the jurisdiction of Philip II. At the time, one particularly zealous
anti-Spanish Adventurer, George Nedham, confidently prophesied that the
Adventurers could live without Antwerp but not vice versa. And although
they were actually back at Antwerp in January 1565, Nedham was proved
right, as he and his fellows settled successively at Hamburg (1567–78), Emden
again (1578–87), Stade (1587–98, 1601–11) and Middelburg (1587–1621).

More significant still for the future was the activity of English traders, both
back in the regions from which they had been temporarily excluded, like the
Baltic and Mediterranean, and beyond them into completely new areas of
the globe such as Russia, southern Asia, Africa and America. Certainly, it is no
accident that whereas Henry VIII had shown little interest in the geographical and commercial expansion urged on him by men like Robert Thorne
and Sebastian Cabot, the disruption of traditional markets after 1551 turned
statesmen and merchants alike to look outwards. Hakluyt's *Principal Voyages*,
published in 1589 and between 1598 and 1600, are often regarded primarily
as an expression of the nation's new geographical curiosity, but he himself
took it for granted, as he put it in his dedication to Robert Cecil of 1599, that
'our chiefe desire is to find out ample vent [sale] of our wollen cloth'. Not
everyone, it is true, shared Hakluyt's preoccupation with finding 'vent', and it
can be argued that a more powerful motive for extra-European trade was the
ongoing search for luxury imports such as silks and spices. But it is striking
that the first significant ventures in the expansion of overseas trade occurred
in the early 1550s, under Edward VI and his sister Mary, though the shortness
of their reigns and the longevity of Elizabeth I have ensured that the shift is
always considered 'Elizabethan'. Indeed, the opening of trade with Morocco
is traditionally, and probably correctly, dated from 1551, the very year of the
Antwerp slump.

All the while, of course, as the more adventurous cast greedy eyes on the
Spanish and Portuguese monopolies over the lands of the New World, or
rich profits from Africa after the first Guinea voyage of 1553, others continued to think of developing their interest in the Baltic or Mediterranean,
or further afield with Turkey and Russia. In the last case, the first voyagers
of 1553 had reached the White Sea, travelled overland to Moscow and started
Anglo–Russian trade almost by accident. But in 1587, which was admittedly
an exceptional year, the Muscovy Company and its 201 founder members
were responsible for imports officially valued at £13,500, which may actually have been little more than half the actual amount. In 1558, moreover,

Russia had conquered the Baltic port of Narva, which was much frequented by English merchants and was added to the Muscovy Company's monopoly sphere in 1566, while, around the same time, the Northern War of 1563–70 between Sweden and a coalition of Denmark–Norway, Lübeck and the Polish–Lithuanian commonwealth weakened the Hanseatic League at precisely the point when troubles in the Netherlands were distracting the Dutch carriers from their share of Baltic trade. As a result, English ships penetrated the area more and more frequently during the 1560s, and in 1578 the Hanseatic merchants in England were reduced to the same footing as other foreigners. Only the following year, Elizabeth formally constituted sixty-five English merchants as the Eastland Company, which traded primarily with Poland, operating through the port of Gdańsk or, after 1581, through the small neighbouring port of Elblag.

In fact, the decline of the Hanseatic League had been long heralded, divided as it was into three increasingly distinct groups of cities. The leadership of Lübeck, on the one hand, had been discredited by a crushing naval defeat at the hands of Sweden and Denmark in 1535, and her participation three decades later in the Northern War against Sweden's rising empire ultimately brought more loss than gain. Likewise, the initial suspension of Hansard privileges in England in 1552, though only temporary, was a sign of growing general weakness, which was exacerbated by increasing Dutch and even south German competition in the Baltic during the mid-century. By the 1560s, the Hansards had lost their control of English cloth to north-east Germany, and from this time on English merchants, from both London and the east coast ports, handled the bulk of the trade. Indeed, the creation of the Eastland Company did not so much create a new outlet for English cloth, but rather organised and canalised the efforts of merchants already active in the Baltic, affording them some protection against piracy and a united front against Hanse resistance. In 1598, the famous Steelyard was closed in London, and though by 1600 more than 80 per cent of the ships passing through the Danish Sound were Dutch, the benefits of the Baltic trade to England remained undeniable. Naval supplies, consisting of flax, cordage, hemp, iron, pitch, tar and so on, as well as grain, flowed in, as cloth flowed out, carried by ships – registered mainly in London, Hull and Newcastle – numbering 920 in the years 1591 to 1600.

As English seamen returned to the Baltic, furthermore, so their compatriots were continuing to re-enter the Mediterranean. Hakluyt averred in his dedication to Robert Cecil that English ships had trafficked regularly with Sicily, Crete and Chios from 1511 to 1552 'and somewhat longer', until 'intermitted, or rather given over', as a result of the Turkish captures of Chios in 1566 and Cyprus in 1571. But while the interruption is an undisputed fact, Hakluyt's causes and chronology are misleading, since English ships were apparently absent from the Mediterranean between 1553 and 1572, along with French and Netherlandish vessels – and not because of Turkish hostility. Instead, the answer lay in the Indian summer enjoyed by Venice and other Mediterranean states that resumed their own carrying trades. In 1569, English cloth was also being carried by ships of Dubrovnik, though Venice's involvement in war with Turkey between 1570 and 1573 gave England its chance once more. For from 1573 onwards, English ships regularly visited Livorno at the invitation of the grand duke of Tuscany, with cargoes of cloth, lead and tin. After which, they were regular traders, too, in the western and central Mediterranean: at Sicily by 1580; Malta from 1581; and Marseilles from 1590. Indeed, by 1582, the homely 'cole of Newcastle' was for sale in Malta, while only a year afterwards, the government even asserted its growing self-confidence by the establishment under royal charter of the Venice Company.

The next step, as it transpired, was to trade directly with the expanding Turkish empire, a clear case of politics and commerce before religion for a queen who had ordered national thanksgivings for the Christian naval victory at Lepanto in 1571. Sir Francis Walsingham was apparently urging commerce with Turkey in or before 1578, and in 1578–79 two London merchants, Sir Edward Osborne and Richard Staper, sent the secret agent William Harborne to Constantinople to make contact with Sultan Murād III, who was interested in English lead and tin for armaments. As a result, Murad promised safe conduct to all traders of 'the domain of Anletār', followed in 1580 by a grant of unrestricted trading facilities throughout his empire, on terms almost identical to those enjoyed by France. Next year, Elizabeth duly incorporated the Turkey Company, which merged with the Venice Company in 1592 to form the Levant Company. By 1599, it had twenty ships in Italian waters alone, consolidating the opening up the Muslim Mediterranean, which, five years earlier, had already led one English visitor to Aleppo to deem a description of the state and trade of the town unnecessary, 'because it is so well known to most of our nation'. Less orthodox traders, operating outside the Levant Company, also did a lively business in arms and slaves for both Venetians and Turks, and there were those too, regrettably, who combined legitimate attacks on Spanish shipping with indiscriminate piracy at the expense of French and Italian merchants also. Yet in the main – notwithstanding the sultan's initial interest in lead and tin, and a new demand in England for Turkish carpets that saw the Countess of Salisbury purchase no fewer than thirty-two of them at Hardwick Hall by 1601 – Anglo–Turkish trade continued to consist essentially of the exchange of cloth for raw silk.

Contrary to appearances, however, it is still by no means altogether certain that all these developments, taken together, represented any really significant overall expansion of England's trade with Europe, even in the reign of Elizabeth. Though no full and reliable figures exist for a comprehensive picture, those available for London's cloth exports, for example, suggest a relative stability from 1574 onwards, but at a level nevertheless below the mid-century peak. There were severe depressions in the early 1560s and the early 1570s, and a crisis in 1586–87, while data for customs receipts also suggest considerable fluctuations in the 1590s, though smuggling and customs evasion undoubtedly increased greatly after the introduction in 1558 of a new Book of Rates by Mary Tudor, which made such activities more profitable and the risks worth taking. Equally, the second half of the century was also marked by restrictive practices, not least of which was the raising of the Merchant Adventurers' entrance fee from ten to a hundred marks in 1555, thus shutting out provincial merchants. True, the Adventurers could not prevent interlopers from trading at Hamburg, and even the Russia Company was unable to maintain a strict monopoly. But the revival of exclusivism was nevertheless ongoing after the crisis of 1550–51. Another, more monopolistic, charter was obtained by the Adventurers in 1564, and a further sign that Elizabethans were not always the enterprising and adventurous traders of popular myth came with the introduction at some unknown later date of a 'stint of trade' that limited individual merchants to the export of a specified number of cloths per year, varying with the seniority of the merchant.

A similar lack of openness to change was also evident, as has been noted, in commercial methods and organisation. The joint-stock company was indeed an innovation, and increasing use was also made of resident agents abroad. Such men might, on the one hand, be aspiring merchants, perhaps lacking sufficient capital to set up business in their own right, and therefore opting to act for one or more principals in a foreign port, sometimes on a commission basis. This was the position, for example, of Thomas Malliard, 'factor' for Thomas Howell at Seville in 1521, and of Blasé and Thomas Freman, factors to Thomas Sexton in Danzig in the 1550s. Alternatively, a young man still barely in or out of his apprenticeship might also perform the role, and it was in this capacity that Thomas Washington worked for Thomas Kitson at Antwerp in 1536. By 1589, indeed, there had appeared a manual for the instruction of such individuals, *The Merchants avizo* by John Browne of Bristol, which combined much sound practical information with a rich coating of pious imprecations. Yet the employment of such agents made it possible for the sixteenth-century English merchant to be stay-at-home and sedentary; it did not make him an international tycoon. Nor, for that matter, did the innovation of the joint-stock company survive very long in either the Russian or the Levant trade, and it was equally true that no English business house of the Tudor period attained either the scope or complexity of Augsburg banking organisations like those of the Fuggers and Welsers, or even of the fifteenth-century Medici. Though English merchants made increasing use of bills of exchange, marine insurance was slow to develop, and its status at law dubious. Double-entry book-keeping, which had been known in Italy for two centuries, was also so poorly applied, in spite of the appearance of textbooks on the subject from 1543 onwards, that one particular author justified the merits of his treatise on the grounds that the ledgers of the owners of lesser firms were:

> so grossly, obscurely and lewdly kept, that after their decease neither wife, servant, executor nor other could by their books perceive what of right appertained to them to be received of other, neither what justly was due by them unto another.

It was for precisely such reasons that English merchants, even the greatest of them, still lagged behind their more outstanding European rivals in terms of wealth, the size and complexity of their business, and their grasp of commercial techniques. Indeed, in these respects the situation of 1485 remained substantially unchanged.

And then, of course, there is finally the question of the impact of war with Spain upon England's status as a European trading power. Predictably, the conflict between 1585 and 1604 was not without repercussions, since the English merchants involved – incorporated as the Spanish Company in 1577 – had apparently been increasing Anglo–Iberian trade steadily from 1574 onwards. Significantly, a Spanish spy in England reported only one year into the conflict that 'the whole country is without trade, and knows not how to recover it; the shipping and commerce here having depended upon the communication with Spain and Portugal'. Yet it was said at the time that by 1593 the merchants of London, Bristol and Southampton had managed to circumvent the Spanish embargo by shipping cloths to Seville under the colour of Flemish goods. Furthermore, privateering during the eighteen years of war may well, according to some estimates, have brought in returns at least as great as the total value of Iberian trade before the outbreak of hostilities – some £100,000 or so per annum, accounting for 10–15 per cent of England's imports. A single Portuguese carrack captured by Drake in 1587 carried a cargo worth nearly £114,000, and the Spanish spy of 1586 had not only exaggerated the importance to England of the Iberian trade, but misleadingly dismissed the kingdom's trade with France as insignificant. In fact, more than one quarter of the tonnage of imports entering London in the nine months from October 1601 to June 1602 came from France, slightly ahead of the Netherlands total.

Even so, contemporary commentators like William Harrison, as well as the more sober testimony of commercial inventories, confirm a notable increase in luxury imports, which are likely, it seems, to have been purchased on the back of a growing balance of payments shortfall. Certainly, the customs accounts had convinced Cecil that in 1559–61 London's overseas trade was in deficit, while about 1580 he was still observing 'that yerly the forayn commodities doo surmount the commodities of the land'. Notwithstanding the buoyancy of the Baltic trade, the second largest after Germany and the Netherlands, Sir Henry Knivet told the Commons in 1593 that England remained poor 'because we brought in more foreign wares than we vented commodities'. And while ample supplies of captured Spanish silver continued to be made available to the Tower Mint during the 1580s and 1590s, it was hardly insignificant that England patently failed to fill the gaps in its overseas commerce by boosting its diplomatic representation abroad. The idea that rulers should have permanent residents at each other's courts, able to help with commercial as well as political matters, had been developed in fifteenth-century Italy, and slowly spread to the larger states of western Europe. As a result, Spain maintained an English embassy from 1495 to 1584, while England under Henry VIII, Edward and Mary maintained a network of embassies in the courts of the Holy Roman Empire, the Netherlands, France and Venice. Yet religious divisions born of the Reformation broke these contacts, so that by 1570 the only English ambassador resident on the Continent was in France.

War and religious divisions had, in fact, from some perspectives brought Tudor England almost full circle in its relations with Europe. But if England's window on the Continent had again been partially shuttered, its front door, ironically enough, had been opened more widely than ever by precisely the same forces. For Flemish and Walloon immigrants, fleeing war and religious persecution in the Netherlands, were from the 1560s onwards arriving in ever greater numbers. And as they migrated, they brought with them the skills that helped the diversification of English cloth manufacture that had been needed for some time. Broadcloth continued to dominate, but lighter cloths, more suitable for the Levant and other warm climates, were now increasingly necessary, and these 'new draperies' would prove the speciality of England's newcomers, who settled especially in Norwich and the surrounding area. The production of bays, says, grograms and other cheap light cloths proceeded apace from the 1560s, and for evidence of the contribution of alien settlers to this process, one need look no further than the records of the Norwich Cloth Halls, which show an increase from around 3,400 cloths a year in 1566–70 to 36,300 in the years 1584–88. Not until the middle of James I's reign would broadcloths cease to dominate the export trade, but

long before his predecessor's reign was out, her second city had been transformed. For in 1565, the Privy Council had invited thirty families of Dutch
and Flemish 'strangers' to settle in Norwich, after which their numbers rose
to some 3,000 persons in 1569, 4,000 in 1571, and 6,000 in 1579, about one
third of the city's population – proportionately a much greater influx of alien
immigrants than any other known example in English history.

5

IMMIGRATION

Moreover, a great number of artificers and other strangers, not born under the King's obeisance, do daily resort and repair to the city of London, and other cities, boroughs and towns of the said realm, and much more than they were wont to do in times past, and inhabit by themselves in the said realm with their wives, children and household …

> From a statute of 1483 forbidding the
> illegal entry of foreigners to the realm

Though still a comparative rarity and, as such, generally distrusted by most people, 'strangers' from Europe were not altogether unknown in England when the kingdom's first Tudor monarch mounted his throne. As early as the reign of Henry III, a writ had been issued for the introduction of foreign 'moneyers' at the Mint, and under Edward I some two to three hundred artisans, mainly Italian, were later employed there. Previously, Richard of Cornwall, King John's second son, had introduced Germans to his duchy's mines, while in the following century, under Edward III, we hear too of clockmakers from Delft as well as linen weavers from Flanders who, according to one tradition, may well have introduced clogs to south-east Lancashire. In the same reign, two weavers from Brabant obtained authority to settle in York, and a certain 'Thomas Blanket' set up looms in Bristol to begin manufacture on a significant scale. Cloths of distinct makes, suggestive of foreign craftsmen, were also being produced as far afield as Kendal, Guildford and Devonshire. And by the time of the Peasants' Revolt, there were more significant settlements of Flemings in Norfolk, whose recent arrival was a sufficiently major cause of vexation to contribute to the rising itself. For at Snettisham, a band of insurgents, headed by a man from Lynn, entered the town with the deliberate intention of killing any Flemings that could be found, while three foreigners imprisoned at Yarmouth suffered summary execution for no more, it seems, than their place of birth.

As the trickle continued over the next century, moreover, there was sometimes resentment among the migrants' own countrymen, as in 1453 when the inhabitants of the Walloon city of Dinant complained how three copperfounders had secretly emigrated to England, raising fears that they might establish a rival source of manufacture to that of their homeland. Similar concerns were evident, too, almost a hundred years later when Muranese glassmakers became the subject of a bitter diplomatic stand-off between the English and Venetian governments. For by the mid-sixteenth century glassmakers on the island of Murano were considered such an asset to the Venetian state that they were forbidden from leaving on pain of assassination. And not without good reason, perhaps, since France, Spain, the Holy Roman Empire and England, too, remained not only entirely captivated by their product but wholly unable to match its quality domestically. When attempts to emulate the quality of Venetian glass in England had begun in the 1530s, for instance, several glassmakers from the Netherlands established a factory in Southwark on the south bank of the Thames. But it failed to flourish, so that in 1549 Edward VI finally succeeded in approving a contract for eight Muranese glassmakers under Josepo Casselari to establish a furnace at the House of the Carmelite Crutched Friars, which had been dissolved by Henry VIII eleven years earlier. Within twelve months, the Venetian authorities had insisted upon their return, and the English government, unwilling to give up its newly acquired craftsmen, imprisoned them and forbade their release until 1551.

In general, however, such incidents were rare and the arrival of foreigners had continued its slow but steady course, notwithstanding the temporary expulsion of Italian merchants in 1456 after a London riot. During the reign of Henry VII, Flemish workmen were established at Seend in Wiltshire, while an Italian, Anthony Bonvis, obtained permission to introduce an improved method of spinning into Devonshire. There was a grant also to two other Italians – 'John de Salvo' and 'Anthony Spynile', a resident of Southampton – to bring in foreign cloth-makers. Most notably of all, there was the arrival around 1495 of the Italian Giovanni Caboto – better known in England as John Cabot – who would command the first English voyage to reach the mainland of America. Taking up residence in Bristol – the only English port with a history of exploratory expeditions in the Atlantic – Cabot had finally been granted letters patent on 5 March 1496, giving him:

… free authority, faculty and power to sail to all parts, regions and coasts of the eastern, western and northern sea, under our banners, flags and ensigns, with five ships or vessels of whatsoever burden and quality they may be, and with so many and with such mariners and men as they may wish to take with them in the said ships, at their own proper costs and charges, to find, discover and investigate whatsoever islands, countries, regions or provinces of heathens and infidels, in whatsoever part of the world placed, which before this time were unknown to all Christians.

And the result was a voyage to the New World in 1497, which would justify Cabot's earlier unsuccessful odyssey to Seville, Valencia and Lisbon in search of patronage. For, as an entry in the chronicle of the city of Bristol for 1496–97 recorded:

This year, on St. John the Baptist's Day [24 June 1497], the land of America was found by the Merchants of Bristow in a shippe of Bristowe, called the Mathew; the which said ship departed from the port of Bristowe, the second day of May, and came home again the 6th of August next following.

In this case, as well as others, the potential services of foreign immigrants with superior skills and knowledge seemed undeniable, particularly if their expertise could then be successfully transmitted to native Englishmen. The discovery of America and the importation of silver from the New World had, for example, not only turned attention all over Europe to the possibility of discovering precious metals nearer home, but given a considerable impulse to the metallurgical arts generally. And since France, and especially Germany, were in advance of their European counterparts in both engineering and chemical science, the result in England was to be the continued arrival of foreign technicians and workers during the reign of Henry VIII. 'Tynners' from Brittany were employed at the tin mines of 'St Hersie' in Cornwall, while Frenchmen from Croys made their way across the Channel, we are told, to labour in England over a period of forty years in:

moynes of iron, lead and other metals as well of the King's highness as others of his faithful subjects by virtue of a commission to one William Pexwell, merchant of Bristol.

By 1500 copper, too, was being extensively worked by Dutchmen at Treworthy, Perrin Sands, St Just, and Logan in Cornwall, though their efforts were later accompanied by a suggestion from Sir Thomas Smith that they be replaced by Cornishmen who were prepared to work for less. Even so, Henry VIII did not hesitate in 1528 to appoint Joachim Hochstetter of Augsburg principal surveyor and master of all mines in England and Ireland, or to empower him to come over with six other Germans to commence operations and to erect smelting houses. Indeed, though this appears to have achieved little at the time, by 1571 Hochstetter's son Daniel had himself become master of the royal mines, with what would prove to be altogether more momentous consequences for the industry.

And in the interim several other Germans were brought over, partly for the purpose of mining, and partly to work at the Mint. Among them was Johannes Kundelfinger in 1550, and Daniel Ulstatt of Augsburg and his partners. But such was the rumoured potential for extracting both gold and silver, as well as copper, that in 1563 a fully fledged German mining company was created. Under the direction of Daniel Hechstetter and Thomas Thurland, operations began at Keswick and elsewhere in Cumberland, and permission was sought to bring in some three to four hundred workmen – which was not only granted but accompanied by a guarantee that the promoters were to be offered significant tax exemptions encompassing all payments of tenths and fifteenths. Not altogether surprisingly, Englishmen too, like William Humphrey, a paymaster of the Royal Mint, sought to cash in on the potential bonanza by forging partnerships with their enterprising German counterparts. In Humphrey's case, the product was alum and the location Ireland, his partner an engineer by the name of Christopher Shutz; while in the Isle of Wight a rival prospector for alum, Cornelius de Vos, was equally keen to venture his capital and labours on what ultimately proved a fruitless quest. Yet Henry VIII had certainly remained undaunted by the occasional business failure of this kind, fully appreciating, albeit with some frustration, that alien expertise had become indispensable in a range of spheres. Peter Baude, for example, a French gun-founder, had been in the country since the outset of the reign, and by 1533 was casting 'brass' – that is, 'bronze' – cannon for the king, passing on his skill to two Englishmen, Robert and John Owen. And when English emissaries sallied forth to secure the hand of Anne of Cleves in 1539, they were also charged not only with buying heavy guns but procuring the services of expert gunners to teach the English how to use them. In the event, Henry liked neither his wife nor the gunners, but he dispensed more readily, it seems, with the former, tolerating the gunners until almost the end of the reign, by which time the iron smelter Ralph Hogg and the rector of Buxted, William Levett, in co-operation with Peter Baude, were proving successful gun-founders in their own right.

However, the preparedness of the first two Tudors to employ foreigners did little, it seems, to stifle the common grumbles and complaints of the day about newcomers, which were no less evident among municipalities and municipal guilds. Regulations at Shrewsbury, for instance, revealed a growing vigilance against 'foreigners', which in this case included both 'aliens' from without and outsiders from within, and the same antagonism is displayed in contemporary ordinances produced by the tailors and coopers of Southampton. Elsewhere, when the government of Worcester was reconstituted in 1497, there were similar traces of ill feeling, all of which was encapsulated in later statutes of 1512, 1523 and 1524 associated with Henry VIII. The first of these acts was directed specifically against aliens engaged in cordwainery, claiming that they had cheated the 'King's liege subjects' by the production of poorly wrought goods. But the second and third were wider in scope, deeming aliens as no more than a necessary, and hopefully short-term evil, on the grounds that Englishmen were not inventive, and therefore dependent upon the introduction of improved methods from abroad until those methods had been successfully assimilated – a view endorsed, at least in principle it seems, by Sir Thomas Smith in his *Discourse of the Commonweal*:

> Yea, wheare as a towne is decayed and lackes artificers to furnishe the townes with suche craftes as other weare sometime well exercised theare, or might be by reason of the satuation and commoditie of the same towne, I would have better craftes allowed oute of other places where they be plenty, to come to these townes decayed to dwell, offringe therein theire fredome, yea theire house rent free, or some stocke let therein of the common stocke of such townes. And when the towne is well furnished of such artificers, then to staie the comminge of forreners.

As always, of course, Smith's use of 'forreners' is crucial, but if he had indeed intended to confine his observation to the employment of native Englishmen, to whom this term was commonly applied, at least one anonymous author of the reign of Henry VIII was unambivalent in his wish to welcome European workers with open arms. Indeed, the author of *How the comen people may be set to worke an order of a Comen Welth* was to urge that 'all workers of artificialite (i.e. skill)' should be 'set to worke as well strangers as Englyshemen', on the grounds that 'good workmanship of all artificialite is most comely seen in strangers'. The further reason, argued the writer, was that the excessive import of foreign goods had precluded the sale of home manufactures, with the result that strangers, with constant practice, had perfected themselves in various arts at the expense of Englishmen who had lost 'all corage to study for such feats'. As such, the antagonism of the entire treatise was directed not so much against either immigrant craftsmen or indeed the native workforce itself as against those merchants, alien or otherwise, who flooded the kingdom with foreign commodities in their own self-interest.

And those self-same complaints about the damaging impact of imports remained ongoing, just as they had before Sir Thomas Smith gave them their classic expression in 1549. The early fifteenth-century author of the *Libelle of Englyshe Polycye* had been echoed by Clement Armstrong in the 1520s, who had deplored the excessive importing of 'strange merchandise and artificial fantasies'. Smith, however, would note in detail two decades later how the long list of imported consumer goods had risen more than 30 per cent in the seven years before his book was published, though until home-bred craftsmen were of sufficient skill and numbers, there seemed no other solution in his opinion than to bow to commercial pressure, regardless of any potential antagonism that this might create for the requisite newcomers. For the acceleration of immigration in the second half of the sixteenth century was particularly marked, as economic necessity, coupled to religious persecution across the Channel, took effect. And though they mostly left again at the accession of his elder sister, a surge in continental Protestants was particularly apparent during the reign of Edward VI, while a larger and more permanent influx arrived from the 1560s onwards, fleeing persecution in the Netherlands, France and Germany, and even Spain and Italy. By 1553, indeed, the French ambassador considered that there were 15,000 French, Flemish and German Protestants in London alone, while in 1560 Philip II's ambassador put the number of Flemish Protestant families in England at 2,000 or some 10,000 people.

More reliable statistics still, meanwhile, are available for 1563, at which time the Privy Council itself commissioned detailed figures for the growing minority of immigrants to the capital. The results, certified by the Lord Mayor, indicated a total of 4,534 'strangers' dwelling in London, Westminster, Southwark and the suburbs, though the number was clearly growing significantly, if a further count submitted by the Bishop of London only four years later is to be believed. For according to this estimate, covering the same area minus Southwark, there were 4,851 immigrants, rising the following year to a total of 6,704. The great majority at this stage were some 5,225 Netherlanders, displaced by war with Spain, and a further 1,119 French. Together these two groups constituted what appears to have been some 7–8 per cent of the capital's population. But they were also joined by a growing body of German artisans who became another prominent component of the social flux that was to have such a significant impact on so many areas of Tudor culture. Excluded by the City of London, along with Dutch and Flemish craftsmen, on the basis that they were not members of a trade guild, most came to settle in Southwark, where their skills were put to good use in both the joinery and leather trades. And the resulting transformation was palpable. For at a time when there was still only one bridge across the Thames, John Norden's map of London in 1593 demonstrates conclusively how far the development of the area south of the river had gone as a result of the immigration that had proceeded in the interim – not least after 1572 when the Spanish destroyed the great commercial city of Antwerp, giving London first place among the North Sea ports.

As the century progressed, therefore, the ongoing internal migration to London from all over England and Wales was supplemented by significant waves of skilled foreigners, encouraging the capital's population to increase from an estimated 50,000 in 1530 to about 225,000 in 1605. And in other places, too, a not dissimilar trend was occurring, most notably at Norwich, home to the second largest immigrant community in the kingdom, where foreigners actually formed a much higher proportion of the population still. In 1565, the Privy Council had invited the settlement of no more than thirty families of Dutch and Flemish 'strangers' in the East Anglian city, in an effort to revive the ailing textile industry, which had languished in the aftermath of the destruction caused by Ket's rebellion in 1549. Trade on Norwich's Market Place had, indeed, dwindled so much subsequently that the municipal authorities were left with no choice other than to pay for the clearance of weeds accumulating there. Yet by 1569, the number of Dutch weavers producing 'russels' and 'sateens' had risen to as many as 3,000 (including 1,132 Flemings and 339 Walloons), and by 1571 to 4,000 – all packed into a fixed housing stock that necessitated a subdivision of dwellings that had before long yielded tragic consequences. Peaking at 6,000 in 1579, the immigrant influx by then amounted to more than one third of the city's 16,000 inhabitants – representing a proportionately much greater influx of alien immigrants than any other known example in English history. And though their numbers were reduced by a dreadful outbreak of bubonic plague that year, which inflicted a particularly heavy toll of some 45 per cent on the overcrowded immigrant families, by 1583 their community had nevertheless recovered to 4,679.

In fact, there had always been some movement of people between Norwich and Europe. Nicholas le Mouner of Amiens, for example, appears in the city's court roll of 1287 when he bought a house in Fyebridge, from which he probably participated in the local woad trade. And if the length of his life is any guide, he appears to have thrived well enough, dying around 1330 after living unmolested with his wife and family. Yet as altogether more substantial numbers arrived in the reign of Elizabeth I, the epidemic of 1579 and the overcrowding that precipitated it were by no means the only challenges facing le Mouner's successors – notwithstanding their exemplary conduct and wide-ranging contribution. Organised by a committee known as Governors of the Drapery and by their church leaders, they had taken every reasonable step to co-operate with their English hosts, appointing twelve 'politic men' (eight Dutchmen and four Walloons) to liaise with them. They worshipped unobtrusively in the Blackfriars church in St Andrew's Hall, looked after their own sick and poor, and brought a number of skills other than weaving to their new city of residence. A silver communion cup, made in about 1580 for his church by a Dutch goldsmith called Peter Peterson, still exists today in the city's Castle Museum, and in the 1570s there are two references to the employment of Dutch physicians in the city – something made all the more significant by the fact that only nine medical doctors are known to have practised in Norwich between 1501 and 1600. John Cropp came from Flanders as a surgeon in 1567, while his son, also called John, who is mentioned in the letters of Katherine Paston, obtained a licence to practise in 1602. More noteworthy still, perhaps, is the decision of Norwich's muster-master to allow Dutch strangers to serve in the local trained bands, due at least partly, it seems, to their knowledge of gunpowder technology. And there were more varied contributions yet. For the city's first printer was Anthony de Solempne, who came over with his wife and two sons in 1567, while in the following year a Dutch gardener, Joos Brake, was being employed by local gentry to lay out their gardens.

As might be expected, however, not all was plain sailing for the new arrivals. For in 1570, John Throgmorton staged an unsuccessful attempt to raise Norfolk's gentry in a rising against them, and though there was little response from the common people, many limitations were subsequently imposed on the immigrants' activities, including orders issued the year afterwards that they were not to walk the streets after the curfew had rung. It was no small irony, perhaps, that the only work published in English by de Solempne was a broadsheet of poetry written by Thomas Brooke on the night before his execution for involvement in Throgmorton's abortive rising. And it was not until 1598 that the printer and his peers were finally allowed to become freemen on the same terms as natives. Yet the recovery of the community's numbers after the epidemic of 1579 suggests not only its resilience in the face of adversity, but the residing attraction of Norwich as a haven. Above all, second-generation immigrants born in the city were eventually freed from the same restrictions applying elsewhere, with the result that those who came were mainly willing to stay. The goldsmith Peter Peterson's will of 1603, for example – in which he asks to be buried 'in the chapel where I do usually sit in the Parish of St Andrew where I was born in the city of Norwich' – confirms that he was a second-generation immigrant, just like the younger John Cropp. And Anthony de Solempne's perseverance and honest endeavours were suitably rewarded only three years after his arrival when he was made a freeman of the city – albeit on restricted terms – and entitled to sell Rhenish wines. By the 1630s, indeed, florists' feasts, introduced by the flower-loving settlers, were an annual feature of Norwich life, just as canary breeding was to become a century later.

Nor was Norwich the only city outside the capital to experience the short and longer-term effects of foreign migration during the Elizabethan period. The newcomers arrived at a time when urban economies were still comparatively stagnant, and just ahead of the early Elizabethan rise in population. But in contrast to the first half of the century and before, some towns were nevertheless more ready to counter their long-standing prejudices against strangers in general and aliens in particular. In 1567, for example, the corporation of Maidstone welcomed not only makers of says (serges), mockadoes (mock velvet) and other woollen cloths, but also producers of friscadoes (linen, sail-cloth and canvas), as well as paving tiles, bricks and all kinds of armour, not to mention those engaged in 'other arts and sciences which are not [here] known, being both necessary and profitable for the commonwealth'. More specifically, the town authorities asked for sixty families, none of which were to exceed twelve persons, including servants. And although only thirty were eventually admitted, houses were nevertheless found for them to rent, on condition that they limited their activities to the stipulated crafts, while taking only English apprentices, employing only English unskilled labour, and selling only wholesale. As a result, by 1585 there were actually forty-three alien families in Maidstone, comprising 115 adults, who appear to have wrought an impact far wider than their original brief. For, with the help of its alien settlers, Maidstone found that its true vocation lay in the production of linen thread, not only encouraging the cultivation of flax in the surrounding countryside but contributing to the conversion of English people from woollen to linen clothes for everyday wear. Blue linen became, indeed, almost as popular in the summer among ordinary men and women – many of whom later migrated to America – as it already was in France.

Other refugees settled in Canterbury and Sandwich, and by the 1580s there were a further 1,300 at Colchester. At Sandwich, in fact, one third of the population was by then of alien stock, forcing the corporation to restrict immigration to certain favoured occupations, though William Cecil's attempts to resuscitate Stamford, his native town, with a similar infusion were less successful, and York, too, proved largely unaffected – albeit not so much for any intrinsic antipathy to radical Protestants as to its distance from ports of entry like Bristol and Exeter. Instead, and for all the obvious reasons, London continued to prove the obvious magnet for enterprising foreigners – including women too, it seems. For as the growing use of linen continued, so the starch-making industry flourished, and made the fortune of individuals like Mistress Dinghen van der Plasse, a Fleming who in the 1560s taught London women how to make starch from wheat: a particularly prized skill when fine linen fabrics such as lawn and cambric had become popular; and at a time when a Dutchwoman, Mistress Boone, wife of the Queen's coachman, was securing her own reputation by starching the monarch's magnificent, trend-setting ruffs. Such was the success of the new fashion fad and the sums expended on it that by 1585 there was considerable public concern at the sacrificing to 'vanity and pride [that] which would staunch the hunger of many that starve in the streets for want of bread'. Cecil, indeed, would attempt to control it from 1588 to 1601 by introducing a patent of monopoly on starch production. But the impact was limited, and as business-minded foreigners continued to arrive, so their influence expanded in other areas, too – not least of which was the production of new types of glass.

For in the wake of Edward VI's attempts to attract master practitioners away from the island of Murano and their Venetian overlords, a patent for cheaper glass, suitable for use in windows, had been granted to Jean Carré, a native of Arras trading in Antwerp. Sometime earlier in 1552, a London merchant named Henry Smith had obtained a monopoly for this purpose and further permission from the Crown to bring skilled men from Normandy. But the real breakthrough came in 1567 with the arrival of Carré, whose highly skilled and productive alien workforce were paid as much as 18s a day at a time when skilled English stonemasons earned about 1s. For their efforts, Carré's men were expected to produce three cases of glass daily with a selling price of 90s – all of which helped over time to bring about the widespread substitution of glass in place of wooden shutters in quite modest houses throughout London and the south. North of the Trent, 'window cloths' would persist down to 1600, but for many English men and women the outlook from the early 1570s was already, quite literally, decidedly brighter, as Carré's success encouraged native producers like the Strudwick family, yeomen farmers of Kirdford in Sussex who both made and carried glass (to the glaziers) as a secondary occupation. And in the meantime makers of altogether finer glass of the kind used in exquisite goblets – men like Jacopo Verzelini – had flourished on an altogether grander scale still. For by the time of his death in 1606 at the age of 84, Verzelini had not only maintained a monopoly on production – resulting in 1581 in the demolition of a rival furnace set up by would-be native competitors – but accumulated a considerable personal fortune, encompassing, among other things, numerous estates around the area of Downe in Kent, which included the manor of Downe Court, the former home of Henry Manning, Knight Marshal.

Peter Morice meanwhile, who died 1588, was an example of an innovating foreigner who not only made good in England, but contributed significantly to his new homeland's health and well-being. Though some accounts describe him as German, Morice was in fact a Dutch-born engineer who developed one of the first pumped water supply systems for the City of London. Before his arrival, the capital's citizens had been reliant for their water supplies on water from the River Thames, its tributaries, or around a dozen natural springs, including the one at Tyburn, which was connected by lead pipe to a large cistern or tank: the so-called 'Great Conduit' in Cheapside. To ensure that water was not removed for unauthorised commercial or industrial purposes, the city authorities had appointed keepers of the conduits who would ensure that users such as brewers, cooks and fishmongers would pay for the water they used, while wealthy Londoners living near a conduit pipe could obtain permission for a connection to their homes. Unauthorised tapping of conduits was common, however, and for those households without access to a gravity feed, supply still depended upon 'cobs', i.e. water carriers, or water taken directly from the Thames or from its tributary streams. Under the circumstances, improvement was essential, and in 1580, Morice duly applied to city officials for permission to construct an undershot waterwheel and pumps beneath the northernmost arch of London Bridge to supply culinary water to the city. After an impressive demonstration of the power of his pumps, which involved forcing a jet of water over the spire of the Church of St Magnus near London Bridge, he was granted a 500-year lease, at an annual rent of just 10s on one arch, which guaranteed him a level of material comfort and security wholly undiminished by either his foreign origins or intense opposition from the city's water carriers.

Albeit on a rather humbler scale than Verzelini and Morice, perhaps, most other aliens arriving in England also came with at least one eye firmly fixed upon making a healthy living in an industrially backward country where there was little competition. And the same was no less true, for that matter, of those who came first and foremost as a result of religious persecution at home, since England was not, of itself, necessarily the most attractive option in this regard. Certainly, until the sixteenth century there had been little occasion for popular migration in Europe on purely religious grounds, and nor, so far as fifteenth-century England was concerned, was there any warm welcome to be had in any case for the small minority of Europeans who had actually found themselves at odds with Latin Christianity. Lollardy, it is true, had been a significant native heresy, but it had been closely associated with political subversion and social anarchy, and duly suppressed by harsh Lancastrian legislation. During the reign of Henry VIII too, even after the breach with Rome, Lutheranism was strongly out of favour, and the best efforts of Thomas Cromwell to nurture links with European Protestantism would actually play no small part in costing him his head. Only during the reign of Edward VI, therefore, did England first offer the prospect of a general haven for refugees, to be followed by a further significant influx in the 1560s, as powerful sympathisers and patrons emerged at the Elizabethan court, and French and Spanish repression generated more widespread sympathy at lower levels. Before then, large numbers preferred to seek shelter in Hesse, the Baltic provinces and elsewhere. And if alien settlers were indeed to be found manufacturing blankets at Witney in Oxfordshire forty years earlier, it was no coincidence either that, among those punished for heresy in 1521, several were Flemings.

In other respects too, while relations with other powers remained strained, Henry VIII, like his subjects in general, would mainly continue to perceive strangers from Europe as a threat to the realm – though not without a generous application of double standards when necessity required. For in spite of the limited number of naturalisations during the reign, and proclamations like that of 1544, ordering all unnaturalised Frenchmen to depart, Henry remained perfectly content in 1536 to employ London-based foreigners to suppress the rebellion of that year. The capital's French tailors, for example, were armed with arquebuses, and given two groats a day, with one groat of drink money for every mile they marched, while Flemish shoemakers were also enlisted at the same rate, notwithstanding the fact English recruits received only sixpence a day and drink money. And it was not only individuals like Peter Baude, the French 'maker of bombards', and the German gun-founders recruited at the time of Henry's courtship of Anne of Cleves, who found themselves serving as 'providers of the King's instruments of war'. On the contrary, sundry other gunners and armourers from France, Germany and the Low Countries were busily employed for the same purpose in Southwark and Blackfriars. The Frenchman Le Caron and his associates made morris-pikes, while his countrymen worked at Sir Thomas Bowyer's saltpetre works, and an Italian cannon founder named Arcana established a gun foundry at Salisbury Court. At the same time, nearly forty workmen, almost all of them natives of Normandy, were employed at Pelham's, Wybarn's, and other ironworks – all of them becoming 'denizens', i.e. entitled to permanent residency, in 1544.

Men of more peaceful trades also made their way across the Channel – albeit at a comparative trickle – during the same reign. A solitary silk weaver came from Rouen in 1532, and two others a few years later. Dutch tapestry weavers also settled in London, and there were others of the same trade at court. Several glaziers arrived from the Low Countries and France, along with bookbinders and printers, while John Stow later attributed the making of felt hats to Spaniards and Dutchmen working at the beginning of Henry VIII's reign – though a more likely originator is a French felt hat maker arriving from Caen in 1514, followed by others of his trade arriving at intervals during the rest of the reign. As far as the capital was concerned, the newcomers mainly took up residence in the various liberties located in the precincts of monasteries, most of them in Blackfriars and St Martin's, in Westminster, and the borough of Southwark. After the abolition of the college of St Martin's under Henry VIII, furthermore, strangers occupied the houses that were built in its place, and sought to retain the privileges previously attached to it. Invariably, the freedom from the city authorities afforded by the liberties of such religious foundations made them especially attractive to foreigners, as did their sanctuary status, which, while serving as a licensed refuge for offenders, also ensured some protection against attack. Similarly, when monasteries were progressively sold off in the late 1530s, foreigners were not slow to see how they could be exploited for industrial purposes, with the result that in early 1550 Walloon weavers were established even at Glastonbury, the most noble and ancient religious foundation of all.

In this particular case, the break-up of Glastonbury's abbey was a serious loss to the town, and the installation of foreign weavers by the Duke of Somerset, who had been granted the abbey's lands and tenements, made sound economic sense for the entire area. Accordingly, dwellings were established for them, along with money for the purchase of tools and materials for the manufacture of worsted. But their English overseer neglected their interests and they appear to have fared particularly badly after the disgrace of their patron in 1549, since it was found necessary to petition the Privy Council on their behalf. Worst of all, however, was their expulsion upon the accession of Queen Mary, at which time all strangers were commanded to leave the realm. Settling in Frankfurt, where they formed no inconsiderable part of the flow of Marian exiles who assembled there, they would soon fall out once again with their English peers – this time over the Prayer Book issued by Edward VI, which many English refugees regarded as the badge of their national church. The source of the problem, as it transpired, was the single church that had been granted to both communities, with services held in French and English on weekdays, but a common rite enforced on Sundays, which the strongly Calvinist Walloons insisted upon controlling. The result was a Walloon victory, and in the process a lasting effect upon the future religious history of England itself, since the English exiles returning at the accession of Elizabeth I, who were to prove such an influence upon the new queen's religious settlement, had by then been largely won over to the Calvinist theology of their fellow Walloon churchgoers.

Even while at Glastonbury, the Walloons' minister, Valeranus Polanus, had been keen to preserve his community's distinctive religious complexion by employing the liturgy approved at Strasbourg – the so-called *Liturgia sacra, seu ritus ministerii in ecclesia peregrinorum propter Evangelicum Christi Argentinae*. And a similar preference for maintaining familiar religious rites appears to have been exhibited by most settler groups from the time that the 'first refuge' began in earnest under Edward VI. In July 1550, the 'Strangers' Church' of London was founded with royal assent under the leadership of the Polish reformer Jean à Lasco, establishing nothing less than an ecclesiastically independent congregation for the benefit of the capital's various Protestant refugee groups – an event of considerable significance in its own right at a time when the issue of religious uniformity was so hotly contested. Yet the establishment of the new church had broader ramifications still, since it symbolised not only the succour officially extended to foreign Protestants by the English Crown, but the permanence of these foreign communities, numbering perhaps 10,000 in the capital by the time of Edward's death. Before long, the Strangers' Church had divided along linguistic lines, with the former Augustinian priory of Austin Friars serving the Dutch- and Flemish-speaking exiles, the French Church in St Anthony's Hospital on Threadneedle Street ministering to those who spoke French, and the needs of the small Italian congregation being met by the Chapel of the Mercers' Company on Cheapside. Nor did Mary Tudor's proclamation of 17 February 1554 ordering the departure of all foreign residents without denizen status put paid to these churches, since as many as 40–50 per cent of the alien community appear to have stayed put in the capital, either because they had indeed acquired denizen status or were granted exemption through membership of one of the city companies, or because they simply laid low, the Privy Council receiving precious little help from the city authorities in the execution of its campaign against foreigners.

Even so, the legal disabilities applying to foreign refugees would remain a source of grievance, particularly among those arriving in the capital from the southern Netherlands in the 1560s. For while embraced on the one hand by sympathisers and co-religionists as Protestant 'brethren' fleeing Spanish tyranny, the Netherlanders found themselves once more designated under the common law merely as *strangers* of the realm, inferior in status to native Englishmen, notwithstanding the common faith both shared. One kind of discrimination, it seemed, had simply been exchanged for another, and in a letter to the queen from the 'community of strangers in London', dated 29 January 1560, the newcomers voiced their concerns accordingly, explaining the futility of religious liberty without economic freedom:

> Seeing the devotion of your Majesty, [the refugees] cannot believe that you wish those, who, for the sake of true religion and relying on your piety, have come thither, or may come afterwards, as to a free and safe place, to be precluded from the very first from your dominion … The grant of this temple [the Augustinian priory designated for worship by the Dutch] would benefit the strangers little if they had no liberty to reside and to exercise their trade here. Therefore, that no strangers be forced to return to their native country and endanger their lives, the supplicants pray you to allow all those

who ... join their community and submit to ecclesiastical discipline to live here freely without any loss of their property and without molestation of those who let houses to them, and to exercise their trades within doors till they have obtained municipal liberty from your Majesty.

Certainly, much English legal literature of the day, like *A Treatise concerning strangers received into a Commonwealth*, considered the influx 'very Prejudicall to a state' unless carefully regulated:

The Laws of England [declared the treatise concerned, which is now contained in the British Library's Harleian manuscripts] hold Strangers born, in great Suspicion of their fidelitie, toward the State, and therefore do make provision accordingly.

And the discrimination in common law extended equally to civic law and the payment of customs duties alike.

Significantly, Francis Bacon would identify four types of person specified within the kingdom's laws: alien enemy; alien friend; denizen; and natural-born subject. On this model, which may have evolved under the pressure of the movement of population during the Hundred Years War, alien friends had most of the rights of the final category, enjoying protection under the law in return for allegiance to the Crown and an obligation to take all oaths required of other subjects. Yet, in general, aliens faced several disabilities: inability to own, inherit, or bequeath real property; inability to bring legal action related to real property; inability to vote or hold high office, or to own an English ship, though they were subject to customs duties imposed by king and parliament and by corporate cities. And while most economic regulations imposed on aliens dated back to the reign of Richard II, they had been firmly reimposed by Henry VIII's statutes of 1523, 1529 and 1540. Thereafter, with regard to property rights, they were prohibited from leasing property, opening or keeping a shop, or even buying a property for their own use. Likewise, they were not allowed to engage in retail or to buy and sell items among themselves. Paying tax at double rates, they found, too, that their children were normally barred from serving an apprenticeship – a prohibition that applied equally, outside exceptions such as Norwich, to second-generation aliens who were effectively precluded from obtaining citizenship.

Plainly, the assumptions expressed in the poet laureate John Skelton's verse of 1512 resonated no less among the kingdom's ruling elites than they did within the ranks of those London apprentices responsible for the Evil May Day riots five years later:

So many Easterlings [Germans],
Lombards and Flemings
To bear away our winnings
Saw I never.

But given the accompanying restrictions on alien artisans' employment rights, it is hard to see how some flourished at all. For, while they could work and employ up to two alien journeymen without special licence, they were forbidden from taking on alien apprentices and from selling their work from home, notwithstanding their preclusion from ownership of a shop. Equally, there was the continual prospect of expulsion for them to contend with in times of war and political conflict – an impediment to any kind of long-term planning, which applied particularly to those refugees born under the nominal allegiance of a political enemy. In February 1554, non-denizen aliens had been given only twenty days to quit the realm, and in early 1558, when Francophobia peaked as a result of war, a further proclamation was issued authorising any citizen to arrest non-denizen Frenchmen. Even with denizenship acting as a personal safeguard of sorts, some resulting loss of business was virtually guaranteed at such times, and neither, for that matter, was denizen status itself altogether without drawbacks.

Naturally, the power to create such subjects lay with the Crown and the bestowal of a letter patent, but the rights conferred depended upon the specific wording of individual grants, rendering any precise definition of denizen status virtually impossible. Certainly, the required letter patent was sometimes comparatively easy to obtain, since residency qualifications seem to have been considerably flexible. Yet denizens did not enjoy full citizenship rights, nor could those rights that they did possess be backdated to before the grant. Most important of all, denizens remained unable to inherit real property, and their transmission of their status to their descendants also depended entirely upon the wording of the particular grant concerned, which might, for instance, specify only 'heirs male'. It was this last point, indeed, which distinguished denizens from the naturalised subject, although aliens could also become naturalised by a special Act of Parliament 'with the assent of the whole nation'. As a result of the prohibitive expense involved, such promotions were rare, however, and throughout the Tudor period the traditional common law ranking of the monarch's subjects applied: at the top the natural-born subject; next the naturalised alien; after him or her the denizen; and then, on the lowest rung of all, the alien. In the towns, furthermore, immigrants found it extremely difficult to join the ranks of 'freemen', who enjoyed full economic rights and, in particular, the ability to engage in independent commercial activity. Most commonly acquiring their status by serving a seven-year apprenticeship, native freemen could also do so by means of patrimony (descent), marriage, or 'redemption' on the basis of 'extraordinary means' – which few aliens enjoyed – or 'talents' of which most were deemed unworthy.

Nevertheless, the cost of a letter patent granting denization remained comparatively cheap until the 1560s at least, with sums varying from 6s 8d to £1 13s 4d, and many paying at the lower end of the scale. Yet only a minority of aliens in London became denizens during Queen Elizabeth's reign: 13 per cent in 1568, falling to 9 per cent in 1573, and 7 per cent by 1593. More curiously still, this was a time when the number of alien 'householders', i.e. those who had managed to run shops from their homes in spite of official prohibitions, was not only comparatively high but increasing from 21 per cent in 1571 to 24 per cent in 1593. Aware of this trend, the City of London had accordingly ordered all free denizens – i.e. freemen of the capital – and denizens to show their patent and demonstrate upon 'what authority they do occupy within the City', while paying 2d to the Beadle for 'recording their Copy Patent and ... for warning them'. But the requisite letter patent was by then becoming more expensive and time-consuming to receive – not least because the necessity of presenting a petition of application entailed the employment of a scrivener, while the length of time between the initial entry of the grant and its final registration was growing steadily to several months in some cases. By 1582, in fact, the fee had increased dramatically to approximately £2 12s 4d, and this was to prove an amount simply beyond the means of many aliens, especially recent ones. For the 1582 subsidy records reveal that of 1,840 aliens assessed in the capital that year, nearly 74 per cent paid merely the basic poll tax of 8d, on the grounds that they had neither goods worth £3 or more, nor land over the value of £1.

Even their better-off counterparts too, it seems, had often suffered financially due to their failure to transfer resources from abroad at the time of their flight. Many no doubt came to England in the first place without the intention of permanent settlement, making the laborious effort of selling up everything at home seem pointless. Equally, some may have kept property abroad as a form of insurance, lest a similar order of expulsion like that issued in Mary's reign should ever reoccur. But a more common explanation is that most, departing in haste and fearful for their lives, simply did not have time to sell their property, and that short-term property sales would not, in any case, have fetched the full market value. Justinne Ploiart wrote from Tournai to her brother Guillaume le Myeulx, who was living in London in February 1570, explaining how she would love to leave but could not find someone to take care of his business. And Guillaume Coppin, once a well-to-do merchant in Valenciennes, was only one among many whose fortunes were drastically altered by the decision to take what he believed would be temporary shelter in England away from his family. After he made drastic revisions to his will in 1572 – because 'by the trouble that passed in the lowe countries I lost a great deale of my goods which god has lent me' – his wife finally had to settle for the limited remains of his goods rather than the 2,700 *livres* originally promised her, while his son, who was to have had 1,400 *livres*, was left only 300, plus another 400 'when liberty shall be in the low countries and that profit and sale of my goods which are at Valenciennes may be made'. Six years in exile in England had not, then, diminished Coppin's hopes of an eventual return to his homeland, though they had certainly eroded the prospect of what awaited him there, and guaranteed the comparative discomfort of his stay, as he tried to maintain his family's interests abroad.

In the meantime, the same forces responsible for bringing Coppin and others to London were also serving to disrupt English trade, especially the embargoes of 1563–64 and 1568–73, as well as the sack of Antwerp in 1576. During 1560–72 an average of 92,600 cloths were exported annually from London, down by one-fifth from the average of 115,200 cloths in the 1550s. And this decline coincided with an enormous increase in native migration to the capital, over and above that resulting from the arrival of aliens. From 80,000 people in 1550, the figure had risen to 120,000 in the 1580s, before reaching 200,000 in 1600, making it hardly surprising that complaints about additional strangers from Europe should have risen accordingly. When the Earl of Warwick appealed in 1580 that certain aliens, under the adopted names of John Leonard and Henry Rodes, be granted freedom of the city, even he was squarely rebuffed by the Lord Mayor:

Our number of poor artificers is so great, and eaten out of their trades and livings by strangers and foreigners, that they do greatly grudge against us for overready granting of freedoms whereby we are constrained in duty and conscience and for avoiding of great misliking of governance to stay such grants.

Increasing popular pressure was clearly no longer ignorable by the municipal authorities, and by 1587 it was equally tangible at higher levels still, when the case of an Italian named Frederico, who had leased a house in London's Bear Lane, was contested by an Englishman called Jones. When judges ruled against the newcomer, his compatriots appealed, only for Sir Francis Walsingham to instruct the Lord Treasurer on 20 May that no such further leases be granted 'until her majesty's pleasure be known'.

Nor was this the only occasion when central government found it necessary to intervene, though it did so mainly with commendable caution and moderation, given the undoubted delicacy of the circumstances. On the one hand, there were repeated complaints about alien shops, which were intended to be kept 'closed' and shuttered, so that passers-by would not be tempted away from English goods. The implication was that aliens should produce only for wholesale purposes to English retailers. But it was nevertheless found necessary in 1566 for the Chamberlain of the City to be instructed in 'quiet manner', to place lattices before the windows of all alien shops opening onto the capital's streets and lanes. Even so, the trouble persisted, and in 1568 an alien was duly ordered to shut up a cordwainer's shop in Cornhill 'in the heart of the city'. More troubling still were the practices employed by some aliens to avoid such restrictions altogether. In some cases, they moved to secret or cheaper places, which had the added advantage of cheaper rents, and so it was that in March 1574 a Frenchman told the Goldsmiths Company how there were 'diverse strangers goldsmiths working some within shoemakers, some within tailors, some within saddlers, and others within others' – a particularly alarming development when the Company considered it necessary for their members to work in public areas as a safeguard against dishonesty. But as late as January 1593, an alien goldsmith was found working in a 'garret in a linen draper's house in St Martin's'. And guilds too, it seems, had difficulty dealing with what they deemed the sharp practice of alien competitors.

The Weavers of London, for instance, claimed that strangers and foreigners lived in:

> dwellings [which] are in chambers and odd corners, being divers families in one house [where they] do and may live at far smaller expense, and work for lesser gains, and sell for less profit ... And thereby have almost got all the work and employment of the said Trade of weaving.

Immigrants also, it was suggested, refused to be inspected, because when bailiffs and the Weavers Company's warden came round, they 'shut their doors against them', and illegally retailed not only their own wares but those of their counterparts in Canterbury, Norwich and elsewhere, travelling, we are told:

> from shop to shop, in London and Westminster and other places, furnishing the mercers and haberdashers therewith, and often retailing such silkwares at the houses of the Nobility and Gentry.

Apprenticeship regulations too, it seems, were being undermined by individuals feigning English parentage in order to dodge the regulation of 1574 prohibiting English masters from taking on children of alien origins. In September 1582 Bryan Savell, a clothworker, was ordered to discharge a certain Bryan Marrowe, the son of Peter Marrowe, stranger. As this was 'done in ignorance', Savell was ordered to pay a fine of only 20s. But when William Tyrone employed William Marrowe, the penalty was 40s, while Christopher Barker, stationer, was dealt with even more severely. For, in addition to a fine of 20s, he was ordered to print 'at his charges' 200 copies of the relevant Act 'for the services of the City'. Significantly, the successful conviction of this case was the work of an informer, since the City subsequently paid a reward of 10s to Gilbert Lyle, merchant tailor, 'being half the sum of 20s received of Xofer Barker'.

More controversial still than their employment as apprentices, however, was the broader issue of whether children born in England of alien parents should be regarded as English at all. It was objected by the authorities of London in 1576, for example, that:

> sundry persons being strangers … have of purpose brought over their wives from the parts beyond the seas, to be delivered with child within this city, and in other places of this realm of England, and thereof do take testimonials thereby to win those children the liberty that other Englishmen do enjoy.

It was contended, likewise, that a child of alien parents should not be regarded as English because:

> he cannot be a perfect loyal subject for that he hath no genealogie of native English but all foreign and strangers unto whom (as to his kindred) nature bindeth him.

From this perspective, it was considered unfair to grant full privileges to those children of strangers who 'retain an inclination and kind affection of their parents'. And so the debate continued until 1604 when it was finally decided to:

> place the children born within this Realm of foreign parents, as aliens and denizens.

Throughout, moreover, concerns about those freedoms that aliens did enjoy continued to exercise the minds of the 'natural born'. In September 1571, indeed, the 'Citizens of London' sent a petition to the queen, outlining seven key grievances, six of which were directed against alien merchants. The first complaint concerned the purchase of property, since, contrary to the requirement that alien merchants should dwell with their free-hosts, i.e. Englishmen, some were buying up the 'fairest houses' in the capital and seeking to 'divide them up and take in lodgers'. Secondly, it was objected that aliens hold goods and 'sell them at their leisure to force up prices', rather than fulfilling the statutory requirement of selling them within six weeks of landing. After which came two grievances centred upon the question of retail and 'foreign buying', for although forbidden to buy and sell merchandise to each other, they 'do freely amongst themselves and colourably deal by others procuring some poor freeman to bear the name'. In addition to such shadow trading, furthermore, they were charged with keeping 'private chambers', in which they sold 'by whole sale and retail', sending chapmen 'to every mans house', as well as fairs. They exported bullion overseas, flouted apprenticeship rules and, last but not least, offended by keeping themselves to themselves, 'severed from us in church, in government, in trade, in language, in marriage, though they be denized or born here among us'.

Such, in fact, was the level of dissatisfaction that the first point of the 1571 petition had actually made reference to an ancient law of hostage, requiring every alien merchant to reside with an English host, who bore responsibility for what amounted to superintending his guest. Five years later, moreover, an office of 'hostager and host' of all foreign merchants in the kingdom was given for twenty-one years to William Tipper, a freeman of the City and a grocer by trade. Italian and Hanseatic merchants were exempted, but the measure was criticised nonetheless – not least by Sir Thomas Smith, the great Elizabethan councillor, who declared it contrary to the 'Magna Carta Angliae' and to humanity. Flemish towns too, particularly Antwerp, expressed their misgivings, and the measure, which proved largely inefficient in any case, was not only soon abandoned, but followed ultimately in May 1587 by a proposition from the Privy Council that equal trading rights and liberties be granted to foreigners, strangers and freemen in London's cloth market. Economic self-interest rather than common humanity was the motive, since it had been calculated in 1582 that the queen would profit to the tune of some £12,000 in customs by allowing immigrants to make cloths 'after the manner of the Low Countries'. But as a result of the disorders of 1581 and subsequent harassment of strangers five years later, the Lord Mayor responded with a clear warning about the 'great hazard and disturbance of the common peace and state of this City', delivering the following firm rebuttal of the Privy Council's suggestion:

It is not unknown to your Honourable what griefs have been conceived and libelled of late against the strangers inhabiting among us ... The cause whereof is the diminishing and deriving away of commodities which otherwise would grow wholly to the freemen of the City and further how these mutinous intents of Apprentices and other have been whetted and set forward by certain other persons aptly disposed and qualified for spoil and sedition. Now this further liberty granted to Strangers what effect it may work in the minds of these stirring and discontented persons we leave to your Honourable to be considered of ...

Nor were attempts at liberalisation any more successful five years later when Sir John Wolley advocated in the House of Commons the application of similar freedoms to those that had brought such benefits to Venice and Antwerp. Bristling at the very prospect, Sir Walter Raleigh was quick to insist that the Dutch were self-seeking rather than worthy objects of charity, and there followed a bill to reinforce restrictions on alien merchants, which was nevertheless thrown out by the House of Lords. Plainly, there was a significant and growing gap in outlook among the country's elites, though in the resulting vacuum alien merchants continued to prosper. For in spite of their opponents' best efforts, a survey of May 1593 still enumerated some 126 alien merchants in the capital, many of whom were engaged in the export of woollen goods made in England. Economic forces, coupled to the sheer impracticalities of control and ongoing turmoil and repression abroad, had created what amounted to an irresistible process across the kingdom that no degree of popular hostility or restrictive practice could stem. In Norwich, the economic 'privileges' of aliens and their duties came to be legally defined, and the boundaries to what they could or could not do were clearly laid down. They could trade with other foreigners, sell their wares at the cloth market from one o'clock to five each day, and were permitted to send cloths to London and other cities. But like their counterparts in the capital, they could neither open shops, have premises opening directly onto the street, nor engage in retailing. Similar rules applied in Canterbury, where trading in the foreigners' commodities was limited to one specific hall. Yet no appreciable lessening of the flow of migrants to both London and the main provincial centres occurred.

What did transpire, however, was a gradual but marked withdrawal of foreign refugees into distinct and increasingly separate communities of their own. Most obvious was the increase in alien church membership. In 1568, the proportion of Dutch and French migrants attending their own churches was roughly the same as those attending English churches, and there were practical reasons for this: sheer convenience on the one hand, coupled to the fact that differences between Calvinist and Anglican services were not in themselves prohibitive. But as aliens experienced increasing antagonism, so the psychological need to protect their communities, culture and social identity appears to have increased accordingly, with the result that by 1593 their attendance at English services had halved. By then 35 per cent worshipped in Dutch churches, 34 per cent in French churches, and only 14 per cent in

English, while just over 3 per cent attended no church at all, and the remaining denizen populace were excluded from the figures. Stranger churches, predictably, were meeting places for the newly uprooted, and sources of social and emotional support for fellow countrymen. Equally, they served as centres of exchange for information concerning developments at home. But most important of all were the economic benefits provided by such churches, since they were sources of alms and relief, and their ministers were both representatives of their congregation's interests and mediators with the host population, frequently petitioning the queen and Privy Council in defence of their privileges and for protection against informers.

Yet however understandable their reluctance may have been, the failure of strangers to integrate was to remain a long-standing charge raised against them. As early as 1444, the English goldsmiths had complained how their alien counterparts took as their servants 'aliens born and never of English nation'. And it was true that between 1449 and 1469, fifteen alien goldsmiths in London took thirty-two apprentices, nearly all of them boys with Dutch names – a trend that is further confirmed by the subsidy records of 1483, which suggest that no English servants were employed in alien households. A hundred and ten years later, some success had been achieved, when a survey reported that 1,671 English servants and outworkers were employed by alien masters. But the process was a slow one and in 1571, according to another survey, all 879 male servants employed by alien masters were themselves of alien birth. Nor, if some commentators are to be believed, were these people familiarising themselves more generally with their new homeland, for, as Peter Mundy observed in the preface to his *Itinerarium Mundii* of the following century:

a straunger May live in England Many yeares and perhaps nott know Whither there are any Otters or badgers in the Countrie or noe, because hee hath nott seene Nor enquired after such, and soe consequently off some Customes, as pressing to Death etts.

Clearly, the perception that foreigners remained in but not of England would subside no more quickly than the notion that, as one petition to Parliament of 1641 put it, they 'doe thus domineere over us in our owne Trades'.

By then the fears of English apprentices who produced the petition had also extended to the 'fearfull dangers, perilous plots and conspiracies which have, and are still pretended by the papists against us', and there was a further reference to how the capital, once 'renowned in the gazing eye of the world', has suffered a loss of its international reputation as a result of alien influence:

Yet the Rights and Liberties thereof being somewhat detracted and abused, as also the Lawes and ancient Customes thereof being extenuated by some malignant and ill-affected persons, it [London] now becomes much deplorable in the sight of all men.

But another petition of the same year also returned to the perennial theme that had so exercised Elizabethan minds half a century and more before, railing against 'forreiners which keepe their residence within the liberty of this City, which in lower rooms or chambers having friends nigh unto them, take away our Custome'. Even in the midst of the greatest period of instability in seventeenth-century London, at the height of the crisis that would eventually spawn the civil war, the question of aliens still retained a place in the political mix. For in what seems to be a draft of a petition from 'the apprentices and journeymen' of the capital, dated July 1647, it duly appears as the last of eight issues cited. Predictably, the first seven address subjects of national concern, such as the implementation of the conditions specified in the Solemn League and Covenant. Yet, surely enough, the eighth represents one more complaint against the 'great abuses and insufferable injuries' caused this time by 'the sale of freedomes' to those 'Foreigners intruding into the suburbs and places near adjacent'.

No longer was the term 'forreigner' as ambiguous as it had once been, and while Londoners continued to resent native migration from the provinces, it was still the ongoing, albeit declining, arrival of newcomers from overseas, as well as the offspring of those who had first settled here, that provoked most concern and antagonism. But just how 'xenophobic', therefore, were Englishmen in general and the Tudors in particular when it came to their responses to visitors and immigrants? Certainly, generalisations are hazardous – both within and across classes, and no less so across and within regions. Important, too, is the need to distinguish between what Englishmen *said* and *did*, just as it is necessary to bear in mind the context of their behaviour at any specific juncture. Not infrequently, the historical sources are themselves questionable, and the sentiments expressed contradictory. Eighteen years before Henry VII ascended the throne, Leo of Rozmital reported after his stay in England how 'in no place were we held in so great honour as there, for both by the King and by all his subjects, wherever we travelled, we were treated kindly and honourably'. Yet the same commentator would conclude that he had 'nothing more to write about the English except that (as it seems to me) they are treacherous and cunning, plotting against the lives of foreigners …' – all of which was no less confusing than the statement three centuries later by L'Abbé Le Blanc, who accepted in one breath that 'a Frenchman is much better received in London, than an Englishman at Paris', but that 'the bulk of the English nation bear an inveterate hatred to the French'.

In between times, foreigners themselves were frequently apt to draw a keen distinction between their reception among gentle and common folk. Writing in 1561, the Dutch physician Levinus Lemnius reflected as follows on his experience of the English:

> Every gentlemen and other worthy person showed unto mee (being a straunger borne and one that never had been there before) all pointes of most friendly curtesy, and taking me first by the hand lovingly embraced and bad me ryghte hartely welcome ... Therefore, franckely to utter what I thinke of the incredible curtesie and friendliness in speche and affability in this famous realme, I must need confess, it doth surmount and carye away the prick and price of all others.

'They that half suspect and have not had the full triall of the maners and fashions of this countrey,' he added, 'will scarcely be perswaded to believe.' And in 1602, Friedrich Gerschow, tutor to Philipp Julius, Duke of Stettin-Pomerania, was no less impressed by the friendliness and helpfulness of England's elites, whom he found 'polite in manners and gestures'. Yet whenever visiting or resident foreigners felt threatened or insulted, the blame was invariably laid squarely upon the shoulders of 'the common sort', 'the apprentices', 'the mob', 'the meaner sort of people' or their like. In 1497, Andreas Franciscus reported that Londoners 'look askance at us day by day, and at night they sometimes drive us off with kicks and blows of the truncheon', while Giacomo Soranzo, Venetian ambassador, wrote in August 1554 how 'the nobility are by nature very courteous, especially to foreigners, who however are treated with very great arrogance and enmity by the people'. On his visit to England in 1545–46, Nicholas Nuncius drew a similar distinction between his genteel hosts and 'the street boys and apprentices' of London, which was echoed in 1592 by Jacob Rathgeb, private secretary to the Duke of Württemburg. Even Englishmen themselves like Fynes Moryson noted with embarrassment how visitors to his country's capital 'are sometime arranged by the insolency of the baser sort of Prentisces, serving men, Dray men, and like people'.

Turning from words to action, moreover, there is little doubt, as we have seen, that invective and gestures could sometimes result not only in individual acts of violence but in shocking civil disorder, though descriptions, even here, were often prone to exaggeration, as demonstrated by the old ballad describing the Evil May Day riots of 1517:

For thousands came with Bilboe blade,
As with an army they would meet,
And such a bloody slaughter made
Of foreign strangers in the street,
That all the channels ran with blood ...
And hundreds hang'd by martial law,
On sign posts at their masters' doors ...

But the contemporary chronicler Edward Hall suggests an altogether more balanced picture, revealing that although about 1,000 people were involved in the disturbance and an unknown number of aliens' houses attacked, no life at all was taken. Likewise, only thirteen rioters, plus a broker named John Lincoln who had been a prime instigator of the troubles, were actually convicted of treason and executed. Certainly, the fury and intensity of the upheaval is indisputable. But the concerted response of the city authorities, the ensuing charges of high treason rather than riot and the draconian punishment handed down by Lord Edmund Howard of half-hanging, mutilation and live disembowelment are likely to explain the lack of future disorder, since there is no evidence of any outright breach of the peace on such a scale throughout the remainder of the sixteenth and into the early seventeenth centuries.

In any case, the next serious threat of trouble in the capital came only after the mid-century spike in immigration, when it was reported that:

500 or 600 men waited on the Mayor and Aldermen of London, complaining of the late influx of strangers, and that by reason of the great dearth they cannot live for these strangers, whom they were determined to kill up through the realm, if they found no remedy.

Remedy, moreover, was indeed found in the form of a survey of strangers conducted by the mayor and aldermen, and the enactment of precautionary and restrictive orders, which appear to have prevented any actual disturbance. Equally, despite the suggestion of the Spanish ambassador that the cause of the trouble was the sight of a thousand foreigners gathering at Austin Friars, a more potent underlying source was the prevailing political crisis and severe social distress, both of which had provoked fears of a more general insurrection in London and its neighbouring counties, and resulted in the mustering of the armed bands. Four years later, in response to a Crown proclamation authorising the harassment of French subjects at English ports after the breakdown of Elizabeth's alliance with the Huguenots, a number of Frenchmen were imprisoned in London, and it would take two further proclamations before the resulting commotions died down. But when other threats of violence were reported in 1567, 1586–87, 1593 and 1595, they came to nothing.

In 1567, John Stow recorded that 'a great watche' was kept in London for the week following 17 February, and that:

> the occasion of this watche was thrwghe a portar who went about to dyvars prentises, tellynge them that nyght folowynge wowlde be ye lyke stire against straungers as was at Evyll May Day …

Significantly, however, Stow also recorded how some of these apprentices informed their masters, who in turn informed the Lord Mayor of what was afoot. As a result, the porter responsible for the rumour was hanged in Cheapside the Friday following, and a survey of the number of strangers was taken, which was distributed to the capital's Livery companies to be read to their members. Once again, the threat of disorder had been nipped in the bud, and it was by such straightforward means that periodic restlessness among 'the poorer sort' was kept firmly in check over the next two and a half decades – until, that is, the last significant threat to the immigrant communities of Tudor England eventually occurred in 1593. By which time, their difficulties had become so marked that on 10 August Petrus Plancius wrote from Amsterdam to Assuerus Regenmortell in London, encouraging resettlement from England to Harderwijk, 'as it is rumoured that the ill feeling of the English against the Netherlanders increases more and more …'

A popular libel of that year, recorded in the fourth volume of Strype's *Annals of the Reformation*, contained the following diatribe:

> Doth not the world see, that you, beastly Brutes, the Belgians, or rather Drunken Drones, and faint-hearted Flemings; and you, fraudulent father, Frenchmen, by your cowardly Flight, from your own natural Countries, have abandoned the same into the Hands of your proud, cowardly enemies, and have by a feigned Hypocrisy, and counterfeit shew of Religion, placed yourselves here in a most fertile Soil, under a most gracious and merciful Prince.

And the invective was also accompanied by an explicit warning:

> Be it known to all Flemings and Frenchmen, that it is best for them to depart out of this Realm of England, between this and the 9th of July next. If not, then to take that which follows. For there shall be many a sore Stripe. Apprentices will rise to the number of 2336. And all the Apprentices and Journeymen will down with the Flemings and Strangers.

A rhyme set upon the wall of the Dutch churchyard advised all strangers to 'Conceive it well, for Safe-guard of your Lives, Your Goods, your children, and your dearest wives'. And when Parliament went on to debate a bill restricting foreigners' rights to sell by retail, Sir Walter Raleigh once again lost no opportunity not only to echo the popular hostility in general circulation, but to add a new dimension, firmly rooted in international political and economic rivalry:

> For first, such as fly hither have forsaken their own King; and Religion is no pretext for them, for we have no Dutchmen here, but such as came from those Princes where the Gospel is preached … The Dutchman by his Policy hath gotten Trading with all the World into his hands, yea he is now entering into the Trade of Scarborough Fishing, and the Fishing of the New-found-Lands … They are the people that maintain the King of Spain in his Greatness. Were it not for them he were never able to make out such Armies and Navies by Sea; it cost her Majesty sixteen thousand pounds a year for the maintaining of these Countries, and yet for all this they Arm her Enemies against her.

Conveniently blurring the distinction between the Catholic southern and Protestant northern Netherlands, Raleigh had affirmed that refugees from those provinces in rebellion against Spanish rule had actually fled a government sympathetic to their cause, while others had arrived, in effect, from a territory not only loyal to Philip II but key to the success of his empire, which England was struggling, at considerable expense, to resist.

Notwithstanding its manifest distortions, it remained, in the context of the time, a powerful argument, and on 27 March 1593, the bill under discussion, which had apparently been brought forward by the City of London, was indeed carried in the House of Commons by a majority of 162 to 82 voices. Yet on this occasion, too, there were dissentient voices, such as those of Sir John Wolley who declared how:

> this Bill should be ill for London, for the Riches and Renown of the City cometh by entertaining of Strangers, and giving liberty unto them.

Sir Edward Dymock, in his turn, was inclined to lay blame for the problems of English retailers firmly upon the shoulders of 'our home Ingrossers', while claiming that it was native, rather than alien merchants, who were mostly responsible for the export of English coin. Others pointed to the religious and moral example of the stranger community, and invoked scriptural precept as grounds for a more tolerant attitude. Sir William Cecil also counselled moderation, though the most significant event of all was to occur four days after the bill's acceptance by MPs, when it was comprehensively rejected by the House of Lords. By which time, 'several young men' associated with the initial offending libel had been not only placed in the stocks, but carted and whipped as an example to other would-be troublemakers.

Even under circumstances of extreme economic dislocation – involving prolonged dearth, plague, atrocious weather, and further plague – London therefore avoided the kind of violence against alien settlers that the authorities feared so intensely. When Anthony Munday finished his play, *The Book of Sir Thomas More*, in 1601, the Master of Revels, Edmund Tilney, whose role included stage censorship, forbade its performance, as a result of its depiction of the Evil May Day riots. In a speech purportedly revised by Shakespeare himself, More delivers the following rebuke to the aggressive mob, which is baying for the banishment of foreigners:

> You'll put down strangers,
> Kill them, cut their throats, possess their houses,
> And lead the majesty of law in lyam
> To slip him like a hound;
> Alas, alas! Say now the King,
> As he is clement if th'offender mourn,
> Should so much come too short of your great trespass
> As but to banish you: whither would you go?
> What country, by the nature of your error,
> Should give you harbour? Go you to France or Flanders,
> To any German province, Spain or Portugal,
> Nay, anywhere that not adheres to England,
> Why, you must needs be strangers, would you be pleas'd
> To find a nation of such barbarous temper
> That breaking out in hideous violence
> Would not afford you an abode on earth.
> Whet their detested knives against your throats,
> Spurn you like dogs, and like as if that God
> Owed not nor made not you, not that the elements
> Were not all appropriate to your comforts,
> But charter'd unto them? What would you think
> To be us'd thus? This is the strangers' case
> And this your mountainish inhumanity.

Relying on human empathy to make his point, the fictitious More therefore asks the on-stage crowd, and by extension the theatre audience, to imagine what it would be like to be an asylum seeker undergoing forced repatriation. But Tilney's instructions to the author can be still be seen in the margin of the original folio submitted to him:

> Leave out the insurrection wholly and the cause thereof, and begin with Sir Thomas More at the Mayor's sessions, with a report afterwards of his good service done being Sheriff of London upon a mutiny against the Lombards – only by a short report, and not otherwise, at your own perils. E. Tilney.

Sensitivities were plainly still such that the efforts of moralising playwrights might not be well received by the 'meaner sort'.

Yet notwithstanding such misgivings, and taking into account the scale of the influx, the process of immigration was certainly met with higher levels of tolerance – both in London and in other towns – than stereotypes of Tudor England have often tended to suggest. When Norwich's conspiracy 'to expulse the strangers from the city and the realm' was discovered in 1570, it had as much to do, arguably, with the rising of the Northern Earls and the disgrace of the Duke of Norfolk as it did with the alien population, which was then on its way to a peak of 40 per cent. Nor would there be any further evidence of violence against foreigners until 1685. At Sandwich, where by 1574 aliens accounted for 2,400 alongside an indigenous population of 4,900, we likewise search in vain for violence, though by 1582 measures had been introduced to encourage the removal of those not of the Flemish congregation. Rye, too, had found itself in the 1580s with an influx of strangers, numbering in excess of 1,500 out of a population of perhaps 4,000, which had made prices 'so excessive dere' and left 'divers houses being too much pestered with them'. But while plans were laid in 1586 for the removal of some, the town's mayor and jurats still felt able to accommodate 1,000 and to extend to them 'all the courtesy' they were due, regardless of their general poverty and the considerable number of mariners from Dieppe that had also swollen numbers. In Colchester, the addition of roughly 1,000 foreign residents to a town that housed only 4,000 led the corporation in 1580 to require the removal of all who were not members of the Dutch congregation, as well as those who had arrived within the past fortnight. No more were to be admitted without the written consent of the aldermen and bailiffs, since 'there are a great number of strangers inhabiting within this town presupposed more than the town can well sustain and bear'. Yet this was the only occasion when expulsion of any kind was suggested, and smaller immigrant communities elsewhere, which were arguably more vulnerable in view of their size, remained largely free from harassment. This was certainly true for the small French-speaking community of Southampton, which by 1596 constituted just 297 out of a population of 4,200, and applied equally to places like Maidstone and Yarmouth.

As the seventeenth century dawned and the Tudor age gave way to the Stuart, indeed, England's 'strangers' were already on their way not only to acceptability but respectability, perceived increasingly as members of civil societies who had arrived for conscience's sake and now conformed themselves to the law. At Canterbury in 1623, the Dean and Chapter would testify that the Walloon congregation:

> for many yeeres past, and still do very religiously, obediently, orderly and civilly demeane and behave themselves towards God and all the Kings Majesties officers, and others in these parts for any thing we have heard to the contrary.

And in the same declaration, there was a further testament to their industry and diligence and the good example they set. At the height of his dispute with the foreign churches in the 1630s, moreover, even Archbishop Laud was prepared to accept that 'their Congregations were beneficiall to the English, especially poor', and that the congregations at Colchester, Canterbury and Sandwich in particular 'did set a great number of English at work'. Clearly, there had been many contradictions in attitudes to foreigners in Tudor England, and a good deal of residing ambivalence. But the newcomers were staying and by the end of Tudor age, English men and women not only knew it, but were increasingly inclined to accept it.

6

MINDS AND CREEDS

What, my lord, shall we build houses and provide livelihoods for a company of buzzing monks, whose end and fall we ourselves may live to see; no, no, it is more meet a great deal that we should have a care to provide for the increase of learning and for such as by their learning shall do good in church and commonwealth.

Bishop Hugh Oldham, patron of Corpus Christi College,
Oxford, to Bishop Richard Foxe, 1517

In its culture, as in its geography, England in the early sixteenth century still lay stubbornly on Europe's edge. Separated from the continental land mass by a narrow channel of water, at one point not much more than 20 miles across, it had somehow escaped the impact of major European developments, or received them late and altered by their sea journey. Indeed, for those who read the history of the first Tudor's reign against the background of the Italian Renaissance, it is difficult from some perspectives to believe that they belong to the same world. Already, when the Battle of Agincourt was fought, Ghiberti was at work on the Baptistery doors of Florence's cathedral, Brunelleschi was 38 and Alberti 11. Seventy years later, when Richard III was killed at Bosworth, Botticelli, Perugino and Ghirlandaio were at the height of their careers. And when Henry VII breathed his last, at the time that the last glories of the Perpendicular style were rising in King's College Chapel and Bath Abbey, Michelangelo was painting the Sistine Ceiling, Raphael the *Stanze*, and the foundations of Bramante's new St Peter's were freshly laid. Even Henry's tomb – with its bronze effigies of himself and his wife, fashioned by Pietro Torrigiani of Florence – was no more at best than an augury for the future. Lying within a screen still in the old style, created by the English artist Laurence Imber, it had not been begun until three years after the king's death, and the choice of Torrigiani was in any case his son's. Nor were native artists quick to follow its example. On the contrary, the classical sarcophagus at Westminster, decorated with candelabra shapes, wreaths, winged putti and childlike angels of pure Italianate beauty, would, it seems, merely impress rather than inspire. And when the Renaissance style eventually became popular at the end of the century, it would involve a typical compromise of traditional elements and Italianate features adapted via France and Flanders.

That England should have been thus marginalised, both intellectually as well as artistically, was hardly surprising. For communication, whether by land or sea, with the great Italian cities was still primitive, and the condition of the kingdom was hardly conducive to the cultural refinements evolving elsewhere. A land of small towns, fifteenth-century England had no tradition of urban culture when Henry VII fought his way to power, and while the heads of the great baronial families looked to war and internal territorial expansion as their most rewarding enterprises, there was little prospect of aristocratic patronage for art or literature. The English nobility was rural in wealth, influence and outlook – a world, if not a universe, removed from the cultured patriciate of Florence. And lone individuals like Humphrey, Duke of Gloucester, youngest brother of Henry V, could hardly make good the difference. Remembered today for his patronage of Oxford and in particular 'Duke Humfrey's Library' in the Bodleian, to which he contributed 280 precious manuscripts, he was a patron of the poets John Lydgate and John Capgrave among others, and corresponded with many leading Italian humanists, in addition to commissioning several translations of Greek classics into Latin. His friendship with Zano Castiglione, Bishop of Bayeux, also led to many further connections on the Continent, including Leonardo Bruni, Pietro Candido Decembrio and Tito Livio de Forli. But the poets of pre-Tudor England, unlike their continental counterparts, were never members of a royal court. Instead they were mainly monks, baronial officials and civil servants. And if a minority of late medieval English chroniclers such as Thomas of Walsingham might boast some literary credit, the rest were mainly content to record no more than the repetitive trivia of municipal officialdom.

The legends of gods and heroes, the tenets of astrology, and the stories of Boccaccio had all been available a century earlier and provided material for Chaucer, as well as Gower's *Confessio Amantis* and Lydgate's *Troy Book*. Old texts in the new 'humanist' script had also found a market in England by the third quarter of the fifteenth century, while John Shirwood, Bishop of Durham, not only knew Greek as well as Latin, but built up an important private collection of classical texts, which by 1464 included a copy of Pliny's *De Viribus Illustribus* in the new script. A handful of other churchmen like William Grey, the future Bishop of Ely, and even a baronial leader like John Tiptoft, Earl of Worcester, had also come back from Italy with new attitudes to culture. Yet any prospect of widening the field of patronage was effectively swallowed by the very wars with France that eventually cost Humphrey of Gloucester his life. And when those wars were followed by the internal conflict known to posterity as the Wars of the Roses, waged by the English magnates who had at last been driven from their French territories, any prospect of serious cultural intercourse with Europe duly withered on the bough. For the resulting poverty and instability were reflected at the royal court itself where no fifteenth-century monarch other than Edward IV enjoyed more than a decade of settled power. Nor would matters alter suddenly when Henry VII finally arrived to impose his will on a kingdom that still presented a potential to defy its monarch. The humanist Bernard André was appointed King's Librarian in 1492 and Latin Secretary three years later, and in 1499 Erasmus visited England for six months, befriending scholars like John Colet and Thomas More who were among a new breed of their countrymen anxious to assimilate the 'New Learning' from abroad. But these remained little more than ripples in a slow-flowing stream, not least because large-scale intellectual discourse through print had not existed before the middle of the fifteenth century.

In July 1485, William Caxton issued Malory's *Morte d'Arthur* from his printing house in the precincts of Westminster Abbey at the Sign of the Red Pale in Tothill Street, near the dwelling houses of many of the rich wool merchants who were his patrons. And by 1491 he had gone on to issue ninety-three works in all, not only sowing the seeds for the emergence of modern English prose as almost a second classical language, but popularising vernacular literature and creating a native reading public. A capable translator from three languages – French, Latin and Dutch – Caxton was responsible for the publication of effectively all the English poetry, romances, chronicles and devotional works then extant. And as Governor of the English Nation at Bruges, an association of merchants who dealt not only in wool but also in spices, he had also travelled. In 1471, indeed, he first saw one of the new printing presses at Cologne, and went on to print his first book at Bruges four years later – an English version of the French *Tale of Troy*. After which, translations of Boethius and Cicero – along with the *Sayings of the Philosophers*, which was translated from the French by the king's brother-in-law Lord Rivers – would follow from his Westminster press.

But for all his broader significance, Caxton remained, from certain perspectives, a populariser who made insufficient use of the new art of printing by an over-emphasis upon what amounted, by European standards, to comparatively lightweight works. Of those books that survive, 45 per cent are religious, 12 per cent are official publications, and only 29 per cent (including works by Chaucer and Gower) strictly literary. Not until 1510, moreover – some nineteen years after his death – did Caxton's presses abandon his favoured black-letter type for one based on the Italian script already widely adopted abroad. In breaking new ground, he was looking backward all the while, it seems, and it is of no small significance, perhaps, that his most noteworthy successors in England's capital were almost all foreigners. Working from premises in Westminster, Southwark, St Paul's Churchyard, Fleet Street and elsewhere, men like Peter Treveris from Trier in Germany, the Dutchman Steven Mierdeman and Julian Notary, a native of Vannes on the south coast of Brittany, eventually helped a handful of Englishmen such as William Rastell and Robert Wyer both to generate and satisfy the needs of what would eventually become a burgeoning reading public. Yet in 1530 it was still a Frenchman, Thomas Berthelet, who was appointed King's Printer by royal charter. A resident in the parish of St Dunstan in London's famous printing quarter where Fleet Street lay, Berthelet would assume responsibility for the printing of royal proclamations and statutes, and by 1549 had been awarded his own coat of arms for his sterling efforts on the government's behalf.

More than any other, however, it was a native of Alsace, Wynkyn de Worde, and to a lesser degree Richard Pynson of Normandy, who took printing in England along new paths. Both, it seems, had been Caxton's assistants. But de Worde improved the quality of Caxton's work as a typographer and moved English printing away from its late-medieval beginnings toward a recognisably modern model. Where Caxton, for instance, had depended more heavily upon noble patrons to sustain his enterprise, de Worde shifted his own emphasis to the creation of relatively inexpensive books for a commercial audience and the beginnings of a mass market. Equally, where Caxton had used paper imported from the Low Countries, de Worde exploited the cheaper product of John Tate, the first English papermaker. As a result of the consequent reduction in costs, de Worde was therefore able to publish more than 400 books in over 800 editions, including children's books, works on good housekeeping and animal husbandry, as well as a range of romantic novels and poetic works, including those of John Skelton. And while only twenty of Caxton's editions contained woodcuts, around 500 of de Worde's were illustrated. In all, Pynson printed more than 500 books during his lifetime – including a translation of the German Narrenschiff by Sebastian Brant – and would himself attain the rank of King's Printer in 1506 at an annuity of two pounds later rising to four, before achieving the rare distinction of naturalisation seven years later.

Between them Pynson and de Worde actually printed about two-thirds of all books entering the English market between 1500 and 1530, working alongside other foreigners like Jean Lettou, William Machlinia and Jean Barbier. Yet the Act of 1523, forbidding any alien to take apprentices other than Englishmen and limiting them to two foreign journeymen, would have an effect upon their activities hardly less damaging than another measure, passed eleven years later, forbidding the importation of foreign books. As a result, it was left to Englishmen such as John Rastell to pick up the mantle as best they could with works that included *The Pastyme of People, the Chronycles of dyvers Realmys and most specially of the Realme of England* (1529), a text dealing with English history from the earliest times to the reign of Richard III. But their output was less skilfully executed and less wide-ranging in scope, and in the meantime the interest in classical literature, which had already made such headway in much of Europe, continued to languish accordingly. For between 1479 and 1520, only thirteen translations from Latin into English were published, of which six were translated indirectly from French. All of them were moralistic, some narrative in tone, but the absence of drama, history, satire, lyric or rhetoric remains striking. Aside from Boethius and Cicero, the authors selected were Aesop, Cato, Frontinus, Lucian, Ovid, Sallust, Terence and Virgil, but Catullus, Horace, Juvenal, Livy, Lucan, Plautus, Seneca, Statius and Tacitus – to name only the more obvious examples – were omitted. Equally, the style of the translations is poor and the quality of the English, with the exception of work by Caxton and Alexander Barclay, is hesitating and marred by a tendency to multiply synonyms in order to blanket the precise meaning of the Latin. More often than not, the intention was simply to instruct the kingdom's elites in the principles of governance and especially the virtues of martial prowess – as was the case with Barclay's translation of Sallust's *Jugurtha*, which makes clear in its dedication to Thomas Howard, 1st Earl of Surrey and victor of Flodden, how the Jugurthine war should be taken as a piece of practical advice 'bothe pleasaunt, profitable and right necessary: but especially to gentlemen whiche coveyt to attayne to clere fame and honour: by glorious dedes of chivalry'.

And this same strictly utilitarian approach was echoed throughout the first half of the sixteenth century. In 1544, Sir Anthony Cope published an account of Hannibal and Scipio, based largely on Livy's *History* and dedicated to Henry VIII at the very time that England was embroiled in war with both France and Scotland. On this occasion, the author observed how the example of the two worthy captains of Carthage and Rome, would help men to:

learne bothe to dooe displeasure to theyr enemies, and to avoyde the crafty
and daungerous baites, which shall be layde for them.

Elsewhere, too, history was used by English translators as little more
than a wider tool of instruction for their rulers. John Brende, for example, printed Quintus Curtius's *History of the Acts of Alexander* in 1553 and
dedicated it to the Duke of Northumberland, with the specific aim of
demonstrating 'how daungerous it is to begin *alteracions* [i.e. altercations]
in a common welth', while Nicholas Smith's translation between 1554
and 1558 of Herodian's *History of the Roman Emperors* was intended, in
effect, as a practical manual highlighting the characteristics of good and
bad rule. Important portions of Thucydides, Livy, Caesar and others were
likewise turned into competent English, only to be used as guidebooks
for governors, alongside Cicero's *De Officiis*, which was translated in 1540
by Whytington and more significantly by Grimald in 1553, for the purpose of serving as a general guide to social conduct. In all cases, the aim
was narrowly didactic rather than literary. And in the process, the figures
of classical epic were represented to all intents and purposes as modern
Europeans, no different in motive, speech and action from contemporary
fifteenth- and sixteenth-century figures. As a result, the fictitious characters of Virgil's *Aeneid*, no less than pseudo-historical heroes like Hannibal,
Scipio and Alexander, not to mention the actual nature and operation of
ancient states themselves, all became quite literally lost in translation for
would-be English readers.

In the meantime, however, the first stirrings of a more adventurous spirit – and one more akin to developments associated with the 'New
Learning' abroad – were at least beginning to be felt in England's universities.
Cambridge, on the one hand, was slowly shedding its former reputation as
the cosy nesting place of unguided youth, and gradually becoming a place
of more exacting standards and competition. No longer quite the home to
riotous high jinks and dissolute living it had undoubtedly become after the
fleeting brilliance of its medieval heyday, it was emerging, in fact, as a more
ordered and rigorous society, as a result of reforms that Bishop John Fisher,
in particular, would bring to fruition after his appointment as the university's
vice chancellor in 1501. Under Fisher's influence, colleges such as St John's
and Corpus Christi were established, and the first freshening breeze of an
altered approach to instruction began for the first time to blow away the cob-
webs from Cambridge's ancient cloisters, though, as the bishop himself would
freely acknowledge in an oration before Henry VII delivered in 1506, there
had been much ground to make up when he first arrived as a callow student
twenty-three years earlier:

At the time when your majesty first showed your concern for us, learning had begun to decline among us. This may have been the result of constant litigation with the town, or of the frequent plagues that beset us so that we lost many of our leading scholars, or of the lack of patrons of learning. Whatever the cause, we should indeed have been reduced to despair had not your majesty shone down upon us like the rising sun itself.

For a scholar of Fisher's uncompromising rigour and hard-edged honesty, of course, the characteristically blunt reflection on Cambridge's recent past was hardly surprising. But he was not alone in bemoaning his university's previous shortcomings, and in a letter of 1516 to his old pupil Henry Bullock of Queens' College, Erasmus himself commented that 'about thirty years ago, nothing was taught at Cambridge but Alexander [de Villa Dei], the *Parva Logicalia*, as they are called, those old dictates of Aristotle, and the questions from Scotus'.

By contrast, Oxford had for some time boasted a closer connection with developments abroad, and assembled a more glittering array of scholars immersed in the intellectual ethos of the Italian Renaissance. William Grocyn, reader in divinity at Magdalen from 1481 to 1488, had, for example, studied at Florence under Demetrius Chalcondylas and Politian, before returning to Oxford to deliver what is likely to have been the first ever set of lectures on the Greek language delivered there. Thomas Linacre too, that other great champion of English humanism, who was also at Oxford between 1480 and 1485, had graduated in medicine from the University of Padua, and thereafter spent some further time in Italy as a member of Lorenzo the Magnificent's 'academy' before returning to his homeland. There he eventually taught Thomas More and gave Erasmus his grounding in Greek. Taking the whole Italian world – including Rome, Venice, Bologna and Vicenza – within his sphere of interest, he would become physician to Henry VIII and founder of the Royal College of Physicians, while John Colet, Dean of St Paul's, was another who had returned from study in Italy in 1496, bringing with him a new style of scriptural exegesis, applying the principles of Renaissance classical scholarship to biblical texts. Even the occasional nobleman, indeed, like William Blount, 4th Baron Mountjoy, who was appointed 'companion of studies' to the future Henry VIII in 1499 for the purpose of reading history with him and improving his Latin composition, felt the influence of these figures. For in addition to befriending Grocyn and Colet, he had been accompanied by his chaplain and Richard Whitford, a fellow of Queens' College, to complete his formal studies in Paris, after which Erasmus became one of his tutors.

Instrumental to the exposure of Oxford to new influences had been the administrator, diplomat and scholar, Bishop Richard Foxe, who was not only a great sponsor of humanist studies within the university, but the founder in 1517 of Corpus Christi College. Within the preamble of the college's founding statutes, he had made clear his views on the function of learning:

> We have no abiding city here, as saith the Apostle, but we seek one to come in heaven at which we hope to arrive with greater ease and dispatch if while we travel in this life, wretched and death-doomed as it is, we rear a ladder whereby we may gain a readier ascent. We give the name of virtue to the right side of the ladder, and that of knowledge to the left ... We, therefore, Richard Foxe, by Divine Providence, Bishop of Winchester, being both desirous ourselves of ascending by this ladder to heaven and of entering therein and being anxious to aid and assist others in a similar ascent and entrance, have founded, reared and constructed in the University of Oxford, out of the means which God of his bounty hath bestowed on us, a certain bee garden which we have named the College of Corpus Christi, wherein scholars, like ingenious bees are by day and night to make wax to the honour of God, and honey, dropping sweetness, to the profit of themselves and of all Christians.

More significant still, however, was Foxe's commitment to the employment, where necessary, of foreign scholars to deliver the four pillars of Latin, Greek, Hebrew and Divinity, upon which the college's curriculum was to rest:

> And if no person in our College shall be found competent in the judgement of the President and the electors for the office of any lecturer vacating, or if any person in our College be found competent, and yet a stranger shall be found more learned ... then we will that he shall be preferred to that office and as public lecturer before all the fellows and scholars of our College ...

Yet the priorities of the founder of Oxford's newest and most prestigious college were, of course, themselves indicative of England's late start in emulating the scholarly achievements of its European counterparts, not to mention the comparative shortfall in native talent. Linacre, for example – along with Richard Croke, Richard Pace and, perhaps, Grocyn – was one of the very few who had really assimilated the new philology that was so central to uncovering the true meaning of classical and indeed biblical texts in Europe. He had sat at the feet of Politian, as well as meeting Ermolao Barbara in Rome, and his mastery of Greek was such that Aldus gladly included his Latin translation of Proclus on the sphere in the *Scriptores astronomici veteres*. Some of the Greek commentators of Aristotle, and especially Simplicius and Alexander of Aphrodisia, are also known to have aroused Linacre's interest, though it was his Latin translations of Galen that gave him a European reputation, while his Latin syntax proved hardly less famous and was widely used in teaching in European schools. In other respects, however, the approach of many of England's leading scholars lay far less obviously at the cutting edge of what was occurring across the Channel.

Certainly, the first elements of a sea change in outlook were at work, which was evident also at the royal court, where the papal collectors, Giovanni Gigli and Polydore Vergil found patronage, along with their countryman, Pietro Carmeliano, who became the first holder of the office of Latin Secretary, established by Henry VII. Even more influential in encouraging England's links with intellectual developments abroad was Thomas Wolsey, who ensured advancement within the state bureaucracy for lay scholars and churchmen like Richard Pace, Richard Morrison, John Clement, Richard Sampson and Cuthbert Tunstall – all of whom had travelled widely in pursuit of the New Learning. At the same time, Cardinal's College, Oxford, was another impressive testament to Wolsey's hopes for the spread of liberal humanism among the next generation, some of whom, like Thomas Starkey, would soon be gathering far away in Padua, to continue their apprenticeship in scholarship in places like the household of Reginald Pole, kinsman and future critic of Henry VIII. Yet John Colet, for example, who exerted so great an influence on Erasmus, was primarily a theologian with a leaning towards humanism of the more esoteric kind, represented by Ficino and Pico, rather than the more critical type associated with Barbaro and Politian. In Italy, moreover, Colet learnt no Greek, and continued thereafter to believe that the prime task of the humanist agenda was simply to rid theology and biblical interpretation of the misapprehensions spawned by medieval scholasticism. Even Thomas More, for that matter, never visited Italy. Certainly, he had attended Linacre's course on Aristotle's *Meteor* during his truncated residence at Oxford, and both Linacre and Grocyn had taught him Greek, after which his work on Plato and translations of Lucian would confirm his undoubted mastery of the language. But the fact remained that the author of *Utopia* and the man usually hailed as England's greatest home-grown humanist was not a philologist in any strict sense and belonged once again with Colet, among those for whom the New Learning was essentially a religious tool, subservient to Christian revelation, rather than a broader instrument for uncovering the treasures of classical learning in general.

In fact, the teaching of Greek at English universities began only in 1511 when Erasmus arrived in Cambridge, and thereafter it was left mainly to Henry Bullock to keep its study alive until the appointment of Richard Croke to a readership in 1518. A pupil of Grocyn who had also been taught by Erasmus at Cambridge and Aleandro in Paris, Croke was a pure-bred philologist who had previously lectured at Cologne, Louvain and Leipzig, and whose edition of Ausconius was actually the first humanist edition of a Latin poet by an Englishman. But for all his merits, Croke, no more than the author of *Utopia*, could match the standing of Guillaume Budé in France or figures like Johannes Reuchlin in Germany, let alone the galaxy of Italian trailblazers who preceded them. And neither could Oxford or Cambridge, for all their recent progress, bear genuine comparison to their competitors abroad. Paris, for example, had stood for centuries as the main bulwark of scholasticism in Europe, while continuing to attract the best minds from other countries. But in 1458, the study of Greek also began there and by 1508, when the Italian scholar Aleandro was lecturing to large audiences on Greek, Latin and Hebrew, the New Learning was firmly established. Upon Aleandro's departure in 1516 to take up the post of Vatican Librarian, moreover, Budé was already poised to assume not only the leadership of French humanism, but arguably that of European scholarship in general. Certainly, no English scholar could bear serious comparison to his achievements.

Originally a law student at the University of Orléans, the Frenchman had in fact developed an interest in Latin and Greek in the 1490s and began learning the latter language from an elderly tutor at around the age of 24. In 1502, he started an exhaustive investigation into the *Pandects* of Justinian, the basic textbook of Roman law, corrected the entire text, added an explanatory commentary and published the whole in 1508. He then wrote a treatise on classical numismatics, which was published in 1515 under the title *De Asse*. Both were works of immense erudition in their own right, earning him the title 'marvel of France' from Erasmus – and rightly so, since the annotations to the *Pandects* referred not only to the law, but also to the language, literature and society of the ancients, while the treatise on currency shed light on a dense and hitherto unknown subject. Writing with equal facility in both Latin and Greek, Budé would be instrumental in persuading Francis I to found the Collegium Trilingue – afterwards the Collège de France – and the library at Fontainebleau, which was ultimately removed to Paris to become the origin of the Bibliothèque Nationale. He would also, in 1529, produce *Commentarii linguae Graecae*, an extensive collection of lexicographical notes, which further boosted the study of Greek literature in his native country, and later persuaded Francis I to refrain from a prohibition upon printing that had been urged by the Sorbonne in 1533. Widely hailed as the most erudite scholar of the entire Renaissance, Erasmus would write thus of him:

> You have preferred to be understood by the learned, I, if I can, by the many; your aim is to conquer, mine to teach or persuade.

And the same could well be said for Budé's German counterpart, Johannes Reuchlin, a Bavarian born in 1485, who started as a scholar of Greek but established his reputation ultimately as a student of Hebrew. Like Colet in England, his aim was to open the Bible, and in particular the Old Testament, to criticism and to balance what both he and Erasmus considered the excessive contemporary absorption in pagan literature. But the more conservative aspects of his approach were executed with a depth of philological inquiry that led him to produce the first Hebrew grammar in western Europe, and made him the foremost Hebrew scholar of his day, an authority on medieval Jewish philosophy, and one of the founders of New Testament criticism. He published two treatises, *De Verba Mirifico* (1494) and *De Arte Cabbalistica* (1517), and his Latin dictionary became a mainstay for early English translators such as John Skelton, who used it extensively in making his version of Diodorus Siclius's *Bibliotheca Historica*.

Undoubtedly, as the century progressed, England found itself more fully abreast of the intellectual climate established in Europe, not least because of developments in education. For by the 1550s the belief that learning was largely the preserve of clerics was already a thing of the past. On the one hand, there remained the old grammar schools, often refounded on the basis of ecclesiastical predecessors like Westminster School, the King's School, Canterbury, and the King's School, Worcester. But many grammar schools were new, arising from the initiative of town authorities, who often petitioned the Crown for funds from the grant of monastic lands or obtained the necessary money from other sources. At Hull, Chelmsford and elsewhere new grammar schools came into existence – including one at Stratford, where Shakespeare may in due course have become a pupil – and by 1600 there were some 360. Girls too, albeit in a minority of cases, were being equipped with the educational tools required to access the best elements of learning and culture in the wider world. The last Tudor ruler herself, like Lady Jane Grey, was a case in point. At the age of 12, Elizabeth was said by the Italian poet Pietro Bizari to be 'a perfect mistress of the Italian tongue', in the learning of which Signor Castiglione was her principal master. Roger Ascham, moreover, confirmed her ability not only in Italian, but in French, Spanish and Latin, and she herself is reported to have said (in French) that she was half Italian – '*me semble que je suis demie Italienne*'. Equally accomplished were the daughters of Sir Anthony Cooke, one of whom, Mildred, became the mother of Sir Robert Cecil, Secretary of State under Elizabeth I, Lord Treasurer under James I. Another daughter, Anne, would become the mother of Sir Francis Bacon.

And in the meantime a change in the whole direction of educational outlook was affecting not only the universities but remoulding the objectives for which an education was sought in the first place. If theology remained – at least in theory – queen of the arts, she found her court dwindling steadily in the face of gathering competition from mathematics, astronomy, cosmography and philosophy, as Oxford and Cambridge both began to attract more and more sons of the nobility and gentry. Usually staying no more than a year or two and often exhibiting the time-honoured bad habits of their social class along the way, they would nevertheless gain at least a passing acquaintance with broader intellectual horizons than their forebears, as well as a familiarity with the more exacting standards of contemporary learning. For by now students were not only being taught different things, but being instructed more intensively, on the growing assumption that scholarship was just as much a means of entry into State office as it had once been a precondition for advancement within the Church. Outlining a plan to reform the teaching at Cambridge in a letter to Bishop Ridley of 1549, Edward Seymour, Duke of Somerset, expressed the new outlook thus:

> We are sure that you are not ignorant how necessary that study of civil law is to all treaties with foreign princes and strangers, and how few there be at this present to do the king's majesty's service therein.

If England was to prosper in the wider world beyond her shores, she could no longer, it seems, rely on the brawn and bravery that was such an object of contempt among Shakespeare's Frenchmen in *Henry V*, who spoke contemptuously of their adversaries' love of beef and lack of 'any intellectual armour'.

Yet the scale of England's educational 'revolution', even at this point, should not be overestimated. 'Eloquence without godliness,' warned Thomas Becon, 'is a ring in a swine's snout,' while Sir John Cheke, Regius Professor of Greek at Cambridge and tutor to Edward VI, placed no less emphasis upon the study of the scriptures than upon the secular philosophy of the ancients. Even the most influential educationist of the day, Sir Thomas Elyot, was to observe in *The Book named the Governor*, published in 1531, how intellectual training should be set within certain specific limits. 'Continual study,' he warned, 'without some manner of exercise shortly exhausteth the spirits vital.' In his view:

> … The most honourable exercise … and that beseemeth the estate of every noble person, is to ride surely and clean on a great horse and a rough, which undoubtedly not only importeth a majesty and dread to inferior persons, beholding him above the common course of other men, daunting a fierce and cruel beast, but also is not little succour, as well in pursuit of enemies and confounding them, as in escaping imminent danger, when wisdom thereto exhorteth.

Plainly, there were distinct limits in Tudor England to the principle of educa-tion for education's sake and limits no less to the rank of those for whom education should be made available. For if grammar schools were expand-ing in number, so events in Europe had also increased the emphasis among England's elites for the maintenance of hierarchy and order. Elyot was of the generation, after all, which had witnessed in 1525 the dreadful consequences of the Peasants' Revolt in Germany, and this had been the time, too, of the Anabaptists who menaced the whole established order with their biblical commonwealth in Münster, a revolutionary, egalitarian society of terrifying significance. Fully conscious of the need to prevent any popular misapprehen-sions about his book, it was not entirely coincidental that Sir Thomas More had preferred to publish *Utopia* in Latin, and nor should it be forgotten that Cromwell's Injunction of 1538, ordaining that an English Bible be placed in every parish church, was followed by the statute of 1543, stringently restrict-ing Bible reading to a narrow section of the community.

But while education would remain the preserve of gentlemen in Tudor England, it was also perceived increasingly as their most distinctive hallmark. It was better, wrote one contemporary, 'for the ploughman's son to go to the plough, and the artificer's child to apply the trade of his parent's vocation,' while the gentleman's children 'are meet to have the knowledge of govern-ment and the rule of the commonwealth' – a view echoed by Sir Thomas Smith, writing in 1561:

> For whosoever studieth the laws of this realm, who studieth in the universi-ties, who professeth liberal sciences, and to be short, who can live idly and without manual labour, and will bear the port, charge and countenance of a gentleman, he shall be called master, for that is the title which men give to esquires and other gentleman.

With a cultured court presided over by a queen who saw herself in a special role as a patron of the arts, and a nobility that, for all its masquerades and formal splendours, was increasingly an educated class of service, it was inevita-ble that the minds of gentlemen as a whole should become more accessible to a much broader range of cultural influences. And since these influences were almost exclusively European in origin, the implications were equally inescap-able: namely, that Europe itself should be perceived henceforth as the home of new and civilised ideas rather than an unfamiliar realm of weird and far from wonderful ways.

Unsurprisingly, of course, the old prejudices were not to vanish overnight, any more than the hair-raising travellers' tales of the hazards – physical and moral – of continental travel, which lost nothing of their piquancy for successive generations. Even late in Queen Elizabeth's reign, William Cecil was to warn his son against crossing the Alps, where a man would learn nothing but atheism, blasphemy and vice. But in cultural and intellectual terms at least, the changing ethos was amply reflected in the new interest in translations, dating from the 1560s. Versions of Italian romances, for example, poured forth from a variety of quarters at the same time that the works of Petrarch, Boccaccio, Tasso and Ariosto were becoming almost as revered as those of Homer and Virgil. In the first half of the century, by contrast, the dissemination of Italian literature in English versions had hardly begun, and while the content of Castiglione's *Il Corregianio* (The Courtier) was known to upper-class Englishmen like Sir Thomas Wyatt and Henry Howard, Earl of Surrey, Hoby's version did not appear until 1561. Thereafter, the real 'courtiers' in the Italianate tradition would prove to be Raleigh and Philip Sidney, and the most powerful imitators of Italian poetry and music the late Elizabethans. Hitherto, with the notable exception of Chaucer, the standard of native verse and prose and indeed the English language itself had left much to be desired, as John Skelton reflected early in the century:

> Our natural tongue is rude
> And hard to be ennewed
> With polished terms lusty.
> Our language is so rusty,
> So cankered and so full
> Of forwards and so dull,
> That if I would apply
> To write ornately,
> I wot not where to find
> Terms to serve my mind.

Of the earlier poets, he found the English of Gower 'old', with his matter vastly superior to the manner in which he expressed himself, while Lydgate was diffuse and difficult to follow. Only 'that famous clerk' Chaucer – 'pleasant, easy, plain, no word he wrote in vain' – was worthy of comparison to his European counterparts. Yet in 1569, at the age of only 17, Edmund Spenser was to produce a translation from Petrarch that heralded, arguably, the wealth of later outpourings from Sidney, Marlowe, Raleigh, Bacon, Donne, Jonson and, of course, Shakespeare.

Key to all was patronage, derived from five main sources, which had hitherto been in short supply compared to Italy as well as France. For apart from the queen herself, both the great provincial nobility and State office holders, as well as courtiers and indeed the wealthy citizens of London, endorsed the new embrace with mainstream European culture in a way that had been only dimly foreshadowed in the preceding decades. Spenser, in particular, understood the situation perfectly by accompanying the printed version of the *Faerie Queene* (1590) with dedicatory sonnets to the Lord Chancellor, ten noblemen, three knights and two noble ladies, along with a final verse to 'all the gracious and beautiful ladies in the court'. Significantly, one of those patrons mentioned was the Earl of Essex, head of the faction to which Spenser himself belonged. But there were lesser courts scattered throughout the provinces where the landed aristocracy likewise exercised a considerable cultural influence, which took its most visible form in the building, or vast extension, of castles and palaces incorporating European influences of various kinds. Burghley House in Northamptonshire, with its 360ft-long front, built in 1577–84, was a truly international creation, which depended for its construction upon German workmen, Flemish designs and French textbooks such as Philibert de l'Orme's *Nouvelles Inventions* (1561). Montacute in Somerset, built between 1588 and 1601 for Edward Phelips, a successful lawyer and Master of the Rolls, was another provincial building reflecting, albeit more modestly, what by then were becoming the customary continental influences. And then, of course, there was Sir Thomas Gresham's Royal Exchange, erected between 1566 and 1570 and designed by the Flemish architect, Henri de Pass. All were different, yet each could only have been built in the more cosmopolitan Elizabethan age.

Not all structures were so successful, perhaps. Kirby Hall in Northamptonshire, begun for Sir Humphry Stafford in 1570, employed as its chief mason Thomas Mason who, in attempting to display in spectacular measure the influence of the Renaissance in English architecture, eventually helped to produce what was arguably an extraordinary mixture of sophistication and bucolic ignorance. But while earlier buildings, for reasons of political insecurity and tradition, had turned inward on themselves, often emphasising defence at the expense of refinement, places such as Longleat were outward-looking both literally and figuratively, reflecting self-confidence, security and ostentation. For they were constructed not only with their owners in mind, but to host and impress the queen herself as she progressed between them. On the most famous of these occasions, at Kenilworth in 1575, she stayed for three weeks to a veritable festival of the arts. But there were numerous other times and places where her visits acted as a cultural spur. Whether in London at the Inns of Court on Lord Mayor's Day, at the universities or St Paul's School, the effect was the same. The Inns of Court put on the work of Shakespeare and Ben Jonson, while some noblemen like the Earl of Leicester kept their own company of players. At the same time, other leading men in Church and State encouraged both native and European scholars to live as tutors and secretaries in their households. Thomas Whythorne, the composer, lived under the patronage of Matthew Parker, Archbishop of Canterbury; John Harte, the antiquary and spelling reformer, lived as a tutor to William Cecil's wards, as did other distinguished scholars such as Lawrence Nowell and Sylvius Frisius.

Yet in assimilating continental norms and influences, Elizabethan England never fully lost sight of its own. Certainly, a spell in Italy, especially Venice and Padua, was by now considered an important phase in the education of any poet. Indeed, to Sir Philip Sidney, as to so many of his contemporaries, such visits proved indispensable. His poem *Arcadia* is indebted not only to the Greeks Heliodorus and Homer but to Sannazaro, too, and he seems likely to have met Tasso during this same great formative period. But the same work is no less medieval and Protestant in tone. Even more striking as an example of the merging of continental approaches with English domestic culture is Spenser's *Faerie Queene*, which, in reflecting the contemporary Italian epic, nevertheless reaches back to Chaucer and Malory, and at the same time presents as its central figures an Arthur who is essentially Spenserian and Tudor, and a Gloriana who is, of course, Elizabeth herself. So, too, with Shakespeare who, in many respects, can be seen as the culminating point of the English Renaissance in the whole range of culture. The extensive study of classical models dating back to the influence of humanism upon education earlier in the sixteenth century; the influence of Terence, Seneca, the classical poets, the modern Sannazaro and Petrarch; the abundant material of the ancient histories available in Sir Thomas North's translation of Plutarch's *Lives*; the whole humanist dream of the perfectibility of human reason; all these, and much else originating in Europe, finally gave form, thought and substance to the magisterial achievements of the bard. But in Shakespeare as in many of his contemporaries, this was combined with quintessentially English elements, so that in *Macbeth*, *Hamlet* and *Lear*, his material was drawn in many cases not from the classics but from the great school of English historians of which the chronicles of Raphael Holinshed, published in 1577, was the best example. Shakespeare's comedies likewise show his debt to the Elizabethan rediscovery of the classics, but *A Midsummer Night's Dream* is arguably as English as anything the language has produced.

In painting, moreover, continental influences were much less marked. In 1506 Baldassare Castiglione was sent on a diplomatic errand to England by the Duke of Urbino, Guido da Montefeltro, who had been created a Knight of the Garter. As a token of gratitude, he brought with him a picture of St George, specially painted for Henry VII by Raphael, in which the saint wore the Garter. Significantly, however, it was the first Italian painting by an important artist to reach England, and it would remain an isolated item. Half a century later, indeed, the Tudor court's painters were still foreigners: William

Scrots from Brussels, Antonio Mor, and the Flemish-born Hans Eworth (1520–74), all of whom provided a service and fulfilled a need, but left no English protégés. The Queen of Hungary lent Mary Tudor a portrait of her husband Philip, painted by Titian, until she had 'the living model in her presence'. But it was perhaps the only great Renaissance painting in England at the time, and even Hans Holbein the Younger – who worked in Henry VIII's court from 1526 to 1528, and again from 1532 until his death from the plague in 1543 – complained how in England 'the arts freeze'. Born in Augsburg, one of the main centres through which Italian influence would penetrate Germany, Holbein was confined in the main to depictions of Henry VIII straddling the Privy Chamber (1537) and portraits of hard-faced courtiers like Sir Henry Guildford and unimaginative officials such as Sir Richard Sachaverell, along with the anonymous men and women who served such individuals. Significantly, Holbein established no native school of painters. Instead, it was through his designs for triumphal arches, gold and silver goblets, book bindings and similar applied decorations that he did most to plant the elements of a Renaissance style in England. And after his passing, the portraits of the aristocracy and gentry continued to be painted by foreigners such as Marc Gheeraedts of Bruges. In fact, the only significant English artists, even of this later period, were miniaturists, such as Nicholas Hilliard (c.1547–1619) and Isaac Oliver (c.1556–1617) – the second of whom was in any case the son of a Huguenot refugee.

Musically, by contrast, the English were less insular – until, that is, the breach with Rome took its toll upon both styles and the nature of patronage. Half a century before Henry VII ascended the throne, the English composer John Dunstable, who worked in both England and France, was influential across Europe. Writing in around 1440, the Burgundian poet Martin le Franc praised Dunstable's music, approving of its *contenance angloise*, i.e. 'English aspect', characterised by the use of 'sprightly consonance' and sophisticated harmonies. And the reign of Henry VIII witnessed a surge in both continental influences and foreign musicians at the royal court. The choir of the king's Chapel Royal, described by a Venetian diplomat in 1515 as 'really rather divine than human', was founded upon a repertoire of works by its English members, including Robert Fayrfax, William Cornish, Avery Burton and Thomas Tallis. But choirbooks of continental motets were copied for Henry and Catherine of Aragon, and the melody for Henry's own 'Pastime with good company' is likely to have been drawn from a chanson published in Paris in 1529. Likewise, the lutenist and composer Philip Van Wilder arrived from the Netherlands not only to play and instruct in his own right, but to run a group of 'singing men and children' in the Privy Chamber. And with him came others, like the Bassano family, a group of Jewish recorder players recruited by Thomas Cromwell as part of the preparations for Henry VIII's marriage to Anne of Cleves. Victims of the Spanish Inquisition, they were ultimately given refuge in England, since they 'owed loyalty neither to the pope nor to Luther'.

Yet the self-same religious tensions that had helped secure a place at the royal court for the Basanos would also serve to stifle other influences from abroad, not least because ecclesiastical patronage of music itself underwent a marked decline. As the madrigalist Thomas Whythorne put it:

> in time past music was chiefly maintained by cathedral churches, chantries, guilds, fraternities &c. But when the abbeys and colleges without the universities with guilds and fraternities, &c. were suppressed, then music went into decay.

Under Elizabeth I, of course, the company of the Queen's Musick, directly employing some sixty musicians, boasted some greatly distinguished performers and composers including Thomas Tallis, Thomas Morley and William Byrd. But while further patrons such as the Earl of Leicester, Christopher Hatton and William Cecil also came forward to fill the gap, along with networks of others like the Kytsons and Petres in East Anglia, and the Talbots and Cavendishes in the north, support in general declined. And in consequence the flow of foreign musicians declined accordingly. Unlike their English counterparts, Italian gentlemen who had no knowledge of music, reflected Thomas Whythorne, were considered 'rudely and basely brought up', and Whythorne's own autobiography tells a depressing story of travel from one tutor's post to another, plying his trade in private houses where musicians were treated merely as minstrels, and considered by beggars and rogues 'to be their companions and fellows'. The madrigal, invented in Italy, became, it is true, the most popular musical form in Elizabethan England, while its most gifted exponent, the lutenist John Dowland, achieved international fame as a result of appointments at the courts of Germany, Italy and Denmark. But, as religious divisions grew, Dowland would subsequently find himself under suspicion of espionage on his travels, while composers like William Byrd would have no choice but to adapt musical styles in accordance with the changing political dictates of the day. In riding out the tumultuous religious changes of the reigns of Edward VI, Mary I and Elizabeth, Byrd, indeed, would prove infinitely adaptable in tailoring his musical repertoire to suit the prevailing climate at any one time, and when so much musical output was connected to church ceremonial, it could hardly have been otherwise.

Another kind of tension, however, was evident in England's first responses to the new scientific thought slowly emerging on the Continent. In 1543 the

Polish monk Nicholas Copernicus published his *Revolution of the Heavenly Spheres*, but it was not until 1576 that Thomas Digges became the first Englishman to come down firmly in print upon the side of Copernicus's theory. In *A Perfect Description of the Celestial Orbs* Digges described how:

> in this our age one rare wit (seeing the continual errors that from time more and more have been discovered, besides the infinite absurdities in their Theoricks, which they have been forced to admit that would not confess any mobility in the ball of the Earth) hath by long study, painful practice, and rare invention delivered a new Theorick or model of the world.

Nor, perhaps, was it surprising that, as a protégé of John Dee, Digges should have stood out as a proponent of such ideas, since Dee himself, unlike many of his English contemporaries, had indeed travelled widely. In 1548 he was studying at Louvain after graduating at St John's College, Cambridge, and becoming an original fellow of Trinity College. And further study followed in Brussels, along with a lectureship, while still in his early twenties, on Euclidean geometry at the University of Paris. He studied, too, with Gemma Frisius, became a close friend of the cartographers Gerardus Mercator and Abraham Ortelius, and mixed likewise with leading continental mathematicians such as Federico Commandino in Italy. But in other respects England's links with developments abroad remained tenuous. On the Continent, the Netherlander Andreas Vesalius, who lectured at Padua, had published the first book of modern anatomy, *On the Fabric of the Human Body*, in 1543 in Basle. And as the century progressed some similar work based on personal observation in connection with gunshot wounds was produced by Englishmen like John Gale and William Clowes, both of whom had seen active service abroad. More significantly, John Caius, now remembered chiefly for the foundation of Gonville and Caius College, lectured and dissected at Cambridge after study under Vesalius and Giovanni Batista Monte at Padua. Yet as late as 1577 the chief surgeon of St Bartholomew's Hospital was still content to rewrite a fourteenth-century treatise on the subject of anatomy, while Elizabethan England's most significant scientist of all, William Gilberd, conducted his work on magnetism without ever leaving his country's shores. Admired by both Kepler and Galileo, he was criticised nevertheless by Francis Bacon, who also, incidentally, refused to acknowledge Copernicus at a time when heliocentrism had become widely accepted elsewhere.

Paradoxically, in fact, the breach in relations with the Roman Catholic Church, which had acted as such a brake on the development of scientific thought in the first place, did not serve to liberate Englishmen intellectually to nearly the degree that might have been expected. On the contrary, the

problems raised by the work of Copernicus, which threatened the whole cos-
mological system of the Church, as well as the medical researches of Vesalius
and his successors that undermined hallowed concepts of the human body,
not to mention new work emerging in mathematics and geography, all bred
grave doubts on the English side of the Channel too, which John Donne in
the early seventeenth century was to express so vividly. Francis Bacon might
indeed set out, on the one hand, to lay down a universal system of knowledge based on inductive reasoning, while William Harvey is rightly hailed
for breaking new ground in the fundamentals of human anatomy, but these
vanguard figures of the intellectual revolution dawning in Europe found
themselves curiously at odds with radical Protestants at home, for whom –
like the Roman Catholics they so vehemently opposed – the Bible remained
the unchallengeable source of authority about man, God and the world order.
In Parliament, pamphlet and sermon alike, many of these so-called 'Puritans'
preached in fact on behalf of a conservative conception of society pre-dating
the Renaissance that remained stubbornly resistant to much of what they
saw in the secular world around them – elements that had originated abroad.
And their intransigence was accompanied by ongoing restrictions on free-
thinking, reinforced by the kind of episcopal control differing surprisingly
little from what had gone before. As such, the very forces that had initially
loosened the stranglehold of Rome on religious belief would therefore serve
in England's case not so much to broaden intellectual liberation as to counter
it, and in doing so, leave the country more separate from Europe than ever
now that its spiritual links had been ended.

It was no small irony, of course, that the Roman Catholic Church had
never been more securely entrenched in England than upon Henry VIII's
succession in 1509. On the one hand, the so-called '*Ecclesia Anglicana*' – a term
encompassing the entire clerical estate within the kingdom – was not only
firmly protected by sanctions and support from its base abroad, but powerfully
strengthened by wide-ranging privileges and immunities enshrined in native
law and consecrated by long custom. At the same time, its leading bishops
were central to the council of the king, whose bureaucracy, such as it was,
still largely comprised clergymen. The Church's services were necessary, in
fact, on all important occasions in life – at christenings, marriages and funer-
als. But its courts also determined all matrimonial cases, ratified or refused to
ratify all wills, and took cognisance, too, of any and every transgression of the
moral law, rendering both the fornicator and the village scold alike subject
to its punishment. And this was still merely the iceberg tip of Rome's more
general influence upon the fabric of everyday life, since merchant guilds and
craft guilds still boasted their own thriving chantry chapels to succour the
souls of their departed, while, besides administering all charitable funds, the

clergy almost entirely controlled education and hospitals, amply assisted at
other levels by the kingdom's parish churches, which remained indispensable
centres of social life. The English, noted the Venetian ambassador in 1497, 'all
attend Mass every day and say many paternosters in public ... They always
hear Mass on Sunday in their parish and give liberal alms.' And their churches
bore ample testament, it seemed, to the scale of their devotion, since there
was not a single one, according to the ambassador, 'so mean as not to possess
crucifixes, candlesticks, censers, patens, and cups of silver'. Some, like the one
at March in Ely, had been given rich, gay timber roofs, while at Peterborough
fan-vaulted chapels were built on to the east end of the cathedral. And kings
had been more generous still. For Edward IV had lavished considerable sums
on St George's Chapel at Windsor, and even Henry VII's natural parsimony
had not prevented him from providing liberally for his chapel at Westminster.

Church-building and decoration was not in itself, of course, a guaranteed
token of more general religious zeal, let alone unwavering allegiance to the
papacy. Henry Parker, the fifteenth-century Carmelite friar who wrote *Dives
et Pauper*, pointed out that were these things done 'for devotion and for the
worship of God ... I trow this land passed all other lands in worshipping of
God and Holy Church'. 'But I dread me,' he added, 'that men do it more for
pomp and pride of this world to have a name and worship thereby in the
country.' Nor, for that matter, were pre-Reformation churches in England
always as directly centred upon God and his adoration as might otherwise
have been expected. 'In some churches,' wrote one foreigner observer, 'are
suspended the eggs of ostriches and other things which cause admiration
because rarely seen.' Worse than this curio shop function, however, was the
habit of using places of worship as places of general assembly, so that booths
set up in Exeter cathedral during fairs, and at places like St Paul's in London,
became crowded not only with lawyers and merchants, but with pickpockets
and prostitutes intent upon furthering their trades. Elsewhere, the parishioners
of All Saints' Church Gresford in Wales, like so many others throughout the
length and breadth of England, were understandably proud of their miraculous image of the Virgin, which brought queues of pilgrims and offerings
from all over the country, 'by reason whereof ... the church of the said parish
was strongly and beautifully made erect and builded'. Not only that, but 'the
inhabitants of the town and parish, with divers others, were not a little aided
and favoured towards the better sustentation of their living' by the devoted
tourist industry that they sedulously harvested.

But if pious eyebrows were being raised in certain more earnest quarters,
the likelihood of any significant confrontation let alone rift between the
English State and Roman Church remained minimal, not least because the
Church itself was so anxious, wherever possible, to accommodate the wishes

of the princes falling under its theoretical ambit. In 1208, Innocent III had suspended all church services in England, and excommunicated King John, to impose Stephen Langton as Archbishop of Canterbury. Yet Henry II, who had made humble submission to Rome after Thomas Becket's murder, ultimately achieved most of his objectives, while the confrontation between Edward I and Archbishop Winchelsey in 1297, over royal taxation of the clergy, had resulted in a speedy resolution in the king's favour. Even in 1341, when Archbishop Stratford claimed that Edward III was infringing the privileges of the clergy over jurisdiction and taxation, and subsequently excommunicated several Crown servants, the eventual outcome was a compromise solution, in which both sides backed down. And when Clement VI's appointments of clerks to English benefices proved too numerous, the result was the Statute of Provisors – a countermeasure enacted by the government in 1351 and followed by further restrictions four decades later. Churchmen themselves, significantly enough, had protested against papal intrusion at that time, and when Martin V appointed Bishop Henry Beaufort his legate *a latere*, the nomination was successfully rejected by both Henry V and Archbishop Chichele. Thereafter, there was no serious conflict between England and the Holy See, merely disputes over abuse rather than struggles over principle. And nor was it ever likely to be otherwise when so many leaders of the English Church were themselves royal officials, with no taste for constitutional crises, and when hard political reality guaranteed that a king, with the assistance of his lay magnates, could invariably bend the clergy to his will. As a result, English bishops gladly embraced royal authority, and in return kings readily supported churchmen against heresy and lay critics of their role.

If anything, indeed, the first two Tudor kings had been courted even more diligently by Rome than their predecessors, since from the 1480s onwards the papacy needed their support not only to strengthen political control over the Papal States but to mount a crusade against the Turks, who had captured Constantinople in 1453. Innocent VIII, for example, readily issued a bull of excommunication against claimants to Henry VII's throne before granting him a dispensation to marry Elizabeth of York, and later vindicating the marriage between his son, Prince Henry, and Henry's brother's widow, Catherine of Aragon. Equally significantly, both Henry VII and Henry VIII were not only allowed to nominate to the English episcopal bench at will, but to translate bishops from see to see, and to obstruct the collection of papal taxes. The former, indeed, even received papal support for a reduction of the important clerical immunities of right of sanctuary and benefit of clergy (the immunity of the clergy from secular law), so that at the start of the century the Venetian ambassador could write with some conviction how England was virtually independent of the Holy See. Norman historians, he said, recorded that

William the Conqueror did homage to the pope but 'the English histories make no mention of this, and it is a forgotten thing'. And in the meantime, the financial contributions exacted by the Vatican remained comparatively light, since in an average year the early Tudor monarchs were actually deriving two-and-a-half times as much money from the English Church as the pope himself. Large numbers of the laity, in their turn, were regularly applying to Rome for indulgences and dispensations from the requirements of canon law. Indeed, so popular were indulgences that during 1498 and 1499 an estimated 2,000 English priests were obliged to request plenary indulgences from the pope on behalf of their lay parishioners.

Even the sullied reputation of the papacy itself, for that matter, had no more destroyed the allegiance of most Englishmen to the see of Rome than the commitment of their kings to the faith they considered themselves born to protect. Lewd tales heard outside the Flaminian Gate in Rome had certainly lost nothing in the telling by the time they reached English shores, while stories that in Italy were lightly dismissed as little more than merry yarns continued to excite grating indignation in London taverns and Cotswold cottages alike. Some popes, as not a few of the king's subjects well knew, had become far more renowned for their toxicological wizardry than for their pastoral gifts as 'Vicars of Christ', while others, such as Julius II, seemed to confirm the Papacy's widespread reputation for greed and immorality. Not only did this particularly dazzling example of papal excess personally conduct an armed vendetta against his rivals in vice, the Borgias, but he did so in specially commissioned silver armour. Yet when Julius was elected in 1513, the mayor and aldermen of London attended a *Te Deum* at St Paul's in honour of the occasion, and nationwide prayers for the Holy Father and the good of the Church continued to be offered up long afterwards. In 1490, they had been commanded in conjunction with similar prayers for the king and his realm, and even as late as 1527 they were directed to the restoration of the pope's liberty, following the sack of Rome. Less than a decade earlier, moreover, after the subjugation of the Holy Land by Selim the Grim's Ottoman Turks, the very ruler who would break England's links with the papacy was, as we have seen, aflame with enthusiasm for Leo X's earnest appeal for aid from Christian knights.

But beneath such characteristic effusions, there were also tensions with England's most enduring and seemingly indestructible bridge to mainland Europe. For while State and Church remained in comparative harmony, certain sections of the laity were much more hostile to clerical privileges and what was increasingly widely perceived as foreign interference. Common lawyers, on the one hand, detested the right of benefit of clergy and made strenuous efforts to legislate against the practice in the parliaments of 1512 and 1515, while many town corporations resented the rival jurisdiction of ecclesiastical institutions, and on occasion became involved in unseemly disputes with the heads of cathedrals and monastic houses. In 1506, for example, the sheriff and gaol-keeper of Norwich became involved in a brawl with the prior of the city's Benedictine cathedral priory, who was seeking to rescue one of his servants recently arrested by municipal officers. Four years later, Archbishop Warham of Canterbury was acknowledging the laity's hostility, and in 1512 Dean Colet of St Paul's was openly blaming the wickedness of the clergy for such widespread hatred, which would surface so starkly over the case of Richard Hunne, a London tailor who had died suspiciously in the Church's custody after raising a legal challenge in the ecclesiastical courts over payment of a mortuary fee that had involved the confiscation of his infant son's burial robe. So great was the resulting uproar in the City of London that the affair was picked up by the Parliament of 1515, and led ultimately to royal intervention in defence of secular jurisdiction. Before the 1520s were out, furthermore, Simon Fish, a barrister of Gray's Inn, would publish his famous *Supplication of Beggars*, which amply reflected the full venom of the Church's most vociferous critics. In it, amongst other things, he denounced the pope as a 'cruel and devilish bloodsupper drunken in the blood of saints and martyrs of Christ', while the clergy in their turn were depicted as immoral perverters of God's word, causing Fish to beseech his sovereign 'to tie these holy idle thieves to carts to be whipped naked about every market town'.

Whether such extremism was common is no more certain, of course, than sweeping claims about the incidence of clerical malpractice in general. But if Rome was not hated, neither was it loved. And there were other forces at work, from Europe itself, which would further estrange England from its traditional spiritual links to the Continent. For the works of Martin Luther had eventually arrived in England in 1518, about a year after the initial upheaval in Germany that had accompanied the nailing up of the 'Ninety Five Theses' on the door of All Saints' Church, Wittenberg. Introduced by German merchants operating in London, Luther's ideas had soon gained currency among sections of the capital's merchants and within university circles, particularly at Cambridge. And nor did the momentum stop there. For by the mid-1520s William Tyndale's English translation of the New Testament had not only been completed in Antwerp and printed in Germany, but was flowing into England, too. As a result of the direct assistance of Merchant Adventurers in Antwerp, indeed, the author had been provided with both a home on the Continent and financial support. And in the meantime the influx of other heretical works had encouraged Wolsey to conduct a ceremonial burning of Lutheran works outside St Paul's Cathedral in 1521 – the same year in which Henry VIII joined the reaction with his *Defence of the Seven Sacraments*. But neither king nor cardinal could rebottle the genie, as anticlerical misgivings and theological undercurrents ultimately became supercharged by a royal change of heart over, first, the king's marital and then his religious loyalties – all suitably magnified by what was to become, under Thomas Cromwell's influence, a potent burst of State-fuelled nationalism.

No other document would better capture the propaganda slant of the entire Henrician Reformation, with its emphasis upon the pope as a foreign potentate, than the preamble to the 1533 Act in Restraint of Appeals, forbidding legal redress to Rome and trumpeting England's return to her destiny as a great and independent nation, under one supreme monarch answerable to none but God:

> Where by divers sundry old authentic histories and chronicles it is manifestly declared and expressed that this realm of England is an empire, and so hath been accepted in the world, governed by one supreme head and king, having the dignity and royal estate of the imperial crown of the same, unto whom a body politic, compact of all sorts and degrees of people divided in terms and by names of spirituality and temporalty, be bounden and owe to bear next to God a natural and humble obedience ...

Before the following year was out, moreover, the entire process had been sealed by a measure no less emphatic in asserting England's liberty from external interference. For if the Act of Supremacy did not quite reach the power of language of the previous measure, it lost nothing in the boldness and grandiloquence of its central message:

> Albeit the King's Majesty justly and rightfully is and oweth to be the supreme head of the Church of England, and so is recognised by the clergy of this realm in their Convocation; yet nevertheless for corroboration and confirmation thereof, and for increase of virtue in Christ's religion within this realm of England, and to repress and extirp all errors, heresies and other enormities heretofore used in the same, be it enacted by authority of this present Parliament that the King our sovereign lord, his heirs and successors of this realm, shall be taken, accepted and reputed the only supreme head in earth of the Church of England called *Anglicana Ecclesia* ...

Henceforth, one item of Italian political literature above all others gained a special relevance to the English scene when Cromwell set in motion the translation of Marsiglio of Padua's *Defensor Pacis*, a fourteenth-century treatise adumbrating the elevation of secular over ecclesiastical authority. For

England was now turning its back on Europe's 'universal church' once and for all. Hopes for reconciliation remained high, it is true, after the death of Catherine of Aragon in January 1536 and the execution of Anne Boleyn several months later. Yet such expectations were unfounded, as the new course became confirmed by the Act Extinguishing the Authority of the Bishop of Rome in 1536; by the dissolution of the monasteries in the same year; and by the preceding execution of prominent opponents, such as Sir Thomas More, John Fisher and the London Carthusians. Now convinced that the King of England's disobedience was irreversible, Pope Pius III duly activated an earlier bull of excommunication against him, and gave his blessing to the northern rebels involved in the Pilgrimage of Grace.

But if Henry VIII had rejected Rome, he was also unwilling to embrace those same German Protestants who had triggered the assault on the papacy in the first place. 'What serpent so venomously crept in as he who calls the Most Holy See of Rome "Babylon"?' wrote Henry of Martin Luther in his *Defence of the Seven Sacraments*, and the antipathy was mutual, as Luther's sardonic riposte makes clear. 'Junker Heintz will be God and does whatever he lusts,' declared the former Augustinian monk, brushing off the King of England's attack with a show of withering indifference. For Henry had never fully grasped the broader ramifications of Luther's challenge to papal authority in 1517, and rather than accept that Europe would henceforth be irrevocably divided into hostile confessional camps, continued to think of a united Christendom organised into national churches, 'compacted and united together to make and constitute but one Catholic Church or body'. Considering himself an authentic Catholic throughout, he had consequently been reluctant to enter into close association with foreign Protestants until political necessity dictated otherwise in the 1530s – though even here the flirtation would prove brief and ultimately fruitless. Certainly, by the autumn of 1535 England's diplomatic situation seemed dangerous. The pope had drawn up a bull of deposition, though its promulgation had been delayed, and Charles V's victories in north Africa had apparently left him free to contemplate a strike against England, in an effort to avenge his rejected aunt and enforce the Holy Father's ruling on the matter of the divorce. But while Henry's agents were dispatched to Germany in search of an alliance, the scheme to forge links with his Lutheran counterparts nevertheless fell foul of his own intransigence:

The king [observed Thomas Cromwell with an uncharacteristic hint of vexation at his master's behaviour], knowing himself to be the learnedest prince in Europe, he thought it became not him to submit to them; but he expected they should submit to them.

Even in face of a manifest threat to his kingdom's security, the King of England would not, it seems, compromise over theology or, perhaps more importantly still, strike deals with Protestant German princes whom he considered his inferiors. For as dukes or men of lower degree, it was not consistent with his dignity that he should be their 'associate' rather than their 'principal and head'. And when the prospect of foreign invasion lifted with the death of Catherine of Aragon in January 1536, so Henry's overtures to his new European allies died, too.

In the meantime, however, largely under the influence of Cromwell, Thomas Cranmer and indeed Anne Boleyn, Henry had nevertheless come to fancy himself a religious reformer, and in spite of his reservations about Lutheranism, the apparent departure of England from Rome was therefore still by no means over. Initially intended to limit the attractions of William Tyndale and his heretical works, a vernacular Bible had been first been promised as early as 1530, but Miles Coverdale's authorised version of 1535 represented, in fact, an affirmation of the new Church of England's evangelical credentials. One year later, furthermore, Cromwell's first ecclesiastical injunctions had not only urged the clergy to teach the Lord's Prayer, the Ten Commandments and the Creed to their parishioners in English, but denied the need for pilgrimages and attacked the whole cult of relics. Then followed the so-called *Bishops' Book* of 1537 – which moved further away from Roman doctrine by ignoring the notion of the sacrament of the Mass and failing to make belief in transubstantiation obligatory – and a second set of Cromwellian injunctions in September 1538 that, among other things, initiated a campaign to destroy religious shrines. Yet the apparent reorientation towards European Protestantism was by that point already proving uncomfortable for Henry, as demonstrated by his personal involvement in the condemnation of John Lambert's eucharistic heresy in November 1538, along with a subsequent proclamation reaffirming the Real Presence and the necessity of clerical celibacy. And it was the Act of Six Articles in 1539 which would mark, in effect, the death knell for any further dialogue with Germany's Lutherans. Henceforth, denial of transubstantiation was to be punished by burning without opportunity for recantation, while communion in one kind, clerical celibacy, vows of chastity, and votive masses were declared acceptable by God's law – notwithstanding the fact that Henry himself vetoed a claim that auricular confession was also divinely sanctioned. The result was a truly 'national' hybrid religion, reflecting the king's personal idiosyncrasies and his kingdom's separation once more from the dominant religious camps across the Channel. He would flirt from time to time with continental reformers, as whim and occasion demanded, until his death in 1547, but from this point forth England would largely continue a religious law unto itself.

For a time, in fact, the accession of Henry's young son held out the prospect of a new spate of bridge-building with Protestant Europe as a swing to
the religious left took place under, first, the influence of Edward Seymour,
Lord Protector, and subsequently his eventual replacement, John Dudley.
Though only 9 at the time of his father's death, Edward VI was in fact already
a committed Protestant, tutored by the evangelically inclined Richard Cox
and John Cheke and therefore thoroughly familiar with the kind of reform-
minded thinking that had never wholly won over his father. Hailed as the
'new Joshua', by 1549 the boy king had not only composed a treatise on
the pope as antichrist but was making a series of informed notes on theological controversies. And though some aspects of his religious outlook would
remain essentially Catholic in his early years, he was soon to become, from
some perspectives, the Frankenstein product of his own father's lip service
to religious reform. For Edward's education had unintentionally primed
him for changes that his predecessor could never have countenanced, and
rendered him keenly receptive to the leftward leanings of Edward Seymour,
who as Duke of Somerset and the king's Lord Protector would assume the
reins of government during the first phase of his minority. Certainly, the tone
of the court changed dramatically as rituals and beliefs favoured by the old
king were now derided and the winds of change blew altogether more freely
from the Continent. The first Parliament of the reign repealed the heresy
Acts and moderated the treason laws, and in the more permissive atmosphere
hitherto banned books were printed freely. The repeal of Henry VIII's 1543
Act also allowed unrestricted Bible reading, and in September 1547, albeit
against the government's express wishes, a wave of iconoclasm began with
the destruction of images in St Paul's and other London churches by specially
appointed commissioners.

The chantries were closed, two versions of the Book of Common Prayer
were introduced – with the second containing the so-called 'Black Rubric'
explicitly denying transubstantiation – and the Lord Protector himself
became a correspondent of John Calvin in Geneva. But the most significant token of England's apparent spiritual reconnection with Europe and
the nascent Protestant internationalism being fostered there was the influx
of continental intellectuals who now took up influential university posts and
advised the government on the introduction of sweeping religious reform.
Indeed, in the aftermath of Charles V's victory over his Protestant enemies at
the Battle of Mühlberg in April 1547, Edward VI's England was to become
a favoured centre for refugee theologians from all over the Continent. The
Pole John à Lasco took up residence at Lambeth, and Martin Bucer became
professor at Cambridge with his countryman, the Hebraist Paul Fagius, to
assist him. At Oxford, in March 1549, the influential Italian, Peter Martyr,

lectured in defence of the Swiss reformer, Zwingli, while another Italian, Bernard Ochino, became a prebendary of Canterbury Cathedral and received a royal pension from the privy purse. When the first prayer book of the reign was introduced, meanwhile, Bucer, the Strasbourg reformer who fled to England in 1549, produced a list of sixty defects in it, alongside Peter Martyr's own submissions to Archbishop Cranmer. All were encouraged by Heinrich Bullinger from Zürich and by Calvin from Geneva, and in the meantime, conservative English bishops like Cuthbert Tunstall and Stephen Gardiner found themselves imprisoned in the Tower. Edmund Bonner, Bishop of London, was likewise deprived of office for his support of transubstantiation, while in April 1550 Bishop Day of Chichester only saved himself by preaching against the doctrine.

Nor was this the limit of the upheaval. On the contrary, after Somerset's fall in the wake of the 1549 rebellions, the whole process gathered new momentum under his replacement John Dudley, Earl of Warwick and later Duke of Northumberland. Hailed by John Knox, rightly or wrongly, as an 'intrepid soldier of Christ', Dudley allowed reforming divines to formulate a further programme of religious change that began with the new Ordinal of 1550 and reached its climax with the 1552 Prayer Book, the second of Edward's reign, which has remained the basis of the Anglican communion service ever since. Omitting any notion of a sacrificial priesthood (i.e. one able to offer the sacrifice of the Mass), the Ordinal was followed by the removal of stone altars from their traditional place at the east end of churches and their replacement by wooden communion tables positioned in the chancel or nave. Even more significantly, perhaps, the new Prayer Book departed radically from the medieval liturgical tradition, rendering the new English communion service nothing more than a memorial of the Last Supper. Enforced by the second Act of Uniformity of Edward's reign, attendance at Sunday worship now became compulsory, as priestly vestments were forbidden, singing was restricted and ordinary bread was distributed directly into communicants' hands. Baptism, confirmation and burial services were rewritten, and after a complaint by John Knox against the requirement that kneeling be required at communion, the Council itself intervened to circumvent Cranmer's defence of the practice, ordering the insertion in the Prayer Book of an explanation that kneeling did not imply adoration of the eucharistic elements or a bodily presence.

John Calvin's Geneva, it may have seemed to many, was guiding events. But if English sympathies, or at least those of most English men and women outside government circles, lay in Europe at all, they remained more firmly rooted in Rome than the cantons of Switzerland – as even one of Calvin's most ardent adherents openly acknowledged. For as Martin Bucer put it:

Things are for the most part carried on by the means of ordinances, which the majority obey very grudgingly, and by the removal of the instruments of ancient superstition.

What he had witnessed, in effect, amounted to a 'reformation from above' – an attempt by certain sections of the kingdom's elites to impose a continental-style religious regime on a largely reluctant populace. And Bucer's was a viewpoint echoed by English Protestant observers such as Bishop John Hooper of Gloucester. Writing in 1550, Hooper noted that most councillors 'favour the cause of Christ as much as they can', but confirmed, too, how such sympathies had failed to take root more generally:

The people, however, that many headed monster, is still wincing, partly through ignorance and partly fascinated by the inveiglement of the bishops and the malice and impiety of the mass-priests.

In short, the flirtation with the main currents of European Protestantism during the brief reign of Edward VI proved little more than a false dawn. The Duke of Somerset's self-consciously pious correspondence with Calvin had been conducted primarily for political advantage over conservative rivals like Thomas Wriothesley and Stephen Gardiner, and to justify his hungry assault on Church endowments, while the so-called 'Prayer Book rebellion' of 1549 in the kingdom's western counties had finally put paid to his pretensions once and for all. It was no coincidence either that his successor's campaign to remove irreligious objects from parish churches should have yielded such a rich harvest of gold and silver items for its initiators, or that John Dudley himself would die a convert to the Catholic Church when his attempt to alter the line of succession failed in 1553.

Above all, the welcome accorded to Mary Tudor at that time and the enthusiastic response to the re-establishment of links with Rome spoke volumes for the fragility of England's embrace with continental Protestantism. In London and Grantham, the announcement of the queen's accession was greeted by singing of the Latin *Te Deum*; and in the north generally, according to the priest Robert Parkyn, 'the common people' immediately derided married clergy, and 'would point them with their fingers when they saw them'. At Mary's proclaiming in Oxford there was unalloyed celebration, and accompanying threats to Protestants that they would soon be burned. And when John Dudley, the defeated Duke of Northumberland, was taken through London to the Tower on 25 July, 'all the people reviled him and called him traitor and heretic', recorded the *Greyfriars' Chronicle*. Later, as Mary herself passed along the capital's streets on 3 August, the crowds were said to have shouted

'Jesus save the grace!' and brandished images and pictures of the Virgin Mary and saints, while even Edmund Bonner, the conservative former bishop, now became a somewhat improbable – if fleeting – popular hero in the city after his release from the Marshalsea prison. 'All the people by the way bade him welcome home,' we are told, 'both man and woman, and as many of the women as might kissed him.' At Melton Mowbray the altar was rebuilt immediately. At Oxford the chalices were brought out and Masses celebrated, and in Yorkshire, too, there were Masses from the beginning of August, encouraged by Catholic nobles and gentry, regardless of protests from 'such as was of heretical opinions'.

How far the reaction was prompted by genuine enthusiasm for Rome rather than antipathy to the Duke of Northumberland and England's fleeting courtship with European Protestantism is, however, far from certain. A proclamation issued by Mary's rival, the ill-fated Queen Jane, warned how 'this noble, free realm' might now be brought 'into the tyranny and servitude of the Bishop of Rome', while letters dispatched to the provinces by the council declared that Mary's accession would result in 'the bondage of this Realme to the old servitude of the Antichriste of Rome'. That such threats failed in their aim, though, was due more to respect for the rights of legitimate succession than any widespread desire to renew the bond with the papacy. Indeed, many members of England's political nation viewed the prospect of reunion with Rome with grave misgivings, particularly in connection with the dilemma arising from the new queen's plans for the vast amount of ecclesiastical land acquired by the laity during the previous two reigns. Thus, while Mary's first House of Commons readily accepted the restoration of Catholic doctrine and liturgy, there was an awkward refusal initially to repeal Henry VIII's anti-papal legislation, accompanied by an even more awkward delay in the final reconciliation with the Holy See until Pope Julius III had secured the future of secularised ecclesiastical property by guaranteeing the rights of existing lay holders. In November 1553 about eighty MPs opposed the repeal of Edward VI's Protestant legislation, and when the queen's intention to marry her Spanish cousin, Philip, became clear in the same month, the result was a failed rebellion led by Sir Thomas Wyatt. Prompted in part by economic distress and Protestant sympathies, the rising was also inspired by the age-old antipathy to foreigners, which surfaced equally strongly at the royal court itself after the marriage eventually took place in the summer of 1554. 'Not a day goes by,' wrote one Spaniard, 'without knife work in the court,' as English courtiers stood poised at 'daggers drawn' with the queen's Spanish and Italian servants.

And this was not the only manifestation of an antipathy to foreign influence, which was even exhibited ultimately by the queen herself. For while

Parliament agreed to rescind the royal supremacy in November 1554, fears that the papacy might renege on the land settlement were heightened after 1555 by the election of Pope Paul IV, whose lack of tact and sensitivity offended Mary no less than her most influential subjects. A rigid and inflexible man who could hardly have been less suited to cementing the reunion of England and Rome, the new pontiff was soon rattling cages and ruffling feathers at a whole range of levels with his anti-Spanish outlook and hostility to Mary's husband, not to mention his undisguised dislike for her chief religious adviser, Cardinal Reginald Pole – all of which was sorely compounded by his ongoing intransigence over the question of ecclesiastical property. One of Paul's first actions, in fact, was to issue a bull denouncing the alienation of church lands, and it was only the considerable diplomatic efforts of Pole that eventually persuaded him to exempt England from its provisions. Even so, knowledge of the bull added significantly to the strength of anti-papal sentiment generated by the burning of Protestants in the so-called 'Marian reaction', and overshadowed the discussions in the Parliament of 1555 on the restoration of annates and tenths to Rome, forcing the government to redraft its plans so that the disputed taxes would remain in the hands of the English Church.

During the next two years, as Catholicism became increasingly associated in English minds with persecuting excess and the creeping influence of Spanish ambition – a process that had drawn the country into a war with France that would ultimately result in the loss of Calais – further serious disturbance in Anglo–papal relations was somehow avoided. But in 1557 the pope once more took action that severely tested the patience of the queen, for, after breaking diplomatic relations with her husband's kingdom, Paul duly revoked Cardinal Pole's legatine commission and proceeded to order the arrest of Cardinal More, a close friend of Pole and the representative of English interests at the papal court. For good measure, he finally summoned Pole to Rome to answer in person 'certain religious suspicions' – a scarcely veiled reference to the cardinal's earlier alleged flirtation with heresy. And the result was both outrage on Mary's part, and a stubborn refusal to allow him to leave the country, which was followed in turn by a further refusal to receive either the papal nuncio bearing the letters of revocation or any replacement for her favourite. All charges against Pole, she declared defiantly, would be heard in England, using words that, with consummate irony, were strikingly reminiscent of those employed by her father two decades earlier. 'In observance of the laws and privileges of her realm', the case was, it seems, to be referred 'to the cognisance and decision' of her own courts. And notwithstanding endless negotiations and a subsequent improvement in the international situation, Mary's position on this would not alter. On the contrary, when she died in

November 1558, she remained in union with Rome, but at loggerheads with the pope.

All too appropriately, perhaps, the queen's death was followed just a few hours later by the demise of Pole himself who, like Thomas Wolsey previously, had remained torn to the end by his obedience to the papacy and loyalty to his monarch. Yet no such ambivalence accompanied the succession of Mary's younger sister, since Elizabeth I's dubious legitimacy as Anne Boleyn's daughter was no longer an issue, and the Crown's need for money, along with continuing unease about the pope's attitude to expropriated church property, were enough to propel the government once and for all in a decisively anti-papal direction. To all concerned, the immediate appointment of Protestant ministers – a number of whom were Marian exiles – and the introduction of a Supremacy Bill in the Parliament of 1559 came as no surprise. And the resulting religious settlement once again laid the foundations for a uniquely 'national church', steering between the opposing poles of Roman Catholicism and European Protestantism, and thereby wholly meriting the title 'Anglican' in the fullest sense of the term. Choosing the title 'Supreme Governor' rather than 'Supreme Head', Elizabeth assumed, in effect, a quasi-episcopal role, designed to win over Catholic waverers, along with Protestant zealots – who argued that only Jesus Christ could be head of the church – as well as those convinced that the queen's gender debarred her from a more authoritative status. As a result, the ruler was confined to the administration and jurisdiction of the Church of England, with no power to define 'any article or point of religion' – though this would not prevent Elizabeth from intervening personally in religious matters, especially when resistance to more radical continental approaches was called for. Under John Calvin's influence, some of her bishops would, it is true, impose a number of changes against her will: the introduction of clerical marriage; the use of bread rather than unleavened wafers at communion; and the removal of roods and crucifixes from churches. But in January 1565, she ordered Archbishop Parker of Canterbury to impose uniformity of clerical dress and ceremonials on those radicals disobeying her regulations, and in 1595 she would even refuse to allow the publication of the predestinarian Lambeth Articles, though they had been approved by her favoured archbishop, John Whitgift.

In the meantime, the papacy had not been quick to burn its bridges with Elizabethan England. Indeed, although an Act of Supremacy was passed in 1559 shortly after her accession, papal condemnation of Elizabeth was postponed for over a decade, partly as a result of Philip II's reluctance to see the English queen replaced by the pro-French claimant, Mary, Queen of Scots. Until 1568, moreover, there seemed a distinct possibility that Elizabeth might marry Philip's cousin, Charles of Austria, and thereby return England both to the Catholic Church and the Habsburg interest. Yet any prospect of England's reconciliation with Rome was undermined ultimately by the preparedness of Pope Pius V to give his support to Catholic plotters responsible for the Northern Rising of 1569. There followed the bull of excommunication, *Regnans in Excelsis*, which released Elizabeth's subjects from their allegiance to her, but in doing so actually sealed the fate of the Catholic Church in England once and for all. Coming too late to assist the Northern Rising, which had already collapsed by the time it was issued, the bull effectively equated Catholicism with treason, and, in doing so, began the process of alienating the majority of English Catholics, who saw themselves, in spite of their faith, as patriotic servants of the Crown – a standpoint which was only reinforced by papal involvement in subsequent plots, and the eventual outbreak of war with Spain. Financial support from Rome for the Spanish Armada, coupled to the arrival of priests from continental seminaries in the 1570s and 1580s, all of whom were widely perceived as papal spies and fifth columnists, not only did further damage, but confirmed England's separatism irrevocably. For by the end of Elizabeth's reign, the pope, who had enjoyed the loyalty of Henry VII, not to mention the overwhelming majority of his subjects, was regarded by increasingly chauvinistic English men and women as both Antichrist and their sworn national enemy.

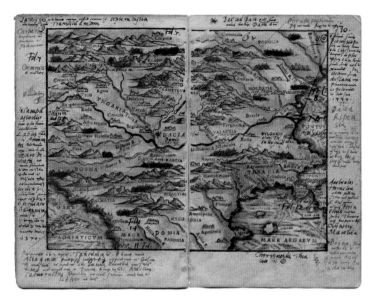

For much of the sixteenth century, European 'countries' continued to be perceived as little more than congeries of regional and local identities, and the approach of a popular textbook – Johannes Honter's *Rudimenta Cosmographica* of 1542 – was typical of its day, illustrating rivers, mountains and major cities but no borders, and reflecting in its place names, all in Latin, the provinces of the Roman and medieval worlds rather than contemporary political realities. A native of Transylvania, Honter's atlas contained thirteen engraved maps showing all known parts of the world, including south-eastern Europe, which is represented here. (Wikimedia Commons)

By the time of this updated version of Geraradus Mercator's 1554 map of Europe, dedicated to Elizabeth I, the idea of the atlas had become firmly entrenched in the budding European consciousness, as sales mushroomed and they became must-have items for any gentleman of sophisticated pretensions. Yet in England, interest in cartography remained comparatively dilatory and narrow in scope – particularly where representations of Europe as a whole were concerned – so that Sir William Cecil was forced to rely for his broader geographical perspective upon a copy of Abraham Ortelius's *Theatrum Orbis Terrarum*, published in 1570. (Wikimedia Commons)

HENRICVS, VII ,

Of all England's Tudor monarchs, Henry VII is rightly remembered as the least inclined by nature to indulge in continental entanglements and adventures. Having spent fourteen years abroad, first in Brittany and latterly in France, he was determined from the outset of his reign not to renew the Lancastrian challenge to the French monarchy. Instead, he would root out lawlessness at home, enrich the monarchy and enhance its prestige until it was no longer the plaything of over-mighty subjects. (Wikimedia Commons)

Thanks to his father's statesmanship, Henry VIII was the first English king in 100 years to succeed unopposed to a stable, peaceful and solvent realm. Yet at the time of his accession, Thomas More readily acknowledged that 'if my head could win him a castle in France … it should not fail to go', and the result was a series of military adventures that stretched his realm's resources to breaking point. Here he meets his ally Emperor Maximilian prior to the French campaign of 1513. (Royal Trust Collection)

Thomas Wolsey not only masterminded the execution of Henry VIII's foreign policy, but became one of the first devotees of continental artistic styles in England. At his urging, agents scoured the markets of Flanders, France, Italy and Venice for all kinds of rich art, and the Florentine Giovanni da Maiano came to work at Hampton Court in 1521 to make a series of terracotta roundels depicting the heads of Roman emperors, which cost, we are told, £2 6s and 8d each. (Wikimedia Commons)

Not altogether surprisingly, images like this detail from Erhard Schoen's *Turkish Atrocities in the Vienna Woods*, 1530, were highly influential, and whenever a Turk featured in English or French plays of the later sixteenth century, he invariably appeared laden with dreadful associations. While Elizabeth I might see fit to endorse trading relations with Constantinople in 1581, she was nevertheless quick to condemn her official ambassador Edward Barton for accompanying Mahommed III on his war of 1593 against Austria, on the grounds that 'he had borne the English armes upon his tent … in the Turkes campe against Christians'. (Wikimedia Commons)

The improvement of access by the River Scheldt, and the comparative ease and cheapness of overland and river communications with the Rhineland and south Germany, made Antwerp a natural meeting place for English exporters and their German customers from the mid-fifteenth century onwards. By 1500, moreover, Antwerp had become the exchange centre for all the great international and intercontinental trades of the day. From England – carried by native Merchant Adventurers and Staplers, as well as Hansards – arrived cloth to be sold, finished and distributed all over northern, central and even Eastern Europe. The Antwerp Bourse, pictured here, at which English traders enjoyed special privileges, was constructed in 1530–31. (Wikimedia Commons)

The Muscovy Company was an English trading company chartered in 1555. As the first major chartered joint stock company, it became the precursor of the type of business that would soon flourish in England and finance the kingdom's exploration of the world. Exercising a monopoly on trade between England and Muscovy until 1698, the company survived as a trading company until the Russian Revolution of 1917, after which it operated as a charity working within the country. (Wikimedia Commons)

Surrounded today by shops and offices, and currently home to the Norwich Puppet Theatre, the Church of St Mary the Less fell out of use in 1544, and has not been in the care of any mainstream denomination since. On its redundancy in the sixteenth century, however, it was sold to Norwich Corporation and became a merchant hall where immigrant Dutch and Walloon merchants sold their cloth until the 1620s. (Wikimedia Commons)

As Lord President of the Council during the troubled minority of Edward VI, John Dudley, Earl of Warwick, had little alternative but to concede to the Treaty of Boulogne with France in March 1550. However, his attempt three years later, as Duke of Northumberland, to alter the legitimate line of succession in favour of Lady Jane Grey risked placing England in a position of permanent cliency to the French king, Henri II. (Wikimedia Commons)

Edmund Grindal, appointed Archbishop of Canterbury on 26 July 1575, was among sixty-seven Protestant English clergy who sought shelter abroad during the reign of Catholic Mary Tudor at places like Basel, Cologne, Frankfurt, Geneva, Padua, Strasbourg, Venice and Zürich, often imbibing the Calvinist ideas, which would become a key feature often associated with Puritanism. Other so-called Marian exiles included William Cecil, Elizabeth Berkeley, Countess of Ormond, Sir Peter Carew and Sir Anthony Cheke, along with some forty merchants, thirty-two artisans, seven printers, three lawyers, three physicians, three yeomen, thirteen servants, and nineteen men with no profession. (Wikimedia Commons)

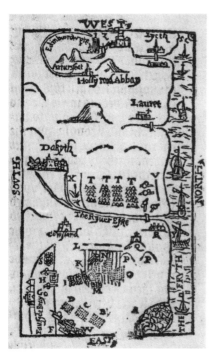

Tudor England's nearest European neighbour was Scotland, which would prove an ongoing security threat, both in its own right and as a result of its connections with the ancient enemy of France. Boasting three universities to England's two, it nevertheless remained for the people of its southern neighbour an almost mythical land inhabited by 'wild Scots' and bounded in the north, or so it was supposed, by a great and impenetrable barrier of snow and ice. In 1548, the English army inflicted a decisive defeat at Pinkie Cleuch (pictured here), adding to previous victories at Flodden in 1513 and Solway Moss in 1542. (Wikimedia Commons)

Beyond the narrow 'Pale' around Dublin, some thirty miles long and less than twenty miles wide, English control was largely nominal, dependent upon Anglo-Irish noble families like the Fitzgerald earls of Kildare and the Butlers of Ormond who differed little from their Gaelic neighbours. In consequence, Ireland became a convenient lever for hostile forces in Europe, especially during the reign of Elizabeth I. In 1579, Irish rebels enlisted the support of Pope Gregory XIII, and fifteen years later, Hugh O'Neill launched the 'Great Revolt', employing infantrymen known as kerns, depicted here by Albrecht Dürer in 1521. (Wikimedia Commons)

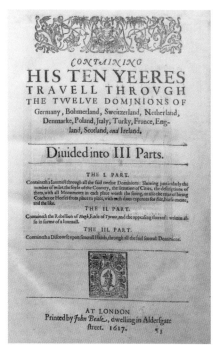

Chief among the new breed of Elizabethan travellers keen to explore Europe was, perhaps, Fynes Moryson, who took ship at Leigh, near Southend, on 1 May 1589, on an expedition around the Continent which would take up the greater part of the next six years, and form the basis for a book recounting his experiences. By the end of 1591 he had reached Prague, after which he retraced his steps to the Low Countries in preparation for a far more extensive excursion still, which would see him briefly enrol as a student at Leyden University on 7 January 1593, and subsequently pass through Denmark and Poland to Vienna, before entering Italy by way of Pontena and Chiusa in October of the same year. (Courtesy of Eamonn de Barca)

As fever mounted steadily against the 'dark Popish Domdaniel' of Spain during the reign of Elizabeth I, two books achieved particular popularity and, in doing so, stirred English audiences to new heights of outrage. One was a curious volume entitled *A Discovery & Plaine Declaration of sundry Subtill practices of the Holy Inquisition of Spain* by Reginaldus Gonsalvius Montanus, the other was John Foxe's *Actes and Monuments*, which in 1570 incorporated an appended section in recognition of the growing interest in 'the extreme dealing and cruel ravening' of the Inquisition. The 'Spanish tickler', pictured here, was used to rip off flesh, removing it from the bone in any part of the body, the face, the back, the breasts, the chest, etc. (Wikimedia Commons)

Traditionally attributed to the artist George Gower, the so-called Armada portrait depicts an idealised Queen Elizabeth I in front of two window-views of the events at sea in 1588. On the left, the glorious English fleet is shown with the flag of St George; on the right, the image is of Spanish ships foundering in the North Sea. The queen has her hand on the globe, with the clear, if premature, message that Spanish world dominion must now give way to the triumph of England's manifest destiny. (Wikimedia Commons)

II

THE TUDORS: RULERS AND STATECRAFT

7

HENRY VII:
PEACE, SECURITY, PRAGMATISM

... this prince is most prudent, ... it seems to me that he thinks he has done
enough in pacifying the kingdom; ... I fancy he will always wish to have
peace with France, though I think if he saw her up to the neck in the water,
he would put his foot on her head to drown her, but not otherwise. There is
nothing fresh in this kingdom, and I do not believe there will be while this
sovereign lives.

Raimondo de Soncino, Milanese ambassador to England, 1497

Of all England's Tudor monarchs, Henry VII is rightly remembered as the
least inclined by nature to indulge in continental entanglements and adventures, though the residing impression of calm and detached, half amused and
half cynical realism that still surrounds him may well result from the fact that
his reign is so much more thinly documented than those of his successors.
Born in 1457, almost at the beginning of the Wars of the Roses, troubled by
ill health in his early years, and forced at the age of 14 to seek safety in exile
from the triumphant Yorkists, he developed that natural wariness towards men
and fortune that can often accompany a delicate and insecure boyhood. Yet
at the age of 28, he would emerge triumphant over Richard III at Bosworth
Field, equipped with all the attributes necessary to hold his newly acquired
crown in hazardous circumstances. He was cool, objective, wary and diplomatic, while capable of instant decision and action – a soldier who fought
with his head and made few mistakes in combat. He had also been well educated in his Welsh boyhood by his uncle the Earl of Pembroke, and though
not a scholar in his own right, the impressive head of his effigy in Westminster

Abbey, sculpted by Pietro Torrigiano, nevertheless suggests a man of powerful intellect not unworthy of the enduring epithet – 'a wonder for wise men' – coined for him by Francis Bacon. Having spent fourteen years abroad, first in Brittany and latterly in France, he was determined from the outset not to go once more upon his travels, particularly by renewing the Lancastrian challenge to the French monarchy. Instead, he would root out lawlessness at home, enrich the monarchy and enhance its prestige until it was no longer the plaything of over-mighty subjects.

Nor, it should be said, had the first Tudor king of England any particularly pressing personal reason for animosity towards the French. On the contrary, they had lent him money for his designs upon his new throne, and it was in the Seine estuary that he had mustered his small expeditionary force for the assault upon his rival Richard. Most of his 2,000 men were, indeed, French, hastily enlisted in Norman villages, and during the first eighteen months of his reign, France would do little to trouble the peace of his realm. For its monarch, Charles VIII, like Archduke Philip of neighbouring Burgundy, was a minor, and the French regent, Anne of Beaujeu, was almost as preoccupied with trouble at home as her Imperial counterpart, whose own regency of the Netherlands was paralysed by widespread rebelliousness, particularly among the great cities of Flanders. A combination of fractious native noblemen, linked to hostile elements in Brittany opposed to subjugation, was in fact seriously challenging Anne's authority, and their encouragement by the Holy Roman Emperor merely resulted in stiffening her own assistance to Emperor Maximilian's Flemish rebels. In consequence, neither he nor the French government were keen for the moment to provoke any additional quarrel with the seemingly peaceable King of England. And to assist Henry's security further, even James III of Scotland, harried by yet another group of turbulent subjects, listened readily to talk of an Anglo–Scottish alliance while keeping in constant communication with his southern neighbour. He dared not abandon, nor would Henry concede, Scotland's long-standing claim to Berwick, and this made a full settlement difficult. But he did agree, all-importantly, to a series of truces that preserved England from any serious attacks across her northern borders during the crucial early phase of Tudor consolidation.

Even so, there remained gathering storm clouds for Henry VII to rue upon. In 1468, Charles the Bold of Burgundy had married Margaret of York, who, as a sister of both Edward IV and Richard III, remained a rabid enemy of all Lancastrians and a ready-made mainstay for any Yorkist pretender. In her dower lands, moreover, she had all the resources necessary to give their ambitions substantial backing, while the troubles of Emperor Maximilian's government in the Netherlands left her largely free to act as whim dictated. Nor, of course, was there any long-term guarantee that the French were likely to remain as friendly to the King of England as they had been when he was an exiled pretender. On the contrary, having driven the English from Normandy and the Burgundians from Picardy, preparations were already mounting for the acquisition of Brittany and perhaps Artois and Flanders too, leaving France's northern shores a glowering menace to England's security. And though the majority of Henry VII's subjects, including the great noblemen, were weary of civil strife and unwilling to risk life or property in doubtful causes against their new ruler, there was also the threat from Ireland to consider, where beyond the narrow 'Pale' around Dublin, some 30 miles long and less than 20 miles wide, Anglo–Irish noble families like the Fitzgerald earls of Kildare and the Butlers of Ormond differed little from their Gaelic neighbours with whom they had intermarried and thereby obtained a free hand to stir what mischief they chose. For although the new English king, like his predecessors since 1200, boasted the title 'Lord of Ireland', the Norman feudal lordships established in the south after Strongbow's invasion in the twelfth century had gradually disappeared in the wake of Gaelic infiltration, and English control over the warring clans, which continued to be led by 'Wild Irish' chieftains obeying Gaelic traditions, remained largely nominal. As a result, the Anglo–Irish lords – long devoted to home rule and the White Rose, and now supported by the military forces of Margaret of York – offered a ready base for any renewed attempts to re-establish the Yorkist cause, which were not, of course, long in materialising.

The only requirement, as Lord Lovell's failed rising early in 1486 had demonstrated, was a suitable royal claimant to set against the fledgling Tudor dynasty, since Richard III had murdered both the sons of Edward IV, while Edward's elder daughter, Elizabeth, had become the new king's wife in January 1486. By this point, equally, Edward's nephew and nearest surviving male kinsman, the Earl of Warwick, was Henry's prisoner and in any case a mere boy, while John de la Pole, Earl of Lincoln, whom Richard III had named as his heir, had too doubtful a claim and too feeble a following to fill his place. But with no legitimate alternative available, there remained of course the possibility of a 'pretender' – a plausible impostor who might, with continental assistance, more than adequately supply the deficiency. And in Lambert Simnel, the 12-year-old son of an Oxford organ builder, the first foreign-sponsored threat to England's new ruling family duly emerged. First presented to the Irish lords in January 1487 in a carefully rehearsed impersonation of the young Earl of Warwick, Simnel's deception nevertheless found support in England only among the Earl of Lincoln, Lord Lovell and a handful of Richard III's supporters who were ready to risk their necks in so doubtful a gamble. Abroad, likewise, no one came forward other than Margaret of York, whose contribution of some 2,000 mercenaries, led by the soldier of fortune

Martin Schwartz with the assistance of Hanseatic ships, still provided no more than the bare nucleus of an army, since the Irish, who made up the rest, were much too ill-equipped to be a likely match for any English force.

Yet despite the paucity of his claim and the weakness of his forces, young Lambert Simnel still went close to loosening the first Tudor's grip upon the throne when, in the summer of 1487, the majority of Anglo–Irish lords rallied to his cause and did homage to him – notwithstanding the fact that Margaret and the English ringleaders were fully aware of his true identity. Crowned thereafter as Edward IV in Dublin, writs were issued in his name, coins were struck bearing his image, and a Parliament was called under his authority. Only Waterford in the south, indeed, held out against him. And although his troops were decisively defeated at the Battle of Stoke on 16 June, twelve days after his landing in England, it had taken a stiff three-hour contest to complete the task. In the process, Simnel himself was captured and Lincoln and Schwartz slain, while Lovell disappeared without trace – perhaps to an uglier fate. But it was clear nevertheless that the recently crowned King of England could no longer afford to ignore the attitudes and activities of his neighbours after even such limited assistance from Europe had enabled so lame a pretender to pose a challenge of this proportion. Though he had early knowledge of what was afoot and acted accordingly – arresting his own mother-in-law and compelling her into a religious house, while parading the real Earl of Warwick through London in an attempt to debunk Simnel's pretences – the initiative had lain squarely with his enemies. He had no naval force capable of intercepting his enemies at sea, and he could not take the risk of leaving England in order to attack them on Irish soil, for fear that another force from the Netherlands might land on the east coast. Instead, he could only gather his army at Nottingham – a convenient staging post for rapid movement towards any part of the western coasts – and await his enemy's actions.

Nor would Henry's eventual leniency towards Simnel himself – who survived another fifty years, first as a kitchen boy and later as a falconer in the royal service – conceal the broader ramifications of what had transpired, since he had hardly time to digest the lessons of one crisis before another in the affairs of the Duchy of Brittany raised them in even sharper relief. Ruled by an ageing and ailing widower, Francis II, Brittany was in fact the last great fief of the French Crown to preserve its independence. But by 1487 the French regent had moved an army there, and gained a further foothold after a victory in July of the following year allowed her to demand a marriage between Charles VIII and Duke Francis's daughter and heir, Anne. Already, since the expulsion of the English in 1453, France controlled several ports from which expeditions could be launched against her old enemy, the most notable of which were Cherbourg, Harfleur, Fécamp and Dieppe, along with

Boulogne, added in 1482. Besides which, there were the prevailing headwinds to consider that would carry any invader across the Channel at considerable advantage. Certainly, England's fighting merchant ships were inadequate to the task of defence, and only the kingdom's ongoing control of Calais provided any reassurance, since without this port, France had no bases on the east of the Straits of Dover with which she could easily bring down a seaborne force on London. Yet with the French conquest of Picardy from Burgundy in 1482, a steadfast buffer against French attacks on Calais had been removed, rendering Brittany – 'a Duchy … situate so opportunely to annoy England either for coast or trade', as Francis Bacon later put it – more critical than ever to English security.

The dilemma could hardly have been starker – not least because the Bretons themselves, unlike the French, were among England's traditional friends, trading amicably and acting on occasion as a military ally. Between the Bretons and the western subjects of the English Crown – the Cornishmen in particular – there was also a sense of racial kinship and even a similarity of language that made mutual support seem natural, while Henry owed a personal debt of gratitude to Brittany that he had not forgotten. Given the threat to England's Channel coast and southern trade, therefore, and notwithstanding the King of England's broadly Francophile inclinations and strategic weakness, action of some kind seemed inescapable. On personal and broader political grounds alike, however, it could not be conducted lightly. Indeed, the entire plan and purpose of the first Tudor's reign might well be ruined by precipitate action. Yet posture he must, as though willing to fight, while convincing Charles VIII – who would attain majority and become ruler of France in his own right in 1492 – that although England could be a serious obstacle to French ambitions on her northern frontiers, she was still essentially a friend prepared to countenance French ambitions elsewhere, particularly in Italy. To demonstrate his potential threat, Henry had already begun by negotiating the Treaty of Medina del Campo with Spain in 1489, and then proceeded to shape more assertively still by asking Parliament for £100,000, sealing treaties of mutual assistance with Emperor Maximilian and Brittany, and sending 6,000 men to occupy Morlaix and Concarneau. Ultimately, after the French had nevertheless occupied additional territory and sealed Anne's marriage to Charles VIII, he would even strengthen his ploy by temporarily laying claim to the French Crown itself, taking an army to France that began the siege of Boulogne in October 1492.

The force concerned, moreover, was to all appearances a formidable one, numbering 26,000 men. But while Henry could very likely have taken the port before winter, he knew too that such an outcome was likely to mark not the end but the beginning of a much greater – and more expensive – war.

And with this in mind, appreciating that the French themselves were anxious to conclude peace in order to fulfil Charles VIII's ambitions in Italy, the circumstances were laid for a mutually advantageous settlement of the kind that had always been the underlying objective. By now in any case, England's ally Emperor Maximilian – a man who always had too many irons in the fire and too little money in his pockets – was away defending the Austrian Habsburg lands against the Hungarians, while Spain's sovereigns, having sent 2,000 men to Brittany in 1490, had withdrawn them before the year was out. Equally disconcertingly, Henry's subjects had paid only £27,000 of the £100,000 voted by Parliament, and in Yorkshire they rose in rebellion rather than contribute at all. Everything, in fact, boiled down to hard cash, as Henry had appreciated from the outset, and the result was four days of negotiation, which culminated in the highly fortuitous Treaty of Étaples of November 1492. Its essence was that the King of France agreed to pay in half-yearly instalments a sum of approximately £150,000 – an enormous amount for the time – so that the war might be conveniently concluded. And while certain English lords and gentry, with visions of plundering marches through France as in days of old, expressed disgust at the wasted expenditure on equipping their followers, their merchant compatriots nevertheless rejoiced and the king himself acquired and retained a financial surplus that was to distinguish him from his successors. No less importantly, French energies and ambitions over the next fifty years were to be expended predominantly in southern Europe, leaving England and the Netherlands largely free from threat for two generations.

Yet while England's king had enhanced his reputation, augmented his income, and won peace by a carefully controlled token show of force, the Treaty of Étaples was no victory in the absolute sense. Indeed, it was from some perspectives a major setback to English interests, since the entire southern shore of the Channel, except Calais, had nevertheless become French. The French monarchy, furthermore, had been immensely strengthened by the reduction of its last great independent fief, and its power to attack England and harass English trade in the longer term had increased immeasurably. For the moment, certainly, Charles VIII had been encouraged to turn away towards Italy by his English counterpart's reluctance to revive the Lancastrian tradition of continental conquest – a reluctance that was to remain the keynote of English policy throughout the reign, securing peace until the succession of Henry VIII. But Henry VII's goodwill could not be guaranteed by itself to ensure France's restraint indefinitely, since French ambition might not always find satisfaction beyond the Alps, and Anne of Beaujeu's support of the Flemish insurgents against Maximilian had made abundantly clear the direction its next turn might take. For the old feud between France and Burgundy was far from dead, and Flanders and Antwerp, the great distributing centres of English cloth, so close to Kent and the Thames estuary, were commercially and strategically of greater importance to England than Brittany had ever been. As such, England's interests and security, no less than the security of the Tudor dynasty itself, required altogether more solid guarantees than a potentially temporary change in French objectives. It required alliances that would provide adequate deterrents to aggression against the Low Countries and Calais, or that would at least make it unnecessary for England to choose again between sacrificing a vital interest and overtaxing her resources in a more or less lone effort at defence.

In this regard, however, alliance with Spain offered real hope, since both sides shared significant mutual interests, permanent as well as temporary. Spain's rulers were, it is true, still closely engaged in their war to recover Granada from Islamic rule, but the end was in sight, after which their territories would be substantially united, with only the small Pyrenean kingdom of Navarre retaining its independence. King Ferdinand, moreover, was a man whose character bore no small resemblance to that of his English counterpart, and, in curbing disorder and centralising government at home, he too foresaw that French aggression might undo his achievements. On the one hand, though he had had been only mildly interested in preserving Brittany, he was keen to recover the Pyrenean counties of Cerdagne and Roussillon, which had fallen into French hands in a period of Aragonese weakness. And there was also, of course, an important Anglo–Spanish commerce for him to foster, with a colony of Spanish merchants in London and a contingent of English merchants traders already established at Seville and its downriver port of San Lucar. Equally, the founder of the Tudor dynasty wished to secure its recognition as one of the established royal families of Europe, which could best be secured by a prestigious marriage alliance, since he had an infant son, Arthur, while Spain's sovereigns had an infant daughter only a few months older. What, therefore, could be more fitting than to confirm the permanence of England's links to Spain by securing a contract for the union of Arthur, Prince of Wales, with Catherine of Aragon – a contract that now became a guiding object of Henry VII's foreign policy.

Indeed, the King of England's warlike posturing over Brittany had been partly staged to further this very objective. For he had already broached the prospective match, to which Catherine's parents had in principle agreed, when English envoys were dispatched to Spain in 1489 to seal the details. They landed on 12 March and had finished the whole negotiation only fifteen days later – quick work by any standard when protracted and ungenerous haggling was characteristic even among friendly diplomatists, let alone the representatives of two such pawky operators as Henry and Ferdinand. Furthermore, the resulting Treaty of Medina del Campo could hardly have been of greater importance to England in particular, since it not only led ultimately to two royal marriages, but founded an alliance that endured with some vicissitudes for eighty years, and went on to secure English security amid unprecedented dangers of a kind never even imagined by its framers. In retrospect, it was an example of the only type of alliance worth making: one based on long-term mutual advantage and substantial commitments on behalf of either party, all of which were clearly laid down at the time of agreement. By the treaty's conditions, the two kingdoms undertook to pledge to protect one another's territories, and not to countenance or harbour any rebels against the other; to join eventually, though not immediately, in war against France; to effect the marriage of the royal children when they were of suitable age, with appropriate stipulations about the princess's dowry; and to allow freedom of commerce and residence, each by the subjects of the other, in all their dominions, with safeguards against the increase of customs duties. Yet there were grey areas, too, since the expression 'all their dominions', while including the Spanish colony of the Canary Islands, did not in fact encompass any other territory outside Europe, as neither party foresaw the immense extension of the Spanish Empire that was to commence with Columbus's first voyage three years later. More ominously still, there were tensions about the making of any separate peace with France that appeared more favourable to Spain than England – so much so, indeed, that Henry saw fit at first to delay ratification of the treaty. But if those who supped with Ferdinand needed to watch their plates, the treaty remained a breakthrough if not a triumph – not least because relations between the two kingdoms had been damaged firstly by the Treaty of Étaples with France, and thereafter by the Holy Roman Emperor's eager collaboration with Margaret of York to promote the designs of a new, more dangerous Yorkist pretender: Perkin Warbeck.

The son of a river Scheldt boatman, Warbeck was from all accounts a physically prepossessing young man of 17 who had launched his deception in Ireland where, like Lambert Simnel before him, he found a ready wellspring of support, following a further plot to release the authentic Earl of Warwick in 1489. Now as before, moreover, the attitude of the Earl of Kildare, an Irish nobleman of Yorkist promotion, who had continued in the office of Ireland's Lord Deputy when Henry VII became king, would be central to events. For during the Simnel rebellion, the earl had already been openly disloyal and taken the lead in recognising the pretender and launching his invasion of England. One of his kinsmen, indeed, had led the ill-fated Irish contingent at the Battle of Stoke and perished with them. Yet the reduction of Ireland as a whole and Kildare in particular in the battle's wake had nevertheless called for more money than any English ruler could reasonably have afforded at that time, with the result that Henry had been forced to settle for no more than a token affirmation of his authority involving the dispatch of 500 men under Sir Richard Edgecumbe to secure the Irish ports and, if possible, the submission of the nobility. In the event, the ports, whose priorities were confined to trade with England, opted to obey the king while there was a prospect of peace and quiet in doing so, and Edgecumbe succeeded in winning them over. But his success with the nobles, by contrast, proved nothing more than nominal. For while an oath of loyalty was indeed forthcoming, it nevertheless sat lightly on the consciences of those concerned, and Kildare himself remained Lord Deputy, though stubbornly refusing to obey Henry's command to come over to England to confer on Irish affairs. Brazenly confident and uncowed, it would have taken nothing short of war to unseat him, which none were ready to contemplate.

And thus things hovered until the arrival in November 1491 of an unlikely but plausible Flemish interloper on board a ship from a Breton port breathed new life into the hopes of a circle of Yorkist malcontents gathered in Cork. Quite when and where the individuals involved first focused their schemes upon the 17-year-old 'Peter', 'Peterkin' or 'Perkin' Warbeck is unknown, but word had it that he was seen walking Cork's streets in fine clothes as an advertisement for the wares of the Jewish merchant to whom he was servant. At which point, the culprits chose to act. For here, they hoped, was their would-be Earl of Warwick, though when asked to participate in the deception, the young man at first refused, altogether denying, according to his own account, that he was of any exalted origin whatsoever. Indeed, only after long argument, he would later claim, were his objections finally overcome by the prime movers in the affair, who were not, as might have been expected, the Earl of Kildare's confederates, but the Mayor of Cork and English Yorkists of the middle rank, along with the Earl of Desmond. And the upshot, as it transpired, was no more than a minor change of plan, in which Warbeck was subsequently presented as the Duke of York, one of the two young princes whom Richard III had murdered in the Tower. Aided by the young impostor's arrival at a juncture when England was virtually at war with France, little else, it seemed, was required, though the French themselves appear to have stirred the coals, welcoming him cordially after his departure from Ireland in 1492. And there was further help from Scotland, since communications with James IV had also been opened up on Warbeck's behalf by the Earl of Desmond. Seeking the border stronghold of Berwick as a prospective gateway for invasion, and boasting a navy of good fighting ships supported by an auxiliary force built up as much by piracy as by trade, the Scottish king, unsurprisingly, was fully alive to the possibilities afforded by the pretender's presence – no less, indeed, than the King of France himself, who proceeded to hold the young man in reserve as a bargaining chip

throughout the summer after his arrival, before cynically banishing him
upon the conclusion of the Treaty of Étaples.

But Warbeck's tale was hardly yet begun. For by now he was already
emerging as a daring adventurer of high intelligence, ability and persuasive-
ness in his own right, soon to find a new home in the Netherlands, where
Maximilian awaited his services and Margaret of York stood willing to welcome him as another nephew rescued from the Tower. Though stricken by
what would prove to be a fatal lack of resolve, recurring at critical moments
when hesitancy meant failure, he would prove able indeed for the next five
years to sustain the guise of a serious candidate for Henry VII's throne, convincing half the statesmen of Europe that he was Edward IV's missing son,
and enlisting in the process not only the support of Desmond and the Irish
Yorkists and James IV of Scotland, but also a series of English notables, including no less a figure than Henry VII's Lord Chamberlain, Sir William Stanley,
younger brother of the Earl of Derby. When Henry dispatched a dossier to
Margaret of York on Warbeck's real origins, moreover, she responded acrimo-
niously, severing diplomatic links and thereby raising the threat to a new order
of magnitude. For although she continued to rule no more than her own
widow's portion of the provinces of Burgundy, her wider threat remained as
tangible as ever, by virtue of her dead step-daughter's marriage to Emperor
Maximilian, which had begotten Archduke Philip, the legitimate successor
to the Burgundian patrimony, who was presently too young to rule in his
own right. Since Maximilian had many other concerns than the Netherlands,
control at this time was therefore effectively shared between himself and
Margaret, and since he too considered himself injured by England's peace
with France, the emperor likewise became a supporter of Warbeck, behaving
consistently as though firmly convinced of the pretender's royal credentials.

Under the circumstances, Warbeck at large in the Netherlands was of
even greater concern to Henry than Warbeck in Ireland. Certainly, the provinces were rich, and the *landsknechts* of Germany could always be had for
an appropriate fee, while the Hanseatic League, with its formidable fleet,
already had good reason to regard the King of England as an enemy. As such,
it was more crucial than ever to extricate Warbeck from his latest sanctuary
as rapidly as possible, and though force of arms was not a viable option, there
remained, nevertheless, other ways for Henry to bell his troublesome cat.
Not least, the middle-class mercantile interest ruling the Flemish cities had
no desire to foment revolution in England, since the quarrel at issue was in
their view strictly dynastic, resulting merely from the personal feud between
Henry Tudor on the one hand and Margaret and Maximilian on the other.
And with this in mind, Henry shrewdly opted to furnish Flemish merchants
with a personal grievance of their own against their overlords by causing an

interruption of trade, which had resulted by September 1493 not only in a full-scale prohibition of English commerce with the subjects of the Archduke Philip, but an expulsion of those subjects from England, and a transference of the Merchant Adventurers' cloth mart from Antwerp to Calais. Thereafter, the sale of English cloth to the Netherlands dried up entirely, and though English merchants were similarly inconvenienced, there was at least in their case the prospect of other markets for their wares. By contrast, the Flemish craftsmen and master clothiers had no alternative source of supply, since the cloth in question was woven but unfinished, not having been smoothed and dyed for the tailor's use. Calculating that they would break before he did, Henry had therefore opted for a simple, punishing and eminently effective strategy of outright economic war.

To the King of England's great good fortune, moreover, his merchants proved willing to pledge him their loyalty, notwithstanding the considerable cost involved. And in doing so they proved in no mood either to tolerate any evasion of trade by 'disordered persons' who might seek to ignore the prohibition. Most obviously suspect in this regard were the members of the Hanseatic League, whose London headquarters, the Steelyard, was obliged to deposit £20,000 as security against illicit trading. But when suspicion mounted regardless, the result was the attack upon the Steelyard of 1494, which culminated in the arrest of eighty assailants, all of whom were released without serious punishment. By which point, Henry's intelligence service was also working far more efficiently than in 1487 to circumvent the danger of foreign intervention. Initially, Sir Robert Clifford, one of the principal Yorkist agents, had been won over and from both him and Henry's own spies full details came to light of what was afoot, with the result that in the autumn of 1494, the entire Yorkist organisation within the kingdom was dealt a devastating blow. Lord Fitzwalter, Sir Simon Mountford, and several others were executed, and in 1495 the further execution of Sir William Stanley provided definitive proof that the Crown had not only the will but also the knowledge and power to deal effectively with even the greatest who might be suspected of dabbling in treason. In one fell swoop, it seems, all danger of a domestic uprising exploitable by hostile continental forces had effectively vanished.

Elsewhere, too, there were encouraging signs for Henry. For although the economic war with the Netherlands needed time to be effective, and Warbeck was left free in the meantime to tour the Holy Roman Empire in the train of Maximilian, there were loyal elements too at work on the King of England's behalf. Warbeck's host, for example, had brought him back to the Netherlands in 1494, but at Antwerp some patriotic Englishmen tore down and trampled in the mud the royal insignia displayed outside the pretender's lodging. That the demonstrators made good their escape, moreover, left little doubt about the underlying sympathies of Antwerp's citizens, as a more assertive approach in Ireland also began to yield dividends. For in the summer of 1492, soon after the Earl of Kildare had given countenance to Warbeck, Henry suddenly dismissed him as Lord Deputy in a stroke evidently timed to coincide with a shift in the dynamics of the perpetual Irish feuds that had on this occasion placed the earl at a temporary disadvantage. Unable to resist, Kildare not only begged the king's pardon but came to England in 1493 to request it in person, and found himself the object of a practical joke that amply reflected the altered political balance. For at a banquet arranged by Henry, Kildare and his followers found themselves served by a cupbearer whose features they recognised at once – the self-same Lambert Simnel, to whom they had once knelt as subjects. 'So the wine be good, I will drink!' Kildare is said to have responded, laughing off the incident as best he might, though not before being treated to a further gibe by his host, who proceeded to prophesy how one day they would crown apes in Ireland.

Apparently tamed by his treatment, Kildare duly returned to Ireland, and soon came back to court for further pleading of his cause, remaining until late 1494. But it would require one more lapse before the earl's loyalty was finally guaranteed, and before that stage was reached there were to be both reforms in the Irish government as well as ongoing tensions that merely confirmed how Ireland, in the longer term, would remain a nagging and largely insoluble problem for Tudor security. Significantly, in September 1494, Henry appointed his 3-year-old second son, the future Henry VIII, Lord Lieutenant of Ireland, and created Edward Poynings Lord Deputy. But trouble was already brewing in Ulster, where the tribal chiefs were in communication with James IV, who had maintained his threat as another possible invader of England in Perkin Warbeck's cause. And when Poynings' small force of 1,000 men arrived in October, it became rapidly clear, as others had already learned to their cost, that native Irish guerrillas could only be held down by overwhelming force of the kind that England was still unable to exert. In fact, it was among the Anglo–Irish lords and within or around the English Pale that the real danger lay, and to compound matters the pardoned Kildare, who was initially supportive of Poynings, soon yielded to the old intoxication. Intriguing with the rebels, he wrote too to the King of Scots, notwithstanding the fact that Warbeck was far away in Flanders, and only Poynings' strength within the Pale and considerable political skill allowed him to arrest and attaint his adversary before dispatching him to England to cool his Yorkist ardour in the Tower of London. Appreciating that Ireland's strength lay in irregular warfare, her weakness in the instability and mutual disloyalty of her chieftains, the Lord Deputy had ultimately managed to split the rebel forces by friendly overtures, while nevertheless acknowledging the bitter truth that outright conquest remained wholly beyond his slender resources.

In such conditions, the immediate outcome from England's perspective was perhaps as much as might reasonably be expected when an Irish Parliament called at Drogheda in December 1494 subsequently enacted the so-called 'Poynings' Law'. By its terms, all English legislation was made valid in Ireland, while the Irish Parliament was neither to meet nor introduce laws without royal approval. After which, a series of further measures followed in tow: enhancing the defence of the Pale; prohibiting the practice of livery and maintenance; establishing a militia among the English colonists; resuming all royal grants made since 1327; and limiting the tenure of important offices to the king's pleasure rather than for life. Yet even in the brief period until early 1496, when Poynings' own tenure as Lord Deputy ended, the limitations of his success were already apparent regarding the most intractable problem of all: the creation of an Irish revenue sufficient to sustain an effective occupying garrison in the long term. Though Kildare had been nullified, it remained as apparent as ever that Ireland could only be held by force, if England herself met the bill, and this alone was enough to ensure that Henry VII had little option beyond a return to the system of ruling through Irish intermediaries. Curiously, perhaps, in Kildare's case at least, the king's faith finally proved justified, since in August 1496 the earl returned from the Tower to Dublin, once more restored to the office of Lord Deputy, which he held without stir to the end of the reign. Yet the threat from the Irish back door would not only outlive the first Tudor, but grow steadily in scale until reaching its climax in the final years of his granddaughter Elizabeth.

Nor, of course, had Perkin Warbeck's shadow entirely receded even now. Undeterred by the execution of Sir Thomas Stanley and other opponents of the Crown in February 1495, Maximilian and Margaret of York had gone on to supply the pretender with ships and soldiers in return for promises of considerable financial and territorial concessions in the event of success. But in spite of a formal agreement with the Burgundian government in December 1494, the eventual assault, if such it can be called, was effectively broken before it started by the impact of the King of England's economic campaign against the Netherlands. A brief and dispiriting sojourn at anchor off the coast of Kent at Deal, where the people were loyal to their ruler and ready and alert, ended wretchedly after Warbeck acted half-heartedly, sending 300 men ashore without landing in person to lead them. Half were killed and the rest dispatched to London for what would amount to small mercy, as the man who had intended to supplant the Tudor dynasty then sailed tamely away down the Channel attempting no further landing on

English soil, to make instead for what was still, at that time, the comparative safety of Ireland. In the process, a further part of his expeditionary force left him before the Munster coast was reached and he was joined by his former friend the Earl of Desmond. He helped him lay siege to the loyal town of Waterford during July and August 1495, when Kildare was in the Tower and Poynings was still Lord Deputy. And once again it was the latter who duly saved the day for his Tudor master, not only taking prompt action to relieve Waterford, but thereby forcing Warbeck to continue his quest wherever fortune might offer – which in this case would prove to be his last best hope: the court of Scotland.

Certainly, though his options had by now diminished considerably, there was to no thought for the moment of surrender on the fugitive's part. On the contrary, received by James IV with open arms, he was duly acknowledged as prospective King of England and married to Lady Catherine Gordon, a suitably high-born bride. In return, furthermore, for the cession of Berwick after victory had been achieved, James also promised his assistance in open war against his southern neighbour. But the Scottish nobles and people were unenthusiastic, and a year would elapse before an invading force of 2,000 men was finally ready to cross the border in September 1496. By which time, crucially, Warbeck had lost his only other ally, the Netherlands, since, amid the constantly shifting sands of continental power politics, Maximilian's anger with Henry had been overtaken by his alarm at Charles VIII's astonishing success in Italy, where the youthful, romantic and adventurous French king had pursued his claim to the kingdom of Naples as a basis for subduing the entire peninsula. Though of no notable ability in his own right, Charles had, of course, agreed the Treaty of Étaples with England in order to forestall the possibility of the invasion of northern France, before proceeding to overrun Naples in 1494 with scarcely a blow struck. And the result was a prolonged and arduous struggle that would rack Europe and dominate its high politics for the next half century after Pope Alexander VI and the north Italian powers of Venice and Milan took fright to side with both Ferdinand of Spain, who continued to balk at the French threat to his Mediterranean interests, and Emperor Maximilian, who was equally keen to advance long-standing Imperial pretensions in the area.

As early as 1495, in fact, the emperor had joined Ferdinand and the pope in a Holy League to drive the French back over the Alps, and while England exhibited no intention of joining the fray, the strategic advantages accruing to her from the hostilities were nevertheless manifest. Certainly, the English king himself was not only keenly abreast of developments in Italy, but acutely conscious of how best to exploit his rivals' preoccupations, so that in 1497 the Milanese ambassador Soncino wrote thus to his master Ludovico Sforza:

In many things I know this king to be admirably well informed, but above all else because he is most thoroughly acquainted with the affairs of Italy, and receives especial information.

And neither his interest nor his judgement would fail him, it seems, as events unfolded thereafter. For eighteen months later, the ambassador commented once more upon Henry VII's shrewd reading of the political balance on the Continent:

In his Highness's opinion he has need of no one, while everyone needs him, and although he clearly sees what may happen to the world, yet he considers it so unlikely as to be practically impossible. In the midst of all, his Majesty can stand like one at the top of a tower looking on at what is passing in the plain. He also seems to believe that even if the King of France became master of Italy, which he would not like, he would be so distracted in ruling it that no harm would ensue either to his Majesty or to his heirs.

By the summer of 1495, moreover, the threat to French communications from the north had indeed forced Charles to retreat from Naples, leaving behind nothing more than a slender force of garrisons, most of which were duly captured after a Spanish landing on the Neapolitan coast.

And while France regrouped the following year, preparing a fresh expeditionary force to relieve the tattered remnants of its predecessor, the Netherlands government, too, demonstrated little heart for sustaining its own dispute with England, which was continuing to harm its economic interests. On the one hand, the emperor's fear of French resurgence remained ongoing, and Warbeck's persistent failure to make headway had further sapped his resolve, so that compromise now seemed inescapable. Whether politics or commerce was the primary drive behind the settlement will remain debatable. But reconciliation duly followed on 24 February 1496 with the treaty known to history as *Intercursus Magnus* – a name first coined by the Flemings and preserved for posterity by Francis Bacon, who later adopted the term from them. By its conditions, English traders were allowed to sell freely in any part of Archduke Philip's dominions, except Flanders, which was nevertheless eventually included in 1502. Similarly, in addition to guarantees of fair and speedy justice in local courts for English merchants, no tolls or customs were to be exacted exceeding rates prevailing over the previous years. Most important of all, however, each government undertook not to countenance the other's rebels – a particularly crucial consideration from England's perspective, which carried additional assurances on the Netherlands' part that

Margaret of York was to be deprived of her dower lands in Burgundy should she refuse to conform.

Henceforth, Perkin Warbeck would be left only with the hope of Scottish assistance, and even this was to prove fleeting since effective countermeasures had also been implemented here. For by his policy of friendship with France, and now by his agreement with the Netherlands, the King of England had, of course, deprived James IV himself of foreign support. And while the French saw fit to dispatch an ambassador to Edinburgh, he, like the Spanish ambassador Pedro de Ayala sent in the summer of 1496, had instructions to work only for peace. Nor was this all. For among a pro-English party of the Scottish nobility, carefully fostered as long ago as 1491 by secret compacts between Henry and figures such as John Ramsay and Archibald Douglas, Earl of Angus, there was further pressure for compromise. Though originally intended to weaken the prospect of Scottish support for France over the Breton question, these links now proved particularly invaluable, as England, freed at last from anxiety about continental rivals, duly turned its undivided attention towards bringing James IV to heel. At which juncture, a brief and inglorious raid across the border by James and Warbeck in September 1496 gave Henry a precious opportunity to call at last upon his subjects to open their purses in defence of their country. In the event, the long-heralded Scottish invasion was over in a week, achieving no vestige of support among potentially disloyal English elements, and advancing only a few miles before melting shamefully under the threat of 4,000 enemy troops advancing from Carlisle. Beforehand, there had actually been an impertinent offer of £1,000 for Henry VII's head – which could only have amused him. For although the City of London responded only sluggishly to their sovereign's requests for money, Parliament, by contrast, subsequently reacted with distinct enthusiasm, voting two fifteenths and tenths in January 1497, as well as an additional subsidy, to provide 'by sea and land two armies royal for a substantial war to be continued upon the Scots'.

Should the promised funds flow readily, the outcome, it seemed, was guaranteed. Yet before the coming hostilities could be prosecuted, of course, any proposed taxes would have to be collected, and the common folk of Henry VII's realm – in the West Country especially – were to prove altogether less forthcoming than MPs. For their part, after all, the people of Cornwall were particularly conscious of their non-English roots, living hard and poorly as they did in their relatively barren peninsula. Deeply isolated from events in the capital and distinguished by a social structure that lacked the stabilising influence of a native nobility, the county's gentry also shared the same political outlook as its farmers and seafarers. And the result was an explosive fusion of class interests triggered by a widespread conviction that the 'outrageous sums' raised by 'crafty means' to pay for a conflict on the far-off Scottish border were wholly unacceptable. From the local perspective, of course, the war seemed only one more aspect of an ongoing struggle between Lancaster and York, and in Cornwall the Yorkists had always been strong. But it was not as Yorkists that Cornishmen finally rebelled. Indeed, at no point did they demand the king's deposition, preferring instead to request the dismissal of his ministers, Cardinal Morton and Sir Reginald Bray. More important by far was the recent recollection of the French war of 1492, which had served only to fill the treasury rather than conquer the enemy. And in consequence the current clamour awaited only a leader, who duly emerged in the figure of Michael Joseph, a doughty blacksmith who took command of the men of St Keverne and brought them to Bodmin, where they were joined by a number of local leaders. Some were gentlemen, and prominent above all others was a lawyer named Thomas Flamank, who clothed the movement with legality by convincing the participants that the king was wrong to collect a tax without first employing the feudal dues to which he was entitled. Whereupon, it seems, the die was well and truly cast.

Resenting the apparently excessive reaction to 'a small commotion made by the Scots', a Cornish rebel host, numbering some 15,000, therefore crossed the Tamar at the end of May – albeit without pillage or violence – gathering support along the way. In Somerset, Lord Audley joined them, with Joseph still in military command, as his men passed on through Wiltshire, Hampshire and Surrey to the edge of Kent, where Flamank expected strong support, since the county had a long tradition of popular uprisings. Yet the men of Kent remained loyal, and when the rebels turned north to London, the king was able to muster the bigger army, in the proportion of two to one. Finally taking post on Blackheath, the Cornish contingent was faced, in fact, not only by Henry himself, who remained the best general in the land, but by Lord Daubeny's troops, freshly recalled from their movement towards Scotland, as well as the militia of the Home Counties under their local leaders. Present, too, were the citizens of London, along with the Earl of Oxford, who had fought at Bosworth and Stoke and seen numerous other campaigns. Certainly, as the royal army poured over London Bridge to assemble in St George's Field, the king among them, there was no great mood for clemency or quarter towards the mob of farmers, fishermen and miners who, according to one chronicler, were by that time actually 'in great agony and variance' as to whether or not to yield to the king's mercy. And nor at the critical moment did Daubeny hesitate to press home the main attack from the westward across Deptford Creek, while Henry deployed the reserve with which to clinch matters, so that by two o'clock that afternoon he was riding back across London Bridge, the summer sun glinting on his armour, to be welcomed in triumph by the mayor and his 'brethren in scarlet'.

There had been a sharp fight at Deptford passage, after which Daubeny forged forward to the heath as perhaps 6,000 rebels deserted, though at one point during a Cornish rally he was actually knocked down and captured, only to be released while the rest of the royal forces gathered for the kill. In all, some 200 rebels thereafter lost their lives in return for a much smaller number of their adversaries, but at least no repetition occurred of the kind of triumphal retribution that had stained other battles in recent memory. On the contrary, though the burial mounds at Blackheath would still be visible for all of two centuries, the common prisoners, tramping in chains behind the king across London Bridge, were mainly dismissed before long to their personal captors for small ransoms sometimes amounting to as little as a shilling. To Thomas More, the entire uprising would seem an almost pitiful affair: 'that disastrous civil war which began with a revolution in the West Country and ended with a ghastly massacre of the rebels'. Yet there was still a price to be paid, and the quarters of Flamank's butchered body were duly set upon each of London's four gates as ghoulish reminders of the penalties of rebellion, while Joseph too, along with Lord Audley, was hanged and mutilated at Tyburn. And there were broader lessons too, of course, for the king himself to ruminate upon. For if Henry had won the day, he had also learnt once more the sobering lesson that too active a foreign policy automatically carried with it domestic perils. True, the events of June 1497 had been less a rebellion than an armed protest march. But the men of Cornwall had nevertheless been able to traverse the breadth of southern England before being crushed ten years and a day after the defeat of Lambert Simnel. Equally worryingly, Perkin Warbeck was still at large, and backed, ostensibly, by the King of Scotland, whose threat remained ongoing.

Of this last point, naturally, Henry needed no reminder. Yet in spite of his ongoing plans for war, his long-standing intention had always been to make of Scotland a friend rather than a foe, so that as far back as 1486 he had first suggested a reconciliation of the two royal houses by means of marriage. In 1495 again, he had offered his elder daughter Margaret as a wife for James IV, and now, as soon as the Cornishmen had been suppressed, he instructed his ambassador, Bishop Fox, to offer peace once more, in return for the surrender of Warbeck and payment of a reasonable indemnity. At the same time, Fox was to suggest a personal meeting between the two monarchs on English soil, which Henry's military preparations, like those against France in 1492, were actually intended to hasten in anticipation of a peaceful settlement that James, however, continued to spurn. For, rather than accept the olive branch on offer, the Scottish king was still intent, as yet, upon seizing the opportunity offered by Henry's difficulties. Indeed, while Warbeck was continuing to explore the possibility of support in Ireland, James crossed the border near Norham Castle, to which he laid siege, regardless of his rival's victory at Blackheath. But as the Earl of Surrey marched north to the relief of Norham, and a squadron of Henry's navy – a new element in England's arsenal – sailed up the east coast, Scotland's ruler duly retreated with the enemy in hot pursuit. After which, a sharp English raid into south-eastern Scotland took place, resulting in a critical reverse for Warbeck, who had already put to sea with a small band of followers before Fox could demand his surrender.

But what the pretender was hoping to achieve as he made his landing at Cork, in a ship appropriately named the *Cuckoo*, is hard to discern. He had arrived, of course, at the scene of his first imposture in 1491, yet this time found even less support in Ireland than he had done in 1495. Disappointed, though still prepared as ever to clutch at straws, he therefore sailed off to Cornwall to see whether any fire remained beneath the ashes of the Cornish revolt, and on 7 September, having been hidden in a cask by the master of his ship, he landed with a few score supporters at Whitesand Bay. Surprisingly, perhaps, a few thousand West Countrymen were even now prepared to risk their heads a second time, only to prove little better than an armed mob and melting before the inevitable counter-blow was struck. Eventually advancing as far east as Taunton, they failed above all to seize Exeter, while Warbeck, not daring with such feeble forces to await the oncoming royal forces, displayed a characteristically faint heart at the moment of decision, slipping away on 21 September and seeking sanctuary at Beaulieu Abbey after failing to break through to the coast. Only a few days later he surrendered to Henry and openly confessed the full story of his deception, including his origins as the son of a Flemish waterman, after which peace returned to Scotland too, since the onset of bad weather ensured that neither side could keep the field. All that remained was for the Spanish envoy, Pedro de Ayala, to mediate a preliminary peace at the end of September, which was extended by a more permanent treaty signed in London in December.

At last, then, James IV was finally detached from the Warbeck adventure – though not before de Ayala had actually tempted the fallen pretender to seek refuge in Spain, in the hope of exploiting his presence in the ongoing marriage negotiations involving Prince Arthur and Catherine of Aragon. Indeed, the envoy had even arranged previously that a Spanish merchantman should give the pretender passage to Ireland, only for Warbeck's subsequent attempt at armed rebellion in Cornwall to render him once and for all too dangerous even for Spanish taste. As a result, he was duly delivered into the hands of the very king he had tried so strenuously to supplant, to be treated for his trouble to a confinement that was by no means as harsh as he truly merited. For all of twelve years, in fact, Henry had struggled against formidable forces, only to prevail by virtue of his judgement, balance, speed of action – and moderation, too. And now, it seems, he palpably had less need than ever for retribution even against his most irksome enemy. For 1497, the middle point of his reign, marked in effect a turning point in his affairs. Henceforth, he might still occasionally feel or feign alarm over stirrings among the Yorkist irreconcilables, as in 1499 when he finally sent Warbeck and the hapless Earl of Warbeck to the scaffold. Equally, he might sometimes allow himself to be deflected from his purposes, as with the Hanseatic towns in 1504, or by the prospect of further Yorkist pretenders at large in foreign lands. But, with Warbeck's failure, the Yorkist danger ceased to be a dominant concern of his foreign policy.

Paradoxically, the trials and challenges of the previous years had actually compelled the king to develop a measured and comprehensive policy towards his continental neighbours. For with Warbeck at liberty, he had been too preoccupied to be tempted into taking advantage of French entanglements in Italy after 1494. And although he had joined Ferdinand, Maximilian and the Pope in their Holy League in July 1496, he did so only at that point when the League was already seeking an agreement with France, and only on condition that it would not involve him directly in war. Even then, therefore, he had effectively reaffirmed his renunciation of the ancient enmity with England's most substantial foe, and more importantly still, he had also been spurred on to create that system of continental alliances that, as the Breton crisis had shown, might still be needed as an insurance against any future French aggression in regions vital to England's security. In particular, he had been able both to reinforce and improve the terms of his alliance with Spain, since Ferdinand's anxiety about Italy had led him to covet the support of a strong England no less than the Tudor dynasty required Spanish friendship to consolidate its own position. And in 1496, Henry's adhesion to the Holy League was duly rewarded by an agreement that Catherine of Aragon should at last marry Prince Arthur as soon as he reached the age of 14 in 1500. The final defeat of Warbeck, which provided a convincing demonstration of England's growing political stability, was followed by the formal betrothal of the pair in August 1497, and two years later they were married by proxy – a ceremony that was repeated in 1500, significantly enough at Spanish rather than English insistence. Thereafter, in October 1501, Catherine finally arrived in England, along with the 100,000 crowns of her dowry, before marrying in St Paul's on 14 November. At which point, the Anglo–Spanish alliance, so hard won in 1489, seemed firm and assured, on terms almost as beneficial to Henry as to Ferdinand and Isabella.

Five years earlier, in 1496, the *Intercursus Magnus*, coupled to membership of the Holy League, had given Henry a second ally on the Continent, the Netherlands, while three years earlier still, the accession of Maximilian as Holy Roman Emperor and the transference of the Netherlands government to his son, the Archduke Philip, had also strengthened relations with England by giving native interests more influence over policy. But this was not all, since Philip's marriage in 1496 to Joanna of Castile, second daughter of Ferdinand and Isabella, had also linked the Netherlands and Spain much more closely together – even more so indeed than the Spanish sovereigns had ever envisaged. For the deaths of their only son Juan in 1497, and of their eldest daughter Isabella in 1498, as well the demise of the latter's only son in 1500, were to leave Joanna heir to both their realms, with the prospect, through her husband, of Habsburg control of both the Empire and Spain at some point in the future. Ultimately, of course, this would bring dangers of its own, but in the meantime, the King of England remained as secure as diplomacy, matrimony and the self-interest of other dynasties could make him. Henceforth, the monarchs of Spain could hardly ignore an attack upon their son-in-law's Netherlands any more than the Holy Roman Emperor might, and with both on England's side in any case, Henry could feel confident that he need no longer fear another setback with France like the one he had suffered over Brittany. To complete the good news, Charles VIII had died without issue in the spring of 1498, and though his cousin and successor, Louis XII, revived the Italian threat in a new form by asserting a claim to the Duchy of Milan, he nevertheless undertook to clear the way for acquiring it by ceding half his Neapolitan claim through partition. And nor, predictably, was this resulting opportunity lost by Henry either, who, apart from enjoying the arrival of temporary peace in Europe, at once demanded and obtained the renewal of the Treaty of Étaples with its guarantees of money payments by France.

Yet Warbeck's activities, though ended, continued to demonstrate the need for security on the 'British' side of the Channel as well as the continental. On the one hand, it was still the case that the fragility of English rule in Ireland offered an irresistible temptation to the King of England's enemies abroad. But the entire Warbeck episode had also emphasised the old lesson that a hostile Scotland could be no less serious a vexation on England's one remaining land frontier, even when such hostility was not actively encouraged by France. In consequence, Henry could no more neglect British affairs than he could the rest of the Continent, though his Irish and Scottish policies, no less than his dealings with mainland Europe, still had to be subordinated to domestic considerations. Plainly, he could not attempt violent and drastic solutions that might overtax his resources and thereby jeopardise the mounting success of his work in England. For the expense of Poynings' administration in Ireland and the expenditure necessitated by the Cornish rising, added to the subsidies required for a Scottish war, made it doubly clear that an English ruler could no more think of trying to conquer Ireland and Scotland than of repeating Henry V's successes in France. Instead, he would have to build a

preponderance of power by courting his enemies rather than by bludgeon-
ing them into submission. And it was for this reason, in fact, that Poynings
had been recalled in 1496 and the Earl of Kildare restored against the advice
of some of the royal council. As a result, Ireland duly succumbed for the rest
of the reign to English government and justice, no longer a drain upon the
king's resources or a happy hunting ground for Yorkist interlopers. But there
could be no denying either that the underlying problems were effectively
shelved rather than solved.

At the same time, Warbeck's ultimate failure enabled Henry to abandon
force and opt for peaceful persuasion with the Scots as well. Whereupon
James IV, deprived for the moment of all foreign encouragement and dis-
heartened by the lukewarm response of his subjects, duly accepted the
generous terms that England was prepared to offer in September 1497 with
the conclusion of the truce of Ayrton. Renewed in 1499, by January 1502 it
had been transformed into a full peace treaty, the first to be made between
the two countries since the breach of 1328. And the results were momentous,
for by the treaty's terms, James finally promised to marry Henry's daughter,
Margaret, the actual celebration of which occurred in August 1503 when
the girl was nearly 14. The Scots, significantly, were not obliged to abandon
their ancient friendship with France, and henceforth, harmony between
Scotland and England would continue to depend upon the maintenance of
Anglo–French goodwill. But the resulting match nevertheless provided the
firmest guarantee of peace that dynastic diplomacy could provide under the
circumstances, and while Henry VII lived the prospects would remain good,
particularly when the new alliance offered wider opportunities besides. For
by the time it was arranged, Margaret's brother, Arthur, had died in April 1502
and only the 11-year-old Prince Henry stood between the new Queen of
Scots and the succession to the Crown of England. As things transpired, the
union of the two crowns was in fact to be deferred for another century by
the survival of Prince Henry and the limited fecundity of his numerous wives.
But from the marriage of Margaret Tudor to James IV of Scotland was born
nevertheless the first notion of a united realm of Britain – 'with sea for its
frontiers and mutual love for its garrison' – which was to allure certain statesmen on both sides of the border until its eventual achievement in 1603.

It was a curious quirk of English history, therefore, that Perkin Warbeck's
six years of adventure between 1491 and 1497 had actually proved of no
inconsiderable benefit to the man who had been its target and the kingdom
he ruled, encouraging Henry VII far along the paths that Lambert Simnel's
rising and the crisis over Brittany had first forced him to explore years earlier.
Indeed, Warbeck's activities had compelled the first Tudor king of England
to develop something very like a systematic network of relationships with

both his continental and his British neighbours, the core of which was a good understanding with France. On the one hand, Henry's steady refusal during these years to regard France's involvement as an opportunity to reopen the Breton question demonstrated that, on his side at least, the Étaples settlement, which was renewed in 1498, was final. And neither – though he continued to employ the empty title of 'King of France' – did Henry make any attempt to make good the territorial claims that had gone with that title in times past. The closeness of his alliance with Spain and of his understanding with the Netherlands provided him, too, with reasonable assurance of adequate assistance if the French should see fit to start a new quarrel by pressing their claims in the Low Countries. And finally, both by loosening the reins in Ireland, which he had previously shown himself more than capable of tightening, and by marrying his daughter to the King of Scots, he appeared to complete his blueprint for the security of his dynasty and the protection of his realm. Indeed, the treaty of peace with Scotland in January 1502, along with the marriage of Prince Arthur to Catherine of Aragon only two months earlier, represented the twin peaks of his foreign policy achievements.

But if the formative period in the development of this overarching policy was by now over, and the remainder of the reign was largely occupied with the maintenance of the 'system' it involved, the twists and turns of events would nevertheless ensure that even Henry, with his newfound freedom from domestic threats, his abundant wealth and his high prestige abroad, could not stand still. On the contrary, his diplomacy became more active than ever from this point onwards and even reached out occasionally towards new projects that seem sometimes to border on the inexplicable – so much so, in fact, that tempting accusations of a return to Lancastrian megalomania, brought on by a combination of his previous successes and the onset of some kind of delusional senility, have sometimes been wrongly levelled against him. True, he was prone at times not only to greater but riskier intervention in continental affairs than formerly. Yet such charges, however superficially appealing, are nevertheless unfounded for one simple reason: that the principles underpinning his policies did not alter in his later years any more than his essentially defensive outlook to the challenges of external events. And if his actions did indeed exhibit a decidedly feverish aspect at times, it was largely because they reflected the swiftly shifting sands of political conditions in Europe, which were regularly thrown into turmoil, not least by a spate of destabilising mortalities among royal families in the early years of the new century. Prince Arthur died in April 1502; Elizabeth of York, Henry's queen, in April 1503; Isabella of Castile in November 1504; and the Archduke Philip of the Netherlands in September 1506. Each in turn produced new problems or led to fresh groupings of powers that explain the extraordinary convolutions of

Henry's later policies, while the loss of those close to him also seems to have taken a particular personal toll as his character undoubtedly grew harsher and he appeared to lose at least some of his remarkable talent for measured leadership. Though she wielded no political power, the king's wife had been well liked and may well have served as a mollifying influence upon her husband's actions, while the loss of old Cardinal Morton in 1500 and Sir Reginald Bray in 1503 also played their part in prompting an apparent decline in the overall quality of rule.

Predictably, Prince Arthur's death had proven a particularly grievous blow to both his father and mother. The news had been brought to them at night by an ageing Franciscan Observant friar who had been instructed by a messenger of the Privy Council to attend his sovereign at the nearby palace of Greenwich without delay. After which, we are told, the royal couple 'took their sorrows together', comforting themselves only with hopes of further offspring. 'God is where he was,' the queen reflected bravely, 'and we are both young enough.' But within a year the queen herself was dead as a result of her very efforts in this regard, expiring nine days after her own birthday upon delivery of a sickly daughter named Catherine who 'tarried but a small season after her mother' – the infant's only mark in history being the purchase of 4 yards of flannel at a shilling a yard to keep her from the perilous draughts of Richmond Palace. In June 1500, Henry's youngest son, Edmund, had also died, with the result that the continuance of the entire Tudor dynasty suddenly came to depend upon the life of one remaining child: Prince Henry, who was not yet 11 years old. Clearly, the line of succession to the throne had become dangerously thin and the execution of Sir James Tyrrell in May 1502 for treason, along with the arrest of Lord William de la Pole and Lord William Courtenay, leaves little doubt that both the king and his subjects were all too acutely aware of how a royal minority and a broken succession might undo at a stroke all that had been so painstakingly achieved since Bosworth Field.

Nor, of course, were foreign observers any less conscious of the consequent change in the King of England's circumstances. Most obviously of all, Arthur's death clearly severed the newly forged matrimonial link between England and Spain, and though negotiations began at once to renew it with a match involving the widowed Catherine and her young brother-in-law, Henry, her parents became confident of their ability to press for better terms. On the one hand, they attempted, albeit unsuccessfully, to stipulate in the new treaty that England should attack France if the French invaded Spain's new possessions in Italy, and it was only after much hard bargaining that agreement was finally reached in June 1503. Two days later, the 13-year-old was solemnly betrothed to Catherine *per verba de praesenti*, and after a year the requisite papal dispensation, permitting the union in spite of the prohibition in canon law of a marriage between a wife and her brother-in-law, was duly obtained from Julius II. But whether Prince Henry was indeed of age to enter into such legally binding contracts was arguable in its own right, and there was, of course, another obstacle altogether more serious than the immaturity of the bridegroom. For if the words of the 1503 treaty are to be believed, rather than the assertions of Ferdinand and Isabella at the time and of Catherine herself twenty-six years later, the previous marriage to Arthur had supposedly been consummated, placing it inside the degrees of consanguinity proscribed by canon law, and thereby rendering Pope Julius's dispensation potentially invalid. It was this, in fact, that explains the year-long delay, and this, too, that would ultimately help shatter England's links with Rome more than two decades later.

Certainly, the lengthy pause in proceedings had not been due to any intrinsic lack of enthusiasm on either the English or the Spanish side, since relations between the two courts were actually more cordial than ever. The death of Elizabeth of York had set Henry VII on a search around the courts of Europe for a second wife by whom he might strengthen the fragile Tudor line, and his choice had turned initially towards the young Queen Joanna, widow of Ferdinand II of Naples and niece of Ferdinand of Aragon, making Spain's good offices essential. Nor was Spanish compliance ever likely to have been an issue after Louis XII acquired Milan in 1500, and Spain incurred his bitter enmity by first agreeing to partition Naples with him in 1501 and subsequently expelling him from his share of the spoils during 1502–03. In response, Louis had cultivated Archduke Philip and Emperor Maximilian, securing their acquiescence, first by promising his infant daughter Claude to Philip's small son Charles, and then by brokering a further compact in 1504 by which the French king promised that Claude should have Milan and Brittany, along with his claims in Naples, were he to die without male heirs. As Claude was not yet 5, Charles not yet 4, and Louis himself, at 42, still apparently capable of fulfilling his procreative responsibilities, there was consequently ample scope to assume that the offer might never be made good. But it was sufficient all the same to secure at least the neutrality of Philip and Maximilian, and more than enough to suggest that the King of France was bent on speedy vengeance against his Spanish counterpart. Threatened by the incensed Louis and now deprived of their Habsburg allies, Ferdinand and Isabella had therefore even greater reason than Henry VII to hasten Catherine's remarriage to the new Prince of Wales – not least when the aged King of England eventually saw fit to toy with the distasteful notion of offering his own wrinkled hand to the Spanish princess, coolly disregarding a discrepancy of thirty years in their ages and the impediment in canon law entailed by their own relationship. 'If the king had been young,' wrote Francis Bacon later, 'a man would have judged him to be amorous,' though the proposal, unsurprisingly, left Catherine's parents aghast. 'Speak of it as a thing not to be endured,' declared Ferdinand.

But it was at this point, in November 1504, just as Pope Julius's dispensation arrived in Spain, that Isabella died and the Spanish kingdoms, first united by her marriage to Ferdinand, threatened to fall apart. For Ferdinand, from the outset, had been only king of Aragon, and in Castile the lawful ruler now became his daughter Joanna, wife of Archduke Philip, who was already drifting rapidly into the camp of her father's arch enemy. Isabella, in fact, had hoped that Joanna might be content to remain in the Netherlands with her husband, effectively ignoring her Spanish inheritance and leaving Ferdinand to administer Castile as regent in her name. But Philip, encouraged by Maximilian, was ambitious for the chance of a crown, and the Castilian nobility in its turn was keen to regain much of its lost independence by playing off daughter against father. As a result, the marriage between the Spanish and Burgundian houses, which had seemed in 1496 to bind Spain and the Netherlands so securely, was teetering dangerously, as was Henry VII's ongoing hopes in England for peace with France. For if Spain disintegrated once more into its component parts, the French would be free to focus their attention upon the Netherlands and thereby present Henry with a repetition in Flanders of the problems that he previously faced in Brittany. And it was this pressing conundrum that explains the tortuous and sometimes sordid shifts of his continental diplomacy during the remaining years of his reign, and, in particular, the urgent, almost frantic, gestures of amity towards France, which in 1505 extended as far as suggestions of a possible marriage alliance.

It accounts, too, for the otherwise inexplicable cordiality of Henry's overtures towards Philip and resulting estrangement from Ferdinand. Doubtless, the increasing importance of the Antwerp market to English cloth exporters played its part. Doubtless, too, Philip acquired a useful diplomatic counter when, in July 1505, he secured in his domains the fugitive Edmund de la Pole, Earl of Suffolk, virtually the last of the Yorkist pretenders. But neither the pull of Antwerp nor the presence in the Netherlands of the White Rose's last faint hope can fully explain the rapidity of the Anglo–Burgundian rapprochement in 1505–06, not to mention the extent, however reluctant, of Henry's abandonment of Ferdinand. Desperately seeking a further counterweight against France, the King of England would have no choice but to favour Philip's attempts to wrest Castile from his father-in-law, lending him £108,000 for the purpose in April 1505, while discussing the possibility of his own marriage to Maximilian's daughter Margaret of Savoy. And as his friendship with Philip and Maximilian grew ever closer, so his relations with Ferdinand deteriorated accordingly, even after the papal dispensation granting

Prince Henry's marriage to Catherine finally arrived. The English king, for his part, retained her dowry as a useful bargaining counter and kept her in relative penury, refusing or evading all her father's requests for completion of the marriage or her return – along with her dowry – to Spain. More significantly still, Henry also arranged in June for his son to register a formal protest that any marriage with his deceased brother's widow was against both his will and conscience, after which negotiations began for an alternative match involving the French princess, Margaret of Angoulême. Isolated, unable to agree with Philip, and despairing of his ability to hold Castile singlehanded, Ferdinand himself was left with no choice than to turn to his old enemy, France, marrying Germaine de Foix, Louis XII's niece, in October 1505 and paying the French king no less than a million crowns for recognition of his rights to the kingdom of Naples.

With the betrothal in the following May of Princess Claude, heiress of Brittany and lately prospective bride of Charles of the Netherlands, to Francis of Angoulême, heir presumptive of France, a new and somewhat improbable alignment of the powers of Europe therefore emerged: Louis and Ferdinand against Philip, Maximilian and the King of England, with Castile as the prize of victory. But perhaps not only Castile. For France's ruler might well consider that the best way of aiding his new ally and advantaging himself was to distract Philip from his Spanish target by attacking Flanders – and in the process threatening his counterpart across the Channel. Acknowledging the possibility, Archduke Philip duly set out in January 1506, along with a large fleet and his wife, to take possession of her kingdom. But midwinter storms after two days at sea swiftly put paid to their plans and left them seeking shelter in Weymouth, where the King of England lost no time in exploiting the heaven-sent opportunity to strengthen and formalise his alliance with Burgundy, inviting the stranded couple to Windsor and entertaining them royally. Whilst there, Philip was installed as a Knight of the Garter, in return for Prince Henry's admittance to the Order of the Golden Fleece, and on the same day, 9 February, a treaty of alliance was signed, by which both sides promised to protect each other's dominions, present and future, and to give no aid to the other's rebels. At once, Philip handed over the unfortunate Earl of Suffolk, whose life Henry promised to spare, followed soon afterwards by English recognition of Philip's claim to Castile, albeit qualified with a proviso that only such troops as the English king deemed fit were to be available for any military assistance. An agreement to facilitate Henry's marriage to Maximilian's daughter, Margaret of Savoy, was also arranged, along with the opening of commercial negotiations, which were to result ultimately in the *Intercursus Malus*, the revised version of the *Intercursus Magnus* signed ten years earlier.

From many perspectives, therefore, Henry had once again managed to drive good bargains. Yet, in doing so, he had not only aligned himself openly and formally with Philip's ambitious projects, but committed himself up to the hilt politically. To his credit, it seemed initially as though his Burgundian investment was paying off handsomely, since Philip and Joanna were indeed warmly welcomed in Castile, and steadily established their hold upon the kingdom during the summer. France, meanwhile, appeared unready to act, forcing Ferdinand to accept Philip as Joanna's regent by the Treaty of Villafranca. But the fateful tale of mortality among princes was not over, and when Philip died in September 1506, so too did the prospective union of Castile with the Netherlands. His possessions in the Netherlands passed, in fact, to his 6-year-old son Charles, whose grandfather, the Emperor Maximilian, duly proceeded as regent to reassume his now familiar duties as Burgundian babysitter. More momentously still, however, in Castile the highly strung temperament of Queen Joanna finally snapped under the shock of her husband's death. For weeks she carried his coffin with her wherever she went, her obvious and morbid insanity rendering her wholly incapable of serving even as no more than a figurehead for Castilian independence. In consequence, Ferdinand resumed the role of regent from which Philip had relieved him, while the King of England's protective web duly dissolved without trace. Having considered Catherine of Aragon as a possible bride and olive branch to Spain, Henry pondered, too, a marriage to the deranged Joanna, as well as the dispatch of English archers to assist Ferdinand's crusade against the Moors in North Africa. But his hopes of rebuilding the broken trinity of England, the Netherlands and Castile were as fragile as his failing eyesight, which was also steadily deserting him as the creeping onset of old age took more and more obvious a toll upon his physical condition.

Instead, he would turn ultimately to the establishment of a triple entente between England, the Netherlands and France, though this itself was far from straightforward, since the Netherlands government was by 1507 engaged in an ongoing quarrel with the Duke of Gelderland, whose French and Scottish connections threatened to give the matter an altogether broader significance. Furthermore, Maximilian's determination to journey to Italy, to receive from the pope the Imperial Crown to which he had first been elected more than twenty years earlier, not only alarmed Venice but also roused French fears for their possession of Milan. Even so, the King of England's new policy still made fair headway, as he confirmed his friendship with the Netherlands by abandoning in 1507 the commercial concessions he had won for English merchants by the *Intercursus Malus*, and subsequently proceeded to mediate a peace between Maximilian and the Duke of Gelderland. More importantly still, he secured in December 1507 the emperor's agreement to a marriage between the young Archduke Charles and his daughter Mary. The kingdom of Castile, on the one hand, was to be the couple's marriage portion – though how this was to be achieved was unclear – and he also pressed his own claim, with equally inflated hopes, for the hand of Margaret of Savoy. Yet when Maximilian agreed a truce with Venice and abandoned his proposed journey to Rome, the King of England actually seemed close to achieving his objectives, even retaining the goodwill of France into the bargain by reviving his former suggestion that his son marry Margaret of Angoulême. Indeed, when the congress of Cambrai met at the end of the year, ostensibly to plan a crusade against the Turks, Henry for a time imagined that this was nothing less than the final step in bringing about a direct understanding between his French and Habsburg allies and the final isolation of Ferdinand.

Almost inevitably, however, events conspired otherwise. For Louis XII, whose chief concern was to safeguard and enlarge his possession of Milan, was not prepared to sacrifice his understanding with Ferdinand, his most dangerous Italian rival, in return for an entente with England and the Netherlands, whose interests and influence in Italy were negligible. In 1505, the French king had already bought Spanish acquiescence to his claims in Milan by recognising Ferdinand's claims in Naples. And now in 1508, under cover of the crusading talks at Cambrai, he undertook to buy off his other Italian rival, Emperor Maximilian, by inducing him to join in the partition of the Venetian republic's mainland territories. The pope was prepared to give the project his blessing, but it was also essential that the project should have Ferdinand's blessing, which was duly won by the offer of the Adriatic towns currently in Venice's possession, and the prospect of simultaneously strengthening his alliance with France and restoring his relations with the Habsburgs. So when the League of Cambrai was formed against Venice in December 1508, it was no small irony that its members were the pope, Louis XII, Maximilian, the Archduke Charles and Ferdinand – without the King of England.

Despite appearances, however, Henry was hardly left in isolation, since the Cambrai powers still proved desirous of his goodwill. France cultivated his friendship; Ferdinand remained ready to talk of Catherine's marriage to Prince Henry; and Maximilian showed his eager desire for English subsidies by allowing the marriage of Charles and Mary to be celebrated by proxy within a week of the conclusion of the League. All, moreover, were bent upon despoiling Italy, where England had no interests to be harmed. Indeed, the humbling of Venice might even benefit England's reviving trade in the Mediterranean, and as a result, this sudden combination of continental powers was actually to prove of greater benefit than any apparent marginalisation it may have entailed loss. Since 1496, or even earlier, the main purpose of Henry VII's designs had been to nurture the friendship of the Netherlands and to provide a deterrent to any French aggression there. The Netherlands apart, there was in fact very little direct conflict of interest between England and France at all, and England had good reason to avoid a dispute that would probably involve a further conflict with Scotland and thus prevent the hoped for isolation of British affairs from continental politics. At the same time, it was only because a clash between English and French interests might arise indirectly out of a French attack upon the Netherlands that Henry had been so eager to build up a deterrent system of continental alliances in the first place. But now, by the League of Cambrai, that danger was removed. Louis, Maximilian and Charles were allies, and Henry could be friends with all. So long as the League lasted, the Netherlands were sure to remain safe from French attack, and the danger that Henry's alliances had been designed to meet was effectively neutralised. Even if that danger should revive with the collapse of the League, moreover, the break-up would surely yield excellent opportunities to rebuild those alliances its existence now made superfluous.

The essential and overriding truth was that England's vital interests were still confined to the regions just across the Channel and the Narrow Seas. For while Italy, where England had few interests and no influence, remained the centre of attraction for the continental powers, there was little danger that any of these powers might seriously threaten England. And no one grasped this more clearly than England's first Tudor ruler, who continued to regard his kingdom's exclusion from the League of Cambrai with comparative indifference. From his perspective, after all, there would be time enough to take up the complicated threads of continental politics when the Cambrai allies fell out, as inevitably they would – notwithstanding the fact that when that time came, he himself would be cold in his tomb and the direction of policy left to altogether less prudent hands.

8

HENRY VIII:
PUISSANCE AND PENURY

Ay, sir, have ye been with Master Henry King? A noble act ye did there! Ye
spent away my money and other men's, like a sort of vagabonds and knaves!
John Brody of Shaftesbury in Dorset to John Williams,
soldier, 1524

On 21 April 1509, Henry VII's creaking descent to the grave finally ended,
whereupon his crown passed to his only surviving son, and a new and
restless spirit began almost at once to inform England's relations with the
Continent. It was not merely that a king of 52 was succeeded by one just
short of his eighteenth birthday: the difference between father and son was
altogether more than a discrepancy between crabbed age and eager youth.
Henry VII had been the child of adversity, schooled by exile and early dangers into a wary approach to life, more anxious to avoid risks than to seize
chances. Henry VIII, by contrast, born six years after the crisis of Bosworth
Field, was the child of prosperity, who could remember only the affluent
and peaceful years of his father's reign, when the consolidation of the Tudor
throne was already well under way. The plain fact was that in this new era
'called then the golden world', Henry VIII had a full hand of aces to play
and ample scope to choose his game. Thanks to his father's statesmanship,
he was the first English king in a hundred years to succeed unopposed to
a stable, peaceful and solvent realm. Furthermore, the second Henry Tudor,
unlike the first, was of 'truly royal stock', embodying as he did the union
of the red and white roses. Last, and by no means least, the new king literally looked the part. The successor to the English throne, it was widely

believed, would be a ruler 'to cleanse every eye of tears and substitute praise for a long moaning', and many foreigners were no less fulsome. 'Love for the king,' said one, 'is universal with all who see him, for his highness does not seem a person of this world, but one descended from heaven.' Thomas More, meanwhile, even vied so gushingly with his praise that one French critic, Germanus Brixius, chided him for disloyalty to the deceased ruler. 'This day,' More had written, 'is the end of our slavery, the fount of our liberty; the end of sadness, the beginning of joy.'

Even at this early stage, however, there were other observers who noted that the young king was 'so made for war that there is no military exercise in which he does not equal (not to say surpass) his soldiers'. Nor was his contempt and hatred for the French even vaguely concealed. Erasmus, who saw him a number of times during his youth, later wrote to a friend how the prince's 'dream as a child had been the recovery of the French provinces'. The writings of Froissart, where all was talk of crushing victories across the Channel, had been eagerly devoured, and in the classroom, likewise, the high points of English valour had all been etched indelibly in his mind. On the one hand, the young prince learned how the great triumph at Crécy had been followed by the capture of Thérouanne's sturdy fortress, and came to know every detail of the siege of Tournai, which Edward III had staged over many weeks. Above all, he dwelt upon the unparalleled exploits of Henry V, 'the flower and glory of all knighthood', who before the Battle of Agincourt had traversed his camp in driving rain, exhorting his dispirited army to rise up and seize victory against all odds. Fixated, too, by the crusades at a time when it was still not finally appreciated that Christendom would never again raise its banners of war in the Holy Land, he had come to see himself, indeed, as a perfect knightly paragon. Having learned to fend off all-comers with sword, spear and poleaxe, he had learned to fight on horseback with Charles Brandon and other 'boon companions' in loud attendance. For the first time, too, he had been fitted with dazzling plate armour fashioned in the smooth, rounded Italian style. Learning to mount and dismount without assistance, he was trained to move at speed under a weight of some 60lb, even in the scorching heat of summer when the rays of the sun made the metal searingly hot, while by the age of 16 he was said to be exercising every day in the lists and gaining his first serious instruction in the use of the lance. At every opportunity, he hacked, thrust and battered at man-sized quintains resembling scimitar-wielding Turks, and became familiar also with the use of guns and gunpowder and the wondrous destructive power of heavy artillery. There was not, it seemed, a single facet of the martial arts that was unknown to him.

Nor, however, is there likely to have been one in which he ever met a telling personal criticism or a serious challenge from his peers. And as the prince's teenaged body steadily achieved heroic proportions, so his adolescent fantasies grew in tandem with his unchecked egotism. Even when glorifying at full tilt at the time of the coronation, Thomas More acknowledged readily of his sovereign master that 'if my head could win him a castle in France … it should not fail to go'. The signs of things to come were, after all, undeniable. At 16, when a French courtier had complimented him on his archery, the prince responded both insultingly and with characteristic naivety by pointing out that the courtier's own shot was 'good for a Frenchman'. And when in September 1509 the Abbot of Fécamp came to congratulate Henry upon his accession, he found himself gratuitously insulted for his trouble. For only the day after his arrival, at a mock battle that he had been specifically invited to attend, the corpulent Frenchman found no place among the official spectators, making it plain, said the Venetian envoy, that Henry 'held the French king in little account'. It was only eighty years, after all, since an English monarch had been crowned in Paris itself, and the throne's new occupant lost no time in commissioning a translation of Titus Livius' life of that resounding legend, Henry V, victor of Agincourt. How better, indeed, for a young King of England to enhance his popularity and win himself renown than by regaining the French lands, perhaps even the French Crown itself, that his Lancastrian predecessors had lost?

Even so, a war policy was not without its risks. South and east, over the water, lay the Great Powers – France, Spain and the Holy Roman Empire – while England, by comparison, still remained a comparatively minor player, in spite of the first Tudor's best efforts. When Henry VIII was born, the King of England ruled less overseas territory, in fact, than for four hundred years. He held not one French province, and Scotland was still a hostile, independent realm. In Ireland, meanwhile, English control remained confined to that thin strip of land around Dublin known as the Pale. Beyond this lay the 'land of war' in which the only rulers, for Englishmen at least, were defiance and danger. Other than their boggy Irish foothold and the Channel Islands, the English kings ruled only Wales, and though they continued to flatter themselves with spurious claims to the throne of France, the land they actually held there was confined to an area around Calais and the castle of Guisnes, about 8 miles in depth from the sea and stretching for some 20 miles or so along the coast. No more than two decades earlier, England's glory years had finally withered on the bough, while the danger from abroad was still as great as ever, since ships of the period continued to have great difficulty sailing into the wind, and southern England remained for most of the year a lee shore, easy to attack and difficult to defend. In such circumstances, Henry VII had wisely followed caution's counsel, so that by the start of the sixteenth century a Milanese envoy could write that he was 'perfectly secure against fortune'. It was England's good luck, in fact, that she had been blessed with a king prudent enough to seek safety in the diplomatic shade rather than risk the white heat of conflict. But now the talk was of 'puissance' and, above all, *virtu*: not the Christian virtue extolled by Erasmus when he dreamed of a new epoch of peace that was 'really golden', but the martial virtue of the Renaissance prince leading boldly at the head of victorious armies amid 'spoils, shouts that rent the heavens, trumpets blaring, and canon thundering'.

In a monarchy where the king ruled as well as reigned, the accession of such a prince as Henry was bound to have far-reaching effects on England's relations with Europe. Not for long was he likely to be willing to trudge in the cautious footsteps of his father. Yet it would ultimately take three long years and more before Henry's knights could finally trample the lilies of France for his greater glory, since he had inherited from his predecessor those self-same councillors who had long governed England 'without sword and bloodshed' abroad. Though their motives varied, each member of the council's inner ring stood resolutely for the measured diplomacy of the previous reign. There was, for instance, William Warham, chancellor as well as Archbishop of Canterbury, who was to marry Henry to Catherine and crowned them both. Described by Erasmus as 'witty, energetic and laborious', he was a pliant, sceptical character who, it was said, 'only read' and would die with merely £30 in hand, 'enough for my funeral'. Frugal and with no apparent interest in pleasure, he seems, in fact, to have seen war as little more than an expensive diversion from the ageing process. Similarly, Richard Fox, Bishop of Winchester, Lord Privy Seal and the man who had baptised Henry, also favoured peace, though more for business' than for goodness' sake, much like Thomas Ruthall, Bishop of Durham, whose narrow devotion to the everyday drudgery of accumulating vast lands made him the richest prelate in the realm. All feared lest, in the words of John Stow, 'such abundance of riches … the King was now possessed of should move his young years into a riotous forgetting of himself'. But though, as Stow added, they 'gate him to be present with them to acquaint him with the politique government of the realm, with which at first he could not endure to be much troubled', even the guile and gravity of such men could not indefinitely quell their master's growing war pangs.

For the time being, however, there were at least other distractions to absorb the new ruler's restless energy and insatiable desire for popularity. Not least, the king's nuptial knot to Catherine of Aragon was finally and impulsively sealed only six weeks after his father's death, notwithstanding the concern of Archbishop Warham, who had raised once more the issue of the bride's previous marriage to Prince Arthur as a possible impediment. Not long afterwards, moreover, two of the very men who had been instrumental in amassing Henry VII's treasure were to be Henry VIII's first victims. For in his first effort to distance himself from his predecessor, the newcomer to the throne had pandered abjectly to public prejudice by inviting all in the kingdom to lay charges of extortion against any of his late father's servants. Richard Empson and Edmund Dudley, the former monarch's infamous tax collectors, were the obvious quarry, though in milking the realm during the previous reign they had been acting under royal instructions throughout and had no difficulty in proving this initially. Even so, a totally fictitious charge of treason was subsequently concocted on the grounds that Empson, allegedly, had 'resolved to seize the government for himself' in collaboration with Dudley, who was said to have 'summoned knights to repair to him with all their power' upon the death of the old king. Sensible precautions honestly conceived were thus neatly recast as conspiracy, and in August both were executed while Henry and his courtiers made merry at Windsor. 'Whoever yet saw any man condemned for justice?' complained Empson vainly at his show trial.

When the time came for bloodshed abroad, however, there was further need for delay. For when Henry mounted the throne, France remained allied with all the other powers of Europe in the apparent harmony of the League of Cambrai. So long as the League lasted, an English attack upon her was obviously out of the question. Nor would Henry find much scope to display his prowess by joining the League while its energies were directed against Venice. Yet if the glory of war was not for the moment an option, the opportunity was still not long in arriving for the young king to posture grandly on the European stage. For within a month of his accession, the Venetian army was decisively routed at Agnadello. 'In one day,' wrote Niccolò Machiavelli, 'the Venetians lost all they had acquired during eight hundred years of effort.' And the result was an appeal to Henry from the defeated city-state that he mediate their peace with the Cambrai powers – an opening that could be exploited in one of two ways, both of which would lead to the centre of European affairs. For if, on the one hand, young Henry could reconcile both sides, he might stand forth as the unifier of Christendom, and as the man who had brought the League of Cambrai back to its original purpose, the defence of Christendom against the infidel Turk. Certainly, the crusading project was one to which Henry at least paid lip service more than once over the next twenty years. But there was also the possibility that Venice's appeal might be exploited to redirect the League of Cambrai not against the Turks but against France, turning it into an alliance to expel the French from Italy and assist England in the recovery not only of her French possessions but of the French Crown itself.

The Venetians, in fact, had been quick to point out this last prospect, and by marrying Catherine of Aragon on 11 June 1509, Henry drew close again to the one continental monarch, Ferdinand, who might be most favourable to such a scheme. By pressing for his sister Mary's marriage to the Archduke Charles, moreover, the King of England sought to secure the Netherlands and Charles's grandfather, Emperor Maximilian. Nor was this all. For if the pope could be reconciled to Venice by Archbishop Christopher Bainbridge's dispatch to Rome, the web would be complete for a new league involving England, Spain, the Netherlands, the emperor, the pope and the Venetians against France. And as this possibility dawned, so Henry prepared accordingly: ordering general musters to check the equipment and preparedness of his kingdom's forces; adding to his father's Yeomen of the Guard a new corps of Gentlemen Pensioners to train and retain skilled captains; and building at once two sizeable ships to augment a royal navy that had already begun to take shape during the previous reign. For while Henry VII had inherited only four 'King's ships' from the Yorkists, which had been designed primarily for trade rather than war, the five handed on to Henry VIII included at least two that were, for their day, powerful and imposing warships. The *Regent*, a four-master of about 600 tons, completed in 1490, carried 225 guns – 180 of them serpentines, the heaviest naval artillery then in use – while the *Sovereign*, completed in the same year, carried 141 guns. And the first Tudor had also developed a naval base for his ships at Portsmouth, where the royal navy's first dry dock was completed between 1495 and 1497. Henceforth, it would be altogether easier for the king's ships to operate for considerable periods of time in the Channel without returning to the main bases in the Medway and the Thames estuary, and they would be better supplied into the bargain by new storage facilities at Greenwich and Woolwich.

But a stiff note of warning to Louis XII against the dismemberment of Venice was as far, for the moment, as any action went. For while young friends among the nobility, like the Duke of Buckingham, might egg Henry on, his old councillors, inherited from his father, continued to restrict him. And there were also, for the time being at least, the pacific inclinations of the queen to consider. For if Catherine was no friend of France, she nevertheless found herself in a dilemma. On the one hand, her unhappy experiences of the previous reign inclined her to bind England and Spain in indissoluble friendship forged by a military campaign against the French in union with the pope – an onslaught that might simultaneously satisfy her husband's appetite for conquest across the Channel and King Ferdinand's ambitions in Italy. But the latter, though alarmed by the growth of French power, was unready to challenge Louis XII with only English support. Instead, he intended to 'continue in amity with the French king … unto the time that the Emperor and he shall be agreed'. He did in December 1509 conclude a treaty with Maximilian settling the succession to Castile upon their mutual grandson, the Archduke Charles. But the emperor, still bitterly hostile to Venice, would not desert France, with the result that Ferdinand, using the Queen of England as Aragon's ambassador in what she herself once described to him as 'these kingdoms of your Highness', laid a restraining hand upon the impetuous young Henry. After which, the war rumours died down and, to the dismay of both the Venetians and Bainbridge, Henry renewed his father's peace treaties with France and Scotland in March 1510.

Nevertheless, by the middle of the next year both Ferdinand and Pope Julius II had become thoroughly disenchanted with the League of Cambrai. Venice had submitted, but France had enjoyed both the pleasure and the profit as Ferdinand and the pope observed impotently from the sidelines. And so it was that Henry now found himself invited by Rome to join a Holy League that would set upon France and hopefully yield – in the name of God, truth and Christian piety – the most unholy profits for all the adventurers involved. Pope Julius's enmity to Venice had in fact been outweighed by fears of France, and having made an alliance with the Swiss cantons in March, he assured himself at least of Spain's benevolent neutrality by formally investing Ferdinand as King of Naples in July. The papal galleys assaulted one French client, Genoa; papal, Swiss and Venetian troops another, Ferrara. So as the diplomatic merry-go-round continued its giddy course, this time the Venetians were papal allies and, as such, they too fanned Henry's ambition to the full. The French king, they said, was 'elate and haughty' and 'wanted to be monarch of the whole world', though behind the scenes, the pope still continued to eye Venice hungrily, and Maximilian continued to vacillate. Only, indeed, when France's client, the Duke of Gelders, fell out with the emperor in the summer of 1511 and Henry dispatched an expedition of 1,500 men under Sir Edward Poynings to his assistance did the emperor's attitude begin to alter. But Spain, in the meantime, remained concerned solely with consolidating her control of Naples and annexing the kingdom of Navarre.

Furthermore, when Henry's envoy in Spain, John Stile, warned him that his father-in-law was only 'afeared for his realm of Naples' and cared not one jot for English interests, the observation fell on deaf ears. By now, indeed, Henry was already contracting with the gun maker Hans Popenruyter of Malines for twenty-four of the 1,000lb naval guns known as serpentines, along with a further two dozen 'courtaulx', which at over 7ft in length were equally substantial. He had even specified their names – Rose, Crown, York and Lancaster among others. 'Night and day and on all the festivals the cannon founders are at work,' reported the Venetian ambassador from London. But while these preparations were unhappy news for Warham, Fox and Ruthall, they were much to the liking, in the meantime, of a rising careerist called Thomas Wolsey who was now to dominate the king's affairs increasingly. For it was he, the king's almoner, who would order the thousands of handguns, the tons of saltpetre and gunpowder, the countless cartloads of victuals and every other conceivable provision for the coming business of war. And it was he, too, who would organise to the finest detail the transport of these items across the heaving Channel and beyond to the field of battle itself. Thus equipped, England's king was bent upon restoring some part of the empire that, until Joan of Arc's crusade, had stretched south of the Loire. All that was wanting was the necessary pretext – and this was not long in coming.

For, having been suddenly turned upon by his former allies and having described his betrayal by the pope as 'a dagger plunged through the heart', the French king promptly besieged the papal forces at Bologna, while assembling at Pisa a schismatic church council with a view to deposing the sharp-witted pontiff. In consequence, by November 1511, Pope Julius II – 'this swarthy and pugnacious Genoese', who once let it be known that he had pulled a galley oar in his youth, and had conducted his holy office ever since like a sailor on leave – finally succeeded in enlisting English help 'to defend the unity of the Church'. Already in the spring of 1510 the Holy Father had dispatched to Henry a golden rose commemorating the Saviour's Passion and signalling the present need for war. But this was only the first of a series of blatant manoeuvres that had progressively inveigled the English king. When the French episcopacy announced itself willing to recognise a rival to the papal throne, Julius responded by threatening to take back the title 'Most Christian King' from Louis and confer it instead upon Henry. And when subsequently the very throne of France itself was dangled before him, the snare was complete and the peace party on Henry's council undermined at a stroke. For the bishops who had so far resisted the king's restless blustering could no longer constrain him when his martial ambitions and dynastic fantasies were thus unexpectedly sanctified. Bitterly denouncing the 'cruel, impious and unspeakable' French attempt to 'lacerate the seamless garment of Christ', Henry would now lead his nation straight into what amounted to a crusade marking the revival of the Hundred Years War and the onset of a fresh conflict that would dominate his reign and outlast his death.

While Emperor Maximilian dragged his feet, moreover, Henry determined to act with his father-in-law alone, and in June 1512 the Marquess of Dorset duly sailed out of Southampton Water bound for Gascony with 7,000 men. Ferdinand, in fact, had joined the League the previous October, but, having reached the port of Fuentarrabia with the intention of attacking Bayonne, Dorset found that his Spanish allies failed to materialise as arranged. Indeed, while France was bracing itself for an English attack, Ferdinand, 'that ancient and politic prince', had sent his troops into Navarre, occupied it successfully and declared an abrupt end to the campaign. In the meantime, the English force, with negligible artillery and faced by novel continental formations of pikemen and arquebusiers, had sweltered through the summer looking hopelessly across the bay of St Jean de Luz. 'Their victual was much part garlic,' said one chronicler, 'and the Englishmen did eat of the garlic with all meats, and drank hot wines in the hot weather, and did eat all the hot fruits that they could get, which caused the blood so to boil in their bellies that there fell sick three thousand of the flux.' A bedraggled force of sullen and demoralised soldiers, 'glad that they had deported out of such a country', therefore limped its way back to England. The expedition had wasted 200,000 ducats and the best part of 2,000 English lives, without striking a single worthwhile military blow. And to compound the insult, Ferdinand now bitterly criticised the English force, which had ultimately mutinied and sailed home without orders. Summoning the captains of Dorset's army to the Palace of Westminster, Henry duly upbraided them in the presence of the Privy Council and Spanish ambassador, ordering them to ask forgiveness of the Spaniard on their knees. Only by such means, it seems, could Henry sustain his pride and maintain his conviction that all would be forgotten if only the next expedition against the French foe was greater still. And surely enough, by the hectic summer of the following year, Catherine of Aragon would write to Wolsey how she and her ladies were 'horribly busy with making standards, banners and badges' for the imminent attack on France.

As a prelude, in Holy Week of 1513 — around the very time that Henry was engaged at the house of the Franciscan Observants in Greenwich in an earnest disquisition with Dean John Colet of St Paul's regarding the virtues of peace — the English fleet would sail down the Thames and out into the Channel under Sir Edward Howard, the 24-year-old son of the Earl of Surrey. Though Maximilian had finally joined the Holy League in November 1512 and agreed the following April to a campaign against France alongside Henry, Ferdinand and the pope, the Spanish king had nevertheless secretly signed a year's truce with the French only a few days earlier. And as the Venetians had already made their peace with Louis in March and Maximilian was a wily — and penurious — ally from whom little could be expected, Henry had accordingly opted for what he could achieve by his own efforts, notwithstanding the fact that the comings and goings of envoys between France and Scotland made it all too probable that these efforts would have to be divided between two fronts. Eighty ships in all ventured forth, including one boat named, with consummate irony, after perhaps the most outspoken advocate of peace in all Europe, Erasmus. In addition to a double complement of sailors, moreover, the fleet carried, according to one particular account, as many as 16,000 soldiers who were to pour over onto the enemy's decks after his ships had been grappled. The objective was Brest and the force of Rhodes galleys, which, with their superior guns and lethal mounted crossbows, had been urgently transferred by the French from patrolling the Barbary Coast and harboured there under the command of Prégent de Bidoux. But Howard was soon writing of misfortunes and hindrances, and a crushing blow was duly delivered when he personally led a force of light rowing craft to assault the galleys in their anchorage in the shallows of Blancs Sablons Bay, north of the Brest entrance, which was inaccessible to the deeper English ships. From his own boat Howard was said to have boarded a galley, only to be forced overboard by morris-pikes and killed before his friends could follow.

It was a bitter blow, but not one that could diminish the war fever of either Henry or, indeed, his subjects, who had already reacted to Ferdinand's lack of co-operation with an outburst of violence against Spanish residents in London. One Venetian observer, Lorenzo Pasqualigo, declared to his brother, with no intentional irony, that there had been no king nobler or more valiant than Henry for a thousand years. And surely enough, wholly undeterred by his admiral's death, Henry proceeded to lay his final preparations for a direct attack on northern France in the traditional fashion from England's bridgehead in Calais. Logistically, the task was formidable. But it was now that Thomas Wolsey, above all others, would show his mettle as an architect of victory. Born at some time between 1470 and 1473, this thrusting son of an Ipswich innkeeper and cattle dealer had first risen to prominence by means of a powerful intellect that not even his bitterest enemies would ever deign to deny. For while John Skelton's references to Wolsey's 'greasy genealogy' were not entirely unfounded, the keenness of his mind had soon been confirmed by the fact that at only 15 he took his degree at Magdalen College, Oxford. Even so, the academic life on offer could not hold him and after a short term as rector of Limington, where tradition has it he suffered the hospitality of the stocks for excessive gaiety at a fair, he began a fleet-footed ascent of the ladder of patronage. Emerging first as chaplain to Henry Deane, Archbishop of Canterbury, he then entered the service of Sir Richard Nanfan, deputy lieutenant of Calais, before becoming a royal chaplain to Henry VII. And such was his obvious impact that by November 1509 he had become both royal almoner and a junior privy councillor. However, it was the backing and execution of Henry VIII's war policies against the older and more conservative heads of the royal council that had won him the king's most passionate advocacy and allowed him to quicken the pace of his promotion to high office at a rate quite without precedent.

And now he would be expected to deliver the shining glory for his master that would either consolidate or dash his fortunes at court. For, after the abortive campaign of 1512 and Edward Howard's subsequent death, this was a conflict transformed from a religious crusade into a naked demonstration of national might and pride. Much to Henry's indignation, Ferdinand had professed himself outraged at English perfidy and remained loud in rebuking his son-in-law for earlier letting his troops desert en masse. English soldiers were, he complained, 'self-indulgent and idle, inconsistent and fickle, rash and quarrelsome and incapable of acting in concert with allies'. Even women, indeed, were heard to decry Henry's armies when Margaret of Savoy muttered dismissively that Englishmen had 'so long abstained from war, they lack experience from disuse, and, as it is reported, they now be almost weary of it'. Not only were English soldiers ill-led and ill-fed, it seems they were also ill-armed – a fact of which Dr Knight, England's ambassador to Spain, was all too aware when he told Wolsey that of the 8,000 bowmen dispatched upon the ill-fated expedition of 1512, only 200 had been properly equipped. In consequence, any army that left English shores would now have to be armed to the teeth and to this end Wolsey scoured all Europe for the necessary weaponry. In Italy especially, he drew up massive contracts for armour – thousands of suits being purchased through the agency of the great Florentine bankers, the Frescobaldi, and from Guydo Portinari and John Cavalcanti, merchants of Florence. From Germany, meanwhile, and still more often from towns in Flanders, such as Malines and Brussels, came a deluge of artillery pieces: not only more serpentines, but brass 'curtals' of some 3,000lb and other smaller guns such as 'bombards' and 'falcons', as well as lightweight swivel guns known as 'murderers', all of which flowed into the ordnance stores at Calais.

To his credit, Wolsey had learnt, too, that any effective army must be full-bellied as well as suitably armed. And the same eye for detail, the same capacity for attending to all aspects of a transaction, the same nose for a good deal, were thus all evident in his purchase of victuals. Throughout the months of February, March and April 1513, stores of food were being steadily poured into Calais in anticipation of the time when England might have as many as 40,000 men operating across the Channel. Moreover, in ordering the slaughter of 25,000 oxen at the end of January, he insisted that only the finest beasts from Lincolnshire and the Netherlands be secured. And once the transaction was done, he duly insisted on securing rebates for the hides and tallow. Amid all, he also found time to ensure that the English soldier's seemingly unquenchable thirst for beer as well as glory would be satisfied, as a network of new brew houses was swiftly erected up and down the length of England, the largest being at Portsmouth. Such were his efforts, in fact, that Bishop Fox prayed God for him to be delivered out of his 'outrageous charge and labour'. But the overall outcome was nevertheless such a triumph of logistical skill that Brian Tuke, Clerk of the Signet, would report eventually how the soldiers were able to live in time of war 'far more cheaply than they lived at home in time of peace'.

And accordingly, at 4 p.m. on 30 June, on a fine midsummer afternoon, Thomas Wolsey's royal master tenderly parted from his queen at Dover in the midst of a fleet of 300 ships, the like of which, said one of his captains, Neptune never saw. It was, in fact, exactly 100 years to the day since Henry V had asserted his claim to the French throne, and it was no coincidence either that both he and his current Tudor successor were each sons of troubled usurpers, seeking to identify their new dynasties with the kingdom they ruled by an aggressive foreign policy. Not one month earlier it was being rumoured that Queen Catherine meant to cross with her husband despite the onset of her fourth pregnancy. Yet she was eventually left behind to rule as regent in her husband's stead, and the parting scene could hardly have been stage-managed more fittingly. 'The king,' said Edward Hall, 'took leave of the Queen and the Ladies, which made such sorrow for the departing of their Lords and husbands that it was great dolor to behold.' And while his wife whimpered touchingly, Henry then stepped forth boldly to realise his destiny at the head of an army finally numbering 25,000 men. Standing in the bow of his royal launch in gleaming German armour, he wore a polished steel headpiece lined with crimson satin and crowned with a rich coronal. But over his armour he had also slipped the tunic of a crusading knight, a simple garment of white cloth fronted with a large red cross. With a jewelled brooch of St George on his crown, the cross of Christ on his heart and the arms of the pope festooned on his banners, the crusading king was therefore off to war at last.

The result was a campaign that would ultimately both flatter and deceive. Early in August, Emperor Maximilian joined Henry with an offer to serve personally as a subordinate general under the flag of St George. Yet while he asked only a simple pikeman's pay for himself, he had arrived nonetheless with barely 2,000 troops in his train, and though Bainbridge related from Rome how the new pope Leo X 'and all other great men here doth look daily to hear that Your Grace shall utterly exterminate the French king', the realities of his master's exploits proved rather more prosaic. For in the upshot, Louis XII was anything but exterminated, and his English counterpart would have to make do with a series of tinsel victories, costing altogether more than they were actually worth. On 16 August, a French attempt to relieve the fortress of Thérouanne was decisively repulsed at a cavalry skirmish that came to be known as the Battle of the Spurs, and seven days later Thérouanne itself surrendered. In the following month, the town of Tournai would also succumb to the threat of English force. 'We ordered our artillery,' Henry boasted to the Duke of Milan, 'to be disposed for the assault. We greeted the inhabitants thereof with some shots, and conceded them, at their request, a two-day truce for the surrender.' In truth, the besieged had considered themselves strong enough to resist with ease, not least because of the great number of cannon in their own possession, but since they had little gunpowder they were hardly as strong as appearances might have suggested. And one eyewitness, Brian Tuke, also recorded how there were actually no French soldiers at all in the captured city – only 'a great amount of peasantry and butchers with no commander-in-chief'. As such, when Henry and Maximilian entered their prize on 25 September in a torchlight procession, with all bells ringing, to be presented with its keys and six barrels of burgundy, the resulting chivalric myth could not mask the deeper realities.

But before his departure that autumn, as the mist descended over Picardy and Flanders, and the English trudged their way home through mysterious towns like Ypres and Dunkirk, which would become so much more familiar to their descendants, Henry had nevertheless concluded a new agreement with Maximilian and Ferdinand, providing for a triple invasion of France by June 1514. The pact was strengthened, too, by a renewal of the agreement that Archduke Charles was to marry the King of England's younger sister Mary, this time by May 1514. And since the French had been driven out of Milan by Swiss and papal forces after the allies' victory at Novara in June 1513, and had also gone on to lose Dijon to the Swiss in September, Henry had good reason to hope, it seemed, that the following year's campaigns might indeed put him once again in possession of a substantial part of the lost Lancastrian lands in France. He could derive considerable satisfaction, likewise, from the crushing victory over the Scots that had been achieved in September by the venerable Earl of Surrey, who, in spite of his eighty years, had crossed the border with a large army and not only routed the enemy but killed their king. Vain and over-confident, James IV had in fact wasted every advantage over the English force and finally seen his men squeezed into an ever-tightening circle at the battlefield of Flodden until they tore the shoes from their feet in a desperate effort to clench their toes more firmly in the blood-soaked hillside. But their final stand was unavailing, and in the aftermath, Scotland was left with a nation of broken families and a new monarch, James V, no more than one year, five months and ten days old.

Such was the scale of the victory that Queen Catherine described it in a letter to Wolsey as 'a matter so marvellous that it seemeth to be of God's doing alone'. But her husband still had much to learn about the broader realities of European politics. For by the end of 1513 Ferdinand was again negotiating secretly with the common enemy and in March 1514 renewed the Franco–Spanish truce. Maximilian, moreover, soon followed suit, while the Medici Pope Leo X, to whom King Louis had submitted in October 1513, was also working for peace, albeit in a more open and honourable fashion. Elsewhere, no progress was forthcoming in Archduke Charles's marriage to Mary, making it increasingly clear that any hoped for conquests by Henry in 1514 would have to be achieved unaided. And the grounds for such pipedreams were in any case decisively undermined by the financial cost already incurred in the most recent campaign. The Venetian Antonio Bavarino reported to his business colleagues that the king had taken with him fourteen wagons laden with gold and four with silver coin – 'facts which sound like tales of romance but are nevertheless true' – while another Italian, Lorenzo Pasqualigo, declared that the sums spent on artillery and camping gear alone could have filled a well of gold. Concluding his account of the first full-scale English invasion of France since the Hundred Years War, even Dr John Taylor, the king's chaplain, rightly reflected that far too much English money, 'which greatly excels foreign coinage in value', had been expended. For in the first three years of the reign, despite the extravagance of the court, annual expenditure had not exceeded £65,000, but by the end of 1512 it had climbed to £286,000 and stood by 1513 at nearly £700,000. Within another year, indeed, Henry and Wolsey had virtually exhausted the limited capital in cash accumulated by Henry VII once and for all, so that by 1516, notwithstanding Wolsey's eventual cutbacks in war expenditure by almost 90 per cent, the reserves were finally consumed.

Ironically, too, the long-term consequences of the expedition were little short of disastrous. The main result, in fact, was to burden England with a troublesome drain on scarce resources that would have been much better devoted to Calais. Certainly, a strong Channel port had numerous advantages in commercial, political and military terms over the unhappy outpost of Tournai, which would cost £230,000 to fortify at a yield of less than half that sum when the French retrieved it in 1518. If, moreover, the previous five years of grinding effort there had been turned instead to Calais, the precious harbour might not have been lost to the French by Queen Mary just over four decades later, while England's position would also have been materially strengthened in the mortal struggle with Spain at the century's end. But the young king with money to burn, who was clay in the hands of older and wiser statesmen, had not been able to wait to flesh his sword.

And by now, in any case, the fulcrum of future control in Europe was already the Holy Roman Emperor's grandson, Charles. Earnest and reserved beyond his 13 years, the simple pleasures of youth had wholly bypassed this Habsburg prince, who now carried the burdens of impending power squarely on his narrow shoulders. Heir to the Imperial throne and, more importantly, heir, too, to the richer holdings of the Spanish Crown through his other grandfather, Ferdinand, he was also nephew to Henry VIII's own wife. And if any further proof were needed of the gangling boy's emergence as the dominant force in the dynastic politics of the day, he had already inherited Flanders and the Netherlands, which were ruled on his behalf for the time being by his other aunt, Margaret of Savoy, daughter of the emperor.

Yet for the moment at least, the King of England did have one worthwhile card to hand in the figure of Thomas Wolsey, who might still prove capable of sustaining the semblance of glory and influence for him. In 1514, after a mere five months as Bishop of Lincoln, the archbishopric of York had fallen into his hands, and only one month later the rich bishopric of Tournai had also become his, in return for his considerable contribution to the French campaign of the previous year. By which time, he was already widely touted for the rank of cardinal on the grounds that 'his merits are such that the king can do nothing of the least importance without him and esteems him among his dearest friends'. Now behaving more than ever like the 'glorious peacock' depicted for posterity by his gentleman usher George Cavendish, the butcher's son from Ipswich had, in fact, been 'taken by preferment as a fish by a worm', not least because the king 'loved nothing worse than to be constrained to do anything contrary to his royal will and pleasure'. 'So fast as other councillors advised the king to leave his pleasure, and to attend to the affairs of his realm,' wrote Cavendish, 'so busily did the almoner persuade him to the contrary; which delighted him much, and caused him to have the greater affection to the almoner.' But Wolsey could also deliver and, as he now demonstrated to perfection, play the game of diplomatic subterfuge and legerdemain with a skill and cynicism worthy of those elder statesmen abroad who had already duped his master so successfully.

For if Ferdinand and Maximilian had shown their double-dealing contempt for their English counterpart before the ink was hardly dry upon the Treaty of Lille, neither had they counted on the diplomatic master-stroke now delivered by the new guiding hand of his policy. In March 1514, Henry's representative, John Stile, was writing in bewilderment from Spain that 'all policy and craft be here used more for their own security … than for any natural love or kindness to their friends'. 'It passeth my poor understanding,' Stile complained, 'and it please your Grace, wants others better learned than I am for to understand them.' Yet, as Wolsey appreciated in a way that perhaps only he could, both Ferdinand and Maximilian had been too clever by half in their continual ruses, for in avoiding real confrontation with France for so long, they had lost their potency and Louis XII was no longer afraid of them. Instead, it was the King of England, swollen with confidence and more pugnacious than ever, who currently represented the most potent menace to French security and, in consequence, Wolsey was able to improvise a 'perpetual peace' with France of the most delectable kind. For while Louis was a gouty widower of 52 who gulped his spittle, he nevertheless hoped for a son, and in the coldly practical world of Renaissance diplomacy where love in marriage was considered no more necessary than loyalty between allies, the newly appointed Bishop of Tournai had the perfect bride in mind: his king's own sister, the Lady Mary, who was 17 and, so we are told, 'a nymph from heaven'. And surely enough, in return for the hapless princess's sacrifice on the altar of marital revulsion, Wolsey's royal master was indeed enabled not only to dish his own deceivers exquisitely, but to retain Tournai and receive from his slobbering former enemy a doubling of the 'pension' accorded by the French to his father under the Treaty of Étaples. There was even, in the resulting agreement, to be a restoration of the ancient privileges of English merchants, as well as guarantees against the Scottish invasion of England, which included a promise from Louis to keep the troublesome John Stewart, Duke of Albany, in France.

The exchange of Thérouanne for Tournai struck deeply, no doubt, in many an English heart, since Thérouanne was nearer to Calais and both easier and cheaper to defend. Nor, of course, was Tournai's connection with Wolsey overlooked by his enemies as word soon circulated that he had personally persuaded the king to keep the city as 'a trophy of his victories'. But whether or not such rumours were founded, the fact remained that Wolsey's pre-eminence was now beyond question. 'I,' he told the Venetian ambassador in no uncertain terms, 'was the author of the peace,' and those well placed to appreciate his influence responded accordingly. The Dutch scholar Erasmus, seeking support and patronage as always, sent a copy of his translation of Plutarch's *De Unitate* and admitted to Wolsey that he hesitated 'to approach so great a man with so petty a gift'. The Earl of Arundel, on the other hand, dispatched 'a morsel of venison' from a deer killed in his own park to grace Wolsey's table, while Sir Henry Vaughan offered 'a Normandy cloth to make sheets for your servants'. Even Lady Margaret Pole, that great Plantagenet figure soon to be restored to the family title as Countess of Salisbury, granted Wolsey an annuity of 100 marks for his counsel and aid, as Cambridge University went further still, electing him its Chancellor, though he stood aside graciously in favour of its most distinguished representative, Bishop John Fisher of Rochester.

Twelve months earlier it would have been inconceivable that the former royal almoner should control the direction of his country's diplomacy. Not least of all, it would have represented an outright slight on the other monarchs of Europe who negotiated only through high-born dignitaries. But Henry would later assure the pope that no one had 'laboured and sweated' more to bring about the diplomatic revolution in European politics than his own Archbishop of York, and by the late summer of 1514, the coming young man, once tipped for further promotion in the murky medium term, had instead arrived with a deafening fanfare in the blinding light of here and now.

Even so, it was not long before the new would-be 'arbiter of Christendom' found himself faced with further revolutions in the affairs of Europe to test his mettle. For on 31 December 1514, less than three months after his marriage to Mary Tudor, Louis XII of France unexpectedly breathed his last. According to David Hume's later explanation, it seems that the sickly king, 'being of an amorous disposition, which his advanced age had not entirely cooled', had been 'seduced into such a course of gaiety and pleasure, as proved very unsuitable to his declining state of health'. But while his wife may well have experienced some initial relief at the demise of her romping burden, the prospects for continental peace were altogether less hopeful. For Louis was succeeded by his ambitious young cousin and son-in-law, Francis I, and within a few months the imposing diplomatic edifice built by Thomas Wolsey in 1514 duly began to crumble. 'This great fellow will spoil everything,' Louis had once said of the man who now occupied his throne, and events for years to come would bear him out, notwithstanding the fact that in April 1515 Francis confirmed his treaty with England, just as he had confirmed the one with the Netherlands the previous month. Strong, healthy and splendidly endowed for life in every way, talking boldly and continually, and seducing women every bit as energetically as he indulged in all other forms of violent exercise, Francis not only patronised scholars and wrote verses of his own, but built more grandly than any other monarch of his day. He was, according to the unanimous view of contemporaries, 'as handsome a prince as the world has seen', and before the first year of his reign was out, this self-same ruler, fatally flawed with all the defects of a spoilt child, had firmly established himself as an infuriatingly dangerous contender for the place that Henry VIII had earmarked as his own in the leadership of the new Europe. Boasting a personal military prowess that Henry himself would never match, Francis also disposed of a power that Henry's island kingdom could not hope to equal.

So it was that on 13 September, at Marignano, the French convincingly overwhelmed the pro-Imperial Swiss and Milanese in the so-called 'Battle of the Giants', which gave their king control of all northern Italy. Not only had they thus secured Milan, but the pope, Venice, Genoa, and eight of the thirteen Swiss cantons now became their allies, just, indeed, as the Scots had done in

May when the Duke of Albany, the infant James V's cousin and heir, deposed
Margaret Tudor as regent after her unpopular marriage to Archibald Douglas,
Earl of Angus. Even after the Venetian ambassador had first told Henry that
Francis had left Lyons and was on his way to Italy, the English monarch stead-
fastly refused to believe that his rival would dare to incur Tudor displeasure.
'The French king,' he declared, 'will not go into Italy this year. I believe he is
afraid of me, and that will prevent him from crossing the Alps.' 'If I choose,'
the boast continued, 'he will cross the Alps and if I choose he will not.' In an
effort to make good this idle claim, Henry had even sent 100,000 gold crowns
to Antwerp to pay the Swiss, but it was all to no avail. And to rub salt into the
English king's festering pride, Francis had also won great personal renown for
his actions in the midst of the hand-to-hand fighting at Marignano. 'For two
thousand years,' the King of France wrote to his mother, 'there has not been
so grand or so hard a battle.'

Nevertheless, Henry's response was simply to cast about for revenge by all
means short of war and to throw good money after bad. Sir Richard Wingfield,
the English ambassador, was accordingly instructed to suborn Emperor
Maximilian into leading a force of 30,000 German and Swiss mercenaries
against the French during the spring of 1516. For initially, when Francis first
crossed the Alps, Maximilian had been too busy paying his attentions to the
Princess of Hungary, who was not yet in her teens. Now, however, at the sight
of English gold, he became more warlike, and in March 1516 duly came down
over the Brenner pass in a bold advance upon Milan before sundry bribes sent
him trudging lamely back to Innsbruck. After seven years of extravagant rule,
Henry thus completed the bankruptcy of his father's treasury, though by then
at least, his right-hand man had won the most prestigious promotion of all –
short, that is, of the papal tiara itself. For on 20 September, 1515, the Venetian
ambassador to England, Sebastiano Giustiniani, was already reporting that 'a
king's courier has arrived here from Rome, having been dispatched with the
news that the Right Reverend of York has been created Cardinal at the suit of
this most serene king who with might and main is intent upon aggrandising
him …' The Italian was quick to add, too, that he himself was keen to keep
the new cardinal 'on the most friendly terms, both by reason of his extreme
influence with the king, and also because he is of a very active and assiduous
mind in matters of business …'

Even Thomas Wolsey, however, could not forestall the next twist in the tan-
gled threads of continental power politics, when, in January 1516, Ferdinand
of Spain, enthusiastically supporting the English king's plan for a pan-
European alliance against France, dealt his final crooked hand by emulating
Louis XII and dying inopportunely. Long ailing, he had expired, according
to Peter Martyr, 'of hunting and matrimony, either of which are fatal to most

men at the age of sixty-three'. And now his successor was Charles, grandson of both Maximilian and Ferdinand himself, and former fiancé of Mary Tudor. By now approaching manhood, unpleasant in features and far from prepossessing in manner, the new King of Spain was already master of the Netherlands, but had never visited the realm that now was his. His personality, moreover, had evolved into a mixture of grandeur and oddity, as complex as the patchwork Holy Roman Empire he would one day go on to inherit, too. Excelling in no particular accomplishment, no gleam of chivalry lightened his character, no prior deeds in war or statecraft declared his fame, or seemed likely to. Lantern-jawed, lisping and ineffectual, he was of worth, it seemed, only by descent. Yet this unlikely figure was now on the verge of confounding his detractors to become Europe's most powerful figure.

Initially, in fact, Charles was wholly prepared to embrace even his archenemy, with the result that at Noyon in August, Spain professed every good will towards France, and invited Emperor Maximilian to join in the reconciliation – a possibility that sent shivers down the spines of both Wolsey and Henry. In the process, he even undertook to marry the infant daughter of the French king, an act that Henry declared scandalous, since the princess was not yet a year old. But more wagon trains of English money, amounting this time to 20,000 gold nobles, were nevertheless dispatched to keep the emperor on side and, equally predictably, Maximilian received them as duplicitously as ever. 'My son,' he is alleged to have chuckled to Charles, 'you are going to cheat the French, and I am going to cheat the English – or at least I shall do my best.' And accordingly, in the spring of 1517, he joined the signatories of the Treaty of Noyon, leaving England, with scarcely concealed contempt, to fend for herself in the diplomatic wilderness before luck, human treachery and Wolsey's consummate skill in exploiting both, served, once again, to salvage his sovereign's irrepressible ego. For by repeating the manoeuvre executed in 1514, Wolsey now made fresh overtures to the French, who were glad to betray their Spanish and Imperial 'allies' before the same trick was played on them.

The result of this spectacular exploitation of adverse events was the so-called 'Peace of London' or 'universal peace' involving a general settlement of the disputes between England, France, the Holy Roman Empire, Spain and the Papacy, as a prelude to a united crusade against the Turks, who were fast encroaching upon central Europe and the Levant. Two days later, proxy marriage celebrations between the infant Princess Mary and the dauphin occurred at Greenwich, and on the following day it was arranged by Wolsey that Henry and Francis should meet each other again near Calais at the place that would become known to posterity as the Field of Cloth of Gold. Fancying himself in a beard no doubt, Henry even swore as a final token of good faith not to shave until the two monarchs met once more. And, not to be outdone in the camaraderie of the moment, Francis, too, pledged his whiskers in unerring friendship. Yet on 19 January 1519, that gay old pauper, Emperor Maximilian, completed a hat-trick of royal mortalities by dying at Weltz, probably from laughter at those gullible enough to have been made fools by him down the years. 'The Emperor,' Pope Julius II had once observed, 'is light and inconsistent, always begging for other men's money which he wastes on hunting the chamois.' And now, as a parting gesture, he had unwittingly succeeded in undoing Wolsey's achievement of 1518, in much the same way that Louis XII's unexpected demise had done four years earlier. For on 28 June – despite all Francis I's intrigues and briberies, and an even more improbable attempt by Henry VIII to win the Imperial Crown for himself – the deceased emperor's grandson Charles, who had become Charles I of Spain three years earlier, now became Charles V of the Holy Roman Empire, thus adding Austria, Germany and the rest of his family's Habsburg patrimony to Spain, Netherlands and Naples, forming an aggregate that threatened to encircle and constrict France on every side. Already wounded by the rejection of his own Imperial candidature and further offended by Charles's refusal to return Navarre, the King of France could never, of course, sit quietly in the shadow of so great a menace. And the result before long was the greatest Habsburg–Valois conflict to date: one in which even the smaller fry, including England, would be forced to take sides.

Yet uncannily, and notwithstanding Thomas Wolsey's unspeakable frustration, his country's position still remained happier than that of most other states, since neither her interests nor her independence were likely to be compromised directly by the impending Habsburg–Valois struggle – especially when both leviathans seemed so evenly matched in 1519. Francis, on the one hand, ruled a strong, compact and obedient kingdom, while Charles administered a much larger, widely scattered and often more loosely held agglomeration of territories, beset in places by peculiarly vulnerable communications. Already, French control of Milan and Genoa had cut one of the vital lines linking the emperor's new and still precariously controlled Spanish kingdoms to his even newer Austrian and Imperial dominions, as well as his ancestral Netherlands. And although it was equally clear from England's perspective that when war came, the main battleground would be far-off northern Italy, now that Milan and Genoa were French, the one remaining line between Spain and the Netherlands – that through the Channel and Narrow Seas – made English support of vital importance to Charles. Nor, better still, could Francis discount the possibility that the King of England might open a second front against him – a prospect that he would be prepared to pay well to avoid. And so it was, from the ashes of the so-called 'universal peace' of 1518, that Wolsey was able against all conceivable odds to pluck a new role for himself and a fresh image for his master: that of honest broker and mediator between Europe's giants, at the fulcrum of a new balance of power between the two.

As a result, in May 1520 Charles duly visited England to allay his concern about the budding Anglo–French friendship that appeared to loom before him – a friendship that, in spite of the hearty welcome extended to the newly elected emperor at Canterbury, was to be spectacularly vaunted less than one month later amid all the chivalric splendour, and hypocrisy, of the meeting between Henry and Francis at the so-called Field of Cloth of Gold just outside Calais. Fortified for his sea crossing by the pension of 7,000 ducats that Charles had just awarded him during his stay, Wolsey would accompany not only his king but a vast train of his country's elite who gathered eagerly for the dazzling extravaganza of junketing and back-slapping humbug that followed. Remarkably, some 5,172 English men and women would be transported across the Channel for the historic encounter between the kings of France and England, which eventually involved, according to one Italian eyewitness, not only an initial physical embrace encompassing twenty hugs, but a degree of culinary excess over the next sixteen days wholly worthy of the event's orchestrator. For whatever the shortcomings of Wolsey's diplomacy, no one at least can fairly deny him his rightful place as the greatest picnic-planner in history. In all, provisions costing £8,831 and a further £1,568 for wine and beer were duly assembled at Calais, and every last detail was personally overseen by the good cardinal himself, from the ordering of 700 conger eels, 2,014 sheep, twenty-six dozen heron and a bushel of mustard, down to the purchase of cream for the king's cakes at a price of £1 10*d* – though no sooner had the English camp at Guisnes Castle been dismantled than Henry and his favourite were hastening to Gravelines for a double-dealing consultation with Charles, refusing the French king's attendance at the meeting.

Uppermost in these ensuing discussions was the question of marriage between Henry's 7-year-old daughter Mary and her Imperial cousin – notwithstanding the young girl's existing betrothal to the dauphin. And while it would take another year for firm agreement to be sealed by the Treaty of Bruges in August 1521, the broader outcome was also beyond doubt. The 'defensive' alliance mooted only a month or so earlier at Canterbury during Charles's visit was duly confirmed, and arrangements were set in place for a further meeting the following year. Nor, in spite of his manifold professions to the contrary at the Field of Cloth of Gold, was the French king himself long in looking to his own interests. For he too was swiftly hatching war – this time in Navarre: a war that, by 1522, Henry would have joined as Charles's ally, promising to keep the Channel open for him in return for a promise of compensation for the French pensions that both he and Wolsey would lose by their treachery. More importantly still, plans were also agreed by the emperor for the conquest and partition of France – a task involving an invasion from Spain in the spring of 1523, along with an attack by Henry from Calais, each ruler at the head of 40,000 men. To crown all, there was a further undertaking on Charles's behalf to conclude his marriage to Henry's only legitimate child at the time of her twelfth birthday. And last but not least, the emperor also undertook to secure Wolsey's victory at the next papal election as soon as the sickly Leo X finally gave up the ghost.

Not surprisingly, the English king was more than satisfied with his cardinal's diplomacy, telling Richard Pace in no uncertain terms how his affairs could not have been better handled. The king's 'contentment with all your acts,' Pace informed Wolsey, 'cannot be so well painted with a pen as it is imprinted in my heart.' And though the cardinal's subsequent attempt for the papacy upon Leo X's death in December 1521 proved abortive, he could nevertheless console himself to some degree with the fact that his commission as legate *a latere* in 1519 had nevertheless been extended and considerably amplified some seven months before Leo's demise. Henceforth, he enjoyed, in effect, powers in England paralleling the pope's own, and would be in a position to use them in the solution of, arguably, his most difficult problem yet: the succession to the English throne. For by 1521 Henry had been married twelve years and, at 36, Queen Catherine's prospects for delivering a male heir were diminishing daily. The king had only to look back across the past century of English history to the reign of Henry VI, or across the border of Scotland since Flodden, to appreciate the scriptural warning, 'woe to thee, O land, whose king is a child'. And the warning was all the more pertinent in the present circumstances when the child was a girl like Princess Mary; when there was no prince of the blood royal to act as regent, as Bedford had done for Henry VI; and when there was no nobleman of such unchallenged pre-eminence that his elevation to that office would be accepted without question. Even were Henry to survive until his daughter came of age, moreover, it could never be forgotten that the only woman who had previously attempted to assert her title as queen regnant – Henry I's daughter Matilda – brought the country nineteen years of civil war. And it was for this very reason that Emperor Charles's hand had been sought so earnestly for Mary in the first place, notwithstanding the fact that the strategy consciously downplayed the pitfalls of England's effective absorption into the Habsburg empire, in anticipation of an altogether rosier prospect of a Catholic world, united under Charles and Mary after the final destruction of France.

Yet the next three years brought little encouragement to Henry's hopes for his daughter's marriage or for the conquest and dismemberment of France, which was so grandiosely envisaged in August 1521. In November of that year, the Imperialists had driven the French from Milan and Tournai, before defeating them in the field at Bocca in April 1522, just one month prior to England's eventual entry into the war. But these preliminary successes merely encouraged Charles to concentrate his efforts in northern Italy, and the negligible achievements of a small force led by the younger Thomas Howard, Earl of Surrey, who would become Duke of Norfolk after his father's death in 1524, spoke for themselves. Beginning in July, the resulting spree of wholesale slaughter initially involved the capture and incineration of Morlaix in the Cherbourg peninsula, though with what aim in mind was far from clear. After which, the son of the victor of Flodden duly ravaged Artois and the country around Boulogne, while finding himself increasingly beset by the great scarcity of basic amenities for his men. Writing bitterly that he had only enough beer for twelve days, he also bemoaned the great shortage of wood for the bake houses. Besides which, it seems, the ships at sea were no better off, since the Earl of Southampton's vessels were without either fish or flesh.

Yet the destruction, at least, was unstinting. For while Henry himself was hawking in Essex and Hertfordshire, Surrey informed the cardinal how:

> all the country we have passed through has been burnt; and all the strong places, whether castles or fortified churches have been thrown down … When we have burnt Dorlance, Corby, Ancre, Bray and the neighbouring country, which I think will be in about three weeks, I cannot see that we can do much more.

Closing his letter with the observation that 'there is universal poverty here, and great fear of this army', he recorded his earnest hope that 'the King's grace and you will be content with our services', which continued to consist of little more than random acts of terror, as at Lottinghen, near Desvres, where English forces incinerated everything they could find over an area of 40 square miles, leaving only one scorched church standing – looking, we are told, 'more like a house of war than the house of God'. That such devastation should have been inflicted upon an area of France already stricken by drought, pestilence and poverty says even more for the baseness of the entire campaign. But quite apart from its most shameful features, the whole enterprise, which the Duke of Vendôme described as a 'very foul war', had continued to assume an almost embarrassing pointlessness as marauding troops struggled vainly to find any broader purpose for their mission. Ultimately, having failed to take the town of Hesdin, the English were eventually prevailed upon by Imperial generals to cease their play, and by 16 October 1522, Surrey was safely returned to Calais, to reflect upon his deadly handiwork with whatever pride he could muster.

In March 1522, meanwhile, some two months before Henry's herald first announced his warlike intentions to the French king, a demand for £20,000 had already been inflicted upon London's merchants, after which royal agents were loosed throughout the shires to ascertain the value of lands and all other items of fixed and movable property. So when Wolsey informed Parliament the following month of his hopes that the Commons would 'cheerfully assist the king in vindicating his Honours' by granting a sum that 'could not be less than £800,000', the response was predictable. For while the art of war was increasing in sophistication continually and its costs climbing accordingly, early efforts to finance the impending hostilities had been left to rely entirely on old expedients that had long grown rusty and deficient. At a time when almost £50,000 had already been earmarked to deal with the danger from Scotland, the land army proposed for France was now expected to number 26,000 English and 8,000 'Almain' infantrymen, along with 8,000 cavalry. And with the whole force's consumption of beer alone calculated to run at the extraordinary figure of some 882,000 gallons for every month of campaigning, it was hardly surprising that the mere cost of provisions was so crippling – particularly when the 'sea army' of some 3,000 men was also expected to consume at least 187 tons of grain, 600 oxen and 18,000 barrels of salt fish, not to mention a further 17,640 gallons of ale. At Wolsey's return to press his demands, therefore, MPs duly met him with 'a marvellous obstinate silence', followed by declarations that if the necessary taxation was forthcoming, loyal subjects would be left with no other choice than 'to barter clothes for cheese and bread'. And the upshot was a grant of little more half the required sum – achieved, even so, only after sixteen days of 'long persuading and privy labouring of friends'.

It was not the last time that king and cardinal would have to stage an almighty about-turn on such matters. But while the whole worthless escapade eventually sucked dry the few remaining sources of money at the kingdom's disposal, there were further pressures to consider. For as Surrey was eagerly swatting scattered French hamlets, so the Duke of Albany arrived in Scotland from France with a force of 5,000 men and marched purposefully towards a defenceless Carlisle. Indeed, though the Earl of Shrewsbury had been sent to improvise what slender resistance he could muster, scarce supplies delayed him at York, and, in consequence, the way to England lay wide open for the invaders to realise at last Scotland's long-awaited moment of destiny. Under the circumstances, there was no alternative for the equally resource-starved commander of England's northern forces, Lord Dacre, but to resort to the diplomacy of desperation by offering a wholly unauthorised truce to the Scots at the very moment when they could have laid waste all before them. And this, by great good fortune, would ultimately prove enough, since the peace party north of the border, feeble as it was, was just sufficient to divide Albany's supporters. In consequence, when Huntley, Argyle and Arran, the leading Scottish earls, proved unwilling to risk another Flodden, and the Gordons resolutely declined to cross the Tweed, the Scottish juggernaut finally faltered, thwarted once and for all by Francis I's reluctance to lend further assistance beyond moral support.

Yet the countless ill omens, setbacks and close scrapes of 1522 still did nothing to arrest the projected main assault on France, which duly lumbered into motion in the late summer of 1523. Largely inexplicably, Henry had been buoyed, it seems, by the revolt of Charles, Duke of Bourbon, against his sovereign. For although Bourbon ranked as France's greatest prince-aristocrat, his rebellion was already some months old and had been treated hitherto by the French king with scarcely concealed scorn. Nevertheless, against all odds, the Duke of Suffolk would still lead his troops to within 40 miles of Paris itself and, from his camp in Compiègne, send word to Henry that there was 'good likelihood of the attaining of his ancient right and title to the crown of France to his singular comfort and eternal honour' – before winter set in with a vengeance. After which, as the frost hardened, so the Imperial soldiers in Suffolk's army began to melt away, leaving him no choice but to send an emissary to his king explaining the necessity of retreat. Even the 'profit of the spoil', which had initially been 'great encouraging to them', he wrote, now held less and less attraction for the English troops, and though Henry had already dispatched a force of 6,000 men under Lord Moulsey to relieve him and was obdurate that the war should be waged to the bitter end, Suffolk acceded to the wishes of his men and broke camp. Bourbon had been held up in the Alps and retreated to Genoa; Charles V did not get through the Pyrenees; and in the meantime Adrian VI had died, prompting Wolsey to stage another abortive attempt to become pope himself.

Further large-scale efforts were now out of the question, and accordingly, in 1524, Charles was informed that he must expect no great help from England. The most that Henry could manage, in fact, was a contribution of £20,000 towards an invasion of Provence from Italy by the Imperial army under Bourbon. But the invasion failed even more completely than its predecessors, and by the autumn Bourbon's army had broken as the French returned to Italy and besieged Pavia. Long before then, even before the rebellious duke had entered Provence indeed, Wolsey had already entered secret negotiations with France, on the assumption that since war was unaffordable, there might yet be hope for a profitable peace. Yet the timing, with what would prove the most consummate irony of all, could not have been less fortunate. For on 24 February 1525, the French army was destroyed and the French king himself taken prisoner, with no English force on hand to share the fruits of victory. In less than two hours at the Battle of Pavia, 8,000 Frenchmen and mercenaries had fallen, and the pick of France's élite, including Fleuranges, Galiot, Montmorency and Henri d'Albret, were captured. 'We have this morning heard from Italy the best news in the world,' declared Archduchess Margaret of Austria to an English envoy, though the emperor himself received the tidings with his usual gravity, prohibiting all celebrations at court, and choosing instead to express sympathy with his French counterpart's misfortune. This was regardless of the fact he had vanquished a mortal enemy, seemingly irreversibly, and done so, moreover, without help, shattering the previous balance of power and thus rendering the King of England an effective irrelevance to his future plans.

In the meantime, however, that same king, in stark contrast to his Imperial cousin, was not only ecstatic at the news of the French defeat but bent at once on gloating and gain. When word reached Henry, he was in bed, though no dream in his head could have matched the one that now became his fantasy. 'You are,' he told the bearer of the glad tidings, 'as welcome as was the angel Gabriel to the Virgin Mary.' Furthermore, upon hearing of the death of his English rival, Richard Pole, in the fighting, he ordered more wine for the messenger and sprang from the sheets to tell his wife, regaling all and sundry with his lofty plans for a final reckoning with the French. 'Now is the time,' he later told an embassy from the Netherlands, 'for the Emperor and myself to devise full satisfaction from France. Not an hour is to be lost.' His ambassadors, Cuthbert Tunstall and Sir Richard Wingfield, were to remind the emperor at once that 'one of the chief and principal things' intended by the Anglo–Imperial alliance 'hath always been to expel the French King from his usurped occupation of the crown of France', and that 'the ambition of France shall always be an occasion to bring all Christian princes and countries unto war, hostility and division'. Charles and Henry should therefore seize the present opportunity 'utterly to extinct the regiment of the French King and his line, or any other Frenchman, from the crown of France', whereupon that Crown should rightfully pass to Henry 'by just title of inheritance'. Likewise, the 'noble countries and great dominions the French King hath and keepeth from the Emperor' were now to be Charles's, along with French claims to 'the Duchy of Milan, Asti, Genoa, the realm of Naples, and other great territories in Italy'.

All this, of course, was to be accomplished by a display of 'force, violence and puissance', involving a 'personal invasion into France this summer', since the task 'is more facile to be done at this time than at any other that ever hath been known or heard of'. With 'the said French King now remaining in captivity, his noblemen, captains and whole army vanquished, slain, destroyed, or taken prisoners', Henry and Charles were to march straight to Paris indeed, bypassing fortresses and strongholds along the way, for a triumphant rendezvous, at which the former would be crowned King of France, hand over his daughter to the latter, and then accompany him to Rome for the formal Imperial coronation by the pope that he had not yet received. Ultimately, or so the King of England fondly contended, 'the whole monarchy of Christendom' would thus 'ensue unto the Emperor':

> For of his own inheritance he hath the realm of Spain and a great part of Germany, the realms of Sicily and Naples, with Flanders, Holland, Zeeland and Brabant, and Hainault and other his Low Countries; by election he hath the Empire, whereunto appertaineth all the rest of Italy and many towns imperial in Germany and elsewhere; and by the possibility apparent to come by my lady Princess [Mary] he should hereafter have England and Ireland, with the title to the superiority of Scotland, and in this case all France with the dependencies.

It was a grand vision, indeed, encompassing all the universalist aspirations that have regularly punctuated European history. And not only would it unite the Continent under a single, centralised authority, allowing a united front against infidel and heretic, it would simultaneously solve the King of England's increasingly pressing succession problem – albeit at the cost of compromising, most probably fatally, his realm's political independence.

But while Henry fantasised, the final impracticality of his projected campaign in France was soon apparent when on 21 March 1525, less than a month after Pavia, commissions went out for the levy of what was described, with no intentional irony, as an Amicable Grant of one sixth of the value of the lands and goods of the laity and one third from the clergy. In response, wrote Edward Hall, 'the poor cursed, the rich repugned, the light wits railed'. And he did not exaggerate. At Cambridge both town and university rose as one in opposition, and a mob of 20,000 milled menacingly when the commissioners sought to make their levies, while, in other parts of East Anglia, Lavenham, Sudbury and Hadleigh were especially affected by the disorders, and there were similar rumblings in Huntingdonshire. Elsewhere, the fear amongst Kentishmen was that should the king indeed conquer France, which they did not believe likely, he would spend all his time and all their money there. In Lincolnshire, news of the levy touched off faggots of rebellion in every town and village, and in London a City councillor quoted to Wolsey's face the statute of Richard III against 'benevolences' of the kind now proposed. Such, indeed, was the scale of general disaffection that both the dukes of Suffolk and Norfolk reported every day from their respective bases at Eye and Norwich on the glowering dissatisfaction of the common people, observing in a letter of 12 May that 'they never saw the time so needful for the king to call his council to determine what should be done'. Nor were their fears assuaged by events in Germany, where Emperor Charles himself was faced by April 1525 with a Peasants' War involving more than 100,000 heavily armed rebels demanding restoration of their ancient manorial rights and citing Martin Luther's doctrines of Christian freedom as justification for their excesses. One Swiss cleric who had seen the rebels at close hand even wrote to the Imperial ambassador in Venice likening the rioting in England to the very events in Germany.

Under such circumstances, it was inevitable that both Henry and Wolsey would confess themselves beaten. The king, 'sore moved', Hall tells us, duly ordered the abandonment of the Grant and acknowledged that all who had opposed it should be accorded full pardon, whereupon the uproar subsided as quickly as it had arisen. In place of the heavy burden of one sixth of all their goods, Henry now asked only 'such as his loving subjects would grant him of their good minds', and left his cardinal to carry the can. 'Well,' he complained, 'some have informed me that my realm was never so rich and that men would pay at the first request, but now I find all the contrary.' And the implication was clear, although the targeting of a convenient scapegoat could not negate two inescapable conclusions: firstly, that any English effort to expel the French king 'from his usurped occupation from the crown of France' was dead in the water; and secondly, that the only course of action now remaining was peace. By the first week in June, negotiations were resumed with the current French regency, and before Tunstall and Wingfield's account of their reception by the emperor reached England, a letter from Henry was on its way to inform them – as they summarised it in their reply – 'that your Highness is not so furnished in your coffers that you may continue the war, nor cannot be helped by your subjects'. The hoped for pageant of a joint journey to Paris and Rome, like the grandiose dream of the Holy Roman Emperor sharing the whole monarchy of Christendom with a Tudor princess, had in fact vanished utterly, even as England's ambassadors were holding their first audiences with Charles. In the event, it mattered little to the emperor when he delivered the ultimate disappointment to his English visitors by informing them that his purpose now was peace rather than war, and that he had no enthusiasm whatsoever for carving out of a defeated France a new Angevin Empire for his belatedly enthused ally. The emperor's coffers, in any case, were as empty as England's, and for this reason he demanded finally that Mary's dowry be sent at once to Spain. When it was not, Charles duly saw fit to write at once to Henry, declaring his release from his engagement to the 9-year-old English princess, and affirming his intention to marry instead the 22-year-old and richly dowered Iabella of Portugal. Failed by Ferdinand in 1514 and now by Charles in 1525, Henry's consequent revulsion with the Spanish alliance went deeper at this point than ever, not only driving him to friendship with France, but propelling him headlong into revolutionary courses with his own marriage that were to prove altogether more portentous still.

9

YEARS OF TRAUMA AND SURVIVAL: EDWARD VI, MARY TUDOR AND THE LEGACY OF THE FATHER

We are at war with France and Scotland, we have enmity with the bishop of Rome … Our war is noisome to our realm and to all our merchants that traffic through the Narrow Seas … We are in a world where reason and learning prevail not and covenants are little regarded.

Bishop Stephen Gardiner to Sir William Paget,
November 1545

The brazen jilting of Princess Mary by Charles V in 1525 marked the great turning point in Henry VIII's reign. For in the summer of that year he began at last to cast off the moorings that had bound him so long to Spain and his wife, and thereafter to loosen not only those connecting his realm to the Continent but ultimately the selfsame links to Rome itself. The man whom he considered his brother-in-arms, the one chosen to be his son-in-law and potential successor, the friend and nephew to whom he had offered loans nearing half a million ducats had not only deserted him, but was seeking reconciliation with the ancient enemy of France. After Pavia, Henry had informed Charles that he rejoiced 'as if he himself had been the victor'. His ambassadors had carried a ring from the Princess Mary, which the emperor had 'put upon his little finger', saying that he would wear it 'for her sake'. The King of England had even professed his readiness to send Wolsey on this tender errand of love, though he had neglected to do so for fear that the cardinal was now 'so growing towards age' that 'so long a journey by sea and land would prove dangerous to him'. What more could have been done to prove Henry's honour and good faith? Yet an insult and betrayal had been delivered that was every bit as dishonourable as the repeated treachery of Charles's grandfathers, Ferdinand and Maximilian.

Spaniards, Flemings, Habsburgs – all were clearly spun from the same twisted yarn, and now they would pay, or so at least Henry hoped. Recompense for his debts to the English Crown was at once demanded from the emperor and the Anglo–Imperial Treaty of Windsor, signed in June 1522, cancelled. On 14 August, moreover, Henry's realm sold its allegiance to Francis, and cashed in on growing fears in Italy of Imperial domination. Though Venice, Florence, Siena, Mantua and the pope had celebrated the routing of the French, all were now in league once more. This time, however, they were uniting against their new foe, and it was with great satisfaction that in September the King of England received the first instalment of a lifetime pension of 100,000 crowns a year from France. It had been guaranteed by the Treaty of the More, signed at Wolsey's own residence on 30 August, as an added result of which, several of Henry's councillors, including the cardinal, received generous pensions of their own and the King of England agreed to mediate for the release of his French counterpart. Not only had Wolsey escaped, it seemed, he had even taken shelter in the very Imperial treachery that, under other circumstances, might well have consumed him. Indeed, the desertion of the emperor had actually deflected attention from the catastrophe of the Amicable Grant, and made the cardinal's expertise seem more indispensable than ever. All hope of future 'amity and good feeling' between England and the Holy Roman Empire was now dead, he fumed to two Flemish envoys representing the Archduchess Margaret. 'I know full well,' he went on, 'that we shall never get assistance from you; but we shall do our best, either by contracting alliance with the Turk, or making peace with the French, or by giving the Princess Mary's hand to the Dauphin …' Every harm, he swore, would be delivered upon the emperor and his confederates, 'so that war between us may last a whole century'.

In the meantime, however, the first public sign of Henry's reaction to Charles's infidelity pointed not only towards novel and drastic solutions of the succession problem, but to a new preparedness to flaunt his own infidelity to his wife. For no sooner had news reached England of the emperor's intention to break his engagement to Mary than the King of England drew his one and only son, the illegitimate Henry Fitzroy, out of the decent obscurity in which he had hitherto been kept, to parade him in court and create him Duke of Richmond on 15 June. The boy's title was that by which Henry's own father had been known before his accession to the throne and its new holder was now given precedence over all the peers of the realm, even over Princess Mary herself. One month later, he was made Lord Admiral of England before becoming Lord Lieutenant of the North soon afterwards and later Lord Lieutenant of Ireland, while the genuinely princely sum of £4,000 a year – a figure far exceeding that made over to his legitimate sister – was allocated for the maintenance of his household. Henceforth, bastard or not, Henry Fitzroy seemed set to succeed his father unless a suitable alternative could be found. As the Venetian ambassador, Lorenzo Orio, freely acknowledged, Henry loved his son 'like his soul' and proudly treated him 'next in rank to his majesty'. And as the boy bathed happily in his father's hope and affection, so the Princess Mary was conveniently packed off to Ludlow to begin her duties as Princess of Wales – away from her mother and increasingly compromised on all fronts.

Nor, of course, was the timing of Henry's decision unconnected with the declining status of the mother herself. On the contrary, it was partly the result of cold anger towards her personally: anger at her consistent failure to produce a male heir to safeguard the succession; anger at the resulting challenge to her spouse's virility; and, above all, anger at the recent treachery of her nephew. By now, her sexual attraction was long lost. Indeed, as early as 1515, a Venetian observer had described her as 'rather ugly than otherwise', while in 1520 the ever-gallant Francis I termed her 'old and deformed'. At her present age of 40, she was past the usual age of childbearing, and her maternal devotion to her daughter made her even more of an encumbrance to the plans of her husband, who also found himself increasingly dogged by theological misgivings about the legitimacy of his marriage. Did not Leviticus xx.21 ordain that 'if a man shall take his brother's wife, it is an unclean thing; he hath uncovered his brother's nakedness; they shall be childless'? And had Henry himself not formally registered a protest against the match in his father's time, echoing other doubts expressed at that juncture about the pope's power to dispense with the law of God on this matter? To cap all, sometime in 1526, the disillusioned husband would be fatally 'struck by the dart of love', as he himself put it, delivered by Anne Boleyn, a self-aware young woman of about 20 – dark-haired, olive-skinned, graceful, elegant, vivacious and 'like enough to have children'. Newly returned from the French court, she had learnt much about the wider world since her departure across the Channel six years earlier, and now she would have a fateful influence not only upon her husband but upon his entire approach to the affairs of mainland Europe.

To the King of England's barely disguised consternation, in February 1526 the French king, who had been transferred from Italy to Spain, was visited amid high ceremony by Charles V and accepted the terms of the Treaty of Madrid for his release. He had failed to make good his escape in the wake of Pavia and now, after a period of illness, succumbed to a truly harrowing settlement. In swearing to submit, he was forced, for example, to surrender the whole of Burgundy – the emperor's most prized objective – and to renounce his claims over Flanders, Artois and the rest of the Low Countries, as well as his rights in Naples, Sicily and Milan. He was also to marry Charles's sister, Eleanor, and to discharge the emperor's debt to the King of England, while providing 5,000 men-at-arms and 10,000 infantry to accompany his enemy to Rome when he went there to receive the Imperial Crown formally. As hostages for the proper execution of the treaty, Francis was compelled, finally, to hand over his two eldest sons, the dauphin and the Duke of Orléans. If fulfilled, the arrangement represented not only the greatest possible victory for the emperor but one which appeared to seal the conclusion of a conflict that had dragged on for more than thirty years. And while Henry VIII grudgingly ordered a *Te Deum* at St Paul's in recognition of a peace that galled him to the core, his Imperial counterpart was already laying plans for a trip to Seville where he would marry Isabella of Portugal and thereby secure her family's accumulated riches in Brazil and the East.

Yet the emperor's victory would prove as hollow as it was dazzling, and by the time that Francis boarded the boat at Bidassoa, which carried him home, he was already intent on renewing the struggle. Upon reaching the French shore, indeed, he rode breakneck for St Jean de Luz and Bayonne, heartily convinced that promises made in captivity carried no authority in either conscience or law. And by May 1526, he had duly enlisted the pope, Florence, Venice and the exiled Ludovico Sforza, Duke of Milan, into the so-called League of Cognac, which the King of England cautiously endorsed by becoming before long its 'Protector'. For, although Wolsey had no real desire to wage war against the emperor, and did not wish to interfere with trade between England and the Netherlands, which was so essential to both countries, he was determined nevertheless to injure Charles and weaken his power. And since Italy was the only place he could do this, he had given the inception of the new league every encouragement – not least because France was to meet two-thirds of the cost of any military operation and Venice the rest. The fact that Henry's involvement as Protector would not be announced until his cardinal saw fit was, of course, another considerable bonus, as was the emperor's broader predicament. For in February, as important German cities deserted the Catholic cause, the Protestant League of Torgau had been formed against him, while in spring the crescent-tipped battle standards of the Turks, draped with human hair, had surged into Hungary, resulting in the slaughter of the flower of the Hungarian aristocracy at Mohács in August.

Meanwhile, the intended annulment of the King of England's marriage to the emperor's aunt was creating an imbroglio of increasing complexity. For in spite of Charles's distractions elsewhere, it was still difficult to envisage how military conditions might be created in Italy that would leave the pope sufficiently free from any Imperial influence to concede to English wishes. And without such conditions, it was equally difficult to believe that diplomatic pressure upon the pope might alone persuade him to agree. Unsurprisingly, the new incumbent in Rome, Clement VII, was neither interested nor motivated by the comparative merits of Henry's case. From his perspective, indeed, the petitions of England's ruler were of value only in terms of the meagre leverage they allowed Rome in its relations with Charles, since the League of Cognac had made little progress in loosening the grip of Spanish troops in Italy during the summer, and Austrian Habsburg soldiers had become even more firmly established in the north. Under the circumstances, the pope's strategy was merely to delay a verdict, in order, as his intimate associate Paolo Giovio put it, 'to nourish the controversy for a while as a means for maintaining in obedience the disposition of the kings'. From September 1526, England was subsidising its Cognac allies in an increasingly desperate effort to prevent Clement from becoming the outright prisoner of Spain, and in April 1527 the subsidy developed into a full-blown Anglo–French treaty, by which Mary Tudor was to marry the French king's son, Henri. But the realities remained stubbornly unaltered – notwithstanding the fact that, at Thomas Wolsey's Hampton Court, French envoys had recently feasted in luxury upon fantastic creations of battling soldiers, leaping knights, guns and crossbows, all brought to life by the cardinal's chefs. And on 6 May 1527, Spanish and German troops duly sacked Rome, killing up to a quarter of the Holy City's population in the process, while leaving the pope, as feared, an effective captive of the emperor.

To compound the irony, the destruction had been wrought by none other than England's former confederate, the Duke of Bourbon. And though the duke himself was shot in the thigh during the onslaught and eventually died in the Sistine Chapel, this had not prevented his famished and unpaid troops from taking a fearful toll upon the Holy City. 'Never,' wrote one commentator, 'was Rome so pilled neither by Goths nor Vandals.' Holy relics and sacred shrines were destroyed, virgins spoiled and wives ravished, while rampaging soldiers 'punished citizens by the privy members to cause them to confess their treasure', and Pope Clement fled in fear of his life to the Castle of San Angelo. Now under siege, it would be impossible henceforth for the pontiff to make even the slightest move without the emperor's permission – unless, that is, Thomas Wolsey could somehow fashion another ploy to salvage his royal master's shipwrecked cause. 'What should I do?' Henry complained to his right-hand man, as he contemplated the pope's capture. 'My person nor my people cannot him rescue, but if my treasure may help him, take that which to you seemeth most convenient.' And within two days, the cardinal had indeed conceived another grand enterprise – perhaps his grandest to date – shot full with complex crossing threads and diverse linking outcomes, all of which, he believed, might rescue an all but hopeless situation and redound once more both to his sovereign's and his own greater glory.

Since the pope was unfree, Wolsey would suggest that a group of independent cardinals commission him to act on the pontiff's behalf, and in this capacity deliver a favourable verdict on the king's 'Great Matter', safe in the knowledge that no higher court existed to which Queen Catherine might appeal. As a prelude, from July 1527, he therefore visited France for three months, paying court to the French king, whom he hoped would prevail on a sufficient number of cardinals to confer the requisite quasi-papal authority. And before leaving for Dover at the head of a splendid retinue, spreading out three-quarters of a mile along the narrow road to the coast, he had drawn up a communication for the pope to sign, bestowing upon him absolute power over ecclesiastical affairs as if he were indeed pontiff – power 'even to relax, limit or moderate divine law' – which meant, in effect, that Clement would be undertaking to ratify all the English cardinal's actions upon regaining his freedom. Beforehand, too, Wolsey had even troubled to consult his astrologer about the most auspicious date for his departure, though his worries, initially at least, seemed largely unfounded. For, according to a Hungarian envoy, the King of France was at a clear disadvantage in the ensuing negotiations – 'destitute of good captains and money' and 'marvellous perplexed' at the pope's captivity, 'not knowing what to do'. As such, the sealing of the Anglo–French treaties agreed to in England three months earlier and the arrangement of a marriage between Henry and a French princess, such as Renée, Francis I's sister-in-law, appeared almost routine.

In spite of early optimism, however, Wolsey's time in France was punctuated with petty frustrations and ill omens, before Charles defeated his characteristically elaborate scheme by the simplest of ploys, allowing the pope to escape his custody in December, so that Henry's cause once more depended solely upon the military defeat of Habsburg troops in Italy. Accordingly, in January 1528 Wolsey declared war on Spain, though this, in truth, was no more than a token gesture of belligerency, delivered without the consent of either his king or the council. And in the event, no military action resulted – only riots in cloth-making areas, such as East Anglia, Wiltshire and Somerset, leading by May to the resumption of trade with the Netherlands. The Merchant Adventurers ignored orders, which under Henry VII they had several times obeyed, to transfer their trade from Antwerp to Calais, while in Kent some men talked of putting Wolsey to sea in a leaky boat. And in the meantime, even the French ambassador admitted that the cardinal seemed to be the only man in England desirous of war in Flanders, so that by June a full truce had been duly agreed with the emperor. Thereafter, all that Wolsey

could do to help his French allies was to forgo the payment of £53,000 for
Henry's pension and send them £49,000 in cash, along with a jewel worth
£10,000. Since Francis was already committed, his army, under Odet de Foix,
Vicomte de Lautrec, would have to go it alone – which it duly did.

Yet the ensuing successes, initially at least, were little short of remarkable,
with a stunning series of victories in the Milanese, the Papal States and Naples.
Though Milan itself did not fall, the Genoese joined Lautrec, while Andrea
Dorea's fleet gave Francis command of the western Mediterranean, cutting
off the Imperial army in Italy from Spanish help. So when Lautrec marched
south, he was not only able to shut up the enemy in Naples, but to free Rome
itself – a prospect that had seemed virtually inconceivable after England's
defection less than a year earlier. In the process, Wolsey had once more failed
dismally – only to reap the richest possible rewards. For Clement VII's behaviour had moved like a barometer recording the fortunes of the French army,
and as soon as the Imperial enemy was locked suitably tight in Naples, he duly
dispatched Cardinal Lorenzo Campeggio to join Wolsey in hearing the King
of England's divorce suit at Blackfriars in London. On 8 June 1529, moreover,
with Naples in worse straits than ever, he sent Campeggio a secret decretal
commission empowering him, along with Wolsey, not only to hear but also to
settle the case in England by pronouncing – or so it was assumed – the decree
that would finally grant Henry his divorce. At Greenwich, we are told, the
king received the news 'marvellously thankfully, and made marvellous dem-
onstrations of joy and gladness', though the double game was still afoot and
Henry now found himself subject not to the prospect of a glittering new
marriage but to slow diplomatic strangulation – more drawn out, more frustrating, more ingenious, more inexorable and more excruciating than even he
might have devised for an unwitting quarry of his own.

For even before the gout-ridden Campeggio finally reached London
on 28 October amid the boos of the common people supporting the
queen, and after an agonising journey conducted at snail's pace over all of
four months, the international situation had already shifted fatefully. While
Lautrec's death and the defection of Andrea Doria's galleys had bolstered the
emperor's prospects in Italy, there had also been a regrouping of the Italian
states, as Florence once more declared itself a republic. Only by coming to
terms with the emperor, therefore, could the Medici pope now save his own
family, and in consequence he would write to Campeggio in December,
ordering him to burn the all-important decretal commission and thus consign
Henry's hopes and Wolsey's fortunes to ashes. All that was left henceforward
was delay, obfuscation and deception as Campeggio opted to play for time and
wait upon further developments as best he might. The French, after all, still
clung to their holdings in northern Italy, and were intending next spring to

send new forces over the Alps to reinforce them. But even in the north their days were numbered, and on 21 June 1529, their army was utterly routed and run out of Italy altogether, presenting the pope with no choice other than to conclude the Treaty of Barcelona with Charles later that same month. From this point onwards, vowed the pope, he would live and die an advocate of the Imperial cause, and surely enough the legatine court at Blackfriars, whose legitimacy Queen Catherine had denied throughout, was duly revoked to Rome. By early August, the Franco–Imperial Peace of Cambrai had also been signed, and little more than two months later the English cardinal whom George Cavendish would describe as 'the haughtiest man alive' had fallen too – stripped of his glory under the Statute of Praemunire of 1393 on the spurious grounds that he had employed his ecclesiastical authority to impinge upon the legal jurisdiction of the Crown.

By any standards, it was a seismic turn of events. The balance of power was shattered and no illusion now persisted of England's exaggerated influence in exploiting it. Nor, of course, was there any longer a place for a cardinal-legate in the king's new policy, such as it was, and certainly no place either for a foreign minister who could not resist the limelight of continental great power politics, or the pretence of playing as an equal with the two indisput-able leviathans of Christendom. Under the stimulus of his desire to divorce his wife and marry Anne Boleyn, Henry VIII had, in fact, at long last learned the hard, and inordinately expensive, lesson of 1512–14 and of 1522–23 – the lesson, ironically, that his father had grasped by instinct: namely, that England had no need to meddle deeply in European affairs as long as the continental powers remained either at peace and reasonably evenly balanced or sharply divided by their mutual jealousies. If England lay suitably low from this point forth, even the mighty Holy Roman Emperor, preoccupied to break-ing point as he invariably was with the task administering his vast domains, might still leave her to her own devices. And if the king's divorce could not be achieved by storming Rome's implacable resistance in the way that Henry still initially believed after his minister's fall, was there not also the alterna-tive option – soon to be devised by the newcomer Thomas Cromwell – of merely circumventing Rome by sundering altogether those ancient bonds tying England to her?

For at least two years after Wolsey's departure, the government remained effectively rudderless as Henry, at the head of a feckless aristocratic triumvi-rate comprising the dukes of Norfolk and Suffolk, and Anne Boleyn's father, the Earl of Wiltshire, huffed and puffed at the pope. Any semblance of a 'new order' was an unconvincing fiction, and fresh approaches, let alone novel solu-tions, to the central issues of Henry's marital dilemma were not to be had, since none were the men to succeed where Wolsey failed. And it would not be long, predictably, before the king was angrily informing the clique around him how 'Wolsey was a better man than any of you'. Yet in now relying increasingly upon his own inadequate resources, Henry himself was consistently guilty of failing to grasp that it is as much the task of a leader to contain and wait upon events as it is to push them. In consequence, he plunged headlong into a political and religious whirlpool that would result ultimately not only in further foreign war but national insolvency, the full and heavy consequences of which his son and eldest daughter would have to bear. Continually absorbed in the short-term priorities of the present and lacking, too, the skill of adaptation to evolving circumstances, he became to all intents and purposes a slave to his reflexes. 'Junker Heintz will be God and does whatever he lusts,' declared Martin Luther, until Wolsey's fall finally initiated, under Thomas Cromwell, a crucial shift from diplomatic to domestic constitutional methods for achieving the royal divorce. Thereafter, pressure was to be placed upon the pope in England and Westminster rather than in Italy and Rome: by legislation and confiscation at home rather than by military or political action abroad. And in the process, England moved once more from the epicentre to the fringes of European affairs, mainly intent upon holding the ring and preventing the interference by foreign powers in the execution of its domestic priorities. If French enmity with the emperor could be maintained and occasionally exploited as a lever upon the pope, this would have to suffice.

Certainly, as England's engagement in Europe unravelled, so Charles V's interest in England declined accordingly – not least because of the ongoing problems of his empire. For although the Turks were forced to raise their siege of Vienna in October 1529, they continued to menace the empire's eastern marches. In Hungary, John Zapolya became the sultan's vassal and it was not until 1533 that a peace of sorts was finally patched up, still leaving the Turks within 90 miles of Vienna. In the same year, moreover, Turkish envoys were actually welcomed at the court of Francis I, and though no open Franco–Turkish co-operation followed until 1536, the threat to Spain's communication with Italy was so apparent that Charles himself led the expedition to Tunis in 1535, by which time his difficulties with Germany's Protestants were no nearer to lasting solution. The Schmalkaldic League, formed at the end of 1531, committed them to defend their faith by joint political, and if necessary military, action, and at the Nürnberg Diet of 1532 Charles felt compelled to yield them formal toleration until a General Council of the Church could be held to reconcile their differences with Rome. Even so, however, they concluded a secret treaty with France in 1534, and though Francis was afraid to strike until two years later, he had now placed himself in a position to weld all his adversary's difficulties into one formidable whole – which could not, of course, have been better news for England and, in particular, Thomas Cromwell who was now the guiding hand behind the execution of his king's objectives.

Indeed, by the end of 1534, the royal divorce – founded upon an outright breach with Rome and the principle that England was an independent 'empire' in its own right – was securely sealed by a stream of Cromwellian legislation culminating in the Acts of Succession and Supremacy. Before the end of January 1533, Henry had married Anne in secret, and in the following month the introduction of the Act in Restraint of Appeals to Rome marked the death knell of direct papal interference in English affairs. Passed by Parliament in March, the statute went far towards turning the kingdom into a sovereign nation state, and what followed during the next twenty months tied up many of the loose ends. The payment of annates to the papacy was ended in July, and in the early months of 1534 all other such payments were diverted to the Crown by statute. Henceforward, too, new bishops were to be nominated by the king without reference to the pope, from whom all diplomatic recognition was withdrawn, except in his capacity as 'Bishop of Rome'. And during 1536, as Cromwell's dissolution of the monasteries clicked into place, even the definition of heresy became a matter for the royal prerogative with the introduction of the Ten Articles. Thereafter, home-brewed statute supplanted canon law or the broader conscience of any other European authority and became the only valid benchmark for loyal Englishmen. '*Your thinking* should not be your trial,' Cromwell had observed to John Fisher in 1534 as the bishop attempted in vain to carve out a defence over certain self-incriminating comments he had made, 'but the *law* must define whether you utter it or not.' Elsewhere, too, Cromwell would declare how 'an act of parliament, made in this realm for the commonwealth of the same, ought rather to be observed in this same realm than any General Council [of the Church]', adding 'and I think that the Holy Ghost is as verily present at such an act as ever he was at any General Council'.

The result of such thinking was a revolution in England's political relationship with Europe and, hardly less significantly, its spiritual orientation. Hereafter, English men and women were neither guided by the Index of the Roman Catholic Church, nor very much influenced, it might be added, by the baroque tastes that were to become arguably the richest harvest of the counter-reformation. Instead, they evolved their native 'Church of England', guided by Cranmer, Hooker, Parker and others in the more mellow ways of religious humanism – that blending of old and new, of Christian tradition with Greek stimulus and contemporary invention, which, in the days of Erasmus, had been the heartfelt preference of some of the greatest minds of Europe. And though a minority of the king's subjects rejected the changes, even revolting against them in 1536, the rest at least were to acquiesce willingly enough, since the papacy's attempts to undermine this process failed to gather momentum early enough. Not until the rebellion known as the Pilgrimage of Grace was effectively over was Reginald Pole made cardinal in December 1536 and then *legate a latere* in February 1537, while the election of Pope Paul III in September 1534 served mainly to revive the ambitions of Francis I against the emperor. Determined to invade Italy once more and reverse the Peace of Cambrai, the French king, too, posed little resulting threat to English interests – to the extent, indeed, that Henry even rejected an offer of alliance with him in the same month that Paul III assumed the papal tiara. When fighting in Italy resumed in April 1536, moreover, Charles's ambassador returned to London anyway, and England remained free from threat of invasion for the next two years until the truce of Nice was negotiated between Charles, Francis and the pope in June 1538.

On this later occasion, it is true, the threat of a Catholic crusade was to remain acute for ten months until April 1539. In December 1538, Pope Paul had pronounced Henry's excommunication and deposition, and David Beaton, a Scottish representative at the French court, had been made cardinal and sent back to his homeland to organise an invasion from the north whenever France and Spain should invade from the south. Already, moreover, James V of Scotland had married Mary of Guise, and in January 1539, at Aigues-Mortes, Francis and Charles agreed not to negotiate with Henry. Both, indeed, recalled their ambassadors from London in February, while English ships were seized in Netherlands ports, and French and Spanish ships began to mass, as for an invasion, at Boulogne and Antwerp. In response, fortresses were built along the south coast at Walmer, Dover, Calshot, Hurst, St Mawes, Pendennis and elsewhere, and the militias of the southern counties, and of the Scottish border counties, were mobilised. Equally significantly, negotiations began for the hand of the daughter of Duke John of Cleves, which were accompanied by a further wave of repression at home when Henry Courtenay, Marquess of Exeter, and Henry Pole, Lord Montague, were executed along with the abbots of Reading and Glastonbury. Margaret, Countess of Salisbury, was imprisoned for being the mother of Cardinal Reginald Pole, in tandem with a final assault launched on ecclesiastical property, which included the destruction of the shrine of St Thomas Becket at Canterbury to emphasise that 'he was really a rebel who fled the realm to France and to the Bishop of Rome to procure the abrogation of wholesome laws'.

Yet amid the frantic manoeuvrings, the threat of invasion nevertheless lifted in April 1539, and by June 1540 Charles and Francis were once more bitterly at odds over the future of Milan. So confident was Henry thereafter, in fact, that he was soon addressing the emperor as his 'loving brother and most cordial friend' and planning the downfall of Thomas Cromwell as a final gesture of conciliation. The minister had, after all, arranged a marriage to Anne of Cleves that had proved not only unappealing but, in the light of international developments, painfully unnecessary. And accordingly on 28 July 1540, he was gruesomely hacked for his efforts by a bungling headsman who required two blows to complete the task. Soon enough, in fact, Henry would be looking back upon his victim as 'the best servant he ever had' and convincing himself that he had been condemned 'on light pretexts'. And nor, from some perspectives, was he wrong, since Cromwell had at least restrained his master from those foreign adventures that had marred the earlier phase of the reign only to resurface now in a final, unseemly attempt to recapture a lost youth that was all too manifestly gone forever. In 1537, after almost three decades of agonising frustration, Henry had at last begotten a legitimate male heir with Jane Seymour. But she died in the process, and the casual promiscuity of his subsequent bride, Catherine Howard, had rendered him a laughing stock – which could mean only one thing. For now that the exercise of his manhood in the marriage chamber was no longer a pressing requirement or, for that matter, a practical option, Henry would opt instead to prove his mettle on another field of honour. As Thomas Wriothesley remarked at the time, England was 'but a morsel between choppers'. Yet her king was nevertheless irreversibly set upon one last martial bow in the Habsburg–Valois wars, which had already lumbered on for half a century. And nor, to Europe's cost, was he alone in his delusions, since Charles V and Francis I, though similarly shadowed by old age and sickness, were equally intoxicated by a bitter cocktail of chivalric fantasy and base ambition, thus ensuring that the King of England would not be thwarted in his vain attempt to profit from the resulting turmoil.

In Henry's case, the essential preliminary to any final marauding fling against the French foe was, by necessity, the neutralisation of Scotland, and to this end, in an effort to protect his back, he first sought 'full brotherly' alliance with James V of Scotland before quickly settling upon an 'honourable enterprise' to crush him. The resulting military campaign achieved an outstanding English success at Solway Moss in November 1542, which was said to have been so spectacular that it cured Sir William Paget's sciatica in London. Yet in other respects it achieved little of profit. On the field of battle 3,000 English troops had almost casually routed some 18,000 Scots, and in return for the capture of 1,200 Scottish prisoners – including two earls, five lords and 500 gentlemen – only seven Englishmen had been killed. But though the conflict was also followed by the death of King James the next month, Henry consistently missed opportunities to gain ground politically. True, the Treaty of Greenwich, which betrothed James' daughter (the future Mary, Queen of Scots) to Prince Edward, represented an uncharacteristic attempt at subtlety on Henry's part. Yet within the year English demands for physical possession of the princess's person had proved so insensitive that the Scots reaffirmed their alliance with the French and were bent on retribution. Faced with such 'ingratitude', Henry at first responded flaccidly with offers of pensions and then with characteristic brutality when an army under Edward Seymour, Earl of Hertford, was dispatched north to destroy every house and village within 7 miles of Edinburgh. 'Furthermore,' Henry's instructions ran, 'you shall take order with the Wardens that the borderers in Scotland may be still tormented and occupied as much as can be conveniently, now specially that it is seed-time, from which if they may be kept and not suffered to sow their grounds, they shall by the next year be brought to such penury as they shall not be able to live nor abide the country.'

By the end of 1543, the earl's 'great season of notable victories' and 'prosperous adventures' north of the border had indeed been concluded, so that in the summer of the following year, the all-conquering English king – who now, according to one commentator, possessed 'a body and a half, very abdominous and wieldy with fat' – set out for his final odyssey across the Channel, manhandled around the French countryside in a specially constructed litter except for those rare occasions when he was winched by crane into the royal saddle. Under the circumstances, the entire campaign in the 'ungracious dog-holes' of France was, in any case, a wildly improbable enterprise, fought mainly to muffle the ticking clocks that disturbed Henry's sleep and mocked his waking hours. But from the time that it began in earnest, it is nevertheless difficult to discern any coherent plan of attack. Only a week or so after setting out from Calais, the Duke of Norfolk wrote in desperation to the Privy Council that he had expected to know before this where he was supposed to be going, and although Boulogne was captured in September, none of the projected huge gains in northern and south-western France were achieved. Then, to compound matters, the emperor rapidly withdrew from the war, leaving Henry to face a possible French invasion in 1545, along with an actual French landing on the Isle of Wight, the prelude to which was the sinking of the *Mary Rose*. And though Henry's French adventures finally culminated in 1546 with Francis agreeing to uncommonly generous peace terms, the Treaty of Camp, which yielded Boulogne to England for eight years, was in reality no more than a face-saving sop afforded by a French government sufficiently triumphant for generosity. No glory was won, no gain accrued. In short, the English tyrannosaur had once again begotten a tadpole.

And in the meantime, the King of England might have done well to heed the advice given some time earlier to Louis XII of France that in war 'three things must be made ready: money, money and, once again, money'. For a military revolution of sorts was continuing to outstrip royal revenues and the gap between princely posturing and harsh economic reality was now starker than ever. The cost of mercenaries, in particular, was out of control, and armies of 10,000, which once consumed whole kingdoms, had by now swollen drastically. The English force, which campaigned for three months in France in 1544, for instance, consisted of 42,000 men and cost just under £587,000, while the total expense of Henry's wars between 1542 and 1546 amounted to £2,144,000 – some ten times as much as the expenditure on the French campaigns that had followed his accession. Apart from the unexpected length of the wars, the economic planning of Henry VIII's council, such as it was, also foundered on the huge standing cost of maintaining defences at Berwick, Calais, Boulogne and the south-coast ports, while even victory brought with it crippling expenses. Boulogne, for example, would cost another £426,306 to defend at a time when the best that Henry could depend upon annually from his normal peacetime revenues was a mere £200,000. And as the painful reality of his inflated ambitions unfolded, so the king had continued to resort to any and every financial expedient to subsidise his new venture. In consequence, the ruler who had begun his reign safe and solvent now went cap in hand to the money lenders of Antwerp to raise – at rates of 10 and 14 per cent – loans totalling £75,000 at his death. Worse still, he would also need to impose taxes and forced loans upon his country that were heavier than any hitherto, and meet more than half the necessary war expenditure not only by the sale of Crown lands but by a grievous debasement of the coinage. The coins minted in 1544, for example, contained only half their weight in fine silver, while those of 1546 consisted of no more than a third, and though this attempted fraud made the war possible in the short term, it did so, of course, only by stoking rampant inflation later on, and bequeathing a poisonous legacy to the king's hapless successors.

When Henry VIII died in January 1547, furthermore, he left his throne to a 9-year-old son and a government under Edward Seymour, the boy's uncle and 'Lord Protector', which was hardly well placed to rectify the kingdom's plight. Indeed, the dozen years following Henry's death could hardly have provided more ample justification of his anxieties about the succession, as his crown passed first to Edward VI and six years later to Mary, the boy's Catholic elder sister. During their reigns political and religious faction destroyed national unity, allowed social and economic discontents to break into open rebellion, and tempted the continental powers to make England, rather than Italy, their plaything. Weakened by domestic dissensions, the English were not only unable to complete the suppression of Scotland but drove the Scots by their actions more firmly than ever into the arms of France – to such an extent that England herself seemed prone to become under Seymour's successor, the Duke of Northumberland, a dependent client of the French king, or under Mary, a handmaid of Spain. Certainly, as the traumas of the mid-Tudor period ran their course, the entire thrust of the kingdom's foreign relations was determined less by what she herself did than by what others might do to her. And by its end the quasi-chivalric notions of adventures in northern France in pursuit of ancient feudal claims were gone forever – like the solitary overseas possession that England had previously clung to in Boulogne and Calais.

Yet in the earliest days of Edward Seymour's Protectorate after Henry's death, the outer world seemed surprisingly disinclined to impinge upon the new regime. The pope and Cardinal Pole did indeed urge Charles V to intervene at once to place his Catholic cousin upon her brother's throne by force of arms. But the emperor's cousin Ferdinand was tied down in Bohemia by a Protestant revolt, and Elector John Frederick of Saxony, leader of the Schmalkaldic League, remained defiant. Should Charles commit himself to hazardous winter operations across the Channel, he might therefore find himself ranged in the next campaigning season against a triple alliance of France, England and the German Lutherans. And he was in no mood anyway to listen to promptings from Rome, since, at the end of December 1546, the pope had recalled the troops sent previously to assist the Imperial army. At the same time, the papacy had not only refused to sanction further taxation of ecclesiastical revenues in Spain and Italy to help finance the war in Germany, but obstructed the General Council of the Church, called at Trent, from making suitable concessions to Charles's Lutherans that might have helped him achieve a much-needed compromise. Certainly, there was no sign of any significant support for Mary's succession in England itself, while from the point of view of the King of France, the prospect of a suitably weak and ineffective boy king upon the English throne remained infinitely preferable to the alternative of Charles V's half-Spanish cousin.

If Edward Seymour, who was created Duke of Somerset in February 1547, played his hand carefully, therefore, the dangerous legacy bequeathed him by Henry VIII upon his death the previous month might yet be somehow managed. He had, it is true, inherited a patched-up peace of fragile worth with France, an old-established war with Scotland in which he had played a hated role, crippling debts and a debased currency that was already fuelling social tension and unrest. But his first moves were prudent, as he angled for political stability at home by forestalling any undue continental interference in England's affairs. To this end, in March 1547 he gave Charles V further reason to adopt a benevolent neutrality by refusing an offer of alliance from the German Lutherans, notwithstanding the evangelical religious sympathies of both himself and his young king. After which, he succeeded in negotiating a defensive alliance with Francis I, and made the right noises, too, with Scotland, offering diplomacy rather than war. If appearances are to be trusted, indeed, Somerset gave every impression of being genuinely inspired by the vision of a united Great Britain where Scots and English should dwell together in peace and amity, guarded by the encircling sea 'against the envy of less happier lands'. And nor was this the limit of his idealistic rhetoric, as he declared his broader hopes for a Christian commonwealth, lifted above narrow national or class antagonisms, and uncorrupted by 'private profit, self love, money and such like the Devil's instruments'. Though English ships did take supplies into St Andrews, Somerset nevertheless hesitated to give all-out support to the Scottish Protestant rebels entrenched there, since they were a tiny doctrinaire minority. Instead, he spoke of the mutual benefit that a union of crowns would bring to both realms, and pressed only for a renewal of the engagements broken after the Treaty of Greenwich in 1543, which had provided, among other things, for the marriage of King Edward to the infant Mary, Queen of Scots.

But that self-same treaty had, of course, been violated by both sides almost before the ink was dry upon it, and in the aftermath, Somerset had served as Henry VIII's primary angel of vengeance during 1544 and 1545, with the result that the Lord Protector's honeyed words now gained little purchase during an attempt to negotiate at Berwick. On the contrary, the offer was roundly refused by Scotland's current regent, the Earl of Arran, at the very time that the advice of English councillors such as Bishop Gardiner and Sir William Paget to 'let the Scots be Scots', at least until Edward VI came of age, was proving equally ineffectual. For in spite of the fact that continual border raiding and the occasional full-scale invasion had only stiffened Scottish resistance, Somerset was now resolved, regardless of the risks, to renew the option of union by force. The question of England's finances, already staggering under the cost of previous unavailing efforts, was duly swept aside, no less than the military practicalities arising from the absence of a regular standing army. And the whole familiar tragedy unfolded accordingly. For merely to crush the Scots in another Solway Moss or Flodden, and follow such a victory with brief raids into the Lowlands, would clearly fail to break the will of the Scottish nation, while the cost of an occupying army was certain to prove far more expensive still, though no more guaranteed of success. Plainly, the case against involvement was powerful. Yet so too, fatefully, was the often over-looked dilemma arising from a new factor: the death on 31 March 1547 of Francis I, and the succession of his son, Henri II, who was less dazzled by the mirage of conquests in Italy, and more inclined to listen to the Duke of Guise and the Cardinal of Lorraine, who urged through their sister, the Scottish Queen Mother, and their niece, the young Queen of Scots, that the new king should set himself to restore and extend French influence in Scotland.

Like those around him, Henri was known to be galled by the loss of Boulogne, and to have expressed a determination to win it back at the earliest possible opportunity. Nor was he likely, prompted by the Guises, to overlook the fact that Mary, Queen of Scots was a great-granddaughter of Henry VII of England and therefore able to claim a place in the succession next after the schismatic Edward VI and the 31-year-old Princess Mary as well as Anne Boleyn's daughter Elizabeth, who, like her half-sister, had already been declared illegitimate. Were an active Scottish policy to win the hand of the Queen of Scots for his son, the Dauphin Francis, Henri might even achieve an eventual union of the French and Scottish crowns. Better still, in the event of the young King of England's premature death and the ongoing issues concerning the legitimacy of his sisters, there was even the prospect of the Queen of Scots becoming heiress to the English throne itself. For although the will of Henry VIII had negated the Scottish claim, his decision was a domestic one that international diplomacy might yet reverse, especially if the House of Valois, under an able and warlike young ruler, held out the dream of a solid empire of France and the British Isles, cutting the Habsburg dominions in two, and thereby offering unity to all Christendom. In fact, the Valois future was to prove tragically different. But the French dream of '*imperium*' was nevertheless to colour Europe for a dozen years to come, and was hardly one that Protector Somerset could ignore lightly in the summer of 1547 as Henri's naval forces transported troops up Scotland's east coast to the Forth.

In July, they took St Andrews, where the Protestants had been holding out since Cardinal Beaton's murder just over a year ago, and dispatched the survivors, John Knox included, to row as slaves in French galleys. That March, as a token of support, Somerset had sent nearly £1,200 to pay the little garrison of seven score men whom the Earl of Arran had been quite unable to suppress. But once arrived at St Andrews, Leo Strozzi's artillery soon proved overwhelming, as a consequence of which the French were able to achieve in only six weeks what the distracted government of Scotland had been unable to accomplish in six months. Thereafter, the Scottish Queen Mother and the other friends of France were more ascendant than ever, which encouraged them to press home with even greater confidence the advantages of a marriage between the dauphin and the little Queen of Scots. With only a few more troops and only a little extra money from Henri, indeed, it seemed as though Scotland might well become, in effect, another Brittany, while for Protector Somerset across the border, the question was no longer whether or not to 'let the Scots be Scots' but how to prevent them becoming French. Since they could not be persuaded, he concluded finally, they must be compelled, despite the cost. And if they were to be compelled, now was the critical time to do it, while the French were still partially restrained by fear of Charles V after his victory over the Schmalkaldic League at Mühlberg in April 1547.

Accordingly, after a month or more of preparation, on 4 September the Lord Protector invaded Scotland at the head of an army of around 17,000 men, marching swiftly up the east coast while a fleet of thirty-five ships guarding his right flank also brought up supplies and artillery. Once again, however, the sight of English troops succeeded only in bringing together, if not exactly uniting, Scotsmen of all factions, with the consequence that on 9 September, at Musselburgh beside the Firth of Forth, some 6 miles east of Edinburgh, Somerset's force found its way barred by a considerably larger but worse-equipped Scottish host of around 23,000, strongly positioned on a hillside beside the river Esk. Next morning the Scots came down from their vantage point, just as their descendants were to come down against Oliver Cromwell at Dunbar 103 years later – and with equally disastrous results. Caught in Pinkie Cleuch between Somerset's army and the Esk, their left flank under fire from an English warship lying close inshore, they were broken and put to total rout in the swamp where they fought. Throughout, Somerset's 800 foreign hackbutters had fired steadily at their closed ranks of spear-men, who were simultaneously torn with ball and hail shot by fifteen field guns placed on rising ground behind the English line. And the results, as might be imagined, were truly harrowing. In all, some 6,000 of them were recorded slain and 1,500 taken prisoner, against an English loss of less than one-tenth that number. Somerset, though, viewed the carnage with misgiving and stopped his men as soon as he could, since his purpose was a Scottish acknowledgement of English military superiority rather than a bloody victory that would exacerbate the hatred he sought to allay.

It was for this reason, too, that a second sack of Edinburgh was avoided and no move made to occupy it or ravage the defenceless land round about. Significantly, the official English account of the campaign by William Patten, quickly written and published in January 1548, was, by the standards of the day, remarkably humane and emollient in tone, incorporating suitable apos-trophes to the Scots to sink their enmity and join Great Britain:

> Seek we not the mastership of you, but the fellowship ... We covet not to keep you bound, that would so fain have you free from the feigned friend-ship of France.

Nor did Somerset stint on further friendly propaganda north of the border itself, distributing Bibles and doing his best to inspire the spread of Protestantism as he garrisoned the strongholds from the Tweed to the capital and round about as far as Dundee, the islands of the Forth, and the towns across the western territory that soon fell into his hands. In return for freedom of trade between the two kingdoms and the retention by the Scots of their own laws, the offer of marriage between Edward and Mary for the union of the crowns was once again renewed. And there was a further offer to King Henri, involving the surrender of Boulogne in return for the 2 million crowns promised in 1546 for his help in promoting the proposed marriage between the English and Scottish monarchs. All did much to give colour to Somerset's professions of moderation. But he had not secured the country or Mary, Queen of Scots herself, nor had he evicted the French. And the Protestant minority he sought to nurture was woefully insufficient to his needs. John Knox remained tethered to an oar in a French galley, defiant in his misery to the extent of hurling overboard an image of the Virgin brought round for the veneration of the slaves. And he would be back. Yet for the moment there was no appreciable Protestant party in his homeland to trouble the Earl of Arran or his aspiring French overlords, and while that was true the English cause in Scotland could never prosper.

In April 1548, therefore, after due persuasion by Francis of Guise to shift French military effort away from Italy to his own north-eastern frontier, Henri II coolly opted to send heavy reinforcements to Scotland with the specific intention of focusing his kingdom's aggression not only there but upon the northern Rhineland, the Netherlands and the English Channel. As such, after fifty years of comparative security lasting until the final years of Henry VIII's reign, England was once more within the orbit of French ambitions. And as the French king offered a promise of marriage between Mary, Queen of Scots and the dauphin, he made good his proposal with the dispatch of a force of 6,000 men that the English fleet failed to intercept. Predictably, the Scottish nobility accepted the alliance, and in August 1548, while Franco–Scottish troops began the task of besieging Somerset's garrisons, French warships took Mary, Queen of Scots from Clyde to Brest. To compound Somerset's predicament, the profound social and economic tensions at home had created the conditions for two rebellions, in the south-west and East Anglia, which would not only prevent him from reinforcing his Scottish garrisons but sweep him from power the following year, by which time those garrisons had already been withdrawn with great difficulty one by one. For in August 1549, Henri had finally declared war on England, and soon stood poised to take Boulogne. His ships harassed English shipping in the Channel; he encouraged rebellion in Ulster; and the French Queen Mother, supported by French troops, assisted his hunt for those Scottish noblemen who had previously collaborated with the English.

So when Protector Somerset found himself dispatched to the Tower by the regency council in October 1549, to be replaced by John Dudley, Earl of

Warwick and subsequently Duke of Northumberland, it came as little surprise. Ultimately, his attempt to unite the crowns of England and Scotland under 'the old indifferent name of Britons' had been fatally undermined by religious and social divisions already dawning in the previous reign, not to mention the grievous financial effects of five previous years of fighting. And under the circumstances, his successor would have little choice but to administer harsh medicine. Long remembered in history as a politician of diabolical cunning and self-interest, the Duke of Northumberland's foreign policy, at least, was an exercise in pragmatism and national survival. Since there was nothing in the treasury, and the rebellious temper of the kingdom precluded any expectation of further revenue, it was necessary to abandon national honour and to cobble together, as best he might, the most favourable terms for peace with France. Consequently, by March 1550 he had agreed the return of Boulogne to Henri – though the town's dogged resistance had convinced the French king that, in spite of his superiority, he would have to pay 400,000 crowns as the price of peace. And as Charles V hovered on the brink of intervention on behalf of the king's sister Mary, after a ban on the hearing of Mass in her household during January and February 1551, an offer of French protection was also duly accepted, which effectively completed the incorporation of England into its ancient enemy's orbit of influence. The Anglo–Scottish Treaty of Greenwich of 1543, proposing marriage between Edward and Mary, Queen of Scots, was formally dissolved, and the hand of the English king promised instead to Elizabeth of Valois, daughter of Henri, who, as a prelude to the Anglo–French alliance of 1551 was created a knight of the Garter.

Henceforward, from France's perspective, England could be left to ripen from weakness to weakness, as Henri's preparations for war with the emperor, and the preceding Treaty of Chambord with the German Lutheran princes, went forward. Northumberland was his client, and though Somerset was soon opposing the prevailing policy of subservience after his release from the Tower in February 1550, he would be neutralised by the headsman's axe in January 1552 – a victim in large part of his very resistance to his rival's Anglo–French alliance. Nor was this the end of England's troubles. For as the kingdom dissolved once more into faction and dissent, culminating finally in Northumberland's vain attempt to set Lady Jane Grey upon the throne after Edward's premature death from tuberculosis in 1553, the French king continued to observe developments and weigh them imperiously. In 1552, after Charles V's setback in Germany with the Lutherans at the Treaty of Passau, he occupied Metz, Toul and Verdun, pondering whether the time was at hand, too, for a military occupation across the Channel. In particular, he watched Northumberland's attempt to forestall Mary Tudor's succession, confident that the duke's government would not only be powerless thereafter to resist any subsequent demands made upon it, but likely to accept the need for French garrisons to sustain it. For there was good reason to believe that, if Mary could be apprehended swiftly, the coup on behalf of Lady Jane Grey might well be consolidated, and even before his eventual failure, Northumberland had already offered the surrender of Calais as a bribe for French assistance.

In the event, however, none of this was to be. And the result was another twist in the tide of affairs, which saw England suddenly swing from abject clientage to France to the imminent prospect of vassalage to Spain. It would take less than a fortnight for Mary Tudor to sweep aside Northumberland's conspiracy and, in doing so, frustrate Henri II's calculations not only to bolster his position but to employ the duke, in effect, as his viceroy. Beforehand, in May 1553, Northumberland had wedded his son Lord Guildford Dudley to Lady Jane Grey, descendant of Henry VIII's sister Mary through the latter's second marriage to Charles Brandon, Duke of Suffolk. And in June, to pave the way for what followed, the ailing King Edward had been further persuaded to compose a 'device' by which the claims of Mary, Elizabeth and Lady Jane's own mother, Frances, were all set aside in favour of Lady Jane Grey herself and her male descendants. Six weeks later the king was dead and his Protestant successor at once proclaimed queen in preference to Mary Tudor, who duly raised her standard at Framlingham in East Anglia and wrote to the council, demanding her own rightful succession – with lethal effect for her enemies' ambitions. Realising the hurried composition of the 'device' and keenly aware of its obvious legal flaws, people flocked in fact to her cause, while her hapless young rival, who had been a painfully unwilling participant in the whole affair, found herself supported only in the City of London. Whereupon, Northumberland's attempt at military resistance melted under the summer sun, as his soldiers deserted in droves, leaving him not only to surrender at Cambridge on 20 July but to throw up his cap in the market place in loyal salutation of the queen he had tried to defeat. Dumbfounded by the entire turn of events, the French ambassador Noailles wrote how he had 'witnessed the most sudden change believable in men', before adding that 'God alone worked it'. For exactly four weeks after the death of her brother, Mary was in London, Northumberland was lodged in the Tower facing execution, and Lady Jane, along with her husband and a handful of others, including Thomas Cranmer, were in close confinement. According to the Spanish ambassador, Simon Renard, England's new ruler, though 'good', was 'easily influenced, inexpert in worldly matters, and a novice all round'. He might also have added 'stubborn' and 'unimaginative'. Even more importantly, however, she remained not only 37 years of age and past her prime for child-bearing, but half-Spanish and wholly Catholic.

England's new queen arrived on her throne, moreover, at precisely the time that her kingdom had resumed its significance for Charles V. In August 1552, after fleeing across the Alps from a new Lutheran alliance forged by Maurice of Saxony, he had been forced to acquiesce in the Treaty of Passau, which accorded virtual independence, politically and religiously, to the German princes and cities of his empire. At the same time, he had already been made to abandon his hopes of achieving the acceptance of his eldest son, Philip of Spain, as successor to the Imperial throne, leaving his brother Ferdinand to salvage what he could from the wreckage of Habsburg authority. For although still nominally emperor, Charles's control over Germany was now fatally compromised. Worn down by old age and sickness, racked by gout and ruined by galloping consumption of pickled eels, live oysters, Spanish sausages and huge tankards of iced German ale taken at whim both day and night, Charles had in fact been carrying his huge empire on his back like a geriatric tortoise for longer than he could remember. And it was at this time, as he tottered agonisingly on his stick around the Imperial court, reflecting wistfully upon those former fine images of him as a dashing knight-errant, that he was increasingly anticipating his own abdication: first as ruler of the Spanish Empire, which he handed to Philip without fanfare in January 1556; and then as Holy Roman Emperor in 1558, by which time he had already retired to the Monastery of Yuste in Extremadura. There, surrounded by clocks, he lived in seclusion and eventually staged his own funeral some six months before the actual event in September. Intended as an act to 'merit the favour of heaven', the mock interment had been conducted, complete with shroud and coffin, after which he duly arose from the box and withdrew to his apartment – 'full', we are told, 'of those awful sentiments, which such a singular solemnity was calculated to inspire'.

Five years earlier, however, when Mary first ascended her throne, Charles was still enmeshed by worldly affairs, and central to his concerns was the fate of England and its new female ruler. For if the French should master her realm as it had already mastered Scotland, they might soon master the Netherlands, too. Within the empire, no help could be spared, and none could arrive by sea if both France and England were hostile. Equally, the French from Lorraine, with their Protestant allies in the Rhineland and northern Germany, were in a position to cut off any aid from overland. Against a France that controlled the British Isles and the Netherlands, and was linked to the German princes, it would not be easy to hold Italy either. And in the meantime, English privateers were already beginning to reinforce the French off Spain's Atlantic coasts, threatening the ports into which the silver from the American mines flowed. In short, French control of England represented an existential threat to Habsburg power, making her nothing less than the foundation stone of

the new western European empire that Charles was to devote his last years
to consolidating as a bulwark against France and an inheritance for the future
Philip II of Spain. Key to all was marriage between Philip and Mary – a
marriage that she would welcome avidly but would nevertheless take a
grievous toll upon the popularity she enjoyed initially, as fears grew that her
kingdom would become 'a little cock-boat in the wake of the Spanish galleon'. Upon her accession, wrote Robert Parkyn, 'the whole commonalty
(certain heretics excepted) did apply unto the said Lady Mary', and on 19 July,
when she was proclaimed at Cheapside, one chronicler described how there
were 'bonfires in every street in London, with good cheer at every bonfire,
the bells ringing in every parish church, and for the most part all the night till
the next day to noon'. 'For my part,' he avowed, 'I never saw the like.' Yet sixth
months later she barely survived Sir Thomas Wyatt's rebellion, and at the time
of her death in 1558, it was said once again that:

> all the churches in London did ring and at night [the people] did make
> bonfires and set tables in the street and did eat and make merry for the new
> Queen who succeeded her.

The cause of this swift and lasting loss of popularity lay not altogether surprisingly with Mary's marriage and, in particular, its consequences for her foreign
policy. Later generations of Protestant Englishmen, brought up on John Foxe's
Book of Martyrs, might think of her chiefly as the Bloody Mary who burned
for their faith not far short of 300 of her subjects. Yet they remembered, too,
that she had lost Calais to the French. And it remained her Spanish marriage and the loss of the kingdom's last foothold across the Channel, even
more than the fires of Smithfield, that lost her the hearts of English men and
women, though her foreign policy was in part only a manifestation and consequence of the old faith that had been her mainstay during the painful years
after her mother's rejection by her father. The kingdom's closer contact with
the reformers during her brother's reign had done nothing to enamour her
of Protestant ideas, and now the seeming miracle of her succession convinced
her of her divinely ordained mission to reconcile the land with Rome. Within
three weeks of her accession she was secretly corresponding with the pope,
and by early August, when the pope again nominated Cardinal Pole legate for
the reconciliation of England, a papal envoy was already in London, dealing
with her in secret. Though keenly aware, as she told the envoy at the time, that
while most of her subjects were Catholic at heart, few were lovers of the Holy
See, she would nevertheless press ahead doggedly – regardless, likewise, of the
fact that her nobles loved their ecclesiastical lands too dearly to have any real
liking for the restoration of Rome's authority.

It was for these reasons, indeed, that Mary felt, as her father had in the 1520s, that a queen regnant required a king consort to support her in the man's world of sixteenth-century politics. But there was more to it than that. For if she died childless, her successor would be that heretical half-sister Elizabeth, Anne Boleyn's daughter, who would surely undo her work. So she must marry, beget an heir, and speedily at that, since her age made childbearing not only problematic but a potentially fatal undertaking. Any prospective husband had therefore to be someone who could not only support her in the present but protect her child and preserve the old religion, were she not to survive. And no English subject could satisfy these requirements. Certainly, those suggested had little to recommend them. Cardinal Pole, himself a candidate, was 53, unwilling and still by law a traitor, while Edward Courtenay, Earl of Devonshire and grandson of Edward IV, was making up for fifteen youthful years in the Tower in ways that did not at all amuse the strait-laced queen. But chiefly the two were ruled out because Mary needed as husband a prince with truly princely power. In consequence, even such otherwise eligible foreign candidates as Don Luis of Portugal, Duke Emmanuel Philibert of Savoy, and the young Archduke Ferdinand of Austria hardly qualified. Instead, it was to her cousin and old-time fiancé, Charles V, that her thoughts first turned, before it became clear that he was now too old and decrepit to make honourable amends for his betrayal of her in 1525. However, his 27-year-old widower son Philip appeared a more than adequate substitute, and on 29 October, after Mary had knelt before the Blessed Sacrament with the Spanish ambassador and a single lady-in-waiting, chanting *Veni Creator*, she duly pledged her hand – breaking the news to her council officially in the ambassador's presence on 8 November.

But the response was not cordial. On the contrary, the first Parliament of the new reign, which sat between October and December, petitioned against the match, and it was clear, too, that there were divisions among the queen's councillors themselves. To some who favoured the marriage, there appeared no alternative, since England seemed destined in any event to become either a Habsburg or a Valois satellite, and the Habsburg option at least brought commercial advantages. Sir William Paget, for example, was certainly of this *politique* turn of mind. Yet the Lord Chancellor, Bishop Stephen Gardiner, who was both a Catholic and a patriot, was undisguisedly opposed. And when Spanish ambassadors arrived in January 1554 – their train snowballed through the streets by the boisterous youth of London – it was soon clear that while the bishop's misgivings were widely shared by the general populace, there would be no retreat on the queen's part. Indeed, as the marriage treaty was speedily drawn up, Gardiner was unable even to raise challenges, though its terms did at least appear to secure the kingdom's independence on matters of neutrality and war, and accorded no power of government to Philip. He would enjoy the title of 'king', but was to observe all English rights and privileges and introduce no foreigners to English offices. If, moreover, he should be at war as ruler of any other dominions, it was to involve England in neither fighting nor paying. And if Mary should die childless, Philip's connection with England was to cease absolutely, notwithstanding the consideration that if any heir were actually to result, it would inherit not only England but the Netherlands and Franche Comté, while Spain and the Italian possessions would go to Don Carlos, the son of Philip by his earlier marriage to Maria Manuela of Portugal.

Superficially at least, the arrangements seemed comparatively equitable from the English standpoint. But the treaty could take no account of what proved to be the queen's doting subservience to the needs and wishes of a husband who would never reciprocate her loyalty or affection. Nor, as events soon demonstrated, could it allay the residing nationalism of Mary's subjects. For if Cardinal Pole would complain bitterly how the emperor could 'not bring himself to believe that I would help him put my country into the hands of a foreigner', there were those, by contrast, who had no intention of allowing such an eventuality. Indeed, a conspiracy involving Edward Courtenay and Sir Thomas Wyatt duly unfolded in January, which consisted of planned uprisings in the south-west, in the midlands and in Kent, and on the Welsh border. Though the plotters were of differing religious backgrounds, hostility to foreign subservience was their common bond, and, regardless of the rebellion's premature launch after its discovery, 4,000 Kentish rebels nevertheless occupied London under Wyatt's leadership. Significantly, too, they were to be foiled only by the queen's personal bravery in standing fast in her capital and urging its citizens to fight, though at least half London's loyal citizens were visibly disaffected as the rebels crossed the Thames on its Middlesex bank after a critical delay at Kingston. Following a skirmish at what is now Hyde Park Corner, moreover, the Earl of Pembroke's defending force actually retreated, while another body of Londoners was chased from Charing Cross. But the gates of the city remained closed, Howard held Ludgate, and Pembroke regrouped to Wyatt's rear, leaving the weary and famished intruders surrounded and ready to surrender. Hitherto, 16-year-old Lady Jane Grey had been spared, but the queen was now hardened by the danger and her execution followed on 12 February, after some seventy-five rebels, including Wyatt, had met a similar fate. At the same time, only a lack of hard evidence implicating her, coupled to her sister's natural instinct for clemency, spared Princess Elizabeth herself in the face of urgent protests from Simon Renard, the Imperial ambassador, that she be executed forthwith.

Yet if the rebellion failed, its expression of public misgivings had been striking, and nor was it long before its participants' worst fears were realised. For
on 4 February, John Rogers, the editor of what was generally dubbed *Matthew's
Bible*, became the first Marian martyr to burn at Smithfield, and in March 1557,
after frequent absences and casual neglect of his wife – to whom he conde-
scendingly referred as his 'aunt' – Philip returned to England to extract from
her a commitment to war against France. He had bided with Mary during
the months of 1555 that she briefly appeared pregnant, but when that hope
vanished in August, he set out from London for Dover and the Netherlands,
leaving his forlorn wife behind him. Five months later he became ruler of
Spain, Spanish America, Naples and the Netherlands, effectively abandoning
his interest in English affairs altogether unless England, or more specifically
its queen, could give him the military support he required. On her accession, ironically enough, Charles V had given his English cousin three pieces
of advice: punish the rebels; beware of France; above all, be *une bonne Anglaise*.
But, as events now proved, the last was what she could never be. For while the
observation of the Venetian ambassador that she scorned her English descent
and boasted only of her Spanish blood, was unfounded, she now conceded
much too easily to her husband's growing insistence upon the military aid
which had been refused between October and December 1555 by the fourth
Parliament of the reign. In May of that year, a Neapolitan and, as such, an
implacable enemy of Spain had become Pope Paul IV. And by July 1556, the
new pontiff had allied with France, shattering the Truce of Vaucelles, which
had brought a temporary halt to hostilities in the Netherlands just over four
months earlier. Now Philip demanded English help in accordance with the
alliance of 1543, and while her council demurred, Mary nevertheless succeeded in winning them round – albeit largely as a result of Henri II's own
miscalculation. For the French king had been keenly observing events across
the Channel, and stirring assorted mischief, which eventually provided the
queen with precisely the pretext for action she needed.

Upon Mary's accession in 1553, it was true, Henri had been largely preoccupied with critical events in the Netherlands and the Rhineland, which
followed hard upon the death of his ally, Maurice of Saxony. Yet his assistance
thereafter was wholly at the service of any and every plot for the overthrow of
the English queen. Rankling at her marriage to Philip, he aided the promoters of Wyatt's rebellion in 1554, and encouraged the plot of Sir Henry Dudley
in 1556 when a distant cousin of the deceased Duke of Northumberland
slipped across the Channel at the behest of the French ambassador de Noailles
in an abortive escapade on behalf of 'our sweet Lady Elizabeth … a jolly liberal
dame and nothing so unthankful as her sister is'. In the event, the endeavour
coincided with the Truce of Vaucelles, and when French backing evaporated,

Dudley made the fatal error of attempting to secure funds by robbing the Exchequer, which led to arrests. But in April 1557, Henri also allowed Sir Thomas Stafford to mobilise a small force in Dieppe for a private invasion of England, and it was this that proved the final straw, even for Mary's reluctant privy councillors. Landing at Scarborough, Stafford's wildcat enterprise was in fact easily and promptly defeated, following the temporary seizure of the town's castle. Yet the would-be invaders had come from a French port, in two ships and with arms provided by the King of France, and such flagrant provocation removed all further obstacles to an outright declaration of war by England in June 1557. In order to ensure the kingdom's participation on Spain's side, moreover, Philip had come over from the Netherlands that spring, and, having achieved his goal, almost solely on the initiative of his wife, he departed forever at the beginning of July, taking with him around 7,000 English troops in support of the much larger Spanish forces already engaged across the North Sea.

Seldom, if ever, had the kingdom gone to war so unwilling and unprepared. It had taken six months' unremitting regal pressure, crowned by the French king's folly to bring it about, and, in the meantime, Mary's Archbishop of Canterbury, the self-same papal legate who had reconciled the realm to Rome, was deprived of his legatine commission, summoned to the Holy City, and even threatened with charges of heresy – an innocent victim and scapegoat of Paul IV's ongoing antagonism to Philip II, cynically administered on this occasion by spite towards his wife's personal mentor and favourite. And in the meantime, Mary's treasury was empty, the necessary naval stores were lacking in the dockyards, and even the kingdom's stock of gunpowder was almost exhausted, leaving her little choice but to opt for a forced loan rather than call Parliament – with predictable results. Soldiers and seamen mutinied and deserted, and civilians abetted them, while Scotland, under the Queen Mother, Guise's sister, entered the war at a time when the border was so sorely ill-defended that the most reliable troops available were a contingent of 3,000 German mercenaries. However, these were intercepted by Philip while crossing the Netherlands en route and promptly added to his own army. Nor, to add salt to the wound, would Mary's husband subsequently declare war on Scotland in order to interrupt Netherlands–Scottish commerce. Indeed, he later impounded for his own use arms and munitions bought in Antwerp for the defence of England. But most significantly of all, he did nothing effective to defend Calais against the attack upon it that the Duke of Guise was busily preparing in the winter of 1557–58 – an attack that would be aided too by what amounted to the almost criminal carelessness of the English government. For when the blow fell on 1 January, the garrison had not been reinforced and the fleet remained laid up for the winter.

Consolations from the outset had been few. In August 1557, the small
English force accompanying Philip to war had helped achieve a notable success at St Quentin, though he lacked the money to exploit his good fortune,
and the victory, in any case, merely served to strengthen French resolve and
lull her enemies to sleep. Likewise, the patched-up peace between Philip and
the pope, which ensued before the end of the year and brought about France's
withdrawal from Italy, resulted only in a strengthening of the French to the
north. In consequence, therefore, they were at liberty to deliver a sudden
stroke in the dead of winter against Calais, which duly arrived after forty-five
warships, along with a siege train and a large army, landed at Boulogne. By
comparison, the English 'ships and barks in the Narrow Seas' were only five
in number and crewed by no more than 400 men, so that for the first time in
half a century sea power was on the side of France. Such, indeed, was the predicament that at Dover the Earl of Rutland hastily levied men from Kent and
Sussex to embark them in local fishing boats in a vain attempt to get through
the French blockade. And in the aftermath, the Calais garrison of 800 men,
protected only by the town's crumbling walls of medieval masonry, found
itself invested on the last day of the year by a force twenty times its number
armed with heavy battering guns. Accordingly, after an honourable defence,
surrender took place on 8 January 1558, to be followed by Guisnes Castle
and the smaller bulwarks of the Pale before the end of the month. Hitherto,
ever since the Norman Conquest, the Crown of England had held some part
or other of continental France, and for more than 200 years its royal standard
had floated most proudly of all over Calais. But the tale was now ended. The
ancient mart for the sale of wool was no more, and the favoured port of entry
for any English invasion of France was gone for ever. Only the incalculable
loss of prestige would reside.

'When I am dead and opened,' Mary famously lamented, 'you shall
find Calais lying in my heart.' And surely enough, as summer merged into
autumn and the people looked forward more and more eagerly to the
accession of her sister, the queen grew steadily sicker in tandem with her
beloved Cardinal Pole, who was also bereft of hope. The action of Paul IV
had galled him grievously, but neither had the pope's Spanish opponents any
good word to say for him. On the contrary, they blamed him for England's
lack of interest in the war and spoke of him as 'the accursed cardinal'. So
perhaps it was only fitting that queen and cleric should die on the same
day, 17 November 1558: Mary in the morning, her mentor in the evening
while the joy bells pealed over London. Beforehand, while his wife lived,
even Philip had feared for his honour at signing Calais away to the King
of France. But now the obstacle was gone and he lost no time in signing
the Peace of Cateau-Cambrésis, at which English participants bargained as

best they could with empty hands. Certainly, they had little to cheer them, though by that time, at least, the King of Spain had neither the will nor the means to obstruct the working of England's Act of Succession. On the contrary, the most that he asked from his former wife's kingdom was that her sister, Princess Elizabeth, should be given in marriage to a Spanish grandee of his choosing – a mere scrap from the feast at which he had apparently eaten his fill.

10

ELIZABETH I:
THE SEMBLANCE OF GLORY

No oblivion shall ever bury the glory of her name, for her happy and renowned memory still liveth and shall for ever live in the minds of men to all posterity, as of one who (to use no other than her successor's expression) in wisdom and felicity of government surpassed (without envy be it spoken) all the princes since the days of Augustus.

William Camden, *Annales: The True and Royall History of the famous Empresse Elizabeth, Queen of England* (1625)

For fifty years after 1494 Italy suffered as the crucible of European warfare, while, 1,000 miles away, foreign policy was a luxury in which England could often choose to indulge or not. By 1558, however, the vortex had shifted to Flanders and the English Channel, and England itself, a little country of 3 million people, was not only bound to be drawn in, but likely to be broken and impoverished, even to lose her identity and suffer that same fate already experienced by the Neapolitans and soon to be endured by the southern Netherlands. In consequence, the forty-five-year reign of England's last Tudor monarch was a time of pessimism, insecurity and agonising national danger under the overshadowing power first of France and then of Spain. By its end, Englishmen had discovered the role of transoceanic enterprise they wished to pursue, but still could hardly believe they would ever be free to fulfil it. They had been divided against each other by the factious ambitions of the Duke of Northumberland and the narrow zeal of Mary Tudor; they had now to live under permanent threat of invasion after half a century of comparative immunity. In the days of the Armada, and afterwards, Elizabethans were less impressed by the magnitude of their victory than by the permanence of their peril and the certainty that the enemy would return, since 'their force is wonderful great and strong' and 'all the world never saw such a force as theirs was'. As such, the legendary popularity of Sir Francis Drake represented little more than a momentary release of pent-up anxieties, a feeling of relief that somewhere some victory had at last been won. And though from 1598 the danger from Spain was no longer so acute, the sense of weary apprehension abided, fuelled first by chronic rebellion in Ireland and equally by chronic poverty at home.

In later years, Raphael Holinshed joined heartily in the myth-making:

> After all the stormy, tempestuous and blustering windy weather of Queen Mary was overblown, the darksome clouds of discomfort dispersed, the palpable fogs and mist of the most intolerant misery consumed, and the dashing showers of persecution overpast: it pleased God to send England a calm and quiet season, a clear and loverly sunshine, a quitset [release] from former broils of a turbulent estate, and a world of blessings by good Queen Elizabeth.

But if he overestimated the last Tudor's achievements, he also over-simplified both the scale and complexity of the problems confronting her at the outset of her reign. Upon her predecessor's passing, England was already, in the view of the Count of Feria, 'the sick man of Europe'. And Elizabeth's subjects, no less than the Spanish ambassador, appreciated full well the scale of the kingdom's plight. Indeed, in *The Distresses of the Commonwealth*, Armagil Waad, a former clerk to the Privy Council who had been deprived of his post in the previous reign, described the condition of the English State thus:

> The queen poor; the realm exhausted; the nobility poor and decayed; want of good captains and soldiers; the people out of order; justice not executed. All things dear. Excess in meat and apparel. Divisions among ourselves. Wars with France and Scotland. The French king bestriding the realm, having one foot in Calais and the other in Scotland. Steadfast enmity but not steadfast friendship abroad.

The realm was unquestionably encircled. Earlier in the year of Elizabeth's accession, the young Queen of Scots, long betrothed to the Dauphin Francis, was at last married to him, strengthening the French tentacles gripping Scotland. Thereafter, a Valois Franco–Scottish kingdom, possibly reaching out to Ireland, was a direct possibility, and in an age where leadership was still considered a strictly masculine preserve, the accession of another female ruler hardly offered solace. It was taken for granted, of course, that Elizabeth would marry, but whom? Any choice posed problems. For if her husband were an Englishman he would create jealousies and counter-loyalties among his peers, whilst her sister's reign had already amply underlined the dangers of a foreign match.

Most perplexingly of all, the heir to the throne, as things stood, was the King of France's new daughter-in-law, Mary Stuart – indeed, by canon law she was the rightful queen already. Henri II, moreover, had lost no time in proclaiming her title and quartering the leopards of England with the lilies of France, raising anew the spectre of a French bloc stretching from the Shetlands to the Pyrenees. Under the terms of the 1543 statute, Mary was, it is true, excluded from the succession, whereas Elizabeth had been included, leaving the next heir, technically, Lady Catherine Grey, grand-niece of Henry VIII and sister of Jane. But all observers agreed that Lady Catherine lacked the requisite qualities, and her marriage in 1560 to the son of the deceased Duke of Somerset had made her the focus of faction rather than national unity. Under the circumstances, the need for a legitimate heir for the new queen in the form of a son could hardly have been more pressing, though as early as 1559, much to the frustration of her councillors, she was already expressing the hope to Parliament that an heir might yet be found 'peradventure more beneficial to the realm than such offspring as may come of me'. Even so, she would remain reluctant to name one, knowing, as she openly professed, 'the inconstancy of the people of England' and 'how they ever mislike the present government and have their eyes fixed upon the next to succeed'. Whatever evils an uncertain succession might one day bring to her kingdom, she reasoned, the present consequence of uncertainty was that Englishmen would rally all the more ardently to their reigning monarch, while her enemies were left to compete with increasing jealousy to frustrate each other's claims to her hand.

In effect, England's present difficulties were so considerable that every present advantage must be seized and the future left to itself, or, more precisely, divine providence. 'The more I reflect,' observed the Spanish ambassador, 'the more I see that all will turn on the husband which this woman chooses.' And it was precisely for this reason, paradoxically, that Elizabeth remained set against marriage from the beginning of her reign, opting instead for the high-risk alternative of withstanding intense pressure both from Parliament and her privy councillors to bank upon her personal survival. On 10 October 1562, she would fall ill with smallpox at Hampton Court, suffering from a fever that left her physicians fearing the worst, and in later years there would be scares of equal or greater magnitude, not least from direct plots upon her life. But the alternative of a foreign husband, like the prospect of a return to Catholicism, was more fraught still with pitfalls, especially when that husband was more likely than not to be a Catholic himself. For the experience of the previous five years had caused most English men and women to associate marriage abroad with the designs of the papacy and the subordination of the kingdom to foreign interests. The queen's subjects were unable to forget 'the late days of Queen Mary when ... the Pope's authority was wholly restored and for the continuance thereof a strange nation ... brought into this land to lord it over us'. And for this reason alone both a reconciliation with Rome, whereby the papacy would recognise Elizabeth's legitimacy, and a marriage alliance with Spain, affording a safeguard against French aggression, remained untenable, notwithstanding the obvious temptations. 'Mere English' was the queen's proud boast, based upon a hundred years of her own English ancestry, and it was to remain so for the rest of her reign. Indeed, Elizabeth's 'Englishness' became the tap root of her success, feeding a national self-consciousness and pride in the kingdom's exclusivity that was born, ironically enough, from its very weakness. Underpinned by prolonged and extensive propaganda, which was itself reinforced by her uniquely 'Anglican' Church, it would create over time a sense of manifest destiny that developed almost seamlessly into that sense of moral superiority so central to the imperial ethic of later years.

Certainly, foreign suitors were not in short supply for Elizabeth. Notwithstanding the disillusionment of his earlier association with Mary Tudor, Philip II, for instance, still saw fit in February 1559 to tender a comparatively desultory proposal of marriage to forestall any potential Anglo–French alliance. But when the Spanish ambassador, de Feria, tried to assure her that she owed her crown to the King of Spain's goodwill and implied that she would be wise to encourage his continued favour, the queen replied boldly that she owed her position only to her people, and proceeded to bar the ambassador even from a room in her palace. Nor, ultimately, were other candidates for the queen's hand to prove any more appealing. The most promising Habsburg suitor was the Archduke Charles, both younger son of Emperor Ferdinand and Philip's cousin. Such a husband held out the prospect of a Spanish military alliance with the least likelihood of a union between the English and Spanish monarchies. But the match entailed religious concessions, which Elizabeth was unwilling to grant, and no Protestant ruler enjoyed sufficient prestige for consideration. In Scotland, James Hamilton, son of the second Earl of Arran, seemed to offer a range of diplomatic advantages, since he was in line of succession to the Scottish throne and stood comparatively free from subordination to both France and Spain. Nor, as Sir William Cecil observed, had the fact altered that 'the best felicity Scotland can have is ... to be made one monarchy with England'. Yet Hamilton was already half-mad and after 1566 incapable of any kind of public life, making him hardly less worthy of the queen's affection than the one man who does undoubtedly seem to have won it: Robert Dudley, scion of the former Duke of Northumberland, whose family had long been an object of general hatred.

Clearly, the problem was a perplexing one. 'The matter,' wrote Cecil, 'is too big for weak folk and too deep for simple.' In the short term, moreover, there were other areas where a policy of delay and prevarication could not suffice at all. For in November 1558 French, Habsburg and a largely impotent group of English negotiators were present at Cateau-Cambrésis, not only terminating the most recent and last of the great Habsburg–Valois wars, but determining the direction of a counter-reformation Europe, in which the intention was 'to bring all Christian Europe to a true accord' – or, in other words, to reverse Protestantism's expansion over the last four decades and, in the process, extirpate heresy once and for all. Cecil, like Thomas Cromwell before and Oliver Cromwell after, believed that religious motives would prevail, that Roman Catholics would unite, and that all Protestants must combine with their European brethren in self-defence. Elizabeth, however, was of the opinion that *politique* motives were likely to win through and that the territorial rivalries of France and Spain would pull them apart – unless, that is, misguidedly aggressive Protestant foreign policies should serve to cement their alliance. Given this, her preferred policy at Cateau-Cambrésis was, in effect, the only one available to her in light of the meagre resources at her disposal: to fan the rivalry of Philip and Henri by carefully exploiting their rivalry for her hand in marriage. And it was for this reason, too, that Elizabeth duly moderated her religious settlement of March 1559, notwithstanding the demands of Parliament for more radical changes than the 'middle way' that eventually resulted. 'I see the heretics are very downhearted,' wrote the Spanish ambassador at the time. But it was a situation that satisfied Elizabeth's needs, as did the eventual peace of Cateau-Cambrésis itself, notwithstanding the final abandonment of Calais – for a token sum of 500,000 crowns – that it entailed. Henceforth, the problem of English defence would be rendered more difficult than ever, since French expeditions to the Firth of Forth or against England's eastern harbours would no longer have to run the gauntlet of the Straits of Dover in such trepidation. At the same time, Calais also gave France a base for commerce-raiding very close to the main shipping route between London and Antwerp. Yet if the treaty marked an inglorious start to the new reign, it was not the new queen's fault, as her subjects knew, and represented nevertheless an early signal both of her prudence and of her cunning. Most important of all, it brought her the precious gift of time.

Nor did the loss of Calais pose the immediate danger that might have been incurred by the loss of Berwick on the Scottish frontier. The border town's defences had been sorely neglected, but the Scots did not attempt its capture, and there were other more substantial traces of comfort in that area for the new queen. For although the French remained powerful, they were not the exclusive element of influence. The young queen was in France, and her mother, Mary of Guise was regent. But the Scottish nobles were as keenly aware as English statesmen of the implications of the Stuart–Valois marriage, which, if it was a pressing threat to English independence, posed an even more immediate menace to Scottish. As early as 1548, there had been an outbreak of violence in Edinburgh between French troops and local people, and ten years later the Earl of Argyle was only one of many making a direct comparison between Scotland and 'the exampill of Brytany':

> The French [he wrote] ar cumin in and sutin down in this realm to occupy it and to put furth the inhabitantis tharoff and siclik to occupy all uther menis rowmes pece and pece and to put away the blud of the nobilitie.

Under the circumstances, some men saw no alternative to rebellion and Anglo–Scottish co-operation in a joint defence against French imperialism. Certainly, the former Earl of Arran, now Duke of Châtelherault, was of this mind, and he and others therefore made no difficulty in signing peace with England in March 1559. By early May, furthermore, John Knox had returned to Edinburgh with the aim of substituting Protestant for Catholic worship, confiscating church property, evicting the French, and perhaps deposing the French-owned Queen of Scots. Four years earlier, he had made many converts, and in 1557 the Scottish Calvinist movement had taken official form as 'the Congregation', whose 'Lords' included a number of peers of the realm. Now, however, the fledgling rebels were openly seeking aid from England, while their noble leaders spoke keenly of outright union by means of Elizabeth's marriage to James Hamilton, the current Earl of Arran and son of the Duke of Châtelherault.

Yet, far from assisting the Queen of England, the prospect of turmoil to the north only compounded her predicament. For if Philip and Henri II were indeed united by any crusading zeal for Roman Catholicism, events in Scotland must surely move them to action. Nor, at the same time, was Elizabeth any more sympathetic than her enemies to the Calvinist programme for ecclesiastical control of the State, which was what, in effect, the Lords of the Congregation had in mind. Profoundly resenting rebels who challenged the legitimate rights of her fellow monarchs, she also distrusted the new Scottish comradeship for England, coming so suddenly after ages of jealousy and hatred, and was decidedly unimpressed by the suitability of young Arran as husband after he came secretly to London on his passage from Geneva to Scotland. But failure to support her fellow Scottish Protestants entailed, at the same time, even more baleful possibilities, since defeat would make their homeland's conquest by the French inevitable and lead equally certainly to the invasion of a disaffected northern England, after which a tale of ruin was bound to unfold. Though he was no more of a military adventurer than the queen herself, Cecil therefore urged intervention, and she was finally constrained to agree with him in mid-summer, by which time the Congregation controlled central Scotland, but stood sorely exposed to the counterstroke that the French were poised to launch. For as large forces gathered across the Channel, there was no means of stopping them at sea, or withstanding them on land, since the success of the rebels so far had been founded on little more than the rage of mobs and rioters against a handful of foreigners. They had virtually no firearms, no organised food supply and no money to supply one.

Even so, Cecil had not found it easy to persuade his sovereign to 'nourish and entertain the garboyle in Scotland'. On the contrary, he had 'had such a torment herein, with the Queen's majesty, as an ague hath not in five fits'. Still relying on Habsburg–Valois rivalry as her main shelter and leverage point, small sums of money – £2,000 in August and £3,000 in November – were paid to the rebels. But the French had sent 1,000 men to Leith and held another 9,500 ready, and it was only on 16 December 1559 that queen and council at last began to yield to Cecil's persuasion more substantially, with the dispatch of Admiral Sir William Wynter to Scottish waters under instructions to get blown into the Firth of Forth and intercept the French 'as of your own courage'. In the meantime, Elizabeth opened marriage negotiations with Archduke Charles in order to ensure Habsburg neutrality – reviving Catholic symbolism in her royal chapel as an enticement – and English troops and guns were mobilised at Berwick, though the Duke of Norfolk refused to march them northwards, and Wynter's force took all of three weeks to reach its objectives in the stormy winter weather. Yet there were consolations, too – and not inconsiderable ones at that. For the eventual arrival of Wynter's men forced the French to evacuate Fife and revived the confidence of the Congregation, bringing waverers over to their side. Equally, the same December gales had wrecked the French expeditionary force off the coast of Zeeland, and bought valuable time for the conclusion at last of what amounted to a formal Anglo–Scottish defence pact, signed at Berwick in February 1560.

Under the terms of the treaty, it was agreed that the joint forces of the two kingdoms should drive out the French, while preserving the monarchy of Mary Stuart, and that Scotland likewise should aid England in its own defence. By now, Elizabeth had received information from Sir Thomas Gresham that the Spanish government in the Netherlands was hopelessly in debt and unable to connive against her interests, while Sir Nicholas Throckmorton, the English ambassador in France, sent news of a growing

Protestant Huguenot movement, and a conspiracy, not limited to Protestants, against the ascendancy of the Catholic Guises. In March, moreover, as an English army of 8,000 advanced towards Leith, the first tremor of the French civil wars that later blunted the acute threat to England's independence duly occurred in the form of the so-called 'tumult of Amboise' – a revolt of a section of the lesser Huguenot nobility against Francis II and the Guise family. And although an English assault on Leith was repulsed, the French not only proved unable to send reinforcements but found their supplies running low. Worse still from the French perspective, Mary of Guise was dying, allowing the triumphant conclusion, in July 1560, of the Treaty of Edinburgh, by which the French and English agreed to evacuate Scotland, and Mary, Queen of Scots recognised Elizabeth as Queen of England. Hereafter, Scotland would be governed by a council of twelve, seven chosen by the absent Queen of Scots and five by the Scottish Parliament that was shortly to meet. Ominously, no word was made of religion, and both Francis and Mary refused to ratify the treaty. But the unexpected shift in the politics of France that had preceded it left Elizabeth in a greater position of security than she could ever have envisaged beforehand.

Cecil himself concluded that 'the benevolence (of the Scots) at this time towards England is so great … as I see not that in long time the French shall recover the mind of Scottishmen against us'. Yet the greatest coup of all for England's security was to be not of Cecil's doing, but God's. For in December 1560 Francis II died prematurely – an event that weakened the power of the Guise, lifted Catherine de' Medici into the position of French regent, and materially increased the likelihood of prolonged civil war in France. Unpopular with the new regent and faced with the prospect of impotence as queen dowager, Mary Stuart would, it is true, now return to her homeland in August 1561 and raise the possibility once more of French influence and Roman Catholicism, which was still the dominant creed in north-central Scotland, from Aberdeen to Skye. But the death of her husband completed the twist in France's fortunes that had begun only five months earlier with the death of Henri II from a jousting accident sustained, ironically enough, at the tournaments held in honour of the marriage between Elizabeth of Valois and the King of Spain. It was Henri who had hatched plans not only to continue the 'Auld Alliance' between France and Scotland but also to absorb Scotland entirely into France. Yet his plans had been undone by nothing more than the fragility of his own life and that of his son after only seventeen months on the throne. For from March 1562, when the Duke of Guise usurped the government and Condé, Coligny and the Huguenots took up arms against him in defence of their religion and the monarchy, France was embroiled in heavy fighting.

Only one year later, furthermore, armed resistance to Philip II's rule began in the Netherlands, never to be ended effectually in the life of any contemporary. Coupled to events in Scotland, England had thus been afforded a seemingly God-given conjunction of circumstances for the defence of its government and religion. North of the border, of course, there was no room for complacency. For although the effective head of state was the illegitimate son of James V and leader of the Lords of the Congregation, James Stuart, Earl of Moray, it was still incumbent upon Elizabeth to detach the Queen of Scots from her French affiliations – notwithstanding Catherine de' Medici's antipathy to Mary's Guise connections and the fact that in 1562 Moray had crushed Earl Huntly of Aberdeen and the Roman Catholic Gordons. As an enticement to her cousin, Elizabeth was prepared in fact to encourage the belief that Mary was her natural successor in every way short of formal recognition. And it was for this reason, too, that Elizabeth even dangled her own favourite, Robert Dudley, before her rival as a suitable husband who might sever her French sympathies once and for all. In the event, Mary saw fit to opt instead in July 1565 for what would prove the disastrous choice of Henry Stuart, Lord Darnley, the grandson of Henry VIII's sister Margaret. Nineteen years old at the time of his marriage, Darnley was technically an Englishman, the son of the Scottish Earl of Lennox, who had been an exile in England since 1544 after supporting the English invasion of his homeland. But he was also a Catholic with a valid claim to the Tudor throne in his own right, and a young man with a deeply flawed and unmanageable disposition, whose shortcomings left some of Elizabeth's councillors in little doubt 'that the peril was greater by this marriage with Lord Darnley … than with the mightiest prince abroad'. Jaundiced, jealous, vain and volatile – resembling 'more a woman than a man' and stricken by inner demons of his own devising, which he could neither tame by infidelity nor dowse with drink – the queen's husband would, indeed, soon become a pox-ridden parody of the dashing blond-haired lover who had first dazzled his bride only two years earlier 'as the properest and best proportioned long man' that she had ever seen.

Yet Elizabeth, paradoxically, could hardly have done more to ease the way for the marriage, first assisting the Earl of Lennox to return to Scotland in September 1564 to recover his estates there, and then allowing Darnley to join his father six months later. Certainly, she cannot have foreseen the turmoil that was to ensue, but is likely to have perceived the marriage as a further means of insulating Scotland from continental affairs, since Mary's cause was unlikely to be so attractive to foreign princes once she could no longer offer herself as a bride with a kingdom as her dowry. Equally, since Mary would ostensibly marry Darnley in defiance of Elizabeth's wishes, it afforded the English queen with a further excuse to ignore her cousin's nagging requests for recognition as her successor. But whatever the motives, it was not long before the full ramifications of the match became manifest. For Moray and his Protestant associates were dismissed from office and fled to England after an unsuccessful rebellion in August 1565, which Elizabeth subsidised but could not make good with military assistance for fear of French intervention. In the event, Mary had turned to Philip II rather than France for advice and protection, and had also requested men and money from the pope, although it was the Scottish queen's collapsing relationship with her husband that finally pushed her realm to the brink when David Rizzio, her favourite and secretary, was murdered with his assistance. Led by the Earl of Morton, the assassins recalled Moray and his allies, while Mary turned to another faction headed by James Hepburn, Earl of Bothwell, who between February and May 1567 murdered Darnley, kidnapped the queen herself and then married her – all, as it appeared, with her consent.

The twists, however, were still not done. For amid the popular reaction to this multiple outrage, Morton won the Battle of Carberry Hill in June 1567, capturing Mary and driving Bothwell into exile, before forcing the queen's abdication in favour of her infant son James VI under the regency of Moray. Just under a year later, Mary escaped from Loch Leven to England, crossing the border at Carlisle in May 1568 after a further defeat by her Scottish enemies at Langside, which effectively extinguished once and for all any likelihood that she might 'recover the mind of Scottishmen' for France. But the end of the Scottish menace in one form was merely the beginning of quite another sort of threat, leading Cecil to tell his own sovereign only the next year how 'the Queen of Scots is and shall always be a dangerous person to your estate'. When she had returned to Scotland from France in 1561 at the age of 18, John Knox claimed to have 'espied such craft' in her 'as I have not found in such age', and now she was firmly ensconced in the kingdom of England, which she had always considered her rightful inheritance. She was a focus for any would-be plotter against her cousin, yet someone whom Elizabeth was unprepared to eradicate, since she was her blood relative and, more importantly still, a rightful monarch of Scotland removed by rebels whose activities could never be condoned. To attempt to restore her would not only be difficult and expensive, but would lose England her new friends north of the border and might, in any case, end in failure. To send her to Europe, perhaps to France, would merely place a valuable piece in the hands of England's enemies. Under the circumstances, the only option was to hold Mary at home – notwithstanding the Rising of the Northern Earls on her behalf in 1569, the excommunication of Elizabeth by the pope in 1570, and the revival of a Marian faction in Scotland that effected the assassination of Moray during the same year and was only finally suppressed in 1573.

For all of eighteen years in fact, until her execution in 1587, Mary Stuart would shadow Elizabeth, and in the meantime, though the possibility of an invasion by France had receded, England's intervention in that country's civil wars had also come at a significant cost. Since the early 1560s, three groups of French nobles had expressed their political ambitions and rivalries in terms of religious ardour. The most powerful were the Guises of Lorraine, half-German, richer than the king himself, and ultra-Catholic, while the Montmorencis had adopted a moderately '*politique*' religious outlook, in contrast to the Bourbon family, strong in the south, next in line of succession to the throne and committed to the Protestant Huguenot cause. Lesser nobles attached themselves to one or other of these three main groups, while the widow of Henri II and mother of Francis II, Catherine de' Medici, who had become regent for her 10-year-old son Charles IX after Francis's death in 1560, attempted to build up the strength of the Crown against the rival noble factions by playing each off against the other. Presiding over the king's council, deciding policy, and controlling all State business and patronage, Catherine was without question the most powerful European woman of the entire century. Yet even she was unable to stem the tide of events resulting from the so-called 'Massacre of Vassy' in March 1562, when the Duke of Guise came upon a Huguenot congregation worshipping in a barn and 'mingled their blood with their sacrifices'. Seventy-four were killed and 104 wounded, and when the duke returned to Paris after what he described as 'the regrettable incident', he found himself cheered in the streets as the first of the French wars of religion, which were to continue intermittently until 1598, erupted around him.

When Louis Bourbon, Prince of Condé, and Gaspard II de Coligny, along with the rest of the Huguenots, took up arms against Guise's usurpation of the government, the appeal for English aid was not long in coming. Nor was it one that could be easily resisted, since an all-out Guisan victory, uniting France, would raise once more the prospect of a French invasion. Cecil, on the one hand, was in no doubt that 'the perils growing upon the overthrow of the Prince of Condé's cause' were manifest, and urged England's ambassador in Paris 'to continue your writing to put the Queen's Majesty in remembrance of her peril if the Guisans prosper'. For Ambassador Throckmorton himself, however, intervention was not only a necessity but an opportunity, on the grounds that 'the protestants ... may be moved to give us possession of Calais, Dieppe, Newhaven [Le Havre], perhaps all three' – a view shared by Sir Thomas Gresham, who had already declared from Flanders how 'now is the time (they say here) to recover those pieces we have lost of late in France, or better pieces'. Accordingly, negotiations were opened and by the secret Treaty of Richmond of September 1562, it was agreed that Le Havre would be held by 3,000 English troops and eventually exchanged for Calais, while a further 3,000 English soldiers would assist the Prince of Condé, bolstered by a loan of 140,000 crowns to the rebels. Only two years earlier, at the time of the 'tumult of Amboise', Cecil had urged against entering 'into that bottomless pit' of expense entailed by force within the King of France's own mainland. But even he now felt that Condé was fighting England's battle as much as the Lords of the Congregation had been in 1560. With Robert Dudley also strenuously urging war, might not the Huguenots therefore be built up as an effective counterpoise to the Guises in France just as the Scots Protestants had been employed north of the border? And in this case, as Throckmorton had pointed out, might not Calais be recovered into the bargain?

The Spanish ambassador, Alvarez de Quadra, commented bitterly of Elizabeth how 'this woman desires to make use of religion in order to excite rebellion in the whole world'. But even if his dubious claim had been founded, he need not have worried unduly about the consequences in France's case, where conditions were starkly different to those applying in Scotland. For in 1560 England had sought no territorial concessions from the Lords of the Congregation, but now, in occupying Le Havre and demanding Calais, French national feeling was outraged. Even the Huguenots, indeed, could not long stomach the indignity, and ultimately, after defeat and capture by the royal forces, Condé himself joined his Catholic enemies to expel the foreigner. Ten months of bitter fighting had inflicted shattering losses on France's leading noble factions, allowing Catherine de' Medici to reassert royal authority, negotiate a settlement and organise a united front against the intruders. And they had also taken a heavy toll upon the intruders themselves, as the English found themselves driven from Dieppe, to leave the garrison of Le Havre – reinforced but dying at the rate of seventy men a day – at surrender point in July 1563. 'They fight like Hectors, labour like slaves, are worse fed than peasants, and are poorer than beggars,' wrote the Earl of Warwick of his men, before south-westerly gales held up the further supplies and reinforcements that might have prolonged resistance for a few more weeks. By the Peace of Troyes, which followed in April 1564, England forfeited her right to the restoration of Calais, and recognised this loss for a payment of only one-third of the price originally agreed in the Treaty of Cateau-Cambrésis.

It was a diplomatic humiliation, following on from a woefully unsuccessful military adventure that impressed upon the Queen of England, once and for all, the dangers of foreign commitments. Henceforward Elizabeth, though always ready to encourage French, Scottish and Netherlands Protestants as useful pressure groups, would openly support them in rebellion solely as a last desperate resort. And this, in fact, was not the only beneficial side effect of the episode. For in attempting to neutralise the religious turmoil around her, Catherine de' Medici had learnt lessons of her own, not the least of which was the need to encourage toleration and acknowledge the importance of seeking an accommodation with the ruler of England, even if that meant doing little for Mary Stuart and denying Charles IX to her as a husband. Since Spain, moreover, was less apt for a rapprochement after Catherine's return to power, that too made the French regent even more desirous of English friendship at a time when the growing madness of Philip II's son, Don Carlos, had also dashed the Queen of Scots' plans for a Spanish marriage. Unable now to hope for a match with the King of France or the Prince of Spain, there was no other continental suitor of sufficient greatness with which Mary Stuart might frighten Elizabeth into recognising her claims. And in consequence, Anglo–Scottish relations were to become still more of a British matter, further disentangled from continental complications. Equally importantly, as an exhausted France again turned in upon itself during the comparatively peaceful breathing space afforded by the new phase of Catherine de' Medici's government, England could look forward with confidence to the prospect of her enemy's imminent descent into further upheaval. For the renewal of civil war in October 1567 and then again from September 1568 until the Peace of St Germain in August 1570 not only maintained France's state of exhaustion, but reduced the influence of the Guises, and advanced the Huguenot Coligny to a central place in government.

The years 1568 to 1570 represented, in fact, a period of broader transition in English foreign policy, as recognition grew that Spain, England's traditional ally, controlled mighty armies newly established in the Netherlands, which represented an increasingly acute threat of their own. Dutch resistance to Spanish influence, fuelled partly by the patriotism of Roman Catholic aristocrats like William the Silent and the religious defiance of Calvinist zealots, had been growing for at least a decade before the outbreak of rebellion in 1567. But Elizabeth had shown little sympathy, pointing out much later in 1601 how, 'when the colour of dissension began first to kindle', she had counselled the rebels 'to contain their passions and rather by humble petition than by violence or arms to seek ease of their grievances'. For not only was she antipathetic to all challenges to legitimate political authority, Spain itself, of course, had long been perceived as England's natural ally – a notion shared no less by Philip II who soon returned to traditional Habsburg fears of France after his brief flirtation with Henri II in 1559 when both kings pondered a crusading mission across the Channel. Henri's death in July of that year had forcefully reminded him that the rule of Protestant Elizabeth was infinitely preferable to the alternative of the Catholic but half-Guise Mary Stuart, and in consequence Spanish ambassadors remained friendly presences at the English court for the next ten years: de Feria until 1559, de Quadra from 1559 until 1564 and de Silva until 1568. 'We are the best of friends,' declared de Quadra of

Cecil, and when de Silva finally left, the queen was genuinely sorry to see him go. Philip, at the same time, had hitherto restrained the pope from excommunicating her and thereby sanctioning her deposition, and though English attempts to impinge upon the Caribbean had strained the relationship, Spain had already recognised at Cateau-Cambrésis that acts of war to the south of the tropic of Cancer did not constitute a *casus belli* for governments in Europe. Indeed, while Sir John Hawkins' expeditions of 1562–63, 1564–65 and 1567–68 might be the cause of indignant diplomatic exchanges, Hawkins' own personal agents were still dealing directly with Philip in 1571 on matters associated with the affairs of San Juan de Ulúa.

But while England's alliance with Spain persisted formally until as late as 1575, the potential fracture lines went much deeper even than the growing commercial rivalry between the two realms. In August 1567, the Duke of Alva arrived in Brussels with 25,000 troops and there followed five years of conflict that foreshadowed all the elements constituting the great twenty-five-year crisis of 1578–1603: Englishmen fighting in the Netherlands; an attack on Spain's bullion shipments from America; a Catholic revival in Scotland; papist assassination plots on England's home front; and rebellion in Ireland. Except that no Spanish Armada was mobilised for an invasion, every other feature of the later crisis was already on display while peace was still technically intact. And the explanation for the impasse was simple. For in 1568 Philip was still in two minds about how to proceed, experiencing growing hostility to Elizabeth but continuing to regard her as a bulwark against Guise power in Europe. By 1580, however, he had come to regard the Guises as subsidised dependants of Spain, and had abandoned his reservations accordingly. Beforehand, too, the Queen of England had herself trodden carefully, never acquiescing in the Spanish military presence in the Netherlands, yet appreciating that an independent Netherlands was sure to be small and weak and open before long to conquest by France. Her aim was to persuade Philip that his kingdom had more to gain from the trade, resources and military support of a semi-autonomous Netherlands than from prolonged warfare, and thereby achieve the withdrawal of Spanish troops, along with a moderate degree of toleration for the sake of public order. In this ideal state of affairs, Spain would retain suzerainty and be ever-ready to invade France across the Pyrenees if the French dared to impinge upon the Netherlands in their own right. And until Philip accepted such an arrangement, England would strive to prevent his victory without assisting his outright defeat – a policy neatly encapsulated by Cecil early in 1578:

Necessary for England that the State of the Low Countries should continue in their ancient government, without either subduing it to the

Spanish nation or joining it to the Crown of France. Profitable to have the State continue as it hath done whereby England may continue both peace and intercourse.

Ten years earlier, in fact, Alva had seemed set to achieve a quick and easy domination, though Cecil was in correspondence with both the Dutch rebels and Coligny in the hope of imposing a long stalemate. Accordingly, a blockade was arranged against Spanish shipping in the Channel, which did not commit the English government to war, but led ultimately to a heated altercation over four Spanish ships forced to seek refuge in Plymouth from French raiders in November 1568. They were carrying £85,000, loaned by Genoese bankers to pay for Alva's army, which was now approaching 50,000 men and had not been paid for months. And although Elizabeth offered to protect the money by providing a military escort to bring it safely by land to London and arranged with the Genoese to take over the loan herself, the response was predictable. For while the Spanish vessels could not leave, as a result of ongoing fears of capture by the French, Elizabeth's 'protection' was nevertheless construed as an act of provocation, and on the advice of Guereau de Spes, Spain's aggressive new ambassador in London, Alva duly confiscated all English ships and goods in the Netherlands, provoking like responses against enemy assets from Elizabeth at home, as well as from Philip in Spain. When English merchants diverted their cloth exports to Hamburg in 1569, moreover, Alva threatened to destroy the convoy designated for the purpose. And while the threat proved vain, relations took a more ominous turn than ever as de Spes now gave encouragement first to the Rising of the Northern Earls and then to the Ridolfi Plot two years later.

The Scottish queen had been in England less than eighteen months, in fact, when the first of the conspiracies on her behalf developed. The plan involved not only her liberation and restoration to Scotland, but also her recognition as Elizabeth's successor and marriage to Thomas Howard, Duke of Norfolk, a conceited, feeble, middle-aged temporiser who nevertheless represented a figurehead of sorts for the old aristocratic order in opposition to the new 'upstart' leadership of men like Cecil and Robert Dudley. Conservative in outlook, Norfolk and his associates opposed the Protestant religious settlement of 1559 as well as the growing bureaucratic powers of the government, which, in their view, reinforced the domination of the north by the south at their expense. But while the duke came quietly to London to be lodged in the Tower after the queen caught wind of his marital conceits, his co-conspirators were made of sterner and more threatening stuff. De Spes, for example, had a hand in matters and the Queen of Scots was also sanguine:

> Tell the Spanish ambassador [she wrote] that if his master will help me, I shall be queen of England in three months, and Mass shall be said all over the country.

Already, the Earl of Sussex had reported 'an intended stir of the people in the north part of Yorkshire', along with his difficulty in raising an army on Elizabeth's behalf. And the touchpaper was duly lit when the Earls of Westmorland and Northumberland, seeing Howard as a symbol of their lost power in the feudal north and Mary as the instrument by which they might regain it, called out their men. Yet while 700 knights joined them at Brancepeth Castle in November and Mass was indeed celebrated in Durham Cathedral, the rebels' plans to occupy York evaporated with the advance of the force of 7,000 men eventually raised by Sussex. Popular support for the conspiracy proved less substantial than expected, and the rebel earls took flight to Scotland, leaving their leaderless men to offer meagre resistance to the harsh restoration of government authority, which entailed the execution of some 800 participants.

Howard, meanwhile, was not only spared but refused to learn from the experience. Released from the Tower, he was in fact swiftly involved in a further plot hatched by Roberto di Ridolfi, a Florentine merchant banker living in London. This time it was hoped that Alva might land men and that Mary would be placed directly upon the throne after Elizabeth's removal by force. But both the Spanish general and his king remained unreceptive to the prospect of placing a Guise upon the English throne, and Elizabeth's intelligence service proved more than equal to the task of uncovering the details – not least because of the role of Sir John Hawkins, who had been approached as a potential participant but proceeded to act as a double-agent collecting information for Cecil. As a result, Norfolk was finally executed in January 1572 after the plot's decisive failure, while Philip implied to de Spes in London that the Queen of Scots was henceforth an effective dead letter in future Spanish policy. 'The thread of the business being cut,' he observed, 'there is no more to say to you about it.' Indeed, as pressure grew in Parliament for her execution, only Elizabeth's perseverance saved her cousin from the same fate as her would-be husband. 'Forthwith to cut off the Scottish Queen's head', ran a note of the Bishop of London, with this particular priority at the top of the list, though it would take another fifteen years before the Babington Plot finally put paid to Mary Stuart's troubled life. In the meantime, she would be shifted continually from castle to castle in the northern midlands, still undoubtedly a menace and, in this capacity, occasionally employed as a lever by Spain, as in 1583 when the largely toothless Throckmorton Plot was hatched on her behalf. Yet by the time of her execution in 1587, she had become a truly spent force, with the kingdom she had once ruled conclusively reconciled to England. For by the Treaty of Berwick of 1586, her son King James was already in receipt of an English pension of £4,000 and of no mind to complain at his mother's treatment indefinitely, as his own claims to be King of England steadily increased over the years to come.

France, meanwhile, had remained in check. The papal excommunication of Elizabeth in 1570 and subsequent Ridolfi Plot, along with the seizure of the Spanish pay ships and Hawkins' voyages had marked, in retrospect, the beginning of the end for the old enmity that been so long a feature of English policy, and initiated an uneasy friendship, which was to become the rule rather than the exception during the next hundred years. Between 1570 and 1572, indeed, the ascendancy of the Huguenot Gaspard de Coligny even prompted plans for a marriage involving the Queen of England and Catherine de' Medici's son Henri, Duke of Anjou, whereby, observed Cecil, 'the Pope's malice with his bulls and excommunications ... would be suspended and vanish in smoke'. And although the project was ultimately dropped, as a result of Anjou's fanatical Catholicism and the fact that, as Robert Dudley noted, 'her Majesty's heart is nothing inclined to marry at all', the more substantial aim of a defensive league was nevertheless achieved by the Treaty of Blois, signed in April 1572. Only one month earlier, Elizabeth had actually opened negotiations with Alva, for fear that France, enjoying a new-found unity, might exploit Spain's difficulties and launch an invasion of the Low Countries. Furthermore, the projected marriage between Henri Bourbon and Margaret of Valois – a Huguenot prince and Catholic princess – had heightened her anxieties. Yet the mutual defence pact agreed at Blois not only afforded England some much-needed protection but also created the potential for a restraining role in the event of Franco–Spanish hostilities – neither of which would finally prove necessary as France dissolved once more into disorder with the slaughter of up to 30,000 Huguenots in Paris in August 1572.

'I think it less peril to live with them as enemies as friends,' wrote Sir Francis Walsingham in the wake of the Massacre of St Bartholomew's Day. But, in spite of acute religious tension between the two kingdoms and a temporary rapprochement with Spain, the Treaty of Blois was nevertheless renewed in 1575, since neither side could afford to neglect the other's offers of friendship. And it was for this reason, likewise, that a fresh marriage project – this time involving Elizabeth and the Duke of Alençon – began first to be broached in the mid-1570s and then actively canvassed in 1579 and 1581. In the event, the fourth son of Catherine de' Medici – and heir to the French throne after his brother became Henri III in 1574 – was a man of *politique* outlook domestically who nevertheless seemed worryingly capable of leading his country into open war against Spain in the hope of seizing Spanish Flanders. And the Queen of England's motive in encouraging his courtship was therefore simple: both to restrain him and to utilise his aggressive ambitions as a lever against Spain. But she was 45, and he was squat and pockmarked. 'The gentleman,' observed Walsingham, 'sure is void of any good favour, besides the blemish of smallpox,' and the duke's friend Jean de Simier was equally sceptical about the sincerity of the courtship. He would not believe it, he said, 'until the curtain was drawn, the candles out, and Monsieur fairly in bed'. In England as a whole, moreover, the marriage was unpopular, as reflected in 1579 by the Puritan John Stubbs's publication of *The Discovery of a Gaping Gulf whereinto England is like to be swallowed by another French marriage if the Lord forbid not the banns by letting her Majesty see the Sin and Punishment thereof.* As retribution for his description of Alençon as 'the old serpent himself in the form of a man come a second time to seduce the English Eve and to ruin the English paradise', the author would lose his right hand – waving his hat with his left, and crying 'long live the queen' after the deed was done. But even this astonishing combination of bravado and Francophobia could not obscure an equally painful truth: namely, that the real threat was already Spanish, and that an outright declaration of war, primarily as a result of the activities of English seamen, could no longer be postponed indefinitely.

Though breaking point had never been reached, Anglo–Spanish commercial rivalry had, of course, continued to strain relations from early in the reign, as England trespassed increasingly upon Philip II's Caribbean preserves. In 1562 and again in 1564 John Hawkins took slaves to Spanish America and brought back cargoes of gold, pearls, sugar and fish – making a profit of 60 per cent. But if Spanish colonists were willing to trade, their government was not, and a third expedition of 1567–68 found the Spanish authorities waiting, with the result that at San Juan de Ulúa, Hawkins was trapped and four of his seven ships lost. Five years later, Drake, who had been present at San Juan, led his own expedition against Nombre de Dios, striking at the land passage that was one of the weak points on the Spanish treasure routes. With the help of the Indians, the town was surprised and sacked, contributing to King Philip's financial difficulties of 1574 and 1575, which in turn caused the great mutiny of his unpaid troops in the Netherlands in July 1576. But as all parties appreciated, Drake had acted with the connivance of his government, and his aggression was only magnified by further provocation in other areas: piracy in the Channel; the behaviour of English sailors in Spanish ports; and the brisk economic tussle of 1563–64, which had led to currency restrictions on both sides. Before long, too, Drake's circumnavigation of the world between 1577 and 1580 would give rise to yet another storm of Spanish protests, as his ships raided freely and his sovereign filled her coffers with the proceeds to the tune of not less than £160,000 – the equivalent of some nine months' ordinary Crown revenue or the yield of a normal parliamentary grant.

During one raid, a landing party had found a man fast asleep on a beach beside thirteen bars of silver. 'We took the silver and left the man,' recalled one of those involved. But if England's ruler expected her enemies to doze equally peacefully while she stepped up her activities in the Netherlands, she was to prove sorely mistaken. As Drake stepped ashore at Plymouth in September 1580, his first question was characteristically direct: 'Is the Queen alive?' And about the same time, Elizabeth was equally explicit about her own foreign policy objectives:

> We think it good for the King of Spain to be impeached both in Portugal and his Islands and also in the Low Countries, whereto we shall be ready to give such indirect assistance as shall not at once be a cause of war.

Yet her hopes for a 'middle way', which had served her so fruitfully in religion, could not apply indefinitely where international power politics was involved, and particularly when the merest flutter of a butterfly's wing might result in who knew what. In 1569 the leader of Dutch resistance, William the Silent, had licensed privateers to prey on Spanish shipping, and in 1572 these so-called 'Beggars of the Sea' were forbidden to use English ports in which to victual and refit, as had been their custom. But Elizabeth's attempt to mollify Spain led merely to the Beggars' seizure of Brielle off the Dutch coast, and six days later the capture of the altogether more important town of Flushing, a deep-water harbour commanding the entrance of the Scheldt and access to Antwerp. At once, the states of Holland and Zeeland rose against the Spanish, and the Revolt of the Netherlands, which had been simmering for five years, was in full flourish, assisted by an army led from France under Louis of Nassau, and the prospect of further aid from Coligny.

Within a month of the seizure of Brielle, furthermore, a small 'volunteer' force from England under Sir Humphrey Gilbert was dispatched to the Low Countries for the dual purpose of expressing support for the rebels against Spain and of preventing the French seizure of Flushing. But the presence of English soldiers in whatever numbers and capacity was of more concern, in effect, to Spain than the French, since Alva, fully appreciating the limited resources at his disposal, was in favour of peace with Elizabeth at almost any price. Even if she broke her promises and continued 'to favour the rebels and pirates', he wrote to Philip in March 1573, 'there is a great difference between open action and underhand'. Hence as early as 1572 the Spaniards had been renewing their overtures for an agreement, the terms of which Cecil made quite clear to de Guaras. Elizabeth would settle accounts about the naval seizures, take measures to reduce privateering and piracy, and no longer shelter Philip's rebels, in return for which Spain must expel English rebels and refugees while assuring English traders freedom from the Inquisition. And although the terms were too stiff for Spain to accept at once, a limited arrangement lasting two years was nevertheless concluded in the spring of 1573, which led first to the reopening of trade and subsequently to the convention of Bristol that, in August 1574, dealt with claims and counter-claims arising out of the seizures. That summer, indeed, by the queen's command – and to Walsingham's consternation – a Spanish fleet was even welcomed in English ports on its way up Channel with supplies and reinforcements for Don Luis de Requesens, who had not only replaced Alva in November 1573 but abolished the so-called Council of Blood in the Netherlands, before opening negotiations with William the Silent on the basis of a return to traditional liberties and forms of government.

By this point, in fact, the difficulty was rather with William than with Spain, since the rebel leader continued to stand out for the one thing that Requesens had no power to grant: liberty of worship for the Netherlands Protestants. And it was this, above all, upon which Elizabeth's hopes for a satisfactory resolution foundered. Realising that the dangers arising from French intervention were greater than ever, as a result of the Duke of Alençon's aggressive posturings, she could not abandon the Dutch, in spite of the consequences for Anglo–Spanish relations, and in December 1576 therefore offered £100,000 to forestall their allegiance to Paris. After the death of Requesens in March, moreover, the rebels found themselves under more pressure than ever from his replacements, Don John of Austria and later the Duke of Parma, leaving Elizabeth no alternative other than to continue her desperate quadrille with Alençon, in an effort both to court and control him. His first army to the Netherlands disintegrated south of the frontier in December 1578, and over the next two years the courtship continued, with Alençon himself in England for a part of the time. But as papal forces, encouraged by Spain, proceeded to land in Ireland and in the following year the first of the Jesuit missionaries set foot in England, it became increasingly unlikely that Elizabeth's kingdom could depend indefinitely upon deft diplomacy and balancing acts, particularly after the Walloon southern Netherlands made peace with Spain in 1579, and the seven northern states, inspired by William the Silent, formed the Union of Utrecht to continue the struggle 'as one province'.

Even so, the final tipping point would not arrive until the Act of Abjuration of 1581, in which the United Provinces of the north finally declared that when a ruler ceases to defend his people from oppression and violence, 'he is no longer a prince but a tyrant, and they may not only disallow his authority, but legally proceed to the choice of another prince for their defence'. The result was an offer of supreme power to Alençon, which on the one hand intensified Elizabeth's courtship of him, but nevertheless prevented her ultimately from avoiding the direct conflict with Spain that both she and Philip II had so strenuously sought to avoid. For in 1583 the duke was persuaded to attempt what amounted to a failed coup d' état in the northern Netherlands, which left the French discredited, and rendered William the Silent the real ruler in the north until his own assassination in July 1585. With the death of Alençon himself the previous May, moreover, there was now a power vacuum in the United Provinces, the delicacy of which was glaringly apparent when discussed by Elizabeth's councillors in October:

> The arguments were very many on either side, on the one part to show the great peril and danger to her Majesty and her realm if the King of Spain should recover Holland and Zeeland as he had the other countries for lack of succour in seasonable time, either by the French King or the Queen's Majesty. And on the other side many difficulties were remembered to depend upon the succouring of them by her Majesty.

It had long been known, of course, that if Philip II's imperial pretensions were to proceed unimpeded, England could expect no more than 'the courtesy of Polyphemus to Ulysses, namely the last to be devoured'. And it had been widely doubted, equally, whether English forces could prevent seaborne invasions from the Netherlands, 'the very counterscarp of England', or repel a veteran army once it had landed. Appreciating the importance in particular of the island of Walcheren that controlled the approaches to Antwerp, Elizabeth and her advisers were therefore as one about the danger of Spanish attack, and in due course Parliament, too, reached the same conclusion that:

> if the Low Countries ... were subdued by the King of Spain ... the Low Countries shall crown him Aeolus and Neptune of the winds and the narrow seas.

Accordingly, negotiations with the Dutch began in November 1584, followed by nine months of hard bargaining. At the outset, it was made clear that the queen would not accept the sovereignty of the United Provinces, and that, while she would help to a limited extent, every penny must be repaid in return for towns held as guarantees. But Spanish pressure increased with the fall of Brussels in February 1585 and finally reached the point of no return with the capture of Antwerp in August. Thenceforth war became the only option, and in the same month there followed the Treaty of Nonsuch, by which Elizabeth, while still refusing a Dutch offer of sovereignty, nevertheless agreed to send and pay for an auxiliary force of 5,000 foot and 1,000 horse, commanded by an Englishman who, along with two other compatriots, was to sit on the Provinces' executive government. But this alone marked only the beginning. For in France, four months earlier, the Catholic League had risen against Henri III, leaving the Queen of England to shoulder alone the burden of a conflict that would not cease until after her death.

By the end of the year, Robert Dudley, Earl of Leicester, was in command of English forces in the Netherlands, and by that time, too, France's Catholic League had concluded the Treaty of Joinville with Philip II by which it was to receive a monthly Spanish subsidy and the Huguenot Henri of Bourbon was to be excluded from the succession. With an eighth civil war looming and no prospect of French pressure on Spain, Leicester's campaign therefore offered little prospect of success, and nor, in the event, did the earl's own conduct assist his cause. For he accepted the United Provinces' offer of 'Governor and Captain-General' against Elizabeth's wishes, wasted his resources to the tune of £236,000 a year, and quarrelled with his most experienced captain, Sir John Norris. And although he did indeed succeed in defending the eastern flank of the Dutch rebels against the offensive of Parma, the Spanish commander, he nevertheless bungled matters once more in 1586 when he fell out not only with Norris, but also with Maurice of Nassau, William the Silent's son. Failing to relieve Sluys, Leicester finally succeeded in allowing the betrayal of Deventer to the enemy, after which, in November 1587, he was recalled to England for good.

Yet this, in effect, still represented no more than the iceberg tip of the Queen of England's predicament. Eighteen months earlier, Walsingham had smugly informed his sovereign that Spain's naval preparations 'will prove nothing this year and I hope less the next'. But the Spanish conquest of Portugal in 1580 and subsequent absorption of its fleet, along with the effective collapse of the French monarchy, had left England the one remaining obstacle to Philip II's hegemony in Europe, and in January 1586 orders were accordingly issued to the Marquis of Santa Cruz to begin detailed planning and preparation for the creation of an Armada with which to execute the *Empresa* or 'Enterprise of England'. Hitherto, the idea of basing England's policy and defence primarily upon insularity reinforced by sea power had proved adequate to uphold her interests and independence, so long as the accustomed jealous equilibrium persisted between the great powers of the Continent. But now, with only the hard-pressed French Huguenots and fragile Dutch rebels between England and the might of Spain, that strategy would be put to the ultimate test.

'It will be no small advantage to your Majesty,' Santa Cruz had written to his king, 'that the game should be played out on the English table, just as she has tried to make Flanders and France the arena.' Yet Philip's task, even so, was far from straightforward. On the one hand, the original plan for a direct invasion was too expensive and English control of the Baltic route created supply problems. To compound matters, Drake's Caribbean voyage of 1585–86 produced credit difficulties for the enemy after he failed in his aim to catch the treasure fleet at the Azores, but nevertheless sacked San Domingo and Cartagena, having calmly completed his fitting out in the Spanish port of Vigo. The result was a loss of confidence among the Italian bankers who funded Philip II's spending and a subsequent rise in the rate of interest, which was accompanied also by an unwelcome necessity to divert valuable stores and equipment to the Spanish Main. Thereafter, in the summer of 1587, Drake further disrupted Spanish preparations by burning thirty ships at Cadiz, and establishing a base at Sagres in Portugal that harried enemy shipping over two months. As a final flourish, he sailed to the Azores and captured a Portuguese carrack, the *San Felipe*, whose cargo, at a value of £114,000, more than covered the cost of his venture. He had weakened the King of Spain's prestige, damaged his already fragile finances and, above all else perhaps, inflicted a delay of unimagined significance upon the *Empresa*. For when at last the Armada sailed, not only had the seasoned staves of its water barrels been destroyed and replaced by rotten ones, but its admiral, Santa Cruz, was dead – to be replaced at the last minute in the spring of 1588 by Alonso Perez de Guzman, Duke of Medina Sidonia, who openly protested that he had 'neither aptitude, ability, health nor fortune' for the expedition and was ultimately appointed against his will.

Nevertheless, in the campaign that beckoned, there was little to reassure the Queen of England as the fate of her realm – and indeed that of Europe – hung in the balance. The Armada had altogether 130 ships, of which thirty-seven were of serious fighting value, the rest being transports and small craft. But Elizabeth's navy was considerably smaller, comprising only twenty-one fighting vessels of 200 tons and over. In addition there were the fighting merchantmen of the Turkey Company and one or two large ships belonging to individuals. But their officers had little to say for these vessels, save that they helped to make a show, while even in terms of guns, where the English anticipated superiority, matters were finely balanced. Medina Sidonia's best ships had more and heavier guns of the short-range type than the queen's, and in longer-ranged weapons were almost as good, thus challenging the age-old assumption that, in neglecting artillery, the Spaniards expected to gain victory by boarding and hand-to-hand fighting. Whether, of course, their gunners were as intimidating as their weapons is another matter, since they were certainly to inflict few casualties while suffering heavily themselves. And there is no doubt either that one particular traditional assumption about the Armada does indeed continue to hold true: namely, that its ships were decisively outclassed in terms of manoeuvrability. For by contrast to the smaller, low-built vessels turned out by Sir John Hawkins, the Spanish galleons, holding more men and guns within their high-charged frames, were especially unwieldy in choppy Channel waters. Likewise, the Spanish transports, the hulks or *urcas*, were slow and unweatherly, and many of them were also unseaworthy through defective hulls and gear. Seasick and lacking fresh water, the 22,000 soldiers, sailors and galley slaves of the Armada therefore faced an existence significantly more daunting than the English enemy awaiting them as they were sighted off the Lizard on 19 July.

The principal Spanish aim, in fact, was not the invasion and full-scale occupation of England, but to end English help for the Dutch and, in particular, to make the Channel safe for the transportation of troops to the Netherlands. If English Catholics might, in the meantime, avail themselves of the opportunity to rid themselves of their heretic queen, then so much the better. Yet when the Armada left Lisbon on 18 May, its strength was certainly insufficient to conquer the country unaided, suggesting instead the lesser goal of an occupation of the south-east prior to a treaty enforcing the abandonment of the Dutch. The plan, therefore, was an economical one and not, in theory, impossible to execute. Medina Sidonia was to rendezvous with the Duke of Parma, convoy the latter's army, embarked in barges, from the Netherlands, and proceed to guard its communications as land operations against England unfolded. But the admiral was forbidden to capture an English port, and this serious strategic handicap was compounded by other drawbacks, not the least of which was the scheme's inflexibility and dependence upon exact co-ordination between the movements of Parma and those of the fleet. All depended, too, upon finding a suitable port in the Netherlands. But Flushing, the best, was in English hands, while neither Dunkirk nor Nieuport, both of which were favoured by Philip, offered adequate deep-water security. In the event, the Armada would anchor off Calais on 27 July, only for its admiral to be informed that Parma would not be ready for another six days, during which time the English used eight fire ships of from 90 to 200 tons to scatter it. No longer was any rendezvous between Medina Sidonia and Parma feasible, especially as the wind now pushed the Spaniards northwards, and by 3 August the Armada's commander was forced to order its return by entering the North Sea, and attempting to pass around Scotland and the west coast of Ireland – a perilous journey in anchor-wrecking gale-force conditions that accounted for the destruction of between half and two-thirds of the fleet.

On the morning of 29 July, after the English fire ships had caused the Spaniards to slip or cut their cables and stand out to sea, their formation lost, a decisive eight-hour engagement was fought off Gravelines, halfway between Calais and Dunkirk. In its wake, the Lord High Admiral, Lord Howard of Effingham, wrote thus to Sir Francis Walsingham in London:

Their force is wonderful great and strong; and yet we pluck their feathers little and little.

And as the havoc wrought by the elements continued all the while, Drake too recorded his satisfaction at the heart of the chase:

We have the army of Spain before us and mind with the grace of God to wrestle a pull with him. There was never anything pleased me better than the seeing of the enemy with a southerly wind northward. I doubt not, ere it be long, so to handle the matter with the Duke of Sidonia as he shall wish himself at St Mary Port among his orange trees.

At St Paul's there was a service of thanksgiving: *Afflavit Deus et dissipate sunt* – God blew and they were scattered – and the fervour, fanned by Cecil's propaganda, was universal. 'It is easier to find flocks of white crows,' reflected the Protestant Petruccio Ubaldini, 'than one Englishman (and let him believe what he will about religion) who loves a foreigner.' The queen, too, minced no words in describing the Spanish plan to James of Scotland as nothing more than a 'tyrannical, proud and brainsick attempt', though Cecil went better still, duly publishing a pamphlet for European consumption, entitled *A Pack of Spanish Lies sent abroad in the world, … Now ripped up, unfolded, and by just examination condemned …* In parallel columns were printed, first Spanish claims, and then the facts. The Spanish had maintained, for instance, that the English had lost sixty-two ships, which provoked the retort from Elizabeth's chief minister that the queen's navy had:

… chased the Spanish as a brace of greyhounds would a herd of deer. The Spanish ships were beaten, spoiled, burnt, sunk, some in the main seas afore Dunkirk, some afore Flushing and the rest chased away until they were chased out of all the English seas, and forced then to run a violent course about Scotland and Ireland … Why durst any report that twenty-two English ships were sunk and forty taken when in truth there was not one sunk or taken?

George Gower, in his turn, was commissioned to paint the Armada portrait, depicting an idealised queen in front of two window views of the events at sea. On the left, the glorious English fleet is shown with the flag of St George; on the right, the image is of Spanish ships foundering in the North Sea. The queen has her hand on the globe, with the clear, if premature, message that Spanish world dominion must now give way to the triumph of England's manifest destiny.

Yet if Elizabethans were for the moment convinced of their status as God's elect, the road ahead would still be paved with more than its share of danger and tribulation. For although the dispatch of the Armada and its defeat marked in some respects the peak of the war between England and Spain, that war had nevertheless hardly begun, and neither country was to achieve such heights of optimism again. The year 1588, indeed, merely broadened the parameters of the conflict as each side strove to encourage the rebellious subjects of the other – Spain in England and Ireland, Elizabeth in the Netherlands – and both deepened their endeavours to tip in their own favour the balance of forces in a divided France. The countries in which they intervened directly were affected decisively, while the protagonists themselves drew nearer, not to victory, but to bankruptcy. And as the strains of intervention multiplied, so even allies became a source of vexation. During the years ahead, support for the Protestant Dutch, for example, would drain the queen's coffers to the tune of £1.5 million. As a result, England would indeed maintain its political interests in the area. But in 1589 the cautious Walsingham was only one among many bemoaning the involvement:

> I wish our fortune and theirs were not so strictly tied as it is, so as we cannot well untie without great hazard.

One year later, furthermore, Cecil was complaining of Dutch double-dealing, and confirming the queen's own frustration with the people she was attempting to assist in the struggle against Spanish domination:

> No enemy can more displeasure [us] than they do by their daily trade to Spain. In very truth her Majesty is herewith tempted greatly both to repent herself of aiding them and to attempt how to be quit of them.

Further armadas were expected, yet the Dutch ports of Brielle and Flushing, as well as Bergen-op-Zoom, which controlled one of the mouths of the Scheldt, were to be garrisoned by Elizabeth's forces at a time when English manpower was also required to prevent key French ports from falling into Guise and Spanish hands. Every year some 5,000 recruits would need to be sent to Europe to keep their total strength to around 10,000 men, and the result was an annual expenditure on defence of approximately £200,000 per annum. Parliamentary grants, in fact, were almost twice as large in the middle 1590s as in the Armada years – about £135,000 per annum as opposed to £72,000 – and social tensions grew accordingly as poverty, inflation and discharged soldiers became a defining feature of Shakespeare's England.

In 1604, one year after Elizabeth's death, her successor James I would finally make peace with Spain, refusing to recognise the Dutch as rebels and reserving the right to trade with them, while also obtaining the privilege of trading freely with Spain's possessions in Europe. Five years later, the Netherlands enjoyed a Twelve Years' Truce with their Spanish foe, and in just under a further three decades Dutch independence was officially enshrined at the Peace of Westphalia. But the long-term success of Elizabeth's other European entanglements were by no means uniformly fruitful. In France, for example, the death of Catherine de' Medici and assassination of the Duke of Guise and Henri III in 1589 had, in one respect at least, simplified a complex situation by furnishing the Protestant Henri of Navarre with the clearest title to the throne. But the Catholic League nevertheless advanced the claims of the King of Spain, as well as those of his children by the French princess Elizabeth of Valois. And when Spanish forces occupied parts of southern Brittany, Elizabeth was forced at once to send men and money in 1589. Nevertheless, while the English contribution was considerable in scale, its achievements were limited. Five expeditions were dispatched, £380,000 was spent, and some 20,000 men were involved (of whom about half never returned) – all in a desperate rearguard effort to oppose the Spanish in Brittany and the Catholic League in Normandy, and to garrison Dieppe and other ports on the Channel coast to prevent their capture by King Philip. In the process, we are told, Henri of Navarre received from the Queen of England 'such aids as never any king hath done the like to any other', only to capture the Crown of France in 1594 by switching to Catholicism. Four years later France had withdrawn from the war against Spain by the Treaty of Vervins.

And in the meantime the shadow of revolt had darkened Elizabethan Ireland more profoundly than ever before. Before the outbreak of war with Spain, three other rebellions had already stretched the meagre resources of the English government in a land that yielded no more than a paltry revenue of £5,000 each year. Between 1559 and 1566 the O'Neill earls of Ulster had been at the epicentre, to be followed by the Fitzgeralds of the south-west from 1569 to 1572 and 1579 to 1583. In the first case, Sean O'Neill had begun to look for help from France and Rome in his quest for the disputed earldom of Tyrone, before being defeated by his old enemy, Hugh O'Donnell, in combination with England's Lord Deputy Sir Henry Sidney. Then it was the turn of James Fitzgerald, who resisted attempts to plant English settlers in the south, first by appealing unsuccessfully for help from Spain, and then enlisting the assistance of Pope Gregory XIII, which led in 1579 to an expedition including papal representatives that seized Smerwick on the Dingle peninsula before the rebel leader himself was killed. Even so, a relief force of Spaniards and Italians arrived in 1580 and held the area until the end of the year, when they were defeated and put to death by Lord Grey of Wilton. By that point English prejudices were already so deeply entrenched that the courtier poet Edmund Spenser could write with conviction of 'the Irishman's mantle': 'a fit house for an outlaw, a meet bed for a rebel, and an apt cloak for a thief.' Nor did Elizabethan men and women in general doubt for one moment that:

> there is no land in the world of so continual war within itself, nor of so great shedding of Christian blood, nor of so great robbing, spoiling, preying and burning, nor of so great wrongful extortion continually, as Ireland.

For the Irish, of course, the cost of resistance was unspeakable, leading one English observer to describe the effect of starvation thus:

> They looked like anatomies of death; they did eat the carrion and one another soon after, insomuch as the very carcasses they spared not to scrape out of their graves.

But they remained unbowed and in the closing years of Elizabeth's reign staged the most spectacular rising of all: the Tyrone rebellion of 1594 to 1603, which is still remembered today – and with good reason – as the 'Great Revolt'.

Led by Hugh O'Neill, who had been brought to England in 1562 in the midst of his brother's earlier uprising and lived there for fourteen years, the rebellion involved a highly trained force of 6,000 men that for two years was barely held in check by Sir John Norris until his death in 1597. The following year, moreover, an English force was cut to pieces at the Battle of the Yellow Ford on the Blackwater River in Ulster. A triumph for the classic tactics of guerrilla warfare, entailing an ambush on marching columns that were unable to change formation quickly enough, the battle led to the loss of 1,300 men for the English – one in four of their total – and confirmed the opinion of the Venetian ambassador in London that Ireland was the Englishman's grave. Yet Elizabeth's fury at her defeat by an Irish leader that she considered no more than 'a bare bush kern' ensured the dispatch in 1599 of an even stronger force, numbering 16,000, under her favourite, the Earl of Essex, who fared no better than his predecessors. For instead of advancing into Ulster as ordered, he peacocked his way through Munster, and, when urged north by the queen, finally signed an immediate truce with O'Neill, which provoked the following despairing barb from her:

> You and the traitor spoke half an hour together without anybody's hearing … To trust this traitor upon oath is to trust a devil upon his religion …

With his men ultimately dying in droves of disease, Essex hurried back to London to defend himself, with nothing to show but wasted time and frittered money. He had spent £300,000 in seven months, almost twice the cost of defeating the Armada, and would cap the end of his career with a vain attempt at a rebellion of his own in 1601, which resulted in his execution. Thereafter, only the efforts of his successor, Charles Blount, Lord Mountjoy, eventually put paid to O'Neill. He gave himself up in 1603, by which time Elizabeth was already dead.

Nor, in the meantime, had even the efforts of English seamen brought much to cheer the queen in her endless conflict with Spain. In 1596 the best equipped of all the forces to leave England achieved a resounding success when Essex, Howard, Ralegh and Vere landed in southern Spain with a fleet of around fifty warships and 6,000 men – including the poet John Donne. With land and sea forces for once co-ordinating effectively, Cadiz was taken and held for a fortnight, while the Spanish were made to sink their *flota* in harbour, compelling them to repudiate their debts in national bankruptcy for the third time in half a century. But only a year earlier, another full-scale expedition had sailed to the Caribbean under Drake and Hawkins, and the results were dismal. Cities were sacked, but little treasure taken, since the Spanish were this time prepared. And as a fitting footnote, perhaps, to the fickleness of renown, Hawkins subsequently fell ill and died off Porto Rico, to be followed by Drake, who contracted dysentery and was buried at sea near Porto Bello 'somewhat to the east of the castle of St Philip'. Since 1591, in fact, when Howard's squadron had been attacked at Flores while lying in wait for treasure ships, the Spanish convoy system had been proving increasingly effective. And even on those rare occasions like that of 1592 when the *Madre de Dios*, a Portuguese galleon from the East Indies, was captured, the filling of the queen's coffers did not always follow automatically. For in this particular case, the vessel was ransacked at Portsmouth and a great part of its cargo, valued at £800,000, disappeared in spite of Cecil's best efforts:

> Everyone I met within seven miles of Exeter [he wrote] that either had anything in a cloak, bag or malle which did but smell of the prizes either of Dartmouth or Plymouth (for I could well smell them also such had been the spoils of ambergris and musk among them) I did (though he had little about him) return him with me to the town of Exeter.

More ominously still, however, the minister remained preoccupied with the imminence of further armadas, and in 1593 told the House of Lords in no uncertain terms how the King of Spain was not only 'now greater than any

Christian prince hath been' but 'maketh these mighty wars not purposely to burn a town … but to conquer all France, all England and Ireland'.

In 1595, four Spanish ships reached Cornwall, and in 1596 and 1597 fleets were dispatched against England and Ireland, only to be turned back by the equinoctial gales. In 1596, indeed, Cecil was making every preparation against a possible invasion – from the holding in readiness of the county levies to such points of detail as the removal of millstones and windmill sails should the enemy make a landing. Now aided by the development of new and faster types of vessels, such as the *avisos* or scouts, the Spanish navy had not only learned from the experience of 1588, but expanded its numbers and borrowed design features from English ships, as Cecil was making clear in 1593:

> It is certain he hath the last two years … made a number of ships of war, as near as he can to the mould and quantity of the English navy, finding by experience his monstrous great ships not mete for the Narrow Seas.

And by then, of course, after the arrival of Spanish forces in Brittany in 1590, Philip II's reinvigorated threat had the added benefit of a new and menacing base of operations. In March 1596, the Spanish siege of Calais set further alarm bells ringing and led to the Treaty of Greenwich in April, whereby Elizabeth agreed to send another 4,000 men to help the French defend the port. But the Triple Alliance signed by England, France and the Dutch Republic the following year was once again a token of stalwart resistance rather than clear-cut evidence of victory in sight, after which Elizabeth rapidly reduced her land commitments, undertaking action only at sea until her death.

Ultimately, the nightmare of Spanish absolutism opposite England's shores would be averted. But it was no small irony that the drama of Tudor defence was to end where it had begun under Henry VII more than a century earlier: namely, with men's minds focused chiefly on Brittany. In 1591, the Earl of Essex led 7,000 men in an attempt to capture Rouen for Henri IV, but in the same year 4,000 others were already in Brittany fighting under Sir John Norris, and as the emphasis shifted, it would require another 7,000 troops to swell this contingent for the next four years in defence of St Malo and Brest. By 1603, moreover, the symmetry in England's position with that of 1490 was apparent at another level. Still the security of the Low Countries remained paramount to English interests, but France was steadily rising from the ashes of her civil wars to become once more the nation and potential threat she had been before 1494 and from 1548 to 1560. On 13 September 1598, Philip II died of cancer at El Escorial, to be replaced by Philip III, but the new king would be unable to resolve his kingdom's predicament, arising from financially unsustainable imperial commitments that could not be abandoned without wrecking the very foundations of his kingship. And in the crisis that eventually unfolded, the old Franco–Habsburg rivalry would emerge as before, with England playing its familiar role on the sidelines, watching vigilantly but intent upon minimal interference. Engagement, it seems, had given place again to withdrawal from Europe, as the kingdom's priorities turned increasingly to expansion further afield. The Continent's partial medieval unity, based on the Catholic Church and the Latin language, was in any case gone forever, which made its divorce from England all the more final – especially when the personal union of England and Scotland under the first Stuart not only united the British Isles but closed the back door to the long-feared invasion that had shadowed his Tudor predecessors. With a navy fit for purpose and set to develop steadily, the small island on Europe's fringe could therefore both sustain its independence and rejoice in its isolation, while celebrating the newly emerging opportunities before it. The circle had been closed, only for others to lay in store.

ACKNOWLEDGEMENTS

The origins of many of the sources and quotations employed in this book are cited as they appear, but others were also located over the years in numerous secondary works. For the latter, I am especially indebted to the research of the late professors John Hale, Fernand Braudel and Richard Bruce Wernham, as well as others like Professor Nigel Goose and Dr Lien Luu, whose efforts more recently have thrown so much light on immigration to Tudor England. With a project of such sweeping scope, where new perspectives are constantly unfolding and fresh information is continually coming to light, I extend my sincere apologies to any whose work I may have failed to highlight. Certainly, the book was daunting to attempt but exhilarating to execute, and at journey's end I feel it only fitting to raise my glass to all concerned, not least my long-suffering spouse and the ever-supportive staff of The History Press, including Mark Beynon, Simon Wright and Alex Waite.

INDEX